The Gendered Cyborg: A Reader

The Gendered Cyborg brings together key writings exploring the relationship between representation, technoscience and gender, through the metaphor of the cyborg. While the contributors argue that the cyborg provides new ways to think about the relationship between culture and technology and between women and machines, they also question whether the cyborg represents a challenge to, or simply another representation of, gendered categories in science.

The articles are grouped into thematic sections, exploring:

- the ways in which Western science has produced and represented gender, and discusses the importance of Donna Haraway's groundbreaking 'Manifesto for Cyborgs'
- the science–gender relationship in contemporary science fiction films such as *Blade Runner* and the *Alien* series
- debates around modern reproductive technology such as ultrasound scans and IVF, and their benefits and constraints for women
- issues relating to artificial intelligence and the Internet.

Editors: Gill Kirkup is Senior Lecturer in Educational Technology at the Open University and co-editor of *Inventing Women: Gender Science and Techology* (1993). Linda Janes and Kath Woodward are both Staff Tutors in Sociology, also at the Open University, and Fiona Hovenden is a Freelance IT Consultant.

Contributors: Alison Adam, Anne Balsamo, Lynda K. Bundtzen, Barbara Creed, Mary Ann Doane, Dion Farquhar, Jennifer González, Evelyn M. Hammonds, Donna J. Haraway, Luce Irigaray, Nina Lykke, Rosalind Pollack Petchesky, Sadie Plant, Londa Schiebinger, Vivian Sobchack, Deborah Lynn Steinberg, Nancy Leys Stepan, Nina Wakeford.

THE GENDERED CYBORG: A READER

This reader provides some of the set readings for a sixteen-week module (D857 Gender, Technology and Representation: Women, Machines and Cyborgs), which is offered by The Open University Masters in Social Sciences programme.

The Open University Masters in Social Sciences

The MA Programme enables students to select from a range of modules, to create a programme to suit their own professional or personal development. Students can choose from a range of social science modules to obtain an MA in Social Sciences, or may specialize in a particular subject area. Thus, D857 Gender, Technology and Representation: Women, Machines and Cyborgs) is one of the modules leading to an MA in Cultural and Media Studies.

At present there are three study lines leading to:

- an MA in Cultural and Media Studies
- an MA in Environmental Policy and Society
- an MA in Psychological Research Methods.

Other study lines being planned include an MSc in Psychology and an MA in Social Policy/MA in Social Policy and Criminology.

OU Supported Learning

The Open University's unique, supported open ("distance") learning Masters Programme in Social Sciences is designed to introduce the concepts, approaches, theories and techniques associated with a number of academic areas of study. The MA in Social Sciences programme provides great flexibility. Students study in their own environments, in their own time, anywhere in the European Union. They receive specially prepared course materials, benefit from structured tutorial support throughout all the coursework and assessment assignments, and have the chance to work with other students.

How to apply

If you would like to register for this programme, or simply find out more information, please write for the Masters in Social Sciences prospectus to the Course Reservations Centre, PO Box 724, The Open University, Walton Hall, Milton Keynes, MK7 6ZW, UK (Telephone 0 (0 44) 1908 653231). Details can also be viewed on our Web page http://www.open.ac.uk

The Gendered Cyborg:
A Reader

Edited by

Gill Kirkup, Linda Janes, Kathryn Woodward and Fiona Hovenden

London and New York

in association with

The Open University

First published 2000
by Routledge
11 New Fetter Lane, London EC4P 4EE

Simultaneously published in the USA and Canada
by Routledge
29 West 35th Street, New York, NY 10001

Routledge is an imprint of the Taylor & Francis Group

Typeset in Perpetua and Bell Gothic by Keystroke, Jacaranda Lodge, Wolverhampton
Printed and bound in Great Britain by TJ International Ltd., Padstow, Cornwall

British Library Cataloguing in Publication Data
A catalogue record for this book is available from the British Library

Library of Congress Cataloging in Publication Data
The gendered cyborg : a reader / edited by Gill Kirkup . . . [et al.].
        p.   cm.
    Includes bibliographical references and index.
    ISBN 0–415–22090–4 (alk. paper). — ISBN 0–415–22091–2 (pbk. :
alk. paper)
      1. Feminist theory. 2. Cyborgs. 3. Feminism and science.
4. Human reproduction—Social aspects. 5. Artificial intelligence—
Social aspects. 6. Science—Social aspects. 7. Technology—Social
aspects. I. Kirkup, Gill.
    HQ1190.G4754 2000
    305.42'—dc21   99-16255
                                                                          CIP

ISBN 0–415–22091–2 (Pbk)
ISBN 0–415–22090–4 (Hbk)

Contents

List of figures   ix
List of acknowledgements   xi
Introduction   xiii

PART ONE   1
Representing gender in technoscience

    Gill Kirkup
    INTRODUCTION TO PART ONE   3

1.1 Londa Schiebinger
    TAXONOMY FOR HUMAN BEINGS   11

1.2 Nancy Leys Stepan
    RACE AND GENDER: THE ROLE OF ANALOGY IN SCIENCE   38

1.3 Donna J. Haraway
    A MANIFESTO FOR CYBORGS: SCIENCE, TECHNOLOGY,
    AND SOCIALIST FEMINISM IN THE 1980s   50

1.4 Jennifer González
    ENVISIONING CYBORG BODIES: NOTES FROM CURRENT
    RESEARCH   58

1.5 Nina Lykke
    BETWEEN MONSTERS, GODDESSES AND CYBORGS:
    FEMINIST CONFRONTATIONS WITH SCIENCE   74

PART TWO
Alien m/others: representing the feminine in science fiction film

89

Linda Janes
INTRODUCTION TO PART TWO

91

2.1 Lynda K. Bundtzen
MONSTROUS MOTHERS: MEDUSA, GRENDEL, AND
NOW ALIEN

101

2.2 Mary Ann Doane
TECHNOPHILIA: TECHNOLOGY, REPRESENTATION, AND
THE FEMININE

110

2.3 Barbara Creed
ALIEN AND THE MONSTROUS-FEMININE

122

2.4 Vivian Sobchack
POSTFUTURISM

136

2.5 Anne Balsamo
READING CYBORGS WRITING FEMINISM

148

PART THREE
Representing reproduction: reproducing representation

159

Kathryn Woodward
INTRODUCTION TO PART THREE

161

3.1 Rosalind Pollack Petchesky
FOETAL IMAGES: THE POWER OF VISUAL CULTURE IN THE
POLITICS OF REPRODUCTION

171

3.2 Deborah Lynn Steinberg
FEMINIST APPROACHES TO SCIENCE, MEDICINE AND
TECHNOLOGY

193

3.3 Dion Farquhar
(M)OTHER DISCOURSES

209

3.4 Donna J. Haraway
THE VIRTUAL SPECULUM IN THE NEW WORLD ORDER

221

PART FOUR   247
Refractions (women, technology and cyborgs)

    Fiona Hovenden
    INTRODUCTION TO PART FOUR   249

4.1 Luce Irigaray
    WHEN OUR LIPS SPEAK TOGETHER   262

4.2 Sadie Plant
    ON THE MATRIX: CYBERFEMINIST SIMULATIONS   265

4.3 Alison Adam
    FEMINIST AI PROJECTS AND CYBERFUTURES   276

4.4 Nina Wakeford
    GENDER AND THE LANDSCAPES OF COMPUTING IN AN
    INTERNET CAFÉ   291

4.5 Evelynn M. Hammonds
    NEW TECHNOLOGIES OF RACE   305

Index   319

Figures

1.1A "His nurse is the earth" from Michael Maier, *Atalanta*   17
fugiens, Oppenheim (1618). By permission of the
Staatsbibliothek zu Berlin – Preufsischer Kulturbesitz

1.1B "The mother of all being" from Charles Cochin and   18
Hubert-François Gravelot, *Iconologie par figures, or
Traite complet des allegories, emblèmes*, &c., (Geneva,
1791, Minkoff Preprint, 1972), s.v. "Nature". Courtesy of
the Pennsylvania State University Libraries

1.1C "Frontispiece to Linnaeus's *Fauna Svecica*" (1746)
By permission of the Staatsbibliothek zu Berlin – Preufsischer   19
Kulturbesitz

1.1D "Sapientia" from a fifteenth-century German manuscript,   20
reproduced in Liselotte Moller, "Nahrmutter Weisheit",
Deutsche Vierteljahrsschrift 24 (1950), fig. 2, facing p. 351

1.1E "Breast shapes among humans" from Hermann Ploss,   22
Max Bartels and Paul Bartels, *Woman: An Historical
Gynecological and Anthropological Compendium*, edited by
Eric Dingwell (St Louis: C. V. Mosby Company, 1936),
vol. 1, p. 399

1.1F "A Hottentot woman with an 'apron' " from François Le   28
Vaillant, *Voyage de François Le Vaillant dans l'intérieur
de l'Afrique* (Paris, 1798), vol. 2, facing p. 349. Courtesy
of the Pennsylvania State University Libraries

1.4A "L' Horlogère" Courtesy of the Bibliothèque des Arts   59
Décoratifs

1.4B "Das schöne Mädchen" (The Beautiful Girl) by Hannah   62
Höch (1919–20), Private collection

1.4C	"Tête mécanique. L'Esprit de notre temps" by Raoul Hausmann (c. 1921), Courtesy of Musée Nationale d'Art Moderne, Centre Georges Pompidou, Paris	64
1.4D	"All you Zombies: Truth before God" by Robert Longo, Los Angeles County Museum of Art, New York (1990). Courtesy of Robert Longo	66
1.4E	"Silent Möbius" Published in *The Cyborg Handbook* (Routledge, 1995)	69
1.4F	"Silent Möbius" Published in *The Cyborg Handbook* (Routledge, 1995)	70
2.1A	Sigourney Weaver as Ripley, Carrie Hen as Newt in *Aliens*	104
2.3A	"The space travellers about to enter the alien ship through its monstrous vaginal portals (*Alien*)" from Barbara Creed, *The Monstrous-Feminism: Film, Feminism and Psychoanalysis* (Routledge, 1993)	124
2.3B	"The egg chamber. The intra-uterine imagery, sign of the abject archaic mother, haunts the *mise-en-scène of Alien*" from Barbara Creed, *The Monstrous-Feminism: Film, Feminism and Psychoanalysis* (Routledge, 1993)	125
2.4A	"*Blade Runner* (Ridley Scott, 1982) More Human Than Human: Relations of resemblance constitute a 'new humanism'" (Courtesy of Ladd/Warner Brothers)	139
2.4B	"*Blade Runner* (Ridley Scott, 1982) Reflexive replicants: Priss" (Courtesy of Ladd/Warner Brothers)	140
2.4C	"*ET: The Extra Terrestrial* (Steven Spielberg, 1982) More Human than Human" (Universal)	141
2.4D	"*Liquid Sky* (Slava Tsukerman, 1983) Aliens R US: Relations of similitude as reversible" (Cinevista)	141
3.4A	"The Virtual Speculum" by Anne Kelly (Stabel, 1924)	223
3.4B	"The Creation of Adam" by Michelangelo, Sistine Chapel (1511–12)	224
3.4C	"Draughtsman Drawing a Nude" by Albrecht Dürer (1538)	228
3.4D	"Venus" by Lynn Randolph (1992)	230
3.4E	"Speculum-Wielding Wonder Woman" *Sister* (July 1973)	238
3.4F	"Wonder Woman for President" *Ms.* (July 1972)	240
4.5A	"DuBois' photographs of Negro Americans"	308
4.5B	"DuBois' photographs of Negro Americans"	308
4.5C	"What color is Black?" *Newsweek* (13 February 1995)	310–311
4.5D	"The new face of America" *Time* (Fall 1993)	313
4.5E	"*Time*'s morphies"	314
4.5F	"Rebirth of a nation, computer-style"	316

Acknowledgements

The editors and publishers would like to thank the following copyright holders for permission to reprint material:

Alison Adam, "Feminist AI Projects and Cyberfutures", published in *Artificial Knowing: Gender and the Thinking Machine*, by Alison Adam, Routledge (1998).

Anne Balsamo, "Reading Cyborgs Writing Feminism", published in *Communication*, 10: 331–44 (1988).

Lynda Bundtzen, "Monstrous Mothers: Medusa, Grendel, and now Alien", published in *Film Quarterly* 40(3) (1987).

Barbara Creed, "Alien and the Monstrous-Feminine", published in *Alien Zone: Cultural Theory and Contemporary Science Fiction Cinema*, edited by Annette Kuhn, Verso (1989), excerpted from "Horror and the Monstrous-Feminine: An Imaginary Abjection", *Screen* 28(2) (1987). Reprinted by permission of *Screen* and Barbara Creed.

Mary Ann Doane, "Technophilia: Technology, Representation, and the Feminine", published in *Body/Politics: Women, Literature, and the Discourse of Science*, edited by Mary Jacobus, Evelyn Fox Keller and Sally Shuttleworth, Routledge, Chapman and Hall Inc. (1990).

Dion Farquhar, "M/other Discourses", published in *The Other Machine: Discourses and Reproductive Technologies*, by Dion Farquhar, Routledge (1996).

Jennifer González, "Envisioning Cyborg Bodies: Notes from Current Research", published in *The Cyborg Handbook*, edited by Chris Hables Gray with the assistance of Heidi J. Figueroa-Sarriera and Steven Mentor, Routledge (1995).

Evelynn M. Hammonds, "New Technologies of Race", published in *Processed Lives: Gender and Technology in Everyday Life*, edited by Jennifer Terry and Melodie Calvert, Routledge (1997). © held by the author.

Donna Haraway, "A Manifesto for Cyborgs: Science, Technology, and Socialist Feminism in the 1980s", published in *Feminisms*, Oxford Readers, edited by

Sandra Kemp and Judith Squires, Oxford University Press (1997), from Linda Nicholson (ed.), *Feminism / Postmodernism*, New York: Routledge, Chapman and Hall Inc. (1990); "The Virtual Speculum in the New World Order", published in *Feminist Review* 55 (Spring) (1997).

Luce Irigaray, "When Our Lips Speak Together", published in *Feminisms: A Reader*, edited by Maggie Humm, Harvester Wheatsheaf (1992). Reprinted from "When Our Lips Speak Together", by Luce Irigaray, *Signs* 6(1) (1980).

Nina Lykke, "Between Monsters, Goddesses and Cyborgs: Feminist Confrontations with Science", published in *Between Monsters, Goddesses and Cyborgs: Feminist Confrontation with Science, Medicine and Cyberspace*, edited by Nina Lykke and Rosi Braidotti, Zed Books (1996).

Sadie Plant, "On the Matrix: Cyberfeminist Simulations", published in *Cultures of Internet: Virtual Spaces, Real Histories, Living Bodies*, edited by Rob Shields, Sage Publications (1996). © held by the author.

Rosalind Pollack Petchesky, "Foetal Images: The Power of Visual Culture in the Politics of Reproduction", published in *Reproductive Technologies: Gender, Motherhood and Medicine*, edited by Michelle Stanworth, Polity Press in association with Basil Blackwell (1987).

Londa Schiebinger, "Taxonomy for Human Beings", an edited version of chapter 2 "Why Mammals Are Called Mammals" and chapter 5 "Nature's Body" from *Nature's Body: Sexual Politics and the Making of Modern Science*, by Londa Schiebinger, Pandora, HarperCollins*Publishers* (1993). Reprinted by permission of HarperCollins*Publishers*.

Vivian Sobchack, "Postfuturism", published in *Screening Space: The American Science Fiction Film*, by Vivian Sobchack, Ungar Publishing Company (1987).

Deborah Lynn Steinberg, "Feminist Approaches to Science, Medicine and Technology", published in *Bodies in Glass: Genetics, Eugenics, Embryo Ethics*, by Deborah Lynn Steinberg, Manchester University Press (1997).

Nancy Leys Stepan, "Race and Gender: The Role of Analogy in Science", from *Feminism and Science*, edited by Evelyn Fox Keller and Helen E. Longino, Oxford University Press (1996) with permission from *ISIS* 77 (1986), 261–77.

Nina Wakeford, "Gender and the Landscapes of Computing in an Internet Café", published in *Virtual Geographies: Bodies and Spaces, Relations*, edited by Crang *et al.*, Routledge (1998).

Every effort has been made to obtain permission to reproduce material. If any proper acknowledgement has not been made, or permission not received, we would invite copyright holders to inform us of the oversight.

Introduction

THE THEME OF THIS BOOK is the interrelationship between representation, technoscience and gender, explored through the metaphor of the cyborg. Since Donna Haraway wrote her original "Manifesto for Cyborgs", the boundary figure of the cyborg has become important in both cultural studies and gender studies by providing new ways to think about the relationship between culture and technology, between people and machines. In this book we will use "technoscience" in the way that Donna Haraway does – as a

> condensed signifier [which] mimes the implosion of science and technology into each other in the last two hundred years around the world . . . [it designates] dense nodes of human and non-human actors that are brought into alliance by the material, social, and semiotic technologies through which what will count as nature and as matters of fact get constituted.
>
> (Haraway, 1997: 50)

Rapid developments in technoscience and the proliferation of theories about its impact on society have been fertile ground for "cyborg" theory to take root. It is now possible to talk about "cyborgism", "cyborgology", even "cyborgization" (Gray *et al.*, 1995), although this book won't.

The genesis (or perhaps parthenogenesis) of this book came out of a taught course that explores the relationship between technoscience, representation and gender. Feminist theory was originally interested in biological science as a set of theories which construct women as deficient, and other technosciences as fields of activity from which women were excluded, at least from powerful positions. The systems and artefacts produced by technoscience were seen as providing the material foundations for gender inequality. The technosciences of the late twentieth and early twenty-first century are proposed as having a different impact and set of possibilities for gender relations and for women. These possibilities increase the human capacities of seeing, hearing, *understanding and communicating*: they are systems for representation. Technosciences represent and at the same time are themselves represented. Marshall McLuhan (1969) understood this in the 1960s but his work contained no gender analysis. Haraway has now provided a gender analysis of technoscience and representation that has captured imaginations.

This book brings together, in a way consistent with feminist scholarship and women's/gender studies, writings from three different disciplines: cultural studies, the social studies of science and technology, and gender theory. The metaphor/image around which these three disciplines weave their critical and explanatory narratives is that of the cyborg, and its companion the monster. The readings chosen explain both why the "cyborg" has provided such a useful theoretical figure, but they also raise questions about the political implications of our enthusiasm for this figure. How do we avoid technophobia, a disease of 1970/1980s feminist writing, or technomania, a disease of 1990s cultural studies? This book aims to present both perspectives through writings which engage with the issue of whether those of us belonging to that contested category "women" will benefit from or be disadvantaged by this new modelling of the relationship between people, machines and systems.

The book is divided into four parts. Part 1 contains writings which give the context for Haraway's cyborg. They look at the history of the production of gender categories through science; categories which the cyborg aims to dissolve. Readings in these parts also begin the critical reflection, which continues though the book, on whether the cyborg is as useful a gender transformative device as has been claimed for it. Parts 2, 3 and 4 expand this debate into areas in which the cyborg has been a fruitful, if flawed, representational device: reproductive technologies, science fiction film, and information and communications technologies.

There is no doubt that the relationship between human beings and technoscience systems and artefacts is changing in a revolutionary way, and will continue to do so for some years yet. But the impact of this for women, as a category and as embodied individuals, is not clear.

References

Gray, C. Hables, Figuero-Sarriera, H. and Mentor, S. (eds) (1995) *The Cyborg Handbook*, New York and London: Routledge.

Haraway, D. J. (1997) *Modest_Witness@Second_Millennium. FemaleMan ©_Meets_OncoMouse™*, London: Routledge.

McLuhan, Marshall (1969) *Understanding Media. The Extensions of Man*, London: Sphere Books.

PART ONE

Representing gender in technoscience

Introduction to Part One

GENDER, ARGUES SANDRA HARDING (1996), is a property of individuals, social structures and symbolic systems. Gender relations are also power relations which lead to unequal access to material resources. This is why a study of gender is more than simply an interesting intellectual endeavour; it is also a political activity. In the 1990s that activity has focused on understanding the representation and creation of gender in symbolic systems. Science is one of the most important symbolic systems in Western culture and it has been clear to feminist critics of science, technology and, in *its* more radical formulation, "technoscience", that gender is very clearly a product of this system (Bleier, 1984).

An empiricist view of Western technoscience would see its main function as producing categories and definitions with which the material world can be described and modelled, and its behaviour controlled and predicted. A poststructuralist view would challenge the importance (and even the reality, in an ontological sense) of the material world, and argue that the categories and definitions that science produces, themselves *produce* knowledge, and that power comes through this production. Whichever way it is seen, power over the material world through knowledge about it is what science has been about since Francis Bacon's "Knowledge is power". Even Fox Keller, who is a key proponent of the view that there is a "residual reality" "vastly larger than any possible representation we might construct" (1992: 74), argues that language produces meaning about this reality rather than simply reflecting it. Technoscientific knowledge contributes to the production of gender through its forms of representation, while itself being a gendered practice. Like the worm Uroborus, it constantly feeds off itself.

There is agreement that gender categories are constructed. 1970/1980s feminist theory argued that gender was a social construction based on a material-biological base: sex difference. Gender was seen as a construction used to justify social inequality. The elaboration of poststructural theory and the critical investigation of the biology of sex difference raised questions about the role of biology as a discourse that created sex difference rather than simply justified it. Biology became another discourse in the construction of gender rather than the material base for it. This left feminist scholars and activists in the uncomfortable position of having apparently deconstructed the category "Woman"; the category which formed the basis of Second Wave feminism. Many, while agreeing that the characteristics of gender categories as we know them are a social construction, would not go so far as to say that "sex/gender" itself is simply a product of discourse. All would agree, however, that it is illuminating to uncover the ways in which Western gender categories have come to be. The deep construction of gender through the casting of male and female into oppositional and hierarchical categories in which the "female" is always the inferior – for example, objectivity/subjectivity, rationality/emotion, Culture/Nature – is evident in many cultures but is especially strong in technoscientific culture. Uncovering the particular way in which this construction has developed in techno-science, from the seventeenth century on, has been a major project of feminist historians of science (for example, Schiebinger, 1989; Tuana, 1993; Fox Keller, 1992). However, uncovering and deconstructing are only the tools of a more radical ambition, which is:

> to undermine the dichotomies themselves – to expose to radical critique a worldview that deploys categories of gender to rend the fabric of human life and thought along a multiplicity of mutually sanctioning mutually supportive, and mutually defining oppositions.
>
> (Fox Keller, 1992: 18)

But once these are undermined, and therefore unserviceable as intellectual tools, it is necessary to construct new conceptual tools to think differently with.

> It is easy enough to say, and to show, that the language of science is riddled with patriarchal imagery, but it is far more difficult to show – or even to think about, what effect a non-patriarchal discourse would have had or would now have (supposing we could learn to ungender our discourse) . . . This . . . is the real task that faces not only feminist critiques of science, but all of history, philosophy and sociology of science.
>
> (Fox Keller, 1986 [1992] p: 48)

It has been in aid of this task that Donna Haraway's 1985 version of the 1960s creature, the "Cyborg" (see reading 1.3), has become a key concept for 1990s thinking about gender, and about the nature of being human in what some have identified as a "posthuman" world (Gray et al., 1995). Haraway's cyborg is not a member of the liberal humanist world. It is not concerned to differentiate itself from other forms of creature, or from machines; its identity does not rest in its individuality. Haraway's cyborg (and, as is discussed later, other versions of "cyborg", contain none of the implications of Haraway's version), like a Rosetta stone, bridges the language of material feminists working on issues of gender and technoscience, and postmodern feminists working with cultural studies and textual deconstruction. It is a theoretical creature that has more currency, and popularity, ten years after it was described by Haraway as a "manifesto" for "socialist feminists". She intended it to be a political creature, but very few who have found it a useful metaphor would see themselves as socialist feminists. Its usefulness for cultural deconstruction of gender has become apparent, but its usefulness as a tool for material change is yet to be proved. Although Haraway famously concludes her article "I would rather be a cyborg than a goddess", the question remains: Is it better to be a cyborg than a woman?

The collection of extracts in part 1 provides a context for Haraway's cyborg by looking in particular at the power of science to create categories of similarity and difference through which we think about being human: male and female. Haraway's cyborg gives us another metaphor to replace "human", but some of the extracts question whether alone it can overcome the problems of our gendered and racialized humanity.

The first extract is taken from Londa Schiebinger's book *Nature's Body* (1993). Schiebinger is a historian of science, and her particular period of interest is the seventeenth and eighteenth centuries. In her first book, *The Mind Has No Sex* (Schiebinger, 1989), she traced the contributions women had made to science and technology before the modern era, and the way that the developing technosciences (of natural history and anatomy in particular) can be seen to be providing a justification, and prescription, for the exclusion of women from the social and intellectual practices of Western technoscience on the grounds of "natural" gender differences. In doing this, she argued, Western technoscience was entrenching unacknowledged sexism. Foucault would argue that the discourses of biology and anatomy were producing meaning through these classification systems, and that this meaning produced power inequalities, rather than simply justified them.

In *Nature's Body* Schiebinger goes more deeply into an analysis of key eighteenth-century natural history taxonomies, where the foundation for our present understanding of the relationship between ourselves as human beings and other types of living thing lies. In this work she is concerned with both gender and race as conceptual creations and material inequalities. In the extract given here she demonstrates how the basic zoological taxonomy that has been in common use for two hundred years, in which human beings are classed as mammals along with other species who suckle their young (and distinguished, for example, from birds or insects), is based on a deliberate privileging of criteria that stress the close relationship between women in particular and other mammals. In constructing his classes of animals Linnaeus deliberately chose a female characteristic as the defining property of mammals. At the same time he created the term *Homo sapiens* ("man of wisdom") to differentiate human beings from other primates. Since medieval times, notes Schiebinger, human beings (especially males) have been seen as distinct from other animals because of their rationality, a characteristic seen by medieval philosophers as particularly male, and lacking in women.

In his new terminology, Linnaeus therefore reasserted that it is a masculine characteristic (and a non-material one) that differentiates human beings from "beasts", while it is a female, biological characteristic that provides commonality with them. This relationship is very important. For Descartes, animals were a kind of machine, made by God, with very small parts. Human beings were not machines/automata like animals because of the power of rational thought and consciousness. When women are put closer to animals they are also placed closer to machines. At its very core, then, the discourse of the discipline which in the twentieth century becomes biology, in its taxonomy of what it is to be human constructs gendered inequality.

Because taxonomies produce meaning it is important to locate the historical process by which they were created. Schiebinger argues that the eighteenth century in Europe was a time of social and political upheaval, when both citizenship and the nature of the family were being redefined. A concern with "natural" rights was also mirrored by a concern with "natural" differences. This new classificatory science provided an argument for the natural place of women as nurturers, both of their own children and of the State.

These biological taxonomies were concerned to sort species and gender into their rightful places. They had a medieval concern to find a "natural hierarchy" that would produce and justify power inequalities, and assert the natural superiority/right-to-rule of white, middle-class European men. So the creation of taxonomies was also focused on identifying and classifying racial difference. The disenfranchising of women by identifying them as closer to "beasts" also extended to the disenfranchising of members of other cultures (and classes of society) by an identification based on different biological indicators. Discussion of the characteristics of non-European women, for example the "Hottentot Venus", cast these women far beyond the defining characteristics of "human". They became seen, and treated, as "monstrous". The "Hottentot Venus" is an example of how technoscience creates monsters from those in some way seen as "outside" the category of "human".

The next reading is from an article by Nancy Leys Stepan on the use of metaphor in scientific theory to disguise the importation of racist and sexist values into apparently "value-free" knowledge. Stepan, a philosopher and historian of technoscience, has written extensively on the construction of the notion of "race" in scientific discourse (Stepan, 1982). She argues that there has been a particular problem with modern science. What technoscience claims for itself as a mirror of reality includes a notion that scientific language and theory is "exact", objective, containing nothing except the unadorned factual words of the "modest witness" (Haraway, 1997). In this positivist discourse about "truth", language is a tool which reflects material reality; theories describe the behaviour of measurable material "stuff". However, argues Stepan, metaphor and analogy are as important in the construction of meaning in technoscience as in any other discourse; the danger is that scientists have been the last to acknowledge their use.

Stepan uses examples from nineteenth-century and early twentieth-century natural history concerning racial and sexual difference that illustrate, when they are read following Schiebinger, the cumulative nature of that particular branch of knowledge. Schiebinger illustrated the eighteenth-century concern with the "chain of being" when it appeared most important to construct difference between white males and non-white males, and all females. Stepan argues that the argument takes a step further by the nineteenth century. Non-white men and all women are no longer seen as simply inferior to white men – they are seen as having similar characteristics of inferiority, and therefore as being like each other. So, for example, skull shape and intelligence (which were understood to be closely connected if not causal) of women, non-white "races" and other primates were seen as having much in common. What becomes visible and desired in the research data is evidence of similarities between these divergent groups, because this supports a theory of some common, biological, causal explanations for inequality. Poststructuralists would argue that these facts/data are themselves constructs of the discourse, and therefore inside it, and can carry no weight of proof or disproof. In Stepan's examples, even from an empiricist position, no data could have challenged the theories proposed because causation was argued to support a metaphorical argument, when the most that could be claimed for the data was correlation. What the nineteenth-century science of race was doing was accepting unexamined metaphors of racial and sexual inequality – that women and non-white races are more like other primates than white men – into an analogical scientific theory by collecting data that supported the theory.

Stepan's reading is also important in putting forward a theory of how metaphor and analogy work. A metaphor does not bring together, through language, two things that have a material or literal similarity; it brings together two diverse ideas or images that interact to construct a meaning that produces the idea that they have something in common. These interaction metaphors, once accepted, produce further associations between aspects of the two things, so that they appear to have even more in common than was originally supposed. Stepan, like Schiebinger, is arguing that the meanings created through the metaphors of race and gender that are embedded in our science and culture have created an acceptance of inequality. Stepan does not argue against metaphors *per se*. In fact she argues that metaphor and analogy are powerful tools for technoscience, which is in the business of constructing systems of implication where they previously didn't exist, and so new metaphors are needed. Haraway's cyborg is seen as potentially one of the most important.

One of Haraway's prime arguments in "A Manifesto for Cyborgs" is for the importance of the cyborg as an ahistorical figure, and as a liberatory metaphor, as well as a description of lived reality. Theorists of gender had searched for the historical and cultural origins of gender inequality; they looked for a time or place when gender was not a basic organizational construct of culture. They tried to imagine what cultural or social changes would be necessary to produce a situation in which gender did not imply structural inequality. Most, argued Haraway, had searched for some holistic unity, some merging of Nature and Culture which might transcend the problem. But, she asserts, there is no Garden of Eden, and gods and goddesses are dead. The solution to the problems inherent in Cartesian gendered dualism is to embrace technoscience for its ability to redraw all category boundaries between human beings and the rest, rather than reject it in favour of a mythic, organic wholeness. She argues that in the late twentieth century three crucial category boundaries have been dissolved by technoscience: the boundaries between human beings and other animals, between animal/human organisms and machines, and between the physical and the non-physical. It is the dissolution of these material boundaries that makes it possible for us to claim the positive identity of cyborg for *ourselves*.

It is questionable whether Haraway's cyborg is an ahistorical construct. She describes it herself as "the illegitimate offspring of militarism and patriarchal capitalism". The cyborg or cybernetic organism was a proposal from the 1960s (Clynes and Kline, 1960) for producing modified humans who could engage in space travel without needing to carry their own "earthly" environment with them. Clynes' cyborgs would remain human beings in a Cartesian sense, their bodies (like machines) would be modified so that their minds (which would remain unchanged) could continue the work of rational technoscience and space exploration, still human, and still gendered. Manfred Clynes makes this very clear in an interview with Chris Hables Grey:

> When he rides a bicycle he virtually has become a cyborg. Initially it's a little hard to learn to ride a bike but once you learn it you do all these things automatically and the bike becomes almost part of you. When *homo sapiens* walks he doesn't pay much attention to how he walks, it's natural. In the same way, when he is on his bicycle it feels natural to a person who knows how to ride a bike . . . But right now I'd like to say – that the cyborg, *per se* – talking now of men and women who have altered themselves in various cyborgian ways – in no way has that altered their sexuality.
>
> (Gray *et al.*, 1995: 49)

It is also the case that others have argued philosophically that the boundary between humans/animals (animate) and machines (inanimate) is a mirage. Hacking claims for Canguilhem, a French philosopher of the 1950s (Hacking, 1998), a notion found in the work of more recent philosophers of technology (Kaufman-Osborn, 1997), that tools and machines should not be seen as in a different category to bodies but as extensions of them. Artefacts and living organs are conceptually the same; machines are animate in the same way that living things are animate, because they are extensions of life. But again it has not been obvious how this challenges the dualism of gender. Only Haraway makes claims for a cyborg identity that will deconstruct and reconstruct the nature of what it is to be human. In a paraphrase of her own words, a promise of monsters (Haraway, 1992).

The final two readings in part 1 argue that Haraway's cyborg is useful, but at the same time challenge her claims for it. Jennifer González analyses images of cyborg bodies for what they say about gender and race. She challenges Haraway on two main points: that cyborgs are outside history, and that they challenge gender and race categories. She presents visual images of "cyborgs" (specifically mechanical cyborgs: techno–human amalgamations) from the eighteenth century to the twentieth century, and argues that each of them demonstrates the particular historical understanding of the nature of bodies and machines (as well as the role of women) of the time in which they were made.

The eighteenth-century *L'Horlogère* is an example of a Cartesian view of the body as mechanism, and very stereotypically, a clock. The female body is objectified and sexual, with its breasts, narrow waist and large hips. González sees this as having a lot in common with the sexual representation of the 1990s comic cyborg Kiddy, who fills a modern male sexual fantasy of the soft sexual female outer body which contains beneath it the powerful machine. It is the same fantasy which produced the "male" cyborg in *Terminator* which exhibits a sexualized, masculine, fleshly outer body, which is revealed, bit by bit as it is damaged, to contain a mechanical skeleton beneath. The female cyborg can also be simply the image of a sexualized slave, as described in the 1993 fax advertisement. In between these González discusses "modernist" images from the 1920s, in which in photomontage and found objects are used to describe the fractured nature of experience and modernist identity. The only image González produces which is not a gendered stereotype is the Longo sculpture. This she describes as hybrid, containing both male and female sexual characteristics, rather than transcending gender. But again she sees this as a particular historical conception, an illustration of the militarized capitalist state of the late twentieth century. She finds no challenge to racial representations in any visual images of cyborgs. For González the "cyborg" body, as represented, is failing in its promise to transcend gender and race categories. At best it is a way of reflecting, at any historical time, the particular contradictions of the lived experience of relating to technoscience.

The final reading, by Nina Lykke, sees the cyborg metaphor as useful for feminist scholars. It supports the activity and validity of feminist technoscience. Lykke notes one major boundary that feminist theory has transcended, that between C. P. Snow's two cultures of the arts and the sciences. This is basically an academic embodiment of the boundary between human and non-human. Since the 1970s Women's Studies (feminist studies or gender studies) has worked as an interdisciplinary knowledge domain, refusing to acknowledge the internal authority of particular disciplines, crossing discipline boundaries as necessary and deconstructing all areas of knowledge as gendered. Women's studies/feminism could therefore be described as cyborg practice, before Haraway named it.

One of the main problems of technoscience for feminism has been to address yet another boundary: that of objectivity versus constructionism in theories of knowledge. Again, argues Lykke, this is a boundary/dichotomy that we must transcend, along with that between the artifactual and the natural, embodied as a choice between cyborg or goddess. Most feminists, she argues, have been happy to choose Haraway's cyborg over a backward-looking "goddess". However, for Lykke the metaphor of "goddess" is also about transcending the boundary between artefact and natural, and between physical and non-physical, a false boundary recognized by Haraway in her machines "made of sunshine" in the 1985 reading (1.3), and also in her own example of Gaia: "itself a cyborg, a complex auto-poietic system that terminally blurred the boundaries among the geological, the organic, and the technological – was the natural habitat, and the launching pad, of other cyborgs" (Haraway, 1995).

Gaia is here claimed by cyberfeminists as well as ecofeminists as an embodiment of the cyborg/goddess.

So, as Haraway's cyborg encourages us to engage in discourses across disciplines and philosophical and political traditions, its strengths and weaknesses as a tool for reconceiving gender and empowering women become clearer, while its usefulness cannot be denied. In the following parts of this book it is taken into the arenas of science fiction film, reproductive technology, and information and communication technology. But the question is raised: What does it do there for "Women"?

References

Bleier, R. (1984) *Science and Gender: A Critique of Biology and its Theories on Women*, New York and Oxford: Pergamon Press.

Clynes, M. and Kline, N. (1960) *Cyborgs and Space*, in Gray, L. H., Figueroa-Sarriera, H., and Mentor, S. (1995), pp. 29–30.

Gray, C. Hables, Figueroa-Sarriera, H. and Mentor, S. (eds) (1995) *The Cyborg Handbook*, New York and London: Routledge.

Hacking, I. (1998) "Canguilhem amid the Cyborgs", *Economy and Society* 27(2/3) May: 202–16.

Haraway, D. (1985) "A Manifesto for Cyborgs: Science, Technology, and Socialist Feminism in the 1980s", *Socialist Review* 80: 65–108.

—— (1992) "The Promises of Monsters: A Regenerative Politics for Inappropriate/d Others", in L. Grossberg, C. Nelson and P. Treichler (eds), *Cultural Studies,* New York: Routledge, 295–337.

—— (1995) "Cyborgs and Symbionts: Living Together in the New World Order", in C. Hables Grey (ed.), *The Cyborg Handbook*, New York and London: Routledge.

—— (1997) *Modest_Witness@Second-Millennium.FemaleMan©_Meets_OncoMouse™*, New York and London: Routledge.

Harding, S. (1996) "Multicultural and Global Feminist Philosophies of Science: Resources and Challenges", in L. H. Nelson and J. Nelson (eds) *Feminism, Science and the Philosophy of Science*, London: Kluwer Academic.

Kaufman-Osborn, T. V. (1997) *Creatures of Prometheus: Gender and the Politics of Technology*, Oxford: Rowman and Littlefield.

Keller, E. Fox (1986) "How Gender Matters, or, Why it's so Hard for Us to Count Past Two", reprinted in G. Kirkup and L. S. Keller (1992), *Inventing Women: Science, Technology and Gender*, Cambridge: Polity Press.

—— (1992) *Secrets of Life, Secrets of Death: Essays on Language, Gender and Science*, New York and London: Routledge.

Schiebinger, L. (1989) *The Mind Has No Sex: Women in the Origins of Modern Science*, Cambridge, MA: Harvard University Press.

—— (1993) *Nature's Body: Sexual Politics and the Making of Modern Science*, London: Pandora.

Stepan, N. (1982) *The Idea of Race in Science: Great Britain, 1800–1960*, London: Macmillan.

Tuana, N. (1993) *The Less Noble Sex Scientific, Religious, and Philosophical Conceptions of Women's Nature*, Bloomington and Indianapolis: Indiana University Press.

Londa Schiebinger

TAXONOMY FOR HUMAN BEINGS

A certain Chinese encyclopedia divides animals into: (a) belonging to the Emperor, (b) embalmed, (c) tame, (d) sucking pigs, (e) sirens, (f) fabulous, (g) stray dogs, (h) included in the present classification, (i) frenzied, (j) innumerable, (k) drawn with a very fine camel's-hair brush, (l) *et cetera*, (m) having just broken the water pitcher, (n) that from a long way off look like flies.

(Jorge Luis Borges, *Other Inquisitions*, 1952)

IN 1758, IN THE TENTH EDITION of his *Systema naturae*, Carolus Linnaeus introduced the term *Mammalia* into zoological taxonomy.[1] Linnaeus devised this term – meaning literally "of the breast" – to distinguish the class of animals embracing humans, apes, ungulates, sloths, sea cows, elephants, bats, and all other organisms with hair, three ear bones, and a four-chambered heart. In so doing, he idolized the female mammae as the icon of that class.

When examining the evolution of Linnaean nomenclature, historians of science have tended to confine their study to developments within the scientific community. They trace the history of classification from Aristotle through the leading naturalists of the sixteenth and seventeenth centuries, the Swiss Conrad Gesner and the English John Ray, culminating ultimately with the triumph of Linnaean systematics. Linnaeus's nomenclature is taken more or less for granted as part of his foundational work in zoology. No one has grappled with the social origins or consequences of the term *Mammalia*. Certainly, no one has questioned the gender politics informing Linnaeus's choice of this term.

It is also possible, however, to see the Linnaean coinage as a political act. The presence of milk-producing mammae is, after all, but one characteristic of mammals, as was commonly known to eighteenth-century European naturalists. Furthermore, the mammae are "functional" in only half of this group of animals (the females) and, among those, for a relatively short period of time (during lactation) or not at all. As we shall see, Linnaeus could indeed have chosen a more gender-neutral term, such as *Aurecaviga* (the hollow-eared ones) or *Pilosa* (the hairy ones).

[. . .]

To appreciate more fully the meaning of Linnaeus's term requires a foray into the cultural history of the breast. Even though Linnaeus's term may have been new to zoology, the female breast evoked deep, wide-ranging, and often contradictory currents of meaning in Western cultures. But, as we shall see, there were also more immediate and pressing political trends that prompted Linnaeus to focus scientific attention on the mammae. Linnaeus venerated the maternal breast at a time when doctors and politicians had begun to extol the virtues of mother's milk (Linnaeus was a practicing physician and the father of seven children). Eighteenth-century middle- and upper-class women were being encouraged to give up their wet nurses; a Prussian law of 1794 went so far as to require that healthy women nurse their own babies. Linnaeus was involved in the struggle against wet-nursing, a struggle that emerged alongside and in step with political realignments undermining women's public power and attaching a new value to women's domestic roles. Understood in broadest terms, the scientific fascination with the female breast helped to buttress the sexual division of labor in European society by emphasizing how natural it was for females – both human and nonhuman – to suckle and rear their own children.

Mammalia – the genealogy of a term

It has been said that God created nature and Linnaeus gave it order; Albrecht von Haller rather mockingly called him "the second Adam."[2] [. . .] His *Systema naturae* treated the three classical kingdoms of nature – animal, vegetable, and mineral – growing from a folio of only twelve pages in 1735 to a three-volume work of 2,400 pages in the twelfth and last edition revised by Linnaeus himself in 1766. In the epoch-making tenth edition, Linnaeus gave binomial names (generic and specific) to all the animals known to him, nearly 4,400 species.

Linnaeus divided animals into six classes: *Mammalia, Aves, Amphibia, Pisces, Insecta*, and *Vermes*.[3] Although Linnaeus had based important aspects of plant taxonomy on sexual dimorphism, the term *Mammalia* was the only one of his major zoological divisions to focus on reproductive organs and the only term to highlight a character associated primarily with the female. The names of his other classes came, in many cases, from Aristotle: *Aves* simply means bird; *Amphibia* emphasizes habitat; *Insecta* refers to the segmentation of the body; *Vermes* derives from the red-brown color of the common earthworm. Scientific nomenclature was a conservative enterprise in the eighteenth century; suitable terms tended to be conserved and new terms derived by modifying traditional ones. Linnaeus, however, broke with tradition by creating the term *Mammalia*.

[. . .]

Linnaeus, in the first edition of his *Systema naturae* (1735), continued to use the traditional term, *Quadrupedia*. He did, however, raise eyebrows and ire by including humans (rather uncomfortably) among quadrupeds. Indeed, it was the question of how to place humans in nature – which Thomas Huxley later called "the question of all questions" – more than anything else that led Linnaeus to abandon *Quadrupedia* and search for something more appropriate.[4] Linnaeus was not, of course, the first in modern times to recognize that humans are animals. In 1555 Pierre Belon had pointed to the similarities in the skeletons of a human and a bird, and in 1699 Edward Tyson had dissected a chimpanzee – his *Homo sylvestris* – revealing the "great affinity" between animal and human anatomy.[5]

[. . .]

Linnaeus's ranking of humans among quadrupeds outraged naturalists. They found repugnant his characterization of rational man as a hairy animal with four feet and four incisors. Georges-Louis Leclerc, comte de Buffon, born the same year as Linnaeus and his principal rival, made the obvious point that many of the creatures included among Linnaeus's *Quadrupedia* were not quadrupeds at all: humans have two hands and two feet; bats have two feet and no hands; apes have four hands and no feet; and manatees have only two "hands."[6] Louis Daubenton, Buffon's assistant at the Jardin du Roi, denounced Linnaeus's entire system as "false" and "inaccurate."[7] Finally, many naturalists rejected as heretical the notion that humans were essentially animals. Holy Scripture, after all, clearly taught that man was created in God's image. It should be recalled that while Aristotle had included humans among viviparous quadrupeds, in the course of the Middle Ages scholastics removed humans from nature, emphasizing instead their proximity to angels.

Natural historians before Linnaeus had struggled long and hard with these problems of classification. John Ray, often credited with developing binomial nomenclature (though he did not employ it systematically), had used the term *Vivipara* to unite whales and other aquatic mammals with terrestrial quadrupeds. Within his subcategory *Terrestria*, he suggested the term *Pilosa* (hairy animals) as more comprehensive than *Quadrupedia* and thus more suitable for joining amphibious manatees with land-dwelling quadrupeds.[8] Peter Artedi, Linnaeus's close friend and colleague, had also called attention to hair in his proposed *Trichozoologia*, or "science of the hirsute animal."[9] Linnaeus might well have chosen the more traditional adjective *Pilosa* for his new class of quadrupeds; in Linnaeus's system hair had the same diagnostic value as mammae. All mammals (including whales) have hair, and it is still today considered a distinguishing characteristic of mammals.

But Linnaeus did not draw on tradition; he devised instead a new term, *Mammalia*. In its defense, Linnaeus remarked that even if his critics did not believe that humans originally walked on all fours, surely every man born of woman must admit that he was nourished by his mother's milk.[10] Linnaeus thus called attention to the fact, commonly known since Aristotle, that hairy, viviparous females lactate. [. . .] In 1758, Linnaeus finally announced the term *Mammalia* with the words: "Mammalia, these and no other animals have mammae [mammata]." He seemed quite unconcerned that mammae were not a universal character of the class he intended to distinguish. "All females," he wrote on the following page, "have lactiferous mammae of determinate number, as do males (except for the horse)."

Mammalia resonated with the older term *animalia*, derived from *anima*, meaning the breath of life or vital spirit.[11] The new term also conformed to Linnaeus's own rules for zoological terms: it was pleasing to the ear, easy to say and to remember, and not more than twelve letters long.[12] For the rest of his life Linnaeus fiddled with his system, moving animals from order to order, creating new categories and combinations to better capture nature's order. Yet he never rechristened mammals.

The term *Mammalia* gained almost immediate acceptance.

[. . .]

Mammalia was adopted by the English as "mammals," though "mammifers" was also occasionally used, and, as one commentator has suggested, the science treating mammals was rather awkwardly rendered as *mammalogy*, meaning literally "a study of breasts" (and not of breast-bearing animals, which would be more properly *mammology* or *mammalology*).[13] The French devised *mammifères*, or the breast-bearers (not *mammaux*, nicely analogous to *animaux*). The Germans refocused matters slightly, creating *Säugetiere*, or "suckling animals," which appropriately drew attention away from the breast and highlighted the act of suckling (though no distinction was made between a mother giving suck and a newborn taking milk). Linnaeus's term *Mammalia* was retained even after the Darwinian revolution and is today recognized by the International Code of Zoological Nomenclature.

[. . .]

How significant are the mammae?

Were there good reasons for Linnaeus to name mammals *mammals*? This question implies a logic uncharacteristic of the naming process. Names of taxa collect over time, and unless there is a technical problem – as was the case with the term *Quadrupedia* – they pass unchanged from generation to generation. Naturalists also name plants and animals for other than empirical reasons. Pleasing plants or animals are often named after a wife or colleague, while a particularly odious species might be given the name of a professional rival (for instance, *Siegesbeckia*, a small and unpleasant flowering weed that Linnaeus named after Johann Siegesbeck, a critic of his sexual system).[14]

Zoological nomenclature – like all language – is, then, to some degree arbitrary; naturalists devise convenient terms to identify groups of animals. But nomenclature is also historical, growing out of specific contexts, conflicts, and circumstances. The historian can fairly ask why a certain term was coined. In creating the term *Mammalia*, Linnaeus intended to highlight an essential trait of that class of animals. Etienne Geoffroy Saint-Hilaire and Georges Cuvier, in their article "Mammalogie" for the *Magazin encyclopédique* of 1795, summed up the practice of eighteenth-century taxonomists, stating that primary organs determine classes, while secondary organs determine orders. In 1827, Cuvier continued to argue that the mammae distinguished the class bearing their name better than any other external character.[15]

Is Cuvier's statement, in fact, true? Does the longevity of Linnaeus's term reflect the fact that he was simply right, that the mammae do represent a primary, universal, and unique characteristic of mammals (as would have been the parlance of the eighteenth century)? Yes and no. Paleontologists today identify the mammary gland as one of at least six uniquely mammalian characters. Linnaeus himself, though, was perhaps overly exuberant in singling out the breast or teat itself – a sexually charged part of the female body – rather than its function. Indeed one could argue that the term *Lactantia* (the lactating ones, derived from Linnaeus's own description of female mammae) would have better captured the significance of the mammae; certainly Linnaeus was wrong to think that the number and position of the teats themselves were significant. But *Lactantia* still refers exclusively to females. *Lactentia* or *Sugentia* (both meaning "the sucking ones") would have better universalized the term, since male as well as female young suckle at their mothers breasts.

The fact remains that the mammae was only one among several traits that could have been highlighted. Even by eighteenth-century criteria, there was not one characteristic alone that could determine class assignment. As Buffon recognized, species – defined for sexually reproducing organisms as members of a group of individuals that can mate and produce fertile offspring – is the only taxon that exists in nature.[16] Even today, this does not mean that higher units (genera, families, orders, classes, and on up) are arbitrary; these must be consistent with evolutionary genealogy.[17] Yet, as we have seen, Linnaeus could have chosen from a number of equally valid terms, such as *Pilosa*, *Aurecaviga*, *Lactentia*, or *Sugentia*. Because Linnaeus had choices, I will argue that his focus on the breast responded to broader cultural and political trends.

Breasts and mother's milk: problematic icons

Long before Linnaeus, the female breast had been a powerful icon within Western cultures, representing both the sublime and bestial in human nature. The grotesque, withered breasts on witches and devils represented temptations of wanton lust, sins of the flesh, and humanity fallen from paradise. The firm spherical breasts of Aphrodite, the Greek ideal, represented an otherworldly beauty and virginity. In the French Revolution, the bared female breast – embodied in the strident Marianne – became a resilient symbol of freedom.[18] From the multibreasted Diana of Ephesus to the fecundbosomed Nature, the breast symbolized generation, regeneration, and renewal.

Linnaeus created his term *Mammalia* in response to the question of humans' place in nature. In his quest to find an appropriate term for (what we would call) a taxon uniting humans and beasts, Linnaeus made the breast – and specifically the full developed female breast – the icon of the highest class of animals. It might be argued that by privileging a uniquely female characteristic in this way, Linnaeus broke with long-established traditions that saw the male as the measure of all things. In the Aristotelian tradition, the female had been seen as a misbegotten male, a monster or error of nature. By honoring the mammae as sign and symbol of the highest class of animals, Linnaeus assigned a new value to the female, especially women's unique role in reproduction.

It is important to note, however, that in the same volume in which Linnaeus introduced the term *Mammalia*, he also introduced the name *Homo sapiens*. This term, man of wisdom, was used to *distinguish* humans from other primates (ape, lemurs, and bats, for example). In the language of taxonomy, *sapiens* is what is known as a "trivial" name. From a historical point of view, however, the choice of the term *sapiens* is highly significant. "Man" had traditionally been distinguished from animals by his reason; the medieval apposition, *animal rationale*, proclaimed his uniqueness.[19] Thus, within Linnaean terminology, a female characteristic (the lactating mamma) ties humans to brutes, while a traditionally male characteristic (reason) marks our separateness.

The notion that woman – lacking male perfections of mind and body – resides nearer the beast than does man is an ancient one. Among all the organs of a woman's body, her reproductive organs were considered most animallike. For Plato, the uterus was an animal with its own sense of smell, wandering within the female body and leaving disease and destruction in its path.[20] The Greek physician Galen and even the great anatomist Andreas Vesalius (for a time) reported that the uterus had horns. Milk production of the female breast had already been seen as linking humans and animals.

[. . .]

Myths and legends also portrayed suckling as a point of intimate connection between humans and beasts, suggesting the interchangeability of human and animal breasts in this respect. A nanny goat, Amaltheia, was said to have nursed the young Zeus. A she-wolf served as the legendary nurse to Romulus and Remus, the founders of Rome. From the Middle Ages to the seventeenth and eighteenth centuries, bears and wolves were reported to have suckled abandoned children [. . .]

In rarer instances, humans were reported even to have suckled animals. [. . .] In the eighteenth century, William Godwin recorded that as Mary Wollstonecraft lay dying after childbirth, the doctor forbade the child the breast and "procured puppies to draw off the milk."[21] The practice of animals suckling at human breasts was also reported outside Europe. Voyagers related that native South Americans kept their breasts active by letting animals of all kinds feed from them.[22] In Siam women were said to have suckled apes.

Linnaeus thus followed well-established Western conceptions when he suggested that women belong to nature in ways that men do not. As Carolyn Merchant has shown, nature itself has long been conceived as female in most Western intellectual traditions.[23] For the seventeenth-century alchemist Michael Maier, the earth was literally a nourishing mother (Figure 1.1A). The identity of woman with the fecund and nurturing qualities of nature was highlighted in the influential eighteenth-century artists and engravers Hubert-François Gravelot and Charles Cochin's personification of Nature as a virgin, her breasts dripping with milk (Figure 1.1B).

It is significant that Linnaeus used the mammiferous Diana of the Ephesians, an ancient symbol of fertility, as the frontispiece to his *Fauna Svecica*, where he first defended his inclusion of humans among quadrupeds (Figure 1.1C).[24] Linnaeus's Diana, half captive in the fecund earth, emerges to display her womb, the center of life, and her nourishing breasts.[25] In this classic image, her curiously immobilized trunk is covered with symbols of both fertility (bees, acorns, bulls, crabs) and chastity (stags, lions, roses). Her pendulous breasts, heavy with milk, represent the life force of nature – mother and nurse of all living things. In ancient statues, Diana's breasts were often carved from a white stone while her head, neck, hands, and feet were made of darker stone.

For Linnaeus to suggest, then, that humans shared with animals the capacity to suckle their young was nothing new. This uniquely female feature had long been considered less than human. But it had also been considered more than human. In the

Figure 1.1A "His nurse is the earth" from Michael Maier, *Atalanta fugiens*,
Oppenheim (1618)
(By permission of the Staatsbibliothek zu Berlin – Preufsischer
Kulturbesitz)

Christian world, milk had been seen as providing sustenance – for both body and
spirit. Throughout the Middle Ages, the faithful cherished vials of the Virgin's milk as
a healing balm, a symbol of mercy, an eternal mystery. As Marina Warner has pointed
out, the Virgin Mary endured none of the bodily pleasures and pains associated with
childbearing (menstruation, sexual intercourse, pregnancy, or labor) except for
suckling. The tender Madonna suckled the infant Jesus both as his historical mother
and as the metaphysical image of the nourishing Mother Church.[26] During the twelfth
century, maternal imagery – especially suckling and nurturing – extended also to
church fathers. Abbots and prelates were encouraged to "mother" the souls in their
charge, to expose their breasts and let their bosoms expand with the milk of
consolation.[27] Even the full breasts of God the Father were said to be milked by the
Holy Spirit into the cup of the Son of God.[28]

In subcurrents of religious traditions, mother's milk was thought to impart
knowledge. Philosophia-Sapientia, the traditional personification of wisdom, suckled
philosophers at her breasts moist with the milk of knowledge and moral virtue
(Figure 1.1D). Augustine of Hippo, too, imagined himself drinking from the breasts
of Sapientia.[29]

[. . .]

Figure 1.1B "The mother of all being" from Charles Cochin and
Hubert-François Gravelot, *Iconologie par figures, or Traite*
complet des allegories, emblèmes, &c., (Geneva, 1791,
Minkoff Preprint, 1972, s.v. "Nature")
(Courtesy of the Pennsylvania State University Libraries)

Figure 1.1C "Frontispiece to Linnaeus's *Fauna Svecica*" (1746)
(By permission of the Staatsbibliothek zu Berlin – Preufsischer
Kulturbesitz)

Figure 1.1D "Sapientia" from a fifteenth-century German
manuscript
(Reproduced in Liselotte Moller, "Nahrmutter Weisheit",
Deutsche Vierteljahrsschrift 24 (1950), fig. 2, facing p. 351)

In a certain sense, Linnaeus's focus on the milk-bearing breast was at odds with trends that found beauty (though not necessarily salvation) above all in the virginal breast. In both Greek and Christian traditions, the ideal breast was an unused one, small, firm, and spherical; the process of milk swelling the breast was thought to deform it. Mythical female figures – the goddesses Artemis and Aphrodite, the martial Amazons (who supposedly burned away one breast so that their bows would lie flat against their chests), and the nursing mother of Christ – were all virgins.[30] Of all the female Virtues, only Charity possessed a nonvirginal body: infants drank maternal bounty, love, and humility from her breasts.[31]

[. . .]

Ideals of the breast, however, changed over time. After roughly the 1750s, the maternal breast vied for a while with the virginal for cultural preeminence. Barbara Gelphi has traced the stunning way in which the maternal breast was eroticized in late eighteenth-century medical literature. Male physicians, including Erasmus Darwin, described in rapturous prose the sensuous pleasures experienced by nursing infants. (Darwin went so far as to attribute to the curvaceous breast filled with milk the origins of the human idea of beauty – an idea impressed on the senses of the infant.) Medical eroticization of the maternal breast paralleled changing fashions in women's clothing, which by the end of the century were designed to expose the full shape of the breast and nipple. Gelphi argues that this new fashion was as much cultivated by women as imposed upon them. While, for legislators, the breast came to guarantee women's disenfranchisement (see below), women, adopting Rousseau's vocabulary of the new domesticity, flaunted their breasts to celebrate their newfound power to nurture the future sons of the state (a power, Gelphi emphasizes, that was restricted to the confines of the home).[32]

Colonial relations also affected perceptions of the breast. Late nineteenth-century anthropologists classified breasts by beauty in the same way that they measured skulls for intelligence (Figure 1.1E). The ideal breast – for all races – was once again young and virginal. Europeans preferred the compact "hemispherical" type, found, it was said, only among whites and Asians. The much-maligned breasts of African (especially Hottentot) women were dismissed as flabby and pendulous, similar to the udders of goats. [. . .]

Thus Linnaeus's fixation on the female mammae, though new to the zoological tradition, emerged from deep cultural roots. [. . .]

Gender politics in taxonomy

Europeans' fascination with the female breast provided a receptive climate for Linnaeus's innovation. But more immediate political concerns compelled him to focus scientific attention on the mammae. His scientific vision arose alongside and in step with important political trends in the eighteenth century – the restructuring of both child care and women's lives as mothers, wives, and citizens. Despite the Enlightenment credo that all "men" were by nature equal, middle-class women were not to become fully enfranchised citizens or professionals in the state, but newly empowered mothers within the home.

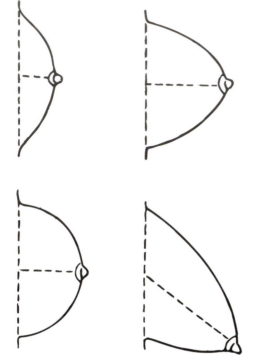

Figure 1.1E "Breast shapes among humans"
(From Hermann Ploss, Max Bartels and Paul Bartels, *Woman: An Historical Gynecological and Anthropological Compendium*, edited by Eric Dingwell, St Louis: C. V. Mosby Company, 1936, vol. 1, p. 399)

Most directly, Linnaeus joined the ongoing campaign to abolish the ancient custom of wet-nursing.[33] The eighteenth century was the heyday of wet-nursing. More Europeans than ever before – including not just aristocrats and wealthy merchants but farmers, clergy, and artisans – sent their children to the countryside to be nursed. By the 1780s, Paris and Lyon were sending up to 90 percent of their children to wet nurses.[34] Although wet-nursing had provided a solution to the problem of child-rearing for middle- and upper-class mothers and fathers, it also resulted in high infant mortality.[35] [. . .]

The preservation of family and maternal duties became important matters of state.[36] For state ministers, the simplest way to increase birth rates was to reduce infant mortality by improving the training of obstetricians, midwives, and, most important, mothers. A central element in this campaign was a series of health and conduct manuals written for women by medical doctors.

In this context, Linnaeus – himself a practicing physician – prepared a dissertation against the evils of wet-nursing in 1752, just a few years before coining the term *Mammalia* and while watching his own children suckle (his wife bore seven children between 1741 and 1757). Linnaeus's work entitled "Step Nurse" (translated into French as "La nourrice marâtre, ou Dissertation sur les suites funestes du nourrissage mercénaire") sounded the themes of the Enlightenment attack on wet-nursing.[37] First and foremost, wet-nursing violated the laws of nature. Nature – herself "a tender and provident mother" – had set the course for female reproduction; digression from her laws endangered both mother and child. [. . .]

In this 1752 pamphlet, Linnaeus also foreshadowed his subsequent nomenclature by contrasting the barbarity of women who deprived their children of mother's milk with the gentle care of great beasts – the whale, the fearsome lioness, and fierce tigress – who willingly offer their young the breast.[38] The idea that women should follow the example of beasts was a common feature of anti-wet-nursing literature flooding Europe.

[. . .]

At the same time many of the attacks on wet-nursing also reiterated age-old myths and superstitions. Linnaeus, for example, cautioned that the character of the upper-class child could easily be corrupted by the milk of lower-class nurses. Using examples drawn from Erasmus, he blamed the bitter, wicked milk of nurses for Nero's addiction to alcohol and for Caligula's tyranny.[39]

While authors of these pamphlets showed genuine concern for the well-being of mothers and children of their own classes, they seldom considered the evils of baby farming for the "lower classes of mankind" (as one influential voice in the anti-wet-nursing movement called them).[40] Children of wet nurses were often neglected or even "disposed of" (for a small fee, no questions asked).[41]

[. . .]

For the enlightened savant, the laws of nature dictated more than the rules for reproductive regimes: they also dictated social order. Medical authority, the legal system, and popular literature worked together to create new interest in maternal breast-feeding. As prescribed in Jean-Jacques Rousseau's influential *Emile*, breast-feeding became fashionable among French upper-class women for a short period in the late eighteenth century.[42] In France and Germany, leading medical doctors advocated laws that would force healthy women to nurse their own infants. The French National Convention decreed in 1793 that only mothers who nursed their own children would be eligible for state aid (women in poor health were exempted).[43] Similar laws were put into effect in Prussia in 1794, just a few years after Frederick the Great installed a modern version of Diana of the Ephesians in his Potsdam garden.[44]

Authors of anti-wet-nursing literature – including Linnaeus, Cadogan, Rousseau, and Anel le Robours – were highly moralistic about returning women to their rightful place as loving and caring mothers. This, despite the fact that Rousseau placed his own five children in foundling homes, not even bothering to record their sex or dates of birth.[45] Women's attempts to contravene the laws of nature were seen as a matter of vanity. [. . .]

Returning to nature and its laws was seen as the surest way to end corruption and regenerate the state, morally as well as economically. [. . .] For the enlightened of Europe, the breast symbolized the synthesis of nature and society, the bond between the private and public worlds.[46]

It is remarkable that in the heady days of the French Revolution, when revolutionaries marched behind the martial and bare-breasted Liberty,[47] the maternal breast became nature's sign that women belonged only in the home. Delegates to the French National Convention used the breast as a natural sign that women should be barred from citizenship and the wielding of public power. In this case, "the breasted ones" were to be confined to the home. In denying women political power, Pierre-Gaspard Chaumette, *procurer* of the Paris Commune, asked indignantly:

> Since when is it permitted to abandon one's sex? Since when is it decent for women to forsake the pious cares of their households and the cribs of their children, coming instead to public places, to hear speeches in the galleries and senate? Is it to men that nature confided domestic cares? Has she given us breasts to feed our children?[48]

[. . .]

The year 1793 marked the fateful repression of women's demands for active citizenship and also, as Lynn Hunt has shown, a turning point in republican images of women. When publicly represented women were no longer cast as the strident Marianne, the symbol of Liberty, but increasingly in motherly roles. Festivals featured parades of pregnant women; women in ceremonies, such as the Festival of the Supreme Being of 1794, were all wives and mothers, many pressing nurslings to their breasts.[49]

[. . .]

Linnaeus's term *Mammalia* helped legitimize the restructuring of European society by emphasizing how natural it was for females – both human and nonhuman – to suckle and rear their own children. Linnaean systematics had sought to render nature universally comprehensible, yet the categories he devised infused nature with middle-class European notions of gender. Linnaeus saw females of all species as tender mothers, a vision he (wittingly or unwittingly) projected onto Europeans understandings of nature.

[. . .]

Race, sex, and the great chain of being

One of the most powerful doctrines governing theories of race in the eighteenth century was the great chain of being. This doctrine postulated that species were immutable entities arrayed along a fixed and vertical hierarchy stretching from God above down to the lowliest sentient being. The historian Winthrop Jordan has shown that the notion of a chain of being became the darling of eighteenth-century conservatives in their attempts to stem the leveling tide of democracy and abolitionism.[50] The conservative British naturalist William Smellie, for example, taught that social hierarchies issued from natural hierarchies. "Independently of all political institutions," Smellie wrote in his 1790 *Philosophy of Natural History*, "Nature herself has formed the human species into castes and ranks."

Europe's anatomists dissected and analyzed the skeletons of animals and humans from every corner of the world in their attempts to substantiate the notion that nature shades continuously from one form to another. Of special interest were the transitional forms bridging the gap between animals and humans. Although different animals vied for a time as the "missing link" (elephants, for their intelligence, and parrots, for their ability to talk), by the eighteenth century naturalists had settled on the ape, and especially the orangutan (still commonly used as a generic name for both chimpanzees and orangutans), as the animal most resembling humankind. What, though, was the "lowest" sort of human? Voyagers, coming into contact with Africans in the course of colonial expansion and the slave trade, had already suggested that the people of this continent resembled the apes who inhabited this same region. (Some went so far as to suggest that the black race originated from whites copulating with apes.)[51] Within this context arose a project central to eighteenth-century anatomy: investigation into the exact relationship among apes, Africans, and Europeans.

Much has been written about the racist implications of the chain of being.[52] What has not been investigated, however, is the place of females in that hierarchy. The notion of a single chain of being stretching throughout nature (and society) created a problem of where to fit women. Scientific racism and scientific sexism both taught that proper social relations between the races and the sexes existed in nature. Many theorists failed to see, however, that their notions of racial and sexual relations rested on contradictory visions of nature. Scientific racism depended on a chain of being or hierarchy of species in nature that was inherently unilinear and absolute. Scientific sexism, by contrast, depended on radical biological divergence. The theory of sexual complementarity attempted to extract males and females from competition with or hierarchy over each other by defining them as opposites, each perfect though radically different and for that reason suited to separate social spheres.[53] Thus the notion of a single chain of being worked at odds with the revolutionary view of sexual difference which postulated a radical incommensurability between the sexes (of European descent).

[. . .]

The Hottentot Venus

The fact that the male body dominated studies of race and the European body dominated studies of sex does not mean that women of color escaped the prurient eye of European anatomists. What is significant, however, is that neither the dominant theory of race nor of sex in this period applied to women of non-European descent, particularly black women. Like other females, they did not fit comfortably in the great chain of being. Like other Africans, they did not fit European gender ideals. As a recent book on contemporary black women's studies put it, all the blacks were men and all the women were white.[54]

[. . .] Certainly African males did not share the traits of heroic manhood presumed inherent in (European) males. African males were thought to be childish, primitive, and sensuous – the obverse of their colonizers. Neither did the gender ideals prescribed for European women extend to African women. Whereas in Europe, middle-class women increasingly became emblems of chaste modesty, black women, by contrast, were thought to embody sexual promiscuity.[55] This European fantasy of the sexual and fecund African woman was reinforced by colonial relations, where European male planters commonly took black and mulatto women as concubines or sold them as prostitutes.

It was therefore doubly determined that the study of black women, as Africans and as women, would focus on their sexuality. Europeans had long been obsessed with the sexuality of Africans – both male and female. [. . .]

African women shared with European women and female apes the incommodious condition of being female in a male world, and thus the scientific gaze fell upon their private parts – breasts and genitalia. As we have seen, the fresh virginal breast was greatly cherished in European culture.[. . .] The breasts of African women took on truly mythic proportions in the male European mind. Some voyagers reported that they hung like "great sacks to the waist," others that they dragged the ground. "Observers" in the colonies reported that some slave women would lay their long breasts upon the ground before lying down beside them to rest. Others imagined that when slave women stooped to work the fields, their breasts made them appear to have "six legs". The most outrageous story passing among European naturalists in the late eighteenth century was that the breasts of Hottentot women were so large that tobacco pouches were made from them and sold in great quantity on the Cape of Good Hope.[56]

[. . .]

In the nineteenth century, the pendulous breast, identified with primitives abroad, was discussed increasingly in terms of class, becoming a staple characterization of the laboring poor at home. Princeton University president Samuel Stanhope Smith traced the origin of what he considered unsightly breasts to the poverty, hardship, and exhausting toil of the lowest classes. Flaccidity increased with age, he noted, because the poor nursed their many children for prolonged periods of time.

Though naturalists had a good deal to say about breasts when considering racial characteristics among females, nothing excited these men more than the elongation of the labia minora, or inner vaginal lips, among the Hottentot. This "Hottentot apron" became the subject of countless books and articles, and much prurient popular and scientific speculation. Linnaeus was so taken with this supposed aspect of Hottentot anatomy that he (quite mistakenly) made it a characteristic of the entire "African" race. [. . .]

Originally called simply a "flap of skin," this supposed aspect of Hottentot genitalia, known for a time by the Latin *sinus pudoris* (translated variously as "loincloth," "veil of shame," or "drape of decency"), was finally domesticated as an "apron" (*tablier* in French; *Schürze* in German). Naturalists hailed the "apron" as a primitive vestige of Hottentots' animal origin. Linnaeus reported finding it also in the female *Homo troglodytes*, his second and lowest species of human. Indeed Linnaeus searched for a similar genital (de)formation in apes, but found none.[57]

From its first sightings in the seventeenth century, the so-called Hottentot apron was pronounced a deformity – a departure from the European norm. John Ovington wrote in his *Voyage to Suratt in the Year 1689* that women sporting these pieces of skin must be hermaphrodites.[58] Voltaire, in the eighteenth century, found the apron so unusual that he argued that these women must belong to a separate species of humans.[59] [. . .]

European naturalists argued amongst themselves about whether the so-called apron actually existed, much as they argued about the existence of the hymen. Few had actually seen African genitalia; much of the information filtering into European universities and academies was second- or third-hand – if not totally fabricated. Blumenbach placed "aproned" women in the same category with beardless Americans, tailed people, centaurs, and sirens – all of which he regarded as figments of travelers' rich imaginations.[60] [. . .]

[. . .] They also wanted to know if these aprons were natural or, once again, the product of female artifice. Many naturalists, including Le Vaillant, suggested that women created these flaps of skin by pulling, pinching, twisting, and wrapping normal labia around little sticks and twigs (for the same inexplicable reasons that Hottentot men cut off their left testicles).[61] [. . .]

Le Vaillant's testimony, however, carried some weight because he produced an illustration of this appendage said to be drawn from life (Figure 1.1F). [. . .]

Elizabeth Helme, one of several English translators of Le Vaillant's work, was of a different mind about the matter. She deleted the eight-page discussion and the illustration of the nude Hottentot woman, explaining in the preface: "I have softened (if I may be allowed the expression) a few passages that possibly might be accounted mere effusions of fancy and vivacity in a French author, but which would ill accord with the delicacy of a female translator, or indeed with the temper and genius of English readers."[62] John Barrow, her compatriot, also criticized Le Vaillant's illustration as more a product of his imagination than a true image of nature.[63]

[. . .] By the early nineteenth century European interest in this aspect of Hottentot genitalia had grown into a grotesque voyeurism to which naturalists were not immune.[64] In 1815, Georges Cuvier, France's premier comparative anatomist, performed his now infamous dissection of the South African woman known as the "Hottentot Venus" to solve once and for all the mysteries of the renowned apron. "There is," he wrote in his report, "nothing more celebrated in natural history."[65] The very name given this woman – Cuvier always referred to her as *Vénus Hottentotte* – emphasized her sexuality. [. . .]

The story of this woman, whose given Dutch name was Saartjie Baartman (her original name has gone unrecorded), has been recounted many times, most recently by Percival Kirby, Stephen Jay Gould, Sander Gilman, and Anne Fausto-Sterling.[66] Baartman was in her twenties when she was transported from the British colony on the Cape of Good Hope to London in 1810 by a ship's surgeon, Alexander Dunlop, who supplemented his income by exporting museum specimens from South Africa. He apparently told her she could make a "grand fortune" by exhibiting herself to the curious in the capital cities of Europe. Upon her arrival in England she became one of the most successful shows of London, displayed (not unlike Madame Chimpanzee) "on a stage two feet high, along which she was led by her keeper, and exhibited like a wild beast; being obliged to walk, stand, or sit as he ordered her."[67] Spectators could catch a glimpse of her "brutal figure" for a mere two shillings. At this time attention focused not on her apron (she was clothed in a costume resembling her skin as nearly as possible) but on her protruding buttocks which, for an extra charge, viewers could poke and prod.

[. . .]

It was in Paris that Sarah Bartmann became the object of intense scientific investigation. In the spring of 1815 she was summoned to the Jardin du Roi by a commission of zoologists and physiologists, where she was examined for three days. Henri de Blainville, professor at the Muséum d'Histoire Naturelle in the Jardin du Roi, set out his purposes in observing her: (1) to provide a detailed comparison of

HOTTENTOTE A TABLIER. *Tom. 1. Pag. 349.*

Figure 1.1F "A Hottentot woman with an 'apron'" from François Le
Vaillant, *Voyage de François Le Vaillant dans l'intérieur de
l'Afrique* (Paris, 1798), vol. 2, facing p. 349.
(Courtesy of the Pennsylvania State University Libraries)

this woman with the lowliest race of humans (the Negro) and the highest type of apes (the orangutan); (2) to provide the most complete possible description of the anomalies of her genitalia.[68]

This investigation required that Bartmann strip naked in the austere rooms of the museum in front of at least three formally dressed men. [. . .] According to de Blainville, the men (apart from de Blainville, Cuvier, and Geoffroy Saint-Hilaire, there is no record of who else was present) had great difficulty convincing Sarah (de Blainville adopted this familiar address) to let herself be seen nude. [. . .]

Bartmann's victory was short-lived. Upon her death from "inflammation" some nine months later at the age of about twenty-six, her body was brought to the museum for further examination. Dissection of her apron – "that extraordinary appendage which nature made a special attribute of her race" – was the first order of business. Cuvier relished this opportunity to resolve the mysteries of her apron, which during her lifetime had been "carefully hidden either between her thighs or more deeply. [. . .]

Cuvier's now notorious memoir described the Hottentot Venus in remarkably unflattering terms. At every turn he found her physique and manner bestial. [. . .] Though by his own report she was gay, had a good memory, and spoke three languages, Cuvier also remarked that while her hands were charming and feet pretty, her ears were small like those of apes. Significantly, her pelvis – the eighteenth-century measure of womanliness – resembled the female ape's. So, too, did her heart.

Like the many apes whose skeletons and skin were sold or donated to natural history museums, Bartmann's body was disassembled and, until quite recently, parts of it – her genitalia preserved in formalin in a bell jar, her skeleton, and a cast of her body – were on display in case number thirty-three in the Musée de l'Homme in Paris (they are now in the museum's storerooms). Her skin was apparently sent back to England, stuffed, and put on display.[69] In 1949, a stereoscopic photograph of her body cast was still available for purchase as a souvenir.

Cuvier's memoir of Sarah Bartmann reveals race and gender dynamics in science at the turn of the nineteenth century. His interest in the body of this South African woman focused on her sexuality; nine of his sixteen pages are devoted to Bartmann's genitalia, breasts, buttocks, and pelvis. Only one short paragraph evaluated her brain. On both accounts – of her sex and her race – Bartmann was relegated to the world of brute flesh.

Notes

1   The tenth edition of Linnaeus's *Systema naturae* and Carl Clerck's *Aranei Svecici* together form the starting point of modern zoological nomenclature. See *International Code of Zoological Nomenclature*, ed. W.D. Ride (London: British Museum, 1985), I.3. The term *Mammalia* first appeared in a student dissertation, *Natura pelagi*, in 1757 but was not published until 1760 (*Amoenitates academicae* [Erlangen, 1788], vol. 5, pp. 68–77).

2   Gunnar Broberg (ed.) (1980) *Linnaeus: Progress and Prospects in Linnaean Research* Stockholm: Almquist & Wiksell International, p. 34.

3   Carl Linnaeus (1758) *Systema naturae per regna tria naturae*, 10th ed., Stockholm.

4   Thomas Huxley, cited in Ernst Haeckel (1907) *Das Menschen-Problem und die Herrentiere von Linné*, Frankfurt: Neuer Frankfurter Verlag, p.8.

5   See Maurice Daumas (1957) *Histoire de la science*, Paris: Gallimard, p. 1352.

6   Georges-Louis Leclerc, comte de Buffon (1749–1804) *Histoire naturelle générale et particulière*, Paris, vol. 14, p. 18.

7   Cited by Jean Baptiste Bory de Saint-Vincent (1825) *Dictionnaire classique d'histoire naturelle*, Paris, vol. 8, p 270.

8   John Ray (1693) *Synopsis methodica: Animalium quadrupedum et serpentini generis*, London. "Animalium tabula generalis", p. 53. See also William Gregory (1908) "Linnaeus as an Intermediary between Ancient and Modern Zoology", *Annals of the New York Academy of Sciences* 18: 21–31, especially 25. Ray's terms were used as adjectives, not nouns – an important distinction at a time when scholastics distinguished between essence and accident. Theodor Gill (1902) "The Story of a Word – Mammal", *Popular Science Monthly* 61: 434–8.

9   Broberg (1983) "*Homo sapiens*: Linnaeus's Classification of Man", in Tore Frängsmyr (ed.) *Linnaeus: The Man and His Work*, Berkeley and Los Angeles: University of California Press, p. 175.

10   Broberg (1983) *Homo Sapiens: Studier i Carl von Linnés naturuppfattning och människolära*, Stockholm: The Swedish History of Science Society, p.176.

11   Gill, "Story of a Word", p. 435.

12   Stearn (1959) "The Background of Linnaeus's Contributions to the Nomenclature and Methods of Systematic Biology", *Systematic Zoology*, 80.

13   Gill, "Story of a Word", pp. 436–7. See also *Dictionnaire pittoresque d'histoire naturelle* (1836) 4, s.v. "Mammifères".

14   Ronald King in Robert Thornton (1799) *The Temple of Flora*, Boston: New York Graphic Society, 1981, p. 9. Linnaeus sometimes named new genera after friends and colleagues, intending to suggest a spiritual likeness between the individual and the plant or animal in question (Benjamin Jackson [1923] *Linnaeus* [London: H.F. & G. Witherby, p. 278). He also ranked his colleagues as "Officers in Flora's Army" according to his evaluation of their scientific merit. His list was headed by "General Linnaeus"; the lowliest rank was assigned to his critic, Johann Siegesbeck (Heinz Goerke [1973] *Linnaeus*, trans. Denver Lindley [New York: Charles Scribner's Sons], p. 108).

15   Cuvier (1817) *Le Règne animal*, Paris, vol. 1, p. 76.

16   Scott Atran (1990) *Cognitive Foundations of Natural History: Towards an Anthropology of Science*, Cambridge: Cambridge University Press, p. 316 nn. 23–4.

17   Stephen Jay Gould, "A Quahog is a Quahog", in *The Panda's Thumb: More Reflections in Natural History*, (New York: Norton, 1980), pp. 204–7.

18   See Lynn Hunt (1984) *Politics, Culture, and Class in the French Revolution*, Berkeley and Los Angeles: University of California Press, especially part 1: also Warner (1985) *Monuments and Maidens: The Allegory of the Female Form*, New York: Atheneum, chaps. 12, 13.

19   Linnaeus saw reason as the principal characteristic distinguishing humans from other animals. In the preface to his *Fauna Svecica* (Stockholm, 1746) he called reason "the most noble thing of all" that places humans above all others. See also H.W. Janson (1952) *Apes and Ape Lore in the Middle Ages and the Renaissance*, London: The Warburg Institute, pp. 74–5.

20   Plato, *Timaeus*, 91c. Plato seemed uncertain whether woman should be classed with brute beasts or rational beings. Ian Maclean (1980) *The Renaissance Notion of Woman: A Study in the Fortunes of Scholasticism and Medical Science in European Intellectual Life*, Cambridge: Cambridge University Press, p. 31.

21   William Godwin (1798) *Memoirs of the Author of a Vindication of the Rights of Woman*, London, p. 183.

22   Hermann Ploss, Bartels, Max and Bartels, Paul (1936) *Woman: An Historical Gynecological and Anthropological Compendium*, ed. Eric Dingwall, St. Louis: C.V. Mosby Company, vol. 3, p. 211.

23   Carolyn Merchant (1980) *The Death of Nature: Women, Ecology, and the Scientific Revolution*, San Francisco: Harper & Row.

24   Linnaeus, *Fauna Svecica*, frontispiece.

25   Neumann (1956) *Die Grosse Mutter*, Zurich: Rhein Verlag, p. 128.

26   Warner (1976) *Alone of All Her Sex: The Myth and the Cult of the Virgin Mary*, New York: Alfred A. Knopf, pp. 192, 200; Warner, *Monuments and Maidens,* p. 283. Whether the Virgin menstruated was much discussed in the Middle Ages; theologians, committed to a new emphasis on Incarnation, argued that she did. Cadden (1992) *The Meaning of Sexual Difference in the Middle Ages: Medicine, Natural Philosophy, and Culture*, Cambridge: Cambridge University Press, pp. 174–5.

27   Bynum (1982) *Jesus as Mother: Studies in the Spirituality of the High Middle Ages*, Berkeley and Los Angeles: University of California Press, p. 115.

28   Warner, *Alone of All Her Sex*, p. 194.

29   The pictorial representation of *sapientia lactans* dates to the early fifteenth century. *Sapientia lactans* was incorporated into the seal of Cambridge University, which shows the naked *Alma Mater Cantabrigia* with milk streaming from her breasts (W. S. Heckscher [1946–7] "Spiritualia sub metaphoris corporalium", *University of Toronto Quarterly* 16: 212 n. 9).

30   On Amazons, see J.A Fabricius, "Dissertatio critica," cited in Thomas Bendyshe (1865) "The History of Anthropology", *Memoirs Read Before the Anthropological Society of London* 1: 415–16. Saints Agnes and Barbara were shown having their breasts cut off as a form of torture in grotesque art of the late Middle Ages (Margaret Miles [1989] *Carnal Knowing: Female Nakedness and Religious Meaning in the Christian West*, Boston: Beacon Press, p. 156).

31   Warner, *Monuments and Maidens*, p. 281.

32   Barbara Gelphi (1992) *Shelley's Goddess: Maternity, Language, Subjectivity*, New York: Oxford University Press, pp. 43–60. See also Jean Block (1984) "Women and Reform of the Nation", in Samia Spencer (ed.) *French Women and the Age of Enlightenment*, Bloomington: University of Indiana Press, pp. 3–18.

33   Dissatisfaction with wet-nursing began in the 1680s. However, the height of the campaign came in the eighteenth century. See Sharp (1671) *The Midwives Book*, London, pp. 353, 361–2; Valerie Fildes (1986) *Breasts, Bottles and Babies: A History of Infant Feeding*, Edinburgh: Edinburgh University Press; and Randolph Trumbach (1978) *The Rise of the Egalitarian Family: Aristocratic Kinship and Domestic Relations in Eighteenth-century England*, New York: Academic Press. Dry-nursing under the mother's direct supervision was also advocated but led to even higher infant mortality.

34   George Sussman (1982) *Selling Mother's Milk: The Wet-Nursing Business in France, 1715–1914*, Urbana: University of Illinois Press, p. 20; see also Nancy Senior (1983), "Aspects of Infant Feeding in Eighteenth-Century France", *Eighteenth-Century Studies* 16: 367; Mary Sheriff, "Fragonard's Erotic Mothers and the Politics of Reproduction", in L. Hunt (ed.) (1991) *Eroticism and the Body Politic*, Baltimore: Johns Hopkins University Press, pp. 14–40.

35   Figures collected by Maxime de Sarthe-Lenoir, Lieutenant Général de Police for

Paris, in the 1770s cited in Senior, "Aspects of Infant Feeding", pp. 367–8. See also George Sussman (1977) "Parisian Infants and Norman Wet-Nurses in the Early Nineteenth Century", *Journal of Interdisciplinary History* 7: 637.

36   In an attempt to curb abuses and decrease infant mortality, wet-nursing in France was regulated by law in 1715 (Sussman, *Selling Mothers' Milk*, p 38).

37   Linnaeus, "Nutrix noverca", trans. by J. E. Gilibert (1770) as "La nourrice marâtre, ou Dissertation sur les suites funestes du nourrissage mercénaire", in *Les chefs-d'oeuvres de Monsieur de Sauvages*, Lyon, vol. 2, pp. 215–44.

38   Linnaeus, "Nutrix noverca", p. 258.

39   Linnaeus, "Nutrix noverca", p. 265. Though this argument was heard less frequently, it was still prominent in the eighteenth century.

40   William Cadogan (1948) *An Essay upon Nursing and the Management of Children*, London, p. 7.

41   Fildes (1988) *Wet Nursing: A History from Antiquity to the Present*, Oxford: Basil Blackwell, p. 193.

42   Rousseau (1762) *Emile: ou De l'éducation*, pp. 254–64. See also Mary Jacobus, "Incorrupible Milk: Breast-feeding and the French Revolution", in Sara Melzer and Leslie Rabine (eds) (1992) *Rebel Daughters: Women and the French Revolution*, New York: Oxford University Press, p. 62.

43   Mary Lindemann (1981) "Love for Hire: The Regulation of the Wet-Nursing Business in Eighteenth-Century Hamburg", *Journal of Family History* 6: 391.

44   *Allgemeines Landrecht* (1794), part II, title II, art. 67, in Susan Bell and Karen Offen (eds) (1983) *Women, the Family and Freedom: The Debate in Documents 1750–1880*, Stanford: Stanford University Press, vol. 1, p. 39.

45   Jean-Jacques Rousseau (1953) *The Confessions of Jean-Jacques Rousseau*, trans. J. Cohen (1978) Harmondsworth, Middlesex: Penguin, p. 333. See also William Kessen (1978) "Rousseau's Children", *Daedalus* 107: 155; ironically, Emile was brought up by a wet nurse in the country (Senior, "Aspects of Infant Feeding", p. 385).

46   Jordanova, *Languages of Nature*, p. 97; Warner, *Monuments and Maidens*, p. 282.

47   See Hunt, *Politics, Culture, and Class in the French Revolution*, chaps. 2, 3.

48   Darline Levy, Harriet Applewhite, and Mary Johnson (eds) (1979) *Women in Revolutionary Paris 1789–1795*, Urbana: University of Illinois Press, p. 219. See also Outram (1989) *The Body and the French Revolution: Sex, Class and Political Culture*, New Haven: Yale University Press.

49   Lynn Hunt (1992) *The Family Romance of the French Revolution*, Berkeley and Los Angeles: University of California Press, pp. 151–91, especially 153–5.

50   Arthur Lovejoy (1953) *The Great Chain of Being: A Study of the History of an Idea*, Cambridge, MA: Harvard University Press, 1964. Winthrop D. Jordan (1968) *White over Black: American Attitudes toward the Negro, 1550–1812*, Chapel Hill: University of North Carolina Press, pp. 217–28.

51   Reported in Petrus Camper (1794) *The Works of the Late Professor Camper on the Connexion between the Science of Anatomy and the Arts of Drawing, Painting, Statuary, etc.*, trans. T. Cogan, London, p. 32, though this was not his opinion.

52   One of the best discussions is found in Jordan, *White over Black*, pp. 215–65.

53   See Thomas Laqueur (1990) *Making Sex: Body and Gender from the Greeks to Freud*, Cambridge, MA: Harvard University Press; and also Londa Schiebinger (1989) *The Mind Has no Sex? Women in the Origins of Modern Science*, Cambridge, MA: Harvard University Press, chaps. 7, 8.

54   See Gloria Hull, Patricia Bell Scott, and Barbara Smith (eds) (1982) *All the Women*

Are White, All the Blacks Are Men, But Some of Us Are Brave: Black Women's Studies, Old Westbury, NY: Feminist Press. One sees these assumptions expressed over and over again today (see Spelman [1988] *Inessential Woman: Problems of Exclusion in Feminist Thought*, Boston: Beacon Press, pp. 114–15).

55 Barbara Bush (1981) "White 'Ladies,' Coloured 'Favourites' and Black 'Wenches'; Some Considerations on Sex, Race and Class Factors in Social Relations in White Creole Society in the British Caribbean", *Slavery and Abolition* 2: 244–62, especially 249; Hazel Carby (1987) *Reconstructing Womanhood: The Emergence of the Afro-American Woman Novelist*, New York: Oxford University Press, pp. 20–39; and Evelyn Brooks Higginbotham (1992) "African-American Women's History and the Metalanguage of Race", *Signs: Journal of Women in Culture and Society* 17: 251–74, especially 262–6.

56 Buffon (1749–1804) *Histoire naturelle, générale et particulière*, 44 vols, Paris, vol. 3, p. 407; Blumenbach (1865) *On the Natural Varieties of Mankind*, trans. Thomas Bendyshe, New York; Bergman, 1969, p. 247 n. 5; C. P. Thunberg (1795) "An Account of the Cape of Good Hope", in John Pinkerton (1808) *A General Collection of the Best and Most Interesting Voyages and Travels in all Parts of the World*, London, vol. 16, pp. 29–30; and Samuel Stanhope Smith (1787) *An Essay on the Causes of the Variety of Complexion and Figure in the Human Species*, Cambridge, MA: Harvard University Press, 1965, p. 82.

57 Linnaeus (1758) *Systema naturae per regna tria naturae*, 10th ed., Stockholm, pp. 22, 24. Winthrop Jordan mistranslated *sinus pudoris* as: "Women's bosom a matter of modesty" (*White over Black*, p. 221); Frank Spencer (1986) also translated it incorrectly as "women without shame" (*Ecce Homo: An Annotated Bibliographic History of Physical Anthropology*, New York: Greenwood Press, p. 78); and most recently, Pieterse has it wrong – "the bosoms of women are distended" (Jan Pieterse [1992] *White on Black: Images of Africa and Blacks in Western Popular Culture*, New Haven: Yale University Press, p. 40). In his "Anthropomorpha" Linnaeus claimed that female troglodytes had these hanging folds of skin (Carl Linnaeus, "Anthropomorpha", respondent C.E. Hoppius [1760] in *Amoenitates academicae* [Erlangen, 1789], vol. 6, description of fig. 4).

58 John Ovington (1696) *A Voyage to Suratt in the Year 1689*, London, p. 497.

59 Blumenbach, *On the Natural Varieties of Mankind*, p. 250 n. 4; Voltaire (1879) *Lettres d'Amabed*, letter 4, *Oeuvres complètes de Voltaire*, Paris: Garnier Frères, vol. 21, pp. 458–9.

60 Blumenbach, *On the Natural Varieties of Mankind*, pp. 249–50; Blumenbach (1779) *Handbuch der Naturgeschichte*, Göttingen, p. 64.

61 Le Vaillant (1790) *Voyage de François Le Vaillant dans L'intérieur de l'Afrique*, Paris, 1798, vol. 2, pp. 351–3; see also Virey (1823) *De la femme*, Paris, p. 30; and Moreau de la Sarthe (1803), *Histoire naturelle de la femme*, Paris, p. 525.

62 François Le Vaillant (1790) *Travels from the Cape of Good Hope into the Interior Parts of Africa*, trans. Elizabeth Helme, London, preface.

63 Barrow (1801) *Reisen in das Innere von Südafrika in den Jahren, 1797 and 1798*, Berlin, 1802, p. 311.

64 Sander Gilman, "Black Bodies, White Bodies: Toward an Iconography of Female Sexuality in Late Nineteenth-Century Art, Medicine, and Literature", in Henry Louis Gates Jr (ed.) (1986) *"Race," Writing, and Difference*, Chicago: University of Chicago Press, pp. 223–61.

65 Cuvier (1817) "Extrait d'observations faites sur le cadavre d'une femme connue à

Paris et à Londres sous le nom de Vénus Hottentotte", *Mémoires du Muséum d'Histoire Naturelle* 3: 259–74.

66   My account of her life has been taken from Percival Kirby (1940) "The Hottentot Venus", *Africana Notes and News* 6: 55-62; and (1953) "More About the Hottentot Venus," *Africana Notes and News* 10: 124–34. See also Edwards and Walvin (1983) *Black Personalities in the Era of the Slave Trade*, Baton Rouge: Louisiana State University Press, pp. 171–82; and Stephen Jay Gould (1985) *The Flamingo's Smile: Reflections in Natural History*, New York: Norton & Company, pp. 291–305; Gilman (1985) *Difference and Pathology: Stereotypes of Sexuality, Race and Madness*, Ithaca: Cornell University Press, pp. 83–8; and Anne Fausto-Sterling, *Making a Difference: Biology and the Social/Scientific Construction of Sexuality* (in preparation).

67   Richard Altick (1978) *The Shows of London*, Cambridge, MA: Harvard University Press, pp. 268–73.

68   Henri de Blainville (1816) "Sur une femme de la race hottentote", *Bulletin des sciences, par la Société Philomatique de Paris*: 183–90, especially 183.

69   In the nineteenth century, the skins of Africans were sometimes taken after death and stuffed for display in natural history museums. The anatomist Bonn at Amsterdam was noted for his beautiful skin collection. See Hans Debrunner (1979) *Presence and Prestige: Africans in Europe*, Basel: Basler Afrika Bibliographen, p. 145.

References

Barrow, John (1801) *Reisen in das innere von Südafrika in den Jahren, 1797 und 1798*, Berlin, 1802.

Bendyshe, Thomas (1865) "The History of Anthropology", *Memoirs Read Before the Anthropological Society of London*: 335–458.

Blainville, Henri de (1816) "Sur une femme de la race hottentote", *Bulletin des sciences par la Société Philomatique de Paris*: 183–90.

Blumenbach, Johann (1865) *On the Natural Varieties of Mankind*, trans. Thomas Bendyshe, New York: Bergman, 1969.

Broberg, Gunnar (1975) *Homo Sapiens L.: Studier i Carl von Linnés naturuppfattning och människolära*, Stockholm: The Swedish History of Science Society.

—— (1983) "*Homo sapiens*: Linnaeus's Classification of Man", in Tore Frängsmyr (ed.) *Linnaeus: The Man and His Work*, Berkeley and Los Angeles: University of California Press.

—— (ed.) (1980) *Linnaeus: Progress and Prospects in Linnaean Research*, Stockholm: Almquist & Wiksell International.

Buffon, Georges-Louis Leclerc, comte de (1749–1804) *Histoire naturelle, générale et particulière*, 44 vols., Paris.

Burrell, Harry (1921) *The Platypus*, Sydney: Angus & Robertson Limited.

Bush, Barbara (1981) "White 'Ladies,' Coloured 'Favourites' and Black 'Wenches'; Some Considerations on Sex, Race and Class Factors in Social Relations in White Creole Society in the British Caribbean", *Slavery and Abolition* 2: 244–62.

Bynum, Caroline (1982) *Jesus as Mother: Studies in the Spirituality of the High Middle Ages*, Berkeley and Los Angeles: University of California Press.

Cadden, Joan (1992) *The Meanings of Sexual Difference in the Middle Ages: Medicine, Natural Philosophy, and Culture*, Cambridge: Cambridge University Press.

Cadogan, William (1748) *An Essay upon Nursing and the Management of Children*, London.

Camper, Petrus (1794) *The Works of the Late Professor Camper on the Connexion between the Science of Anatomy and the Arts of Drawing, Painting, Statuary, etc.*, trans. T. Cogan, London.

Carby, Hazel (1987) *Reconstructing Womanhood: The Emergence of the Afro-American Woman Novelist*, New York: Oxford University Press.

Cuvier, Georges (1817) "Extrait d'observations faites sur le cadavre d'une femme connue à Paris et à Londres sous le nom de Vénus Hottentotte", *Mémoires du Muséum d'Histoire Naturelle* 3: 259–74.

—— (1817) *Le règne animal*, 4 vols. Paris.

Debrunner, Hans (1979) *Presence and Prestige: Africans in Europe*, Basel: Basler Afrika Bibliographen.

Edwards, Paul and Walvin, James (1983) *Black Personalities in the Era of the Slave Trade*, Baton Rouge: Louisiana State University Press.

Fildes, Valerie (1986) *Breasts, Bottles and Babies: A History of Infant Feeding*, Edinburgh: Edinburgh University Press.

—— (1988) *Wet Nursing: A History from Antiquity to the Present*, Oxford: Basil Blackwell.

Gates, Henry Louis, Jr (1986) *"Race," Writing, and Difference*, Chicago: University of Chicago Press.

—— (1989) *Figures in Black: Words, Signs, and the "Racial" Self*, New York: Oxford University Press.

Gelphi, Barbara (1992) *Shelley's Goddess: Maternity, Language, Subjectivity*, New York: Oxford University Press.

Gilibert, J. E. (1770) *Dissertation sur la dépopulation, causée par les vices, les préjugés et les erreurs des nourrices mercénaires"; in Les chefs-d'oeuvres de Monsieur de Sauvages*, Lyon, vol. 2.

Gill, Theodor (1902) "The Story of a Word – Mammal", *Popular Science Monthly* 61: 434–8.

Gilman, Sander (1985) *Difference and Pathology: Stereotypes of Sexuality, Race and Madness*, Ithaca: Cornell University Press.

Gould, Stephen Jay (1985) *The Flamingo's Smile: Reflections in Natural History*, New York: Norton & Company.

Gregory, William (1910) "The Orders of Mammals", *Bulletin of the American Museum of Natural History* 27.

Haeckel, Ernst (1907) *Das Menschen-Problem und die Herrentiere von Linné*, Frankfurt: Neuer Frankfurter Verlag.

Hull, Gloria, Scott, Patricia Bell and Smith, Barbara (eds) (1982) *All the Women Are White, All the Blacks Are Men, But Some of Us Are Brave: Black Women's Studies*, Old Westbury, New York: Feminist Press.

Hunt, Lynn (1984) *Politics, Culture, and Class in the French Revolution*, Berkeley and Los Angeles: University of California Press.

—— (ed.) (1991) *Eroticism and the Body Politic*, Baltimore: Johns Hopkins University Press.

—— (1992) *The Family Romance of the French Revolution*, Berkeley and Los Angeles: University of California Press.

Jackson, Benjamin (1923) *Linnaeus*, London: H.F. & G. Witherby.

Janson, H.W. (1952) *Apes and Ape Lore in the Middle Ages and the Renaissance*, London: The Warburg Institute.

Jordan, Winthrop D. (1968) *White over Black: American Attitudes toward the Negro, 1550–1812*, Chapel Hill: University of North Carolina Press.

Jordanova, Ludmilla (ed.) (1986) *Languages of Nature*, New Brunswick: Rutgers University Press.

Kirby, Percival, (1949) "The Hottentot Venus", *Africana Notes and News* 6: 55–62.

—— (1953) "More about the Hottentot Venus", *Africana Notes and News* 10: 124–34.

Laqueur, Thomas (1990) *Making Sex: Body and Gender from the Greeks to Freud*, Cambridge, MA: Harvard University Press.

Le Vaillant, François (1790) *Voyage de François Le Vaillant dans l'interieur de l'Afrique*, Paris, 1798.

—— (1790) *Travels from the Cape of Good-Hope into the Interior Parts of Africa*, trans. Elizabeth Helme, London.

Levy, Darline, Applewhite, Harriet and Johnson, Mary (eds) (1979) *Women in Revolutionary Paris, 1789–1795*, Urbana: University of Illinois Press.

Lindemann, Mary (1981) "Love for Hire: The Regulation of the Wet-Nursing Business in Eighteenth-Century Hamburg", *Journal of Family History* 6: 379–95.

Linnaeus, Carl (1980) *Praeludia sponsaliorum plantarum*, in N.H. Lärjungar and T. Fries (eds) *Smärre Skrifter af Carl von Linné*, Uppsala: Almquist & Wiksell.

—— (1735) *Systema naturae*, ed. M.S.J. Engel-Ledeboer and H. Engel, Nieuwkoop: B. de Graaf, 1964.

—— (1746) *Fauna Svecica*, Stockholm.

—— (1753) *Species plantarum*, Stockholm.

—— (1758) *Systema naturae per regna tria naturae*, 10th ed. Stockholm.

—— (1752) "Nutrix noverca", respondent F. Lindberg, in *Amoenitates academicae*, Erlangen, 1787, vol. 3.

—— (1760) "Anthropomorpha", respondent C. E. Hoppius, in *Amoenitates academicae*, Erlangen, 1789, vol. 6.

Lovejoy, Arthur (1933) *The Great Chain of Being: A Study of the History of an Idea*, Cambridge, MA: Harvard University Press, 1964.

Melzer, Sara and Rabine, Leslie (1992) *Rebel Daughters: Women and the French Revolution*, New York: Oxford University Press.

Merchant, Carolyn (1980) *The Death of Nature: Women, Ecology, and the Scientific Revolution*, San Francisco: Harper & Row.

Moreau de la Sarthe, Jacques (1803) *Histoire naturelle de la femme*, Paris.

Neumann, Erich (1956) *Die Grosse Mutter*, Zurich: Rhein Verlag.

Outram, Dorinda (1989) *The Body and the French Revolution: Sex, Class and Political Culture*, New Haven: Yale University Press.

Ovington, John (1696) *A Voyage to Suratt in the Year 1689*, London.

Pieterse, Jan (1992) *White on Black: Images of Africa and Blacks in Western Popular Culture*, New Haven: Yale University Press.

Pinkerton, John (1808–14) *A General Collection of the Best and Most Interesting Voyages and Travels in all Parts of the World*, 17 vols, London.

Ploss, Hermann, Bartels, Max and Bartels, Paul (1936) *Woman: An Historical Gynecological and Anthropological Compendium*, ed. Eric Dingwall, 3 vols, St. Louis: C.V. Mosby Company.

Ray, John (1693) *Synopsis methodica: Animalium quadrupedum et serpentini generis*, London.

Rousseau, Jean-Jacques (1762) *Emile, ou De l'éducation*, in Bernard Gagnebin and Marcel Raymond (eds) *Oeuvres complètes*, Paris: Gallimard, 1959–1969.

Schiebinger, Londa (1989) *The Mind Has no Sex? Women in the Origins of Modern Science*, Cambridge, MA: Harvard University Press.

Senior, Nancy (1983) "Aspects of Infant Feeding in Eighteenth-Century France", *Eighteenth-Century Studies* 16: 367–88.

Sharp, Jane (1671) *The Midwives Book*, London.

Smith, Samuel Stanhope (1787) *An Essay on the Causes of the Variety of Complexion and Figure in the Human Species*, Cambridge, MA: Harvard University Press.

Spelman, Elizabeth (1988) *Inessential Woman: Problems of Exclusion in Feminist Thought*, Boston: Beacon Press.

Spencer, Frank (1986) *Ecce Homo: An Annotated Bibliographic History of Physical Anthropology*, New York: Greenwood Press.

Stearn, W.T. (1959) "The Background of Linnaeus's Contributions to the Nomenclature and Methods of Systematic Biology", *Systematic Zoology* 8: 4–22.

Sussman, George (1982) *Selling Mothers' Milk: The Wet-Nursing Business in France, 1715–1914*, Urbana: University of Illinois Press.

Thornton, Robert (1799) *The Temple of Flora*, Boston: New York Graphic Society, 1981.

Trumbach, Randolph (1978) *The Rise of the Egalitarian Family: Aristocratic Kinship and Domestic Relations in Eighteenth-Century England*, New York: Academic Press.

Virey, Julien Joseph (1823) *De la femme*, Paris.

Warner, Marina (1976) *Alone of All Her Sex: The Myth and the Cult of the Virgin Mary*, New York: Alfred A. Knopf.

—— (1985) *Monuments and Maidens: The Allegory of the Female Form*, New York: Atheneum.

Nancy Leys Stepan

RACE AND GENDER: THE ROLE
OF ANALOGY IN SCIENCE

METAPHOR OCCUPIES A CENTRAL PLACE in literary theory, but the role of metaphors, and of the analogies they mediate, in scientific theory is still debated.[1] One reason for the controversy over metaphor, analogy, and models in science is the intellectually privileged status that science has traditionally enjoyed as the repository of non-metaphorical, empirical, politically neutral, universal knowledge. During the scientific revolution of the seventeenth century, metaphor became associated with the imagination, poetic fancy, subjective figures, and even untruthfulness and was contrasted with truthful, unadorned, objective knowledge – that is, with science itself.[2]

[. . .]

One result of the dichotomy established between science and metaphor was that obviously metaphoric or analogical science could only be treated as 'prescientific' or 'pseudoscientific' and therefore dismissable.[3] Because science has been identified with truthfulness and empirical reality, the metaphorical nature of much modern science tended to go unrecognized. And because it went unrecognized, as Colin Turbayne has pointed out, it has been easy to mistake the model in science 'for the thing modelled' – to think, to take his example, that nature *was* mechanical, rather than to think it was, metaphorically, seen as mechanical.[4]

[. . .]

Although the role of metaphor and analogy in science is now recognized, a critical theory of scientific metaphor is only just being elaborated. The purpose of this article is to contribute to the development of such a theory by using a particular analogy in the history of the life sciences to explore a series of related questions concerning the cultural sources of scientific analogies, their role in scientific reasoning, their normative consequences, and the process by which they change.

Race and gender: a powerful scientific analogy

The analogy examined is the one linking race to gender, an analogy that occupied a strategic place in scientific theorizing about human variation in the nineteenth and twentieth centuries.

As has been well documented, from the late Enlightenment on students of human variation singled out racial differences as crucial aspects of reality, and an extensive discourse on racial inequality began to be elaborated.[5] In the nineteenth century, as attention turned increasingly to sexual and gender differences as well, gender was found to be remarkably analogous to race, such that the scientist could use racial difference to explain gender difference, and vice versa.[6]

Thus it was claimed that women's low brain weights and deficient brain structures were analogous to those of lower races, and their inferior intellectualities explained on this basis.[7] Woman, it was observed, shared with Negroes a narrow, childlike, and delicate skull, so different from the more robust and rounded heads characteristic of males of 'superior' races. Similarly, women of higher races tended to have slightly protruding jaws, analogous to, if not as exaggerated as, the apelike, jutting jaws of lower races.[8] Women and lower races were called innately impulsive, emotional, imitative rather than original, and incapable of the abstract reasoning found in white men.[9] Evolutionary biology provided yet further analogies. Woman was in evolutionary terms the 'conservative element' to the man's 'progressive' preserving the more 'primitive' traits found in lower races, while the males of higher races led the way in new biological and cultural directions.[10]

Thus when Carl Vogt, one of the leading German students of race in the middle of the nineteenth century, claimed that the female skull approached in many respects that of the infant and in still further respects that of lower races, whereas the mature male of many lower races resembled in his 'pendulous' belly a Caucasian woman who had had many children, and in his thin calves and flat thighs the ape, he was merely stating what had become almost a cliché of the science of human difference.[11]

So fundamental was the analogy between race and gender that the major modes of interpretation of racial traits were invariably evoked to explain sexual traits. For instance, just as scientists spoke of races as distinct 'species', incapable of crossing to produce viable 'hybrids', scientists analysing male–female differences sometimes spoke of females as forming a distinct 'species', individual members of which were in danger of degenerating into psychosexual hybrids when they tried to cross the boundaries proper to their sex.[12] Darwin's theory of sexual selection was applied to both racial and sexual difference, as was the neo-Lamarckian theory of the American Edward Cope.[13] A last, confirmatory example of the analogous place of gender and race in scientific theorizing is taken from the history of hormone biology. Early in the twentieth century the anatomist and student of race Sir Arthur Keith interpreted racial differences in the human species as a function of pathological disturbances of the newly discovered 'internal secretions' or hormones. At about the same time, the apostle of sexual frankness and well-known student of sexual variation Havelock Ellis used internal secretions to explain the small, but to him vital, differences in the physical and psychosexual make-up of men and women.[14]

In short, lower races represented the 'female' type of the human species, and females the 'lower race' of gender. As the example from Vogt indicates, however, the analogies concerned more than race and gender. Through an intertwined and over-lapping series of analogies, involving often quite complex comparisons, identifications, cross-references, and evoked associations, a variety of 'differences' – physical and psychical, class and national – were brought together in a biosocial science of human variation. By analogy with the so-called lower races, women, the sexually deviate, the criminal, the urban poor, and the insane were in one way or another constructed as biological 'races apart' whose differences from the white male, and likenesses to each other, 'explained' their different and lower position in the social hierarchy.[15]

It is not the aim of this article to provide a systematic history of the biosocial science of racial and sexual difference based on analogy. The aim is rather to use the race–gender analogy to analyse the nature of analogical reasoning in science itself. When and how did the analogy appear in science? From what did it derive its scientific authority? How did the analogy shape research? What did it mean when a scientist claimed that the mature male of many lower races resembled a mature Caucasian female who had had many children? No simple theory of resemblance or substitution explains such an analogy. How did the analogy help construct the very similarities and differences supposedly 'discovered' by scientists in nature? What theories of analogy and metaphor can be most effectively applied in the critical study of science?

The cultural sources of scientific metaphor

[. . .]

The origin of many of the 'root metaphors' of human difference are obscure. G. Lakoff and M. Johnson suggest that the basic values of a culture are usually compatible with 'the metaphorical structure of the most fundamental concepts in the culture'.[16] Not surprisingly, the social groups represented metaphorically as 'other' and 'inferior' in Western culture were socially 'disenfranchised' in a variety of ways, the causes of their disenfranchisement varying from group to group and from period to period. Already in ancient Greece, Aristotle likened women to the slave on the grounds of their 'natural' inferiority. Winthrop Jordan has shown that by the early Middle Ages a binary opposition between blackness and whiteness was well estab-lished in which blackness was identified with baseness, sin, the devil, and ugliness, and whiteness with virtue, purity, holiness, and beauty.[17] Over time, black people themselves were compared to apes, and their childishness, savageness, bestiality, sexuality, and lack of intellectual capacity stressed. The 'Ethiopian, the 'African', and especially the 'Hottentot' were made to stand for all that the white male was not; they provided a rich analogical source for the understanding and representation of other 'inferiorities'. In his study of the representation of insanity in Western culture, for instance, Gilman shows how the metaphor of blackness could be borrowed to explicate the madman, and vice versa. In similar analogical fashion, the labouring poor were represented as the 'savages' of Europe, and the criminal as a 'Negro'.

When scientists in the nineteenth century, then, proposed an analogy between racial and sexual differences, or between racial and class differences, and began to generate new data on the basis of such analogies, their interpretations of human difference and similarity were widely accepted, partly because of their fundamental congruence with cultural expectations. In this particular science, the metaphors and analogies were not strikingly new but old, if unexamined and diffuse. The scientists' contribution was to elevate hitherto unconsciously held analogies into self-conscious theory, to extend the meanings attached to the analogies, to expand their range via new observations and comparisons, and to give them precision through specialized vocabularies and new technologies. Another result was that the analogies became 'naturalized' in the language of science, and their metaphorical nature disguised.

In the scientific elaboration of these familiar analogies, the study of race led the way, in part because the differences between blacks and whites seemed so 'obvious', in part because the abolition movement gave political urgency to the issue of racial difference and social inequality. From the study of race came the association between inferiority and the ape. The facial angle, a measure of hierarchy in nature obtained by comparing the protrusion of the jaws in apes and man, was widely used in analogical science once it was shown that by this measure Negroes appeared to be closer to apes than the white race.[18] Established as signs of inferiority, the facial angle and blackness could then be extended analogically to explain other inferior groups and races. For instance, Francis Galton, Darwin's cousin and the founder of eugenics and statistics in Britain, used the Negro and the apish jaw to explicate the Irish: 'Visitors to Ireland after the potato famine', he commented, 'generally remarked that the Irish type of face seemed to have become more prognathous, that is, more like the negro in the protrusion of the lower jaw.'[19]

Especially significant for the analogical science of human difference and similarity were the systematic study and measurement of the human skull. The importance of the skull to students of human difference lay in the fact that it housed the brain, differences in whose shape and size were presumed to correlate with equally presumed differences in intelligence and social behaviour. It was measurements of the skull, brain weights, and brain convolutions that gave apparent precision to the analogies between anthropoid apes, lower races, women, criminal types, lower classes, and the child. It was race scientists who provided the new technologies of measurement – the callipers, cephalometers, craniometers, craniophores, cranio-stats, and parietal goniometers.[20] The low facial angles attributed by scientists starting in the 1840s and 1850s to women, criminals, idiots, and the degenerate, and the corresponding low brain weights, protruding jaws, and incompletely developed frontal centres where the higher intellectual faculties were presumed to be located were all taken from racial science. By 1870 Paul Topinard, the leading French anthropologist after the death of Paul Broca, could call on data on sexual and racial variations from literally hundreds of skulls and brains, collected by numerous scientists over decades, in order to draw the conclusion that Caucasian women were indeed more prognathous or apelike in their jaws than white men, and even the largest women's brains, from the 'English or Scotch' race, made them like the African male.[21] Once 'woman' had been shown to be indeed analogous to lower races by the new science of anthropometry and had become, in essence, a racialized category, the traits and qualities special to woman could in turn be used in an analogical under-standing of lower races. The analogies now had the weight of empirical reality and scientific theory. The similarities between a Negro and a white woman, or between a criminal and a Negro, were realities of nature, somehow 'in' the individuals studied.

Metaphoric interactions

We have seen that metaphors and analogies played an important part in the science of human difference in the nineteenth century. The question is, what part? I want to suggest that the metaphors functioned as the science itself – that without them the science did not exist. In short, metaphors and analogies can be constituent elements of science.

It is here that I would like to introduce, as some other historians of science have done, Max Black's 'interaction' theory of metaphor, because it seems that the metaphors discussed in this essay, and the analogies they mediated, functioned like interaction metaphors, and that thinking about them in these terms clarifies their role in science.[22]

By interaction metaphors, Black means metaphors that join together and bring into cognitive and emotional relation with each other two different things, or systems of things, not normally so joined. Black follows I. A. Richards in opposing the 'substitution' theory of metaphor, in which it is supposed that the metaphor is telling us indirectly something factual about the two subjects – that the metaphor is a *literal comparison*, or is capable of a literal translation in prose. Richards proposed instead that 'when we use a metaphor, we have two thoughts of different things active together and supported by a single word or phrase, whose meaning is the resultant of their interaction.' Applying the interaction theory to the metaphor 'The poor are the negroes of Europe', Black paraphrases Richards to claim that "our thoughts about the European poor and American negroes are 'active together' and 'interact' to produce a meaning that is a resultant of that interaction."[23] In such a view, the metaphor cannot be simply reduced to literal comparisons or 'like' statements without loss of meaning or cognitive content, because meaning is a product of the interaction between the two parts of a metaphor.

[. . .]

Black's point is that by their interactions and evoked associations both parts of a metaphor are changed. Each part is seen as more like the other in some characteristic way. Black was primarily interested in ordinary metaphors of a culture and in their commonplace associations. But instead of commonplace associations, a metaphor may evoke more specially constructed systems of implications. Scientists are in the business of constructing exactly such systems of implications, through their empirical investigations into nature and through their introduction into discourse of specialized vocabularies and technologies.[24] It may be, indeed, that what makes an analogy suitable for scientific purposes is its ability to be suggestive of new systems of implications, new hypotheses, and therefore new observations.[25]

In the case of the nineteenth-century analogical science of human difference, for instance, the system of implications evoked by the analogy linking lower races and women was not just a generalized one concerning social inferiority, but the more precise and specialized one developed by years of anthropometric, medical, and biological research. When 'woman' and 'lower races' were analogically and routinely joined in the anthropological, biological, and medical literature of the 1860s and 1870s, the metaphoric interactions involved a complex system of implications about similarity and difference, often involving highly technical language (for example, in one set of measurements of the body in different races cited by Paul Topinard in 1878 the comparisons included measures in each race of their height from the ground to the acromion, the epicondyle, the styloid process of the radius, the great trochanter, and the internal malleolus). The systems of implications evoked by the analogy included questions of comparative health and disease (blacks and women were believed to show greater degrees of insanity and neurasthenia than white men, especially under conditions of freedom), of sexual behaviour (females of 'lower races' and lower-class women of 'higher races', especially prostitutes, were believed to show similar kinds of bestiality and sexual promiscuity, as well as similar signs of pathology and degeneracy such as deformed skulls and teeth), and of 'childish' characteristics, both physical and moral.[26]

As already noted, one of the most important systems of implications about human groups developed by scientists in the nineteenth century on the basis of analogical reasoning concerned head shapes and brain sizes. It was assumed that blacks, women, the lower classes, and criminals shared low brain weights or skull capacities. Paul Broca, the founder of the Société d'Anthropologie de Paris in 1859, asserted:

> In general, the brain is larger in mature adults than in the elderly, in men than in women, in eminent men than in men of mediocre talent, in superior races than in inferior races. . . . Other things being equal, there is a remarkable relationship between the development of intelligence and the volume of the brain.[27]

Such a specialized system of implications based on the similarities between brains and skulls appeared for the first time in the phrenological literature of the 1830s. Although analogies between women and blackness had been drawn before, woman's place in nature and her bio-psychological differences from men had been discussed by scientists mainly in terms of reproductive function and sexuality, and the most important analogies concerned black females (the 'sign' of sexuality) and lower-class or 'degenerate' white women. Since males of all races had no wombs, no systematic, apparently scientifically validated grounds of comparison between males of 'lower' races and women of 'higher' races existed.

Starting in the 1820s, however, the phrenologists began to focus on differences in the shape of the skull of individuals and groups, in the belief that the skull was a sign faithfully reflecting the various organs of mind housed in the brain, and that differences in brain organs explained differences in human behaviour. And it is in the phrenological literature, for almost the first time, that we find women and lower races compared directly on the basis of their skull formations. In their 'organology', the phrenologists paid special attention to the organ of 'philoprogenitiveness', or the faculty causing 'love of offspring', which was believed to be more highly developed in women than men, as was apparent from their more highly developed upper part of the occiput. The same prominence, according to Franz Joseph Gall, was found in monkeys and was particularly well developed, he believed, in male and female Negroes.[28]

By the 1840s and 1850s the science of phrenology was on the wane, since the organs of the brain claimed by the phrenologists did not seem to correspond with the details of brain anatomy as described by neurophysiologists. But although the specific conclusions of the phrenologists concerning the anatomical structure and functions of the brain were rejected, the principle that differences in individual and group function were products of differences in the shape and size of the head was not. This principle underlay the claim that some measure, whether of cranial capacity, the facial angle, the brain volume, or brain weight, would be found that would provide a true indicator of innate capacity, and that by such a measure women and lower races would be shown to occupy analogous places in the scale of nature (the 'scale' itself of course being a metaphorical construct).

By the 1850s the measurement of women's skulls was becoming an established part of craniometry and the science of gender joined analogically to race. Vogt's *Lectures on Man* included a long discussion of the various measures available of the skulls of men and women of different races. His data showed that women's smaller brains were analogous to the brains of lower races, the small size explaining both groups' intellectual inferiority. (Vogt also concluded that within Europe the intelligentsia and upper classes had the largest heads, and peasants the smallest.)[29] Broca shared Vogt's interest; he too believed it was the smaller brains of women and 'lower' races, compared with men of 'higher' races, that caused their lesser intellectual capacity and therefore their social inferiority.[30]

One novel conclusion to result from scientists' investigations into the different skull capacities of males and females of different races was that the gap in head size between men and women had apparently widened over historic time, being largest in the 'civilized' races such as the European, and smallest in the most savage races.[31] The growing difference between the sexes from the prehistoric period to the present was attributed to evolutionary, selective pressures, which were believed to be greater in the white races than the dark and greater in men than women. Paradoxically, therefore, the civilized European woman was less like the civilized European man than the savage man was like the savage woman. The 'discovery' that the male and female bodies and brains in the lower races were very alike allowed scientists to draw direct comparisons between a black male and white female. The male could be taken as representative of both sexes of his race and the black female could be virtually ignored in the analogical science of intelligence, if not sexuality.

Because interactive metaphors bring together a *system* of implications, other features previously associated with only one subject in the metaphor are brought to bear on the other. As the analogy between women and race gained ground in science, therefore, women were found to share other points of similarity with lower races. A good example is prognathism. Prognathism was a measure of the protrusion of the jaw and of inferiority. As women and lower races became analogically joined, data on the 'prognathism' of females were collected and women of 'advanced' races implicated in this sign of inferiority. Havelock Ellis, for instance, in the late nineteenth-century bible of male–female differences *Man and Woman*, mentioned the European woman's slightly protruding jaw as a trait, not of high evolution, but of the lower races, although he added that in white women the trait, unlike in the lower races, was 'distinctly charming'.[32]

Another set of implications brought to bear on women by analogy with lower races concerned dolichocephaly and brachycephaly, or longheadedness and round-headedness. Africans were on the whole more longheaded than Europeans and so dolichocephaly was generally interpreted as signifying inferiority. Ellis not surprisingly found that on the whole women, criminals, the degenerate, the insane, and prehistoric races tended to share with dark races the more narrow, dolichocephalic heads representing an earlier (and by implication, more primitive) stage of brain development.[33]

Analogy and the creation of new knowledge

In the metaphors and analogies joining women and the lower races, the scientist was led to 'see' points of similarity that before had gone unnoticed. Women became more 'like' Negroes, as the statistics on brain weights and body shapes showed. The question is, what kind of 'likeness' was involved?

Here again the interaction theory of metaphor is illuminating. As Black says, the notion of similarity is ambiguous. Or as Stanley Fish puts it, 'Similarity is not something one finds but something one must establish.'[34] Metaphors are not meant to be taken literally but they do imply some structural similarity between the two things joined by the metaphor, a similarity that may be new to the readers of the metaphoric or analogical text, but that they are culturally capable of grasping.

However, there is nothing obviously similar about a white woman of England and an African man, or between a 'criminal type' and a 'savage'. (If it seems to us as though there is, that is because the metaphor has become so woven into our cultural and linguistic system as to have lost its obviously metaphorical quality and to seem a part of 'nature'.) Rather it is the metaphor that permits us to see similarities that the metaphor itself helps constitute.[35] The metaphor, Black suggests, 'selects, emphasizes, suppresses and organizes features' of reality, thereby allowing us to see new connections between the two subjects of the metaphor, to pay attention to details hitherto unnoticed, to emphasize aspects of human experience otherwise treated as unimportant, to make new features into 'signs' signifying inferiority.[36] It was the metaphor joining lower races and women, for instance, that gave significance to the supposed differences between the shape of women's jaws and those of men.

[. . .]

The metaphor, in short, served as a programme of research. Here the analogy comes close to the idea of a scientific 'paradigm' as elaborated by Kuhn in *The Structure of Scientific Revolutions*; indeed Kuhn himself sometimes writes of paradigms as though they are extended metaphors and has proposed that 'the same interactive, similarity-creating process which Black has isolated in the functioning of metaphor is vital also in the function of models in science.'[37]

The ability of an analogy in science to create new kinds of knowledge is seen clearly in the way the analogy organizes the scientists' understanding of causality. Hesse suggests that a scientific metaphor, by joining two distinct subjects, implies more than mere structural likeness. In the case of the science of human difference, the analogies implied a similar *cause* of the similarities between races and women and of the differences between both groups and white males. To the phrenologists, the cause of the large organs of philoprogenitiveness in monkeys, Negroes, and women was an innate brain structure. To the evolutionists, sexual and racial differences were the product of slow, adaptive changes involving variation and selection, the results being the smaller brains and lower capacities of the lower races and women, and the higher intelligence and evolutionarily advanced traits in the males of higher races. Barry Barnes suggests we call the kind of 'redescription' involved in a metaphor or analogy of the kind being discussed here an 'explanation', because it forces the reader to 'understand' one aspect of reality in terms of another.[38]

Analogy and the suppression of knowledge

Especially important to the functioning of interactive metaphors in science is their ability to neglect or even suppress information about human experience of the world that does not fit the similarity implied by the metaphor. In their 'similarity-creating' capacity, metaphors involve the scientist in a selection of those aspects of reality that are compatible with the metaphor. This selection process is often quite unconscious. Stephen Jay Gould is especially telling about the ways in which anatomists and anthropologists unselfconsciously searched for and selected measures that would prove the desired scales of human superiority and inferiority and how the difficulties in achieving the desired results were surmounted.

Gould has subjected Paul Broca's work on human differences to particularly thorough scrutiny because Broca was highly regarded in scientific circles and was exemplary in the accuracy of his measurements. Gould shows that it is not Broca's measurements *per se* that can be faulted, but rather the ways in which he unconsciously manipulated them to produce the very similarities already 'contained' in the analogical science of human variation. To arrive at the conclusion of women's inferiority in brain weights, for example, meant failing to make any correction for women's smaller body weights, even though other scientists of the period were well aware that women's smaller brain weights were at least in part a function of their smaller body sizes. Broca was also able to 'save' the scale of ability based on head size by leaving out some awkward cases of large-brained but savage heads from his calculations, and by somehow accounting for the occasional small-brained 'geniuses' from higher races in his collection.[39]

[. . .]

When contrary evidence could not be ignored, it was often reinterpreted to express the fundamental valuations implicit in the metaphor. Gould provides us with the example of neoteny, or the retention in the adult of childish features such as a small face and hairlessness. A central feature of the analogical science of inferiority was that adult women and lower races were more childlike in their bodies and minds than white males. But Gould shows that by the early twentieth century it was realized that neoteny was a positive feature of the evolutionary process. 'At least one scientist, Havelock Ellis, did bow to the clear implication and admit the superiority of women, even though he wriggled out of a similar confession for blacks.' As late as the 1920s the Dutch scientist Louis Bolk, on the other hand, managed to save the basic valuation of white equals superior, blacks and women equal inferior by 'rethinking' the data and discovering after all that blacks departed more than whites from the most favourable traits of childhood.[40]

To reiterate, because a metaphor or analogy does not directly present a pre-existing nature but instead helps 'construct' that nature, the metaphor generates data that conform to it, and accommodates data that are in apparent contradiction to it, so that nature is seen via the metaphor and the metaphor becomes part of the logic of science itself.[41]

[. . .]

A brief conclusion

In this essay I have indicated only some of the issues raised by a historical consideration of a specific metaphoric or analogical science. There is no attempt at completeness or theoretical closure. My intention has been to draw attention to the ways in which metaphor and analogy can play a role in science, and to show how a particular set of metaphors and analogies shaped the scientific study of human variation. I have also tried to indicate some of the historical reasons why scientific texts have been 'read' non-metaphorically, and what some of the scientific and social consequences of this have been.

Some may argue I have begged the question of metaphor and analogy in science by treating an analogical science that was 'obviously pseudoscientific'. I maintain that it was not obviously pseudoscientific to its practitioners, and that they were far from being at the periphery of the biological and human sciences in the nineteenth and early twentieth centuries. I believe other studies will show that what was true for the analogical science of human difference may well be true also for other metaphors and analogies in science.

My intention has also been to suggest that a theory of metaphor is as critical to science as it is to the humanities. We need a critical theory of metaphor in science in order to expose the metaphors by which we learn to view the world scientifically, not because these metaphors are necessarily 'wrong', but because they are so powerful.

Notes

1   A metaphor is a figure of speech in which a name or descriptive term is transferred to some object that is different from, but analogous to, that to which is properly applicable. According to Max Black, 'every metaphor may be said to mediate an analogy or structural correspondence': see Black, 'More About Metaphor', in Andrew Ortony (ed.), *Metaphor and Thought* (Cambridge: Cambridge University Press, 1979), 19–43, on p. 31. In this article, I have used the terms *metaphor* and *analogy* interchangeably.

2   G. Lakoff and M. Johnson, *Metaphors We Live By* (Chicago/London: University of Chicago Press, 1980), 191. Scientists' attacks on metaphor as extrinsic and harmful to science predate the Scientific Revolution.

3   For this point see Jamie Kassler, 'Music as a Model in Early Science', *History of Science*, 20 (1982), 103–39.

4   Colin M. Turbayne, *The Myth of Metaphor* (Columbia: University of South Carolina Press, 1970), 24.

5   See Nancy Stepan, *The Idea of Race in Science: Great Britain, 1800–1960* (London: Macmillan, 1982), esp. ch. 1.

6   No systematic history of the race–gender analogy exists. The analogy has been remarked on, and many examples from the anthropometric, medical, and embryological sciences provided, in Stephen Jay Gould, *The Mismeasure Of Man* (New York: W. W. Norton, 1981), and in John S. Haller and Robin S. Haller, *The Physician and Sexuality in Victorian America* (Urbana: University of Illinois Press, 1974).

7   Haller and Haller, *The Physician and Sexuality*, 48–9, 54. Among the several craniometric articles cited by the Hallers, see esp. J. McGrigor Allan, 'On the Real Differences in the Minds of Men and Women', *Journal of the Anthropological Society of London*, 7 (1869), cxcv–ccviii, on p. cciv; and John Cleland, 'An Inquiry into the Variations of the Human Skull', *Philosophical Transactions, Royal Society*, 89 (1870), 117–74.

8   Havelock Ellis, *Man and Woman: A Study of Secondary Sexual Characters* (London: A. & C. Black, 6th edn. 1926), 106–7.

9   Herbert Spencer, 'The Comparative Psychology of Man', *Popular Science Monthly*, 8 (1875–6), 257–69.

10   Ellis, *Man and Woman* (cit. n. 8), 491.

11   Carl Vogt, *Lectures on Man: His Place in Creation, and in the History of the Earth* (London: Longman, Green, & Roberts, 1864), 81.

12   James Weir, 'The Effect of Female Suffrage on Posterity', *American Naturalist*, 29 (1895), 198–215.

13   Charles Darwin, *The Descent of Man, and Selection in Relation to Sex* (London: John Murray, 1871), ii, chs. 17–20; Edward Cope, 'The Developmental Significance of Human Physiognomy', *American Naturalist*, 17 (1883), 618–27.

14   Arthur Keith, 'Presidential Address: On Certain Factors in the Evolution of Human Races', *Journal of the Royal Anthropological Institute*, 64 (1916), 10–33; Ellis, *Man and Woman* (cit. n. 8), p. xii.

15   See Nancy Stepan, 'Biological Degeneration: Races and Proper Places', in J. Edward Chamberlin and Sander L. Gilman (eds.), *Degeneration: The Dark Side of Progress* (New York: Columbia University Press, 1985), 97–120, esp. 112–13. For an extended exploration of how various stereotypes of difference intertwined with each other, see Sander L. Gilman, *Difference and Pathology: Stereotypes of Sexuality, Race, and Madness* (Ithaca, NY: Cornell University Press, 1985).

16   Lakoff and Johnson, *Metaphors We Live By* (cit. n. 2), 22. The idea of root metaphors is Stephen Pepper's in *World Hypothesis* (Berkeley/Los Angeles: University of California Press, 1966), 91.

17   Winthrop D. Jordan, *White over Black: American Attitudes toward the Negro, 1550–1812* (New York: Norton, 1977), 7.

18   Stepan, *The Idea of Race in Science*, 6–10.

19   Francis Galton, 'Hereditary Improvement', *Fraser's Magazine*, 7 (1873), 116–30.

20   These instruments and measurements are described in detail in Paul Topinard, *Anthropology* (London: Chapman & Hall, 1878), pt. 2, chs. 1–4.

21   Ibid. 311.

22   Max Black, *Models and Metaphor* (Ithaca, NY: Cornell University Press, 1961), esp. chs. 3 and 13. See also Mary Hesse, *Models and Analogies in Science* (Notre Dame, Ind.: University of Notre Dame Press, 1966); Mary Hesse, 'The Explanatory Function of Metaphor', in Y. Bar-Hillel (ed.), *Logic Methodology and*

Philosophy of Science (Amsterdam: North-Holland, 1965), 249–59; and Richard Boyd, "Metaphor and Theory Change: What is 'Metaphor' a Metaphor for?", in A. Ortony (ed.), *Metaphor and Thought*, 356–408.

23 Black, *Models and Metaphor*, 38, quoting I. A. Richards, *Philosophy of Rhetoric* (Oxford: Oxford University Press, 1938), 93.

24 See Turbayne, *Myth of Metaphor* (cit. n. 4), p. 19, on this point.

25 Black himself believed scientific metaphors belonged to the pretheoretical stage of a discipline. Here I have followed Boyd, who argues in 'Metaphor and Theory Change' (cit. n. 22), p. 357, that metaphors can play a role in the development of theories in relatively mature sciences. Some philosophers would reserve the term 'model' for extended, systematic metaphors in science.

26 For an example of the analogous diseases and sexuality of 'lower' races and 'lower' women, see Eugene S. Talbot, *Degeneracy: Its Causes, Signs, and Results* (London: Walter Cott, l898), 18, 319–23.

27 Paul Broca, 'Sur le volume et la forme du cerveau suivant les individus et suivant les races', *Bulletin de la Société d' 'Anthropologie Paris*, 2 (1861), 304.

28 Franz Joseph Gall, 'The Propensity to Philoprogenitiveness', *Phrenological Journal*, 2 (1824–5), 20–33.

29 Vogt, *Lectures on Man* (cit. n. 11), 88. Vogt was quoting Broca's data.

30 Gould, *Mismeasure of Man* (cit. n. 6),103.

31 Broca's work on the cranial capacities of skulls taken from three cemeteries in Paris was the most important source for this conclusion. See his 'Sur la capacité des cranes parisiens des divers époques', *Bulletin de la Société d'Anthropologie Paris*, 3 (1862), 102–16.

32 Ellis, *Man and Woman* (cit. n. 8),106–7.

33 Alexander Sutherland, 'Woman's Brain', *Nineteenth Century*, 47 (1900), 802–10; and Ellis, *Man and Woman*, 98. Ellis was on the whole, however, cautious about the conclusions that could be drawn from skull capacities and brain weights.

34 Stanley Fish, 'Working on the Chain Gang: Interpretation in the Law and Literary Criticism' in W. J. T. Mitchell (ed.), *The Politics of Interpretation* (Chicago: University of Chicago Press, 1983), 277.

35 Max Black, as cited in Ortony, *Metaphor and Thought* (cit. n. 1), 5.

36 Black, *Models and Metaphor* (cit. n. 7), 44.

37 Thomas S. Kuhn, *The Structure of Scientific Revolutions* (Chicago: University of Chicago Press, 2nd edn., 1973) esp. ch. 4; and Thomas S. Kuhn, 'Metaphor in Science', in A. Ortony (ed.) *Metaphor and Thought*, 409–19, on 415.

38 Barry Barnes, *Scientific Knowledge and Sociological Theory* (London: Routledge & Kegan Paul, 1974), 49.

39 Gould, *Mismeasure of Man* (cit. n. 6), 73–112. For another example see Stephen Jay Gould, 'Morton's Ranking of Race by Cranial Capacity', *Science*, 200 (l978), 503–9.

40 Gould, *Mismeasure of Man*, 120–1.

41 Terence Hawkes, *Metaphor* (London: Methuen 1972), 88, suggests that metaphors 'will retrench or corroborate as much as they expand our vision', thus stressing the normative, consensus-building aspects of metaphor.

Donna J. Haraway

A MANIFESTO FOR CYBORGS: SCIENCE, TECHNOLOGY, AND SOCIALIST FEMINISM IN THE 1980s

THIS CHAPTER IS AN EFFORT to build an ironic political myth faithful to feminism, socialism, and materialism. Perhaps more faithful as blasphemy is faithful, than as reverent worship and identification. Blasphemy has always seemed to require taking things very seriously. I know no better stance to adopt from within the secular-religious, evangelical traditions of U.S. politics, including the politics of socialist feminism. Blasphemy protects one from the Moral Majority within, while still insisting on the need for community. Blasphemy is not apostasy. Irony is about contradictions that do not resolve into larger wholes, even dialectically, about the tension of holding incompatible things together because both or all are necessary and true. Irony is about humor and serious play. It is also a rhetorical strategy and a political method, one I would like to see more honored within socialist feminism. At the center of my ironic faith, my blasphemy, is the image of the cyborg.

A cyborg is a cybernetic organism, a hybrid of machine and organism, a creature of social reality as well as a creature of fiction. Social reality is lived social relations, our most important political construction, a world-changing fiction. The international women's movements have constructed "women's experience", as well as uncovered or discovered this crucial collective object. This experience is a fiction and fact of the most crucial, political kind. Liberation rests on the construction of the consciousness, the imaginative apprehension, of oppression, and so of possibility. The cyborg is a matter of fiction and lived experience that changes what counts as women's experience in the late twentieth century. This is a struggle over life and death, but the boundary between science fiction and social reality is an optical illusion. [. . .]

By the late twentieth century, our time, a mythic time, we are all chimeras theorized and fabricated hybrids of machine and organism, in short, we are cyborgs. The cyborg is our ontology; it gives us our politics. The cyborg is a condensed image of both imagination and material reality, the two joined centers structuring any possibility of historical transformation. In the traditions of Western science and politics – the tradition of racist, male-dominant capitalism; the tradition of progress; the tradition of the appropriation of nature as resource for the productions of culture, the tradition of reproduction of the self from the reflections of the other, the relation between organism and machine has been a border war. The stakes in the border war have been the territories of production, reproduction, and imagination. This chapter is an argument for pleasure in the confusion of boundaries and for responsibility in their construction. It is also an effort to contribute to socialist-feminist culture and theory in a postmodernist, nonnaturalist mode and in the utopian tradition of imagining a world without gender, which is perhaps a world without genesis, but maybe also a world without end. The cyborg incarnation is outside salvation history. [. . .]

The cyborg is a creature in a postgender world: it has no truck with bisexuality, pre-Oedipal symbiosis, unalienated labor, or other seductions to organic wholeness through a final appropriation of all the powers of the parts into a higher unity. In a sense, the cyborg has no origin story in the Western sense: a "final" irony since the cyborg is also the awful apocalyptic telos of the West's escalating dominations of abstract individuation, an ultimate sell untied at last from all dependency, a man in space. An origin story in the Western humanist sense depends on the myth of original unity, fullness, bliss, and terror, represented by the phallic mother from whom all humans must separate; the task of individual development and of history, the twin potent myths inscribed most powerfully for us in psychoanalysis and Marxism. Hilary Klein has argued that both Marxism and psychoanalysis, in their concepts of labor and of individuation and gender formation, depend on the plot of original unity out of which difference must be produced and enlisted in a drama of escalating domination of woman/nature. The cyborg skips the step of original unity, of identification with nature in the Western sense. This is its illegitimate promise that might lead to subversion of its teleology as Star Wars.

The cyborg is resolutely committed to partiality, irony, intimacy, and perversity. It is oppositional, utopian, and completely without innocence. No longer structured by the polarity of public and private, the cyborg defines a technological polis based partly on a revolution of social relations in the oikos, the household. Nature and culture are reworked: the one can no longer be the resource for appropriation or incorporation by the other. The relationships for forming wholes from parts, including those of polarity and hierarchical domination, are at issue in the cyborg world. Unlike the hopes of Frankenstein's monster, the cyborg does not expect its father to save it through a restoration of the garden, that is, through the fabrication of a heterosexual male, through its completion in a finished whole, a city and cosmos. The cyborg does not dream of community on the model of the organic family, this time without the Oedipal project. The cyborg would not recognize the Garden of Eden: it is not made of mud and cannot dream of returning to dust. Perhaps that is why I want to see if cyborgs can subvert the apocalypse of returning to nuclear dust in the manic compulsion to name the Enemy. Cyborgs are not reverent: they do not remember the cosmos. They are wary of holism, but needy for connection – they seem to have a natural feel for united front politics, but without the vanguard party. The main trouble with cyborgs, of course, is that they are the illegitimate offspring of militarism and patriarchal capitalism, not to mention state socialism. But illegitimate offspring are often exceedingly unfaithful to their origins. Their fathers, after all, are inessential.

[. . .] I want to signal three crucial boundary breakdowns that make the following political fictional (political scientific) analysis possible. By the late twentieth century in United States, scientific culture, the boundary between human and animal, is thoroughly breached. The last beachheads of uniqueness have been polluted, if not turned into amusement parks – language, tool use, social behavior, mental events. Nothing really convincingly settles the separation of human and animal. Many people no longer feel the need of such a separation; indeed, many branches of feminist culture affirm the pleasure of connection with human and other living creatures. Movements for animal rights are not irrational denials of human uniqueness; they are clear-sighted recognition of connection across the discredited breach of nature and culture. Biology and evolutionary theory over the last two centuries have simultaneously produced modern organisms as objects of knowledge and reduced the line between humans and animals to a faint trace re-etched in ideological struggle or professional disputes between life and social sciences. Within this framework, teaching modern Christian creationism should be fought as a form of child abuse.

Biological-determinist ideology is only one position opened up in scientific culture for arguing the meanings of human animality. There is much room for radical political people to contest for the meanings of the breached boundary. The cyborg appears in myth precisely where the boundary between human and animal is transgressed. Far from signaling a walling off of people from other living things, cyborgs signal disturbingly and pleasurably tight coupling. Bestiality has a new status in this cycle of marriage exchange.

The second leaky distinction is between animal-human (organism) and machine. Pre-cybernetic machines could be haunted; there was always the specter of the ghost in the machine. This dualism structured the dialogue between materialism and idealism that was settled by a dialectical progeny called spirit or history, according to taste. But basically machines were not self-moving, self-designing, autonomous. They could not achieve man's dream, only mock it. They were not man, an author of himself, but only a caricature of that masculinist reproductive dream. To think they were otherwise was paranoid. Now we are not so sure. Late twentieth century machines have made thoroughly ambiguous the difference between natural and artificial, mind and body, self-developing and eternally designed, and many other distinctions that used to apply to organisms and machines. Our machines are disturbingly lively, and we ourselves frighteningly inert.

Technological determinism is only one ideological space opened up by the reconceptions of machine and organism as coded texts through which we engage in the play of writing and reading the world. "Textualization" of everything in post-structuralist, postmodernist theory has been damned by Marxists and socialist feminists for its utopian disregard for lived relations of domination that ground the "play" of arbitrary reading. It is certainly true that postmodernist strategies, like my cyborg myth, subvert myriad organic wholes (e.g. the poem, primitive culture, the biological organism). In short, the certainty of what counts as nature – a source of insight and a promise of innocence – is undermined, probably fatally. The transcendent authorization of interpretation is lost and with it the ontology grounding Western epistemology. But the alternative is not cynicism or faithlessness, that is, some version of abstract existence, like the accounts of technological determinism destroying "man" by the "machine" or "meaningful political action" by the "text". Who cyborgs will be is a radical question; the answers are a matter of survival. Both chimpanzees and artifacts have politics, so why shouldn't we?[1]

The third distinction is a subset of the second: The boundary between physical and nonphysical is very imprecise for us. Pop physics books on the consequences of quantum theory and the indeterminacy principle are a kind of popular scientific equivalent to the Harlequin romances as a marker of radical change in American white heterosexuality: They get it wrong, but they are on the right subject. Modern machines are quintessentially microelectronic devices: They are everywhere and they are invisible. Modern machinery is an irreverent upstart god, mocking the Father's ubiquity and spirituality. The silicon chip is a surface for writing: it is etched in molecular scales disturbed only by atomic noise, the ultimate interference for nuclear scores. Writing, power, and technology are old partners in Western stories of the origin of civilization, but miniaturization has changed our experience of mechanism. Miniaturization has turned out to be about power; small is not so much beautiful as preeminently dangerous, as in cruise missiles. Contrast the TV sets of the 1950s or the news cameras of the 1970s with the TV wristbands or hand-sized video cameras now advertised. Our best machines are made of sunshine; they are all light and clean because they are nothing but signals, electromagnetic waves, a section of a spectrum. These machines are eminently portable, mobile – a matter of immense human pain in Detroit and Singapore. People are nowhere near so fluid, being both material and opaque. Cyborgs are ether, quintessence. [. . .]

In this attempt at an epistemological and political position, I would like to sketch a picture of possible unity, a picture indebted to socialist and feminist principles of design. The frame for my sketch is set by the extent and importance of rearrangements in worldwide social relations tied to science and technology. I argue for a politics rooted in claims about fundamental changes in the nature of class, race, and gender in an emerging system of world order analogous in its novelty and scope to that created by industrial capitalism: we are living through a movement from an organic, industrial society to a polymorphous, information system – from all work to all play, a deadly game. Simultaneously material and ideological, the dichotomies may be expressed in the following chart of transitions from the comfortable old hierarchical dominations to the scary new networks I have called the informatics of domination:

Representation	Simulation
Bourgeois novel, realism	Science fiction, postmodernism
Organism	Biotic component
Depth, integrity	Surface, boundary
Heat	Noise
Biology as clinical practice	Biology as inscription
Physiology	Communications engineering
Small group	Subsystem
Perfection	Optimization
Eugenics	Population Control

Decadence, *Magic Mountain*	Obsolescence, *Future Shock*
Hygiene	Stress management
Microbiology, tuberculosis	Immunology, AIDS
Organic division of labor	Ergonomics/cybernetics of labor
Functional specialization	Modular construction
Reproduction	Replication
Organic sex role specialization	Optimal genetic strategies
Biological determinism	Evolutionary inertia, constraints
Community ecology	Ecosystem
Racial chain of being	Neo-imperialism, United Nations humanism
Scientific management in home/factory	Global factory/electronic cottage
Family/market/factory	Women in the integrated circuit
Family wage	Comparable worth
Public/private	Cyborg citizenship
Nature/culture	Fields of difference
Cooperation	Communications enhancement
Freud	Lacan
Sex	Genetic engineering
Labor	Robotics
Mind	Artificial intelligence
World War II	Star Wars
White capitalist patriarchy	Informatics of domination

This list suggests several interesting things. First, the objects on the right-hand side cannot be coded as "natural", a realization that subverts naturalistic coding for the left-hand side as well. We cannot go back ideologically or materially. It's not just that "god" is dead: so is the "goddess". Or both are revivified in the worlds charged with microelectronic and biotechnological politics. In relation to objects like biotic components, one must think not in terms of essential properties, but in terms of design, boundary constraints, rates of flows, systems logics, costs of lowering constraints. Sexual reproduction is one kind of reproductive strategy among many, with costs and benefits as a function of the system environment. Ideologies of sexual reproduction can no longer reasonably call on notions of sex and sex role as organic aspects in natural objects like organisms and families. Such reasoning will be unmasked as irrational, and ironically corporate executives reading *Playboy* and anti-porn radical feminists will make strange bedfellows in jointly unmasking the irrationalism.

Likewise for race, racist and anti-racist ideologies about human diversity have to be formulated in terms of frequencies of parameters. It is "irrational" to invoke concepts like primitive and civilized. For liberals and radicals, the search for integrated social systems gives way to a new practice called "experimental ethnography" in which an organic object dissipates in attention to the play of writing. At the level of ideology, we see translations of racism and colonialism into languages of development and underdevelopment, rates and constraints of modernization. Any objects or persons can be "reasonably" thought of in terms of disassembly and reassembly: no "natural" architectures constrain system design. The financial districts in all the world's cities, as well as the export-processing and free-trade zones, proclaim this elementary fact of "late capitalism". The entire universe of objects that can be known scientifically must be formulated as problems in communications engineering (for the managers) or theories of the text (for those who would resist). Both are cyborg semiologies.

One should expect control strategies to concentrate on boundary conditions and interfaces, on rates of flow across boundaries – and not on the integrity of natural objects. "Integrity" or "sincerity" of the Western self gives way to decision procedures and expert systems. For example, control strategies applied to women's capacities to give birth to new human beings will be developed in the languages of population control and maximization of goal achievement for individual decisionmakers. Control strategies will be formulated in terms of rates, costs of constraints, degrees of freedom. Human beings, like any other component or subsystem, must be localized in a system architecture whose basic modes of operation are probabilistic, statistical. No objects, spaces, or bodies are sacred in themselves; any component can be interfaced with any other if the proper standard, the proper code, can be constructed for processing signals in a common language. Exchange in this world transcends the universal translation effected by capitalist markets that Marx analyzed so well. The privileged pathology affecting all kinds of components in this universe is stress communications breakdown. The cyborg is not subject to Foucault's biopolitics; the cyborg simulates politics, a much more potent field of operations. Discursive constructions are no joke.

[. . .] One important route for reconstructing socialist-feminist politics is through theory and practice addressed to the social relations of science and technology, including crucially the systems of myth and meanings structuring our imaginations. The cyborg is a kind of disassembled and reassembled, postmodern collective and personal self. This is the self feminists must code.

Communications technologies and biotechnologies are the crucial tools re-crafting our bodies. These tools embody and enforce new social relations for women worldwide. Technologies and scientific discourses can be partially understood as formalizations, that is, as frozen moments, of the fluid social interactions constituting them, but they should also be viewed as instruments for enforcing meanings. The boundary is permeable between tool and myth, instrument and concept, historical systems of social relations and historical anatomies of possible bodies, including objects of knowledge. Indeed, myth and tool mutually constitute each other.

Furthermore, communications sciences and modern biologies are constructed by a common move – the translation of the world into a problem of coding, a search for a common language in which all resistance to instrumental control disappears and all heterogeneity can be submitted to disassembly, reassembly, investment, and exchange.

In communications sciences, the translation of the world into a problem in coding can be illustrated by looking at cybernetic (feedback controlled) systems theories applied to telephone technology, computer design, weapons deployment, or data-base construction and maintenance. In each case, solution to the key questions rests on a theory of language and control; the key operation is determining the rates, directions, and probabilities of flow of a quantity called information. The world is subdivided by boundaries differentially permeable to information. Information is just that kind of quantifiable element (unit, basis of unity) which allows universal translation and so unhindered instrumental power (called effective communication). The biggest threat to such power is interruption of communication. Any system breakdown is a function of stress. The fundamentals of this technology can be condensed into the metaphor C^{3}I, command-control communication intelligence, the military's symbol for its operations theory.

In modern biologies, the translation of the world into a problem in coding can be illustrated by molecular genetics, ecology, sociobiological evolutionary theory, and immunobiology. The organism has been translated into problems of genetic coding and read-out. Biotechnology, a writing technology, informs research broadly. In a sense, organisms have ceased to exist as objects of knowledge, giving way to biotic components, that is, special kinds of information-processing devices. The analogous moves in ecology could be examined by probing the history and utility of the concept of the ecosystem. Immunobiology and associated medical practices are rich exemplars of the privilege of coding and recognition systems as objects of knowledge, as constructions of bodily reality for us. Biology here is a king of cryptography. Research is necessarily a kind of intelligence activity. Ironies abound. A stressed system goes awry; its communication processes break down; it fails to recognize the difference between self and other. Human babies with baboon hearts evoke national ethical perplexity – for animal-rights activists at least as much as for the guardians of human purity. In the United States gay men and intravenous drug users are the most "privileged" victims of an awful immune-system disease that marks (inscribes on the body) confusion of boundaries and moral pollution.

But these excursions into communications sciences and biology have been at a rarefied level; there is a mundane, largely economic reality to support my claim that these sciences and technologies indicate fundamental transformations in the structure of the world for us. Communications technologies depend on electronics. Modern states, multinational corporations, military power, welfare-state apparatuses, satellite systems, political processes, fabrication of our imaginations, labor-control systems, medical constructions of our bodies, commercial pornography, the international division of labor, and religious evangelism depend intimately upon electronics. Microelectronics is the technical basis of simulacra, that is, of copies without originals.

Microelectronics mediates the translations of labor into robotics and word processing, sex into genetic engineering and reproductive technologies, and mind into artificial intelligence and decision procedures. The new biotechnologies concern more than human reproduction. Biology as a powerful engineering science for redesigning materials and processes has revolutionary implications for industry, perhaps most obvious today in areas of fermentation, agriculture, and energy. Communications sciences and biology are constructions of natural-technical objects of knowledge in which the difference between machine and organism is thoroughly blurred; mind, body, and tool are on very intimate terms. The "multinational" material organization of the production and reproduction of daily life and the symbolic organization of the production and reproduction of culture and imagination seem equally implicated. The boundary maintaining images of base and superstructure, public and private, or material and ideal never seemed more feeble.

I have used Rachel Grossman's image of women in the integrated circuit to name the situation of women in a world so intimately restructured through the social relations of science and technology.[2] I use the odd circumlocution "the social relations of science and technology", to indicate that we are not dealing with a technological determinism, but with a historical system depending upon structured relations among people. But the phrase should also indicate that science and technology provide fresh sources of power, that we need fresh sources of analysis and political action. Some of the rearrangements of race, sex, and class rooted in high-tech-facilitated social relations can make socialist feminism more relevant to effective progressive politics. [. . .]

Cyborg imagery can help express two crucial arguments in this essay: (1) the production of universal, totalizing theory is a major mistake that misses most of reality, probably always, but certainly now; (2) taking responsibility for the social relations of science and technology means refusing an anti-science metaphysics, a demonology of technology, and so means embracing the skilful task of reconstructing the boundaries of daily life, in partial connection with others, in communication with all of our parts. It is not just that science and technology are possible means of great human satisfaction, as well as a matrix of complex dominations. Cyborg imagery can suggest a way out of the maze of dualisms in which we have explained our bodies and our tools to ourselves. This is a dream not of a common language, but of a powerful infidel heteroglossia. It is an imagination of a feminist speaking in tongues to strike fear into the circuits of the super savers of the New Right. It means both building and destroying machines, identities, categories, relationships, spaces, stories. Although both are bound in the spiral dance, I would rather be a cyborg than a goddess.

Notes

1   Frans de Waal, *Chimpanzee Politics: Power and Sex among the Apes* (New York: Harper & Row, 1982); Langdon Winner, "Do Artifacts have Politics?", *Daedalus* (Winter 1980), 121–36.

2   "Women's Place in the Integrated Circuit", *Radical America*, 14/1 (1980), 29–50.

Jennifer González

ENVISIONING CYBORG BODIES: NOTES FROM CURRENT RESEARCH

The truth of art lies in this: that the world really is as it appears in the work of art.
(Herbert Marcuse)

THE CYBORG BODY is the body of an imagined cyberspatial existence. It is the site of possible being. In this sense it exists in excess of the real. But it is also embedded within the real. The cyborg body is that which is already inhabited and through which the interface to a contemporary world is already made. Visual representations of cyborgs are thus not only utopian or dystopian prophesies, but are rather reflections of a contemporary state of being. The image of the cyborg body functions as a site of condensation and displacement. It contains on its surface and in its fundamental structure the multiple fears and desires of a culture caught in the process of transformation. Donna Haraway has written,

> A cyborg exists when two kinds of boundaries are simultaneously problematic:
> 1) that between animals (or other organisms) and humans, and 2) that between
> self-controlled, self-governing machines (automatons) and organisms, espe-
> cially humans (models of autonomy). The cyborg is the figure born of the
> interface of automaton and autonomy.[1]

Taking this as a working definition, one can consider any body a cyborg body that is both its own agent and subject to the power of other agencies. To keep to the spirit of this definition but to make it more specific, an *organic cyborg* can be defined as a monster of multiple species, whereas a *mechanical cyborg* can be considered a techno-human amalgamation (there are also conceivable overlaps of these domains). While images of *mechanical cyborgs* will be the focus of the short essays that follow, both types of cyborgs, which appear frequently in Western visual culture, are metaphors for a third kind of cyborg – a cyborg consciousness.[2] This last, is both manifest in all the images included here, and is the invisible force driving their production, what Michel Foucault might call a "positive unconscious."[3] This unconscious is reflected in the spatial and political agency implied by a given cyborg body. Unlike some of my contemporaries, I do not see the cyborg body as primarily a surface or simulacrum which signifies only itself; rather the cyborg is like a symptom – it represents that which cannot otherwise be represented.

The following group of eclectic commentaries is meant to address a sample of the issues which may arise in the consideration of representing cyborg bodies. The images here were chosen not because they are the most beautiful, the most frightening or the most hopeful of the cyborg visions I have found, but because they incarnate what seem to be important features for any consideration of a "cyborg body politics."[4]. This is only a beginning.

Mechanical mistress

Flanked by rows of cypress, demurely poised with a hand on one hip, the other hand raised with a pendulous object hanging from plump and delicate fingers stands "L'Horlogère" (The Mistress of Horology) (Figure 1.4A). From above her head stares the circular face of time, supported by a decorative frame through which her own face complacently gazes. Soft feminine shoulders descend into a tightly sculpted bust of metal. Cinched at the waist, her skirts flounce into a stiffly ornamental "montre emboeté" which rests on dainty feet, toes curled up to create the base. An eighteenth-century engraving, this image by an unknown printer depicts what we today might call a cyborg. The body of the woman is not merely hidden inside the machine (despite the two tiny human feet that peek out from below), nor is the organic body itself

Figure 1.4A "L' Horlogère"
(Courtesy of the Bibliothèque des Arts Décoratifs)

a mechanical replica, rather the body and the machine are a singular entity. In contrast to, but within the context of, the popular depictions of entirely mechanical automata – the predecessors of our modern-day robots – this image represents an early conception of an ontological merging of "cultural" and "natural" artifacts.

Taken as a form of evidence, the representation of an amalgam such as this can be read as a symptom of the pre-industrial unconscious. *L'Horlogère* substantiates an ideology of order, precision, and mechanization. French philosopher Julien Offray de La Mettrie, in his essay "L'Homme Machine" (1748) wrote "The human body is a machine which winds its own springs. It is the living image of perpetual movement."[5] The beating hearts of many Europeans at this time no doubt sounded an apprehensive ticking. Wound up to serve the industrial impulse, the human model of perfection culminated in a mechanized identity. Variations of this ideal continued into the nineteenth century with the expansion of large-scale industrial production. Scholar Julie Wosk writes,

> . . . artists' images of automatons become central metaphors for the dreams and nightmares of societies under-going rapid technological change. In a world where new labor-saving inventions were expanding human capabilities and where a growing number of people were employed in factory systems calling for rote actions and impersonal efficiency, nineteenth-century artists confronted one of the most profound issues raised by new technologies: the possibility that people's identities and emotional lives would take on the properties of machines.[6]

But was this not exactly what was desired by one part of the population – that another part of the population become mechanical? Was this not also exactly what was feared? The artists, depicting an experience already lived by a large portion of the population, were reflecting a situation in which the relation – and the distinction – between the machine and the human became a question of gender and class. Those who had access to certain machines were privileged, those who were expected to behave like certain machines were subjugated. The same is true today.

The pre-industrial representation of *L'Horlogère* thus functions as an early prototype of later conceptual models of the cyborg. The woman is a clock, the clock is a woman – complex, mechanical, serviceable, decorative. Her history can be traced to automatic dolls with clockwork parts dating back to at least the fifteenth century in Europe[7] and much earlier in China, Egypt and Greece.[8] Of the examples which I have found of such automata, a decided majority represent female bodies providing some form of entertainment.

> The idea of automatons as useful servants and amusing toys continued in the designs of medieval and Renaissance clockmakers, whose figures, deriving their movements from clock mechanisms, struck the hours . . .[9]

The history of the automaton is thus imbedded in the mechanical innovations of keeping time, and *L'Horlogère* undoubtedly derives much of her status from this social context. She is clearly an embodied mechanism, but she has the privilege of her class. The imaginative engraver who produced this image undoubtedly wished to portray *L'Horlogère* as aristocratic; as one who could acquire, and therefore represent, the height of technological development. As machine, she displays the skill and artistry of the best engineers of her epoch. The fact that she represents a female body is indicative of the role she is meant to play as the objectification of cultural sophistication and sexuality. Her gender is consistent with the property status of an eighteenth-century decorative artifact.

L'Horlogère is not merely an automaton. As part human, she should have human agency, or some form of human being. Her implied space of agency is, nevertheless, tightly circumscribed. This cyborg appears more trapped by her mechanical parts than liberated through them. If a cyborg is "the figure born of the interface of automaton and autonomy," then to what degree can this cyborg be read as a servant and toy, and to what degree an autonomous social agent? In order to determine the character of any given cyborg identity and the range of its power, one must be able to examine the *form* and not merely the *fact* of this interface between automaton and autonomy. For, despite the potentially progressive implications of a cyborg subject position,[10] the cyborg is not necessarily more likely to exist free of the social constraints which apply to humans and machines already. "The machine is us, our processes, an aspect of our embodiment,"[11] writes Donna Haraway. It should therefore come as no surprise that the traditional, gendered roles of Euro-American culture are rarely challenged in the visual representations of cyborgs – a concept which itself arises from an industrially "privileged" Euro-American perspective. Even the conceptual predecessors of the cyborg are firmly grounded in everyday social politics; "Tradition has it that the golem first did housework but then became unmanageable."[12] The image of *L'Horlogère* thus provides a useful ground and a visual tradition from which to explore and compare more contemporary examples of cyborg bodies.

Signs of changing consciousness

The image of the cyborg has historically recurred at moments of radical social and cultural change. From bestial monstrosities, to unlikely montages of body and machine parts, to electronic implants, imaginary representations of cyborgs take over when traditional bodies fail. In other words, when the current ontological model of human being does not fit a new paradigm, a hybrid model of existence is required to encompass a new, complex and contradictory lived experience. The cyborg body thus becomes the historical record of changes in human perception. One such change may be reflected in the implied redefinition of the space the cyborg body inhabits.

Taking, for example, the 1920 photomontage by Hannah Höch entitled *Das schöne Mädchen* (The Beautiful Girl) (Figure 1.4B) it is possible to read its dynamic assemblage of images as an allegory of modernization. Allied with the Dadaists of the Weimar Republic, Höch provided a chaotic vision of the rapid social and cultural change that followed in the wake of World War 1. In *Das schöne Mädchen* the figure of a woman is set in the midst of a disjointed space of automobile and body parts. BMW logos, a severed hand holding a watch, a flying wig, a parasol, a hidden feminine face and a faceless boxer leaping through the tire of a car surround the central figure whose head has been replaced with an incandescent light bulb – perhaps as the result or condition of her experience.

Figure 1.4B "Das schöne Mädchen"
(The Beautiful Girl) by Hannah
Höch (1919–20)
(Private collection)

Many of Höch's early photomontages focus on what might be called the "New
Woman" in Weimar Germany. These images are not simply a celebration of new,
"emancipated" roles for women in a period of industrial and economic growth, they
are also critical of the contradictory nature of this experience as depicted in the mass
media. "Mass culture became a site for the expression of anxieties, desires, fears and
hopes about women's rapidly transforming identities," writes Maude Lavin in her
recent book *Cut with the Kitchen Knife: The Weimar Photomontages of Hannah Höch*.
"Stereotypes of the New Woman generated by the media could be complex and
contradictory: messages of female empowerment and liberation were mixed with
others of dependence, and the new consumer culture positioned women as both
commodities and customers."[13] Existing across several domains, the New Woman was
forced to experience space and presence in new and ambiguous ways.

Traveling through and across this space could therefore be both physically and
psychologically disorienting. The experience of a disjointed modern space takes form
in Höch's collage as a cyborg body suspended in chaotic perspective (the hand-held
parasol in the image is reduced to one-tenth the size of the figure's floating hair), with
body parts chopped off, and with new mechanical/electric parts added in their place
(the missing hand severed at the figure's wrist reappears holding the watch in the
foreground). It is impossible to tell exactly which spatial plane is occupied by the
body and of what sort of perception this body is capable. Yet, despite her Dadaist
affiliation, Höch's work tends not to be random. Her images produce a discordant but
strikingly accurate appraisal of an early twentieth-century experience of modernism.
Here, existence as a self-contained humanist subject is overcome by an experience
of the body in pieces — a visual representation of an unconscious state of being
that exceeds the space of the human body. Perception is aligned to coincide with
the machine. The effects of such an alignment are made alarmingly transparent
by Virginia Woolf in her 1928 novel *Orlando*. In her description of the uncanny event

of experiencing the world from the perspective of the automobile, her metaphor of torn scraps of paper is particularly appropriate to Höch's use of photomontage.

> After twenty minutes the body and mind were like scraps of torn paper tumbling from a sack, and indeed, the process of motoring fast out of London so much resembles the chopping up small of body and mind, which precedes unconsciousness and perhaps death itself that it is an open question in what sense Orlando can be said to have existed at the present moment.[14]

The questionable existence of Orlando, Virginia Woolf's protagonist who changes gender and who adapts to social and cultural changes across many centuries and continents, is not unlike the questionable existence of the cyborg. It is the existence of a shifting consciousness that is made concrete only in moments of contradictory experience. The attempt to represent and reassemble – but not to repair – the multiple scraps of body and mind that are scattered at such historical junctures has, in fact, been a central activity of modernism.

Photomontage has served as a particularly appropriate medium for the visual exploration of cyborgs. It allows apparently "real" or at least indexically grounded representations of body parts, objects and spaces to be rearranged and to function as fantastic environments or corporal mutations. Photographs seduce the viewer into an imaginary space of visually believable events, objects and characters. The same can be said of assemblage – the use of found or manufactured (often commonplace) objects to create a three-dimensional representational artifact. The common contemporary practice of representing a cyborg through photomontage or assemblage resembles the poetic use of everyday words: the discrete elements are familiar, though the total result is a new conceptual and ontological domain.

One of Höch's compatriots, Dadaist Raoul Hausmann, pictured this new ontological domain in several of his own photomontages and found-object assemblages. Unlike Höch's representations, however, Hausmann's images represent a more cerebral concept of the modern experience. Rather than a body in pieces, he depicts a mechanical mind. His assemblage *Tête Mécanique* (Mechanical Head) (Figure 1.4C) is a particularly appropriate example of a cyborg mind. Also called "The Spirit of Our Times," this assemblage consists of the wooden head of a mannequin to which are attached diverse cultural artifacts. A wallet is fixed to the back, a typographic cylinder in a small jewel box is on one side of the head, a ruler attached with old camera parts is on the other side, the forehead is adorned with the interior of a watch, random numbers and a measuring tape, and a collapsible metal cup crowns the entire ensemble. Timothy O. Benson writes that this assemblage depicts a man imprisoned in an unsettling and enigmatic space, "perceiving the world through a mask of arbitrary symbols."[15] At the same time it functions as a hyper-historical[16] object collection; a testament to Hausmann's own contemporary material culture. The cyborg in this case is not without origins, though it is without origin myths. Donna Haraway contends that cyborgs have no natural history, no origin story, no Garden of Eden and thus no hope of, nor interest in, simplistic unity or purity. Nevertheless, given their multiple parts, and multiple identities, they will always be read in relation to a specific historical context. According to scholar Matthew Biro,

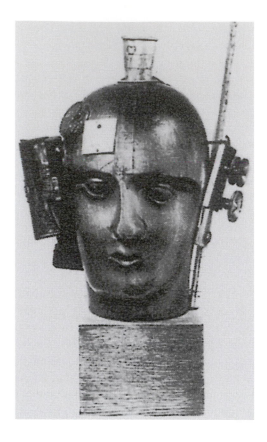

Figure 1.4C "Tête mécanique.
L'Esprit de notre temps" by Raoul
Hausmann (c. 1921)
(Courtesy of Musée Nationale d'Art
Moderne, Centre Georges Pompidou,
Paris)

. . . by fashioning his cyborgs out of fragments of the new mass culture which he found all around him, Hausmann also believed he was fulfilling the primary positive or constructive function he could still ascribe to dada: namely, the material investigation of the signs and symbols bestowed on him by his historical present.[17]

Until the desire to define identities and the power to do so is lost or relinquished, even the most spontaneous cyborgs cannot float above the lingering, clinging past of differences, histories, stories, bodies, places. They will always function as evidence.

The new spatial relations of the human body are thus traced onto the cyborg body. Höch's figure is fragmentary and dispersed, floating in an untethered perspective. Hausmann's figure implies a calculable context that is linear, a cerebral space of measurement and control. Each cyborg implies a new spatial configuration or territory – a habitat. For Höch's *Beautiful Girl*, the world is a space of multiple perspectives, consumer goods, lost identities and fleeting time. The world in which Hausmann's *Mechanical Head* operates is one that links identity to material objects, and is simultaneously an environment in which knowledge is the result of a random encounter with the world of things.

Hausmann himself described this assemblage as representing an everyday man who "has nothing but the capacities which chance has glued to his skull."[18] Sense perception itself is accounted for only to the degree that appears in the image of the cyborg body. Sight, hearing, and tactile senses can only be implied by the body's exterior devices. The *Mechanical Head*, for example, has no ears to "hear" with, only a mechanical ruler and jewel case. *The Beautiful Girl* has neither eyes nor ears, nor mouth to speak with, only a light bulb for illumination. The human head which gazes from the corner of this image is at best the memory of what has been displaced. A new social space requires a new social being. A visual representation of this new being through an imaginary body provides a map of the layers and contradictions that make up a hyper-historical "positive unconscious." In other words, the cyborg body marks the boundaries of that which is the underlying but unrecognized structure of a given historical consciousness. It turns the inside out.

White collar epistemology

Turning the outside in, Phoenix Technologies Ltd. produced an advertisement for their new Eclipse Fax in 1993. The advertisement's lead-in text reads: "Eclipse Fax: if it were any faster, you'd have to send and receive your faxes internally." The text floats over an image of a pale woman's head and shoulders. It is clear from the image that the woman is on her back as her long hair is splayed out around her head. Her shoulders are bare, implying that she is unclothed. Mechanical devices comprised of tubes, metal plugs, cables, hoses and canisters appear to be inserted into her ears, eye sockets and mouth. Two electrodes appear to be attached to the woman's forehead, with wires extending out to the sides, almost like the antennae of an insect. A futuristic Medusa's head of wires, blinded with technology, strapped to the ground with cables and hoses, penetrated at every orifice with the flow of information technologies, this is a subjugated cyborg. Her monstrous head is merely a crossroads. All human parts of the image are passive and receptive. Indeed it seems clear that the blind silence of this clearly female creature is the very condition for the possibility of information flow. This is not a cyborg of possibilities, it is a cyborg of slavery. The advertisement promises that the consumer will be able to send and receive faxes "without being interrupted," and concludes that ". . . to fax any faster, you'd have to break a few laws. Of physics." Here the new technology is not only seen as always available, but also as somehow pushing the boundaries of legality – even if only metaphorically – in the use of the body. This is the bad-boy fantasy prevalent in so many images of feminized cyborgs. The textual emphasis on speed in this advertisement is but a thin veil through which the underlying visual metaphor of information flow as sexual penetration bursts forth. For many, this is already an apt metaphor for cyborg body politics: knowledge as force-fed data.

What *are* the consequences of a montage of organic bodies and machines? Where do the unused parts go? What are the relations of power? Is power conserved? Is the loss of power in one physical domain the necessary gain of power for another? Who writes the laws for a cyborg bill of rights? Does everyone have the "right" to become any kind of cyborg body? Or are these "rights" economically determined? These are questions that arise in the attempt to figure a politics of cyborg bodies. A visualization of this hypothetical existence is all the more important for its reflection of an already current state of affairs.

The power of plenitude

Robert Longo's sculpture/installation entitled *All You Zombies: Truth before God*, (Figure 1.4D) stages the extreme manifestation of the body at war in the theater of politics. The glow of many painted lights hang within the frame of a semi-circular canvas – an opera house or concert hall – that surrounds a monstrous cyborg soldier who takes center stage on a revolving platform. The chasm between the implied context of cultural refinement and the uncanny violence of a body that defies any and all such spaces, visually enunciates the collaboration that is always found between so-called civilization and its barbarous effects. The central figure is a cultural and semiotic nightmare of possibilities; an inhabitant of what Hal Foster has described as "the war zone between schizoid obscenity and utopian hope."[19] In a helmet adorned with diverse historical signs (Japanese armor, Viking horns, Mohawk-like fringe and electronic network antenna), the cyborg's double face with two vicious mouths snarls through a mask of metal bars and plastic hoses that penetrate the surface of the skin. One eye is blindly human, the other is a mechanical void. A feminine hand with razor sharp nails reaches out from the center of the chest, as if to escape from within. With arms and legs covered in one-cent scales, clawed feet, legs with fins, knee joints like gaping jaws, serpents hanging from the neck, insects swarming at the genitals, hundreds of toy soldiers clinging to the entrails and ammunition slung across the body, this beast is a contemporary monster – what Longo has called "American machismo."[20] The cyborg might be what Robert Hughes saw in the Dadaist obsession with war cripples, "the body re-formed by politics: part flesh, part machine."[21] In this light, it may seem to embody the very "illegitimate offspring of militarism and patriarchal capitalism" that Haraway problematizes in her "Cyborg Manifesto."[22] But in fact Longo's sculpture describes a rebellion against these institutions, who are better represented by the familiar corporate or government-owned, sterile, fantasy figures such as RoboCop.

Figure 1.4D "All you Zombies: Truth before God" by Robert Longo, Los Angeles County Museum of Art, New York (1990).
(Courtesy of Robert Longo)

Instead of an asexual automaton, Longo's creature represents a wild manifestation of human, animal and mechanical sexual potency and violence. With one artificially-rounded bare breast, and one arm raised, holding a torn flag to a broken pole, the figure is remarkably reminiscent of Delacroix's *Liberty Leading the People*. Her incongruous presence has the power to capture the imagination of the viewer through an embodiment of a maternal wrath and revolutionary zeal. At the same time the creature is not without his penis, protruding but protected in a sheath of its own armor (the wings of a powerful and no doubt stinging insect). Whether the cyborg is bisexual or not, it certainly has attributes of both human sexes. Interestingly, none of the three critics writing about this work in the exhibition catalogue mention this fact. Indeed, they all fail to acknowledge that the creature has any female attributes at all. Although the body overall has a masculine feel of weight and muscular bulk, this is clearly not a single-sex being. It storms across several thresholds; that between male and female, life and death, human and beast, organic and inorganic, individual and collective. To a certain degree then, this might be considered a hybrid body; a body which "rejoices" in "the illegitimate fusions of animal and machine."[23]

Historically, genetic engineering and cyborg bodies have produced similar fears about loss of human control – if there ever was such a thing – over the products of human creation. Barbara Stafford in her book *Body Criticism: Imagining the Unseen in Enlightenment Art and Medicine*, writes that in the eighteenth century,

> The hybrid posed a special problem for those who worried about purity of forms, interfertility, and unnatural mixtures. Both the plant and animal kingdoms were the site of forced breeding between species that did not amalgamate in the wild. The metaphysical and physical dangers thought to inhere in artificial grafts surfaced in threatening metaphors of infection, contamination, rape, and bastardy.[24]

Robert Longo's sculpture functions as an iconography of this metaphysics. It appears to be the very amalgamation of organic and inorganic elements that is the result of a dangerous and threatening mutation. But what makes this "hybrid" fusion "illegitimate"?

Fraught with many contradictory cultural connotations, the term "hybrid" itself demands some explanation before it can be used in any casual way – as it has been – to describe a cyborg body. The term appears to have evolved out of an early seventeenth-century Latin usage of *hybrida* – a crossbred animal.[25] Now the word has several meanings, among them: a person or group of persons reflecting the interaction of two unlike cultures, traditions, etc.; anything derived from heterogeneous sources or composed of elements of different or incongruous kinds; bred from two distinct races, breeds, varieties, species or genera. These definitions reveal a wide range of meaning, allowing for easy application, but little semantic substance. What makes the term controversial, of course, is that it appears to assume by definition the existence of a non-hybrid state – a pure state, a pure species, a pure race – with which it is contrasted. It is this notion of purity that must, in fact, be problematized. For if any progress is to be made in a politics of human or cyborg existence, heterogeneity must be taken as a given. It is therefore necessary to imagine a world of composite elements without the notion of purity. This, it seems, is the only useful way to employ the concept of the hybrid: as a combination of elements that, while not in themselves "pure" nonetheless have characteristics that distinguish them from the other elements with which they are combined. Hybridity must not be tied to questions of legitimacy or the patriarchal lineage and system of property which it implies. Rather, it must be recognized that the world is comprised of hybrid encounters that refuse origin. Hybrid beings are what we have always been – regardless of our "breeding." The visual representation of a hybrid cyborg thus becomes a test site for possible ways of being in the world. Raging involuntarily even against its own existence, the hybrid figure in *All You Zombies: Truth before God*, stands as its own terrible witness of a militarized capitalist state. As a body of power, active within its multiple selves, though mercenary in its politics, this cyborg is as legitimate as any other.

Passing

When I began to explore visual representations of cyborg bodies, I was originally motivated by a desire to unravel the relationship between representations of cyborgs and representations of race and racial mixtures.[26] I was brought to this point by the observation that in many of the texts written about and around the concept of cyborgs the term "miscegenation" was employed. Not only that, there seemed to be a general tendency to link the "otherness" of machines with the otherness of racial and sexual difference. I encountered statements such as the following:

> But by 1889 [the machine's] "otherness" had waned, and the World's Fair audience tended to think of the machine as unqualifiedly good, strong, stupid and obedient. They thought of it as a giant slave, an untiring steel Negro, controlled by Reason in a world of infinite resources.[27]

> Hence neither the identification of the feminine with the natural nor the identification of the feminine with the cultural, but instead, their uncertain mixture – *the miscegenation of the natural and the cultural* – is what incites, at once, panic and interest.[28]

The history of a word is significant. While the word "hybrid" has come to have ambiguous cultural connotations, words such as "illegitimate" and "miscegenation" are much more problematic. The latter is believed to have been "coined by U.S. journalist David Goodman Croly (1829–89) in a pamphlet published anonymously in 1864."[29] "Miscegenated" unlike "hybrid" was originally conceived as a pejorative description, and I would agree with scholar Stephanie A. Smith that "This term not only trails a violent political history in the United States but is also dependent on a eugenicist, genocidal concept of illegitimate matings."[30] At the same time, this may be the very reason that certain writers have employed the term – to point out the "forbidden" nature of the "coupling" of human and machine. (But, as others have made quite clear, this dependency upon metaphors of sexual reproduction is a problem of, rather than the solution to, conceptions of cyborg embodiment.) Lingering in the connotations of this usage are, of course, references to racial difference.

While there are several images I have encountered of cyborgs that appear to be racially "marked" as not "white" (*Cyborg* by Lynn Randolf being among the better known and more optimistic of these images) none struck me as so emblematic of the issues with which I was concerned as those found by my colleague Elena Tajima Creef in the 1991 Japanese comic book *Silent Möbius* (Figure 1.4E).[31] In part one, issue six, there is the story of a young woman of color. (Her hair is green, and her face is structured along the lines of a typical Euro-American comic-book beauty with big eyes [that not insignificantly fluctuate between blue and brown] and a disappearing nose and mouth. Yet, her skin is a lovely chocolate brown. She is the only character "of color" in the entire issue and she is clearly a "hybrid.") When we encounter her at the beginning of the story she is identified as a member of a futuristic feminine police force who is rehabilitating in the hospital. She is then seen racing off in a sporty jet vehicle after some dreaded foe. After pages of combat with an enemy called "Wire," it appears that she has won by default. She then declares that she must expose something to her love interest, a white young man with red hair. She disrobes, pulls out a weapon of some kind and proceeds to melt off her beautiful skin (looking more and more like chocolate as it drips away from her body), revealing to her incredulous and aroused audience that she is in fact a cyborg. Her gray body underneath looks almost white. She says, "This is my body Ralph . . . Seventy percent of my body is bionic, covered with synth-flesh. Three years ago, after being cut to pieces, I was barely saved by a cyber-graft operation. But I had it changed to a combat graft." "Why?" Ralph asks. "So I could become as strong as Wire, the thing that destroyed my life." But she goes on to say, "Eventually I started to hate this body. I wasn't feminine anymore. I was a super-human thing. I hated this body even though I wanted it. I didn't want to accept it. I kept feeling it wasn't the way I was supposed

Figure 1.4E "Silent Möbius"
(Published in *The Cyborg Handbook*, Routledge, 1995)

to be." As she speaks the reader is given more views of her naked body with gray, cyborg parts laid bare beneath disappearing brown skin. In the end she says, "I think I can finally live with what I have become."[32]

"Kiddy," for that is her diminutive name, is typical of contemporary (mostly male-produced) cyborg fantasies: a powerful, yet vulnerable, combination of sex toy and techno-sophisticate – in many ways not unlike *L'Horlogère*. But she is not an awkward machine with tubes and prosthetics extending from joints and limbs. She is not wearing her power on the outside of her body, as does Robert Longo's sculpture, nor is she broken apart and reassembled into disproportionate pieces, as in the case of Hannah Höch's photomontage. Rather she is an "exotic" and vindictive cyborg who passes – as simply human. It is when she removes her skin that she becomes the quintessential cyborg body. For in the Western imaginary, this body is all about revealing its internal mechanism. And Kiddy is all about the seduction of the strip tease, the revelation of the truth, of her internal coherence; which, ultimately, is produced by the super-technicians of her time. Her "real" identity lies beneath the camouflage of her dark skin – rather than on its surface.

"Passing" in this case has multiple and ominous meanings. Initially this cyborg body must pass for the human body it has been designed to replicate. At the same time, Kiddy must pass for the feminine self she felt she lost in the process of transformation. Staging the performance of "true" identity, Kiddy raises certain questions of agency. Must she reveal the composition of her cyborg identity? Which

Figure 1.4F "Silent Möbius"
(Published in *The Cyborg Handbook*, Routledge, 1995)

seventy percent of her original self was lost? Which thirty percent was kept? Who is keeping track of percentages? (The historical shadow of blood-quantum measurement and its contemporary manifestations looms over these numerical designations. Still serious and painful, especially in many communities of color, are the intersecting meanings of percentage passing and privilege.)[33] What are the consequences of this kind of "passing," especially when the body is so clearly marked with a sign – skin color – of historical oppression in the West? Why does Kiddy feel her body is not the way it is "supposed to be"? Has it been allowed unusual access to technological freedoms? Is the woman of color necessarily a cyborg? Or is Kiddy also only "passing" as a woman of color? What are the possible consequences of this reading? I leave these questions open-ended.

From my encounter with the world of cyborgs, and any cyberspace that these bodies may inhabit, I have seen that the question of race is decidedly fraught. Some see cyborgs and cyberspace as a convenient site for the erasure of questions of racial identity – if signs of difference divide us, the logic goes, then the lack of these signs might create a utopian social-scape of equal representation. However, the problem with this kind of e-race-sure is that it assumes differences between individuals or groups to be primarily superficial – literally skin deep. It also assumes that the status quo is an adequate form of representation. Thus the question over which so much debate arises asks: are there important differences between people (and cyborgs), or are people (and cyborgs) in some necessary way the same? The answers to this two-part question must be yes, and yes. It is the frustration of living with this apparent contradiction that drives people to look for convenient alternatives. As industrialized Western cultures become less homogeneous, this search intensifies. Cyborg bodies will not resolve this contradiction, nor do they – as yet – function as radical alternatives. It may be that the cyborg is now in a new and progressive phase, but its "racial" body politics have a long way to go. At best, the configuration of the cyborg, which changes over time, will virtually chart human encounters with a contradictory, lived experience and continue to provide a vision of new ontological exploration.

Acknowledgements

I would like to thank all of the friends and colleagues who have helped, and continue to help, in my search for images of cyborg bodies, and who have pointed me in the direction of useful literature on the topic; especially Elena Tajima Creef, Joe Dumit, Douglas Fogle, Chris Hables Gray, Donna Haraway, Vivian Sobchack and the Narrative Intelligence reading group at the MIT Media Lab.

Notes

1   Donna J. Haraway, *Primate visions: Gender, Race and Nature in the World of Modern Science*, New York: Routledge. 1989. p. 139.
2   Donna J. Haraway alludes to such a consciousness in her essay "A Cyborg Manifesto," in *Simians, Cyborgs and Women: The Reinvention of Nature*. New York: Routledge. 1991.

3   Michel Foucault. *The Order of Things: An Archeology of the Human Sciences*. New York: Vintage Books. 1973. Foucault explains his project in this text as significantly different from earlier histories and epistemologies of science by suggesting that he wishes to reveal a "positive unconscious" of knowledge — "a level that eludes the consciousness of the scientist and yet is part of scientific discourse" (p. xi). This "positive unconscious" can be thought of as "rules of formation, which were never formulated in their own right, but are to be found only in widely differing theories, concepts, and objects of study" (p. xi). One might also think of this notion as akin to certain definitions of ideology. It is useful for my purposes to the degree that it implies an unconscious but simultaneously proactive and wide-ranging discourse, in this case, of cyborg bodies.

4   See "The Cyborg Body Politic Meets the New World Order" by Chris Hables Gray and Steven Mentor. [In Chris Hables Gray, H. Figueroa – Sarriera and S. Mentor (eds) *The Cyborg Handbook*. New York and London: Routledge. 1991].

5   Julie Wosk. *Breaking Frame: Technology and the Visual Arts in the Nineteenth Century*. New Brunswick: Rutgers University Press. p. 81.

6   Ibid. p. 79.

7   Ernst Von Bassermann-Jordan. *The Book of Old Clocks and Watches*. Trans. H. Alan Lloyd. London: George Allen & Unwin Ltd. 1964. p. 15.

8   "The delight in automatons extended back even earlier to ancient Egyptian moving statuettes with articulated arms, and to the automatons of ancient Chinese, ancient Greek and medieval Arab artisans, as well as to European clockmakers of the medieval and Renaissance periods. . . . Homer in *The Iliad* described two female automatons who aided the god Hephaestus, the craftsman of the gods. The women were 'golden maidservants' who 'looked like real girls and could not only speak and use their limbs but were endowed with intelligence and trained in handiwork by the immortal gods.' " See Julie Wosk, pp. 81–82.

9   Wosk. p. 82.

10 "From another perspective, a cyborg world might be about lived social and bodily realities in which people are not afraid of their joint kinship with animals and machines, not afraid of permanently partial identities and contradictory stand-points. . . . Cyborg unities are monstrous and illegitimate: in our present political circumstances, we could hardly hope for more potent myths for resistance and recoupling." Donna Haraway. "A Cyborg Manifesto," p. 154.

11 Ibid. p. 180.

12 Patricia S. Warrick, *The Cybernetic Imagination in Science Fiction*. Cambridge MA: MIT Press. 1980. p. 32.

13 Maude Lavin. *Cut with a Kitchen Knife*. New Haven: Yale University Press. 1993. p. 2.

14 Virginia Woolf. *Orlando*. New York: Harcourt Brace Jovanovich Publishers. 1928. p. 307.

15 Timothy O. Benson. *Raoul Hausmann und Berlin Dada*. Ann Arbor: University of Michigan Research Press 1987. p. 161.

16 I use the term hyper-historical to connote an object or existence that appears to be synchronous with a very specific moment in history, but that seems to have had no coherent evolutionary past, nor developing future. The concept was originally conceived in order to salvage the seemingly a-historical status of the cyborg in Donna Haraway's description of this term (see *Simians, Cyborgs and Women: The Reinvention of Nature*). She writes that the cyborg has no myth of origin, but I do not

think she means to imply that it has no historical presence. Rather it has a presence that is so entirely wrapped up in a state of contemporary and multiple being that it is an exceptionally clear marker of any given historical moment – even when it makes references to the past.

17   Matthew Biro. "The Cyborg as New Man: Figures of Technology in Weimar and the Third Reich." Unpublished manuscript delivered at the College Art Association Conference, New York 1994.

18   Benson. p. 161.

19   Hal Foster. "Atrocity Exhibition," in *Robert Longo*, ed. Howard N. Fox. Los Angeles: Los Angeles County Museum of Art and New York: Rizzoli. 1989. "It is in the war zone between schizoid obscenity and utopian hope that the art of Robert Longo is now to be found," p. 61.

20   Howard N. Fox. "In Civil War," in *Robert Longo* . . . "Longo describes the monster as an image of 'American machismo,' a confusion of vitality and vigor with warlike destructiveness," p. 43.

21   Robert Hughes. *The Shock of the New*. New York: Alfred A. Knopf Inc. 1980. p. 73.

22   Haraway. "A Cyborg Manifesto," p. 151.

23   Ibid. p. 154.

24   Barbara Maria Stafford. *Body Criticism: Imagining the Unseen in Enlightenment Art and Medicine*. Cambridge, MA: The MIT Press. 1991. p. 264.

25   Random House Dictionary. Unabridged edition. 1993.

26   The term "race" is itself problematic and relies upon a history of scientific and intellectual bias. I use it here because the term has come to have a common-usage definition referring to genetic phenotype. Regardless of my distaste for this usage, I nevertheless recognize the real relations of power that are structured around it. It would be naive to ignore the ways in which this concept is employed and deployed. Here I try to point out the role of the idea of "race" in the conception of cyborg bodies.

27   Hughes, p. 11.

28   Mark Seltzer. *Bodies and Machines*. New York: Routledge. 1992. p. 66.

29   Random House Dictionary. Unabridged edition. 1993.

30   Stephanie A. Smith. "Morphing, Materialism and the Marketing of *Xenogenesis*," in *Genders*, No. 18, winter 1993. p. 75.

31   Elena Tajima Creef is Assistant Professor of Women's Studies at Wellesley College. She discusses *Silent Möbius* in relation to issues of race and representation in "Towards a Genealogy of Staging Asian Difference," a chapter of her dissertation "Re/orientations: The Politics of Japanese American Representation."

32   Kia Asamiya. "Silent Möbius," Part 1, No. 6. Trans. James D. Hudnall and Matt Thorn. Viz Communications Japan, Inc. 1991. pp. 34–36.

33   For a good discussion of passing see "Passing for White, Passing for Black," by Adrian Piper in the British journal *Transition*.

Nina Lykke

BETWEEN MONSTERS, GODDESSES AND CYBORGS: FEMINIST CONFRONTATIONS WITH SCIENCE

I T IS BECOMING MORE AND MORE difficult today for even the most stubborn traditionalists within academia to reject feminist arguments regarding the significance of gender in culture and society. In the so-called "hard" sciences, however, this is not the case. These sciences seem to be more resistant to the intruding feminist subjects than the humanities and social sciences. One of the reasons for this state of affairs is no doubt to be found in still dominant notions of science. If science is regarded as an enterprise which, no more and no less, aims at a value-neutral, progressive discovery of "universal and objective truths" about nature and matter, there is no room for feminism. Feminists can, of course, participate in the important work to change the gender balance in scientific communities, but actions beyond that point will not seem appropriate. The claim that feminist perspectives can be meaningful in the hard sciences, beyond the issue of recruiting more women, involves a radical challenge to the traditional notion of science as a "pure" search for the hidden truths of nature and matter.

In this chapter I will draw a map of some discursive spaces which seem to emerge when feminists confront and challenge science. The map I shall draw will be based on three landmarks: the metaphors of monsters, goddesses and cyborgs. I have chosen these metaphors because they are able to serve as evocative and open-ended markers. Through them I will point out different aspects of critical feminist rethinking concerning the relationship between gender, scientific subjects and the material worlds of artefacts and natural bodies, which have traditionally been cast in the role of passive objects and bearers of the desired "objective truths".

First, I ask the monster metaphor to perform as a representation of boundary phenomena in the interdisciplinary or hybrid grey zone between the cultural and natural sciences. In this zone boundary subjects and boundary objects, monsters which cannot be defined as either human or non-human, challenge established borders between the sciences. This is a zone where confrontations between feminism and science take place. I will draw a map of this zone of monsters as a place where feminist science studies can proliferate in promising ways and activate processes which may transform science.

In the second part of the chapter, two other boundary figures, goddesses and cyborgs (that is, hybrids of machines and organisms), both of which have attracted a great amount of feminist attention and debate, are introduced into the text. They are called forth to serve as metaphors for another border: that between "the artefactual" and "the natural", which traditionally divides non-human phenomena into two separate compartments. Like the border *between* human and non-human, this border *within* the non-human affects feminists in their confrontations with science. "I would rather be a cyborg than a goddess", is the conclusion with which Donna Haraway ends her famous cyborg manifesto (see Reading 1.3). In return, spiritually oriented eco-feminists would argue that a feminist reclaiming of the great goddesses of pre-historic matriarchies may help to redirect society, science and technology away from their present policies of violence – sexism, racism, "naturism",[1] and so on.

Instead of focusing on the apparent dichotomy between these feminist positions, I will ask a cyborg and a goddess to voice both their sameness and their difference. My purpose is to map out a space for a non-dichotomic conversation about feminist alternatives to the traditional scientific reduction of the non-human world to resources and mere objects without subjectivity.

The great divide

As a scholar, I am situated within the "soft" humanities, but oriented towards interdisciplinary work and transdisciplinary efforts at breaking down excessively rigid boundaries between disciplines. When I approach the "hard" sciences from this point of departure, it strikes me how great the divide that seems to separate natural and cultural sciences still is. C. P. Snow's famous diagnosis (Snow, 1965) of the intellectual world of modernity as split into two different cultures seems to be true even today, despite the best endeavours of postmodern and feminist science studies to deconstruct the boundaries. The dichotomy, which is signalled by the popular predicates of "hard" and "soft" sciences, has definitely not lost its significance.

One testimony to this dichotomy is the institutionalized divide between university faculties. Although certain hybrids (such as arts and science programmes) are emerging, the great divide between faculties still seems to hold the majority within academia spellbound. Marking one pole of this divide, the humanities and social sciences supposedly deal with those phenomena that differentiate the universal human being, traditionally identified as "man", from "his" others: things/artefacts and nature. Among these phenomena are the ability to think and the linguistic, aesthetic, ethical, imaginative and social capacities of the human being. At the other pole of the great divide we find the techno-, biomedical and exact sciences. They are expected to explore the non-human, which includes the biological dimensions of the human body, since universal man principally shares them with non-human creatures such as other mammals. Very little interaction takes place across the borders of this demarcation line. Literary and physics departments, for example, seldom act as if they have anything in common other than the infrastructure of university buildings.

"Nature" in literature and "nature" in physics seem to be two totally separate phenomena. One is inscribed in the world of art and language and supposed to be human, while the other is defined as non-human and subject to natural laws.

Modern monsters

A conspicuous characteristic of the great modern divide between human and non-human is that its construction is accompanied by strong hostility to monsters and hybrids in their capacity as boundary figures which adhere to neither the human nor the non-human sphere. As an illustration, I shall call Frankenstein's monster as my first witness.

Mary Shelley's enormously popular horror story about this monster (Shelley, 1968), which has been more or less canonized as *the* myth of modern science monsters, touches strongly on these feelings of fear and aversion to the non-human/human boundary figure. Frankenstein's monster appears as monstrous precisely because he/it is situated on the borderline between human and non-human. The mixture of human and non-human dimensions is what constitutes the monster's monstrosity.

From its conception the monster was supposed to be a true mirror of his human creator, but the result of the scientific birth process, initiated by the scientist Victor Frankenstein, turned into something very different. It became a human yet non-human creature whose borderline existence made him/it appear terrifying.

Shelley's novel makes it very clear that the monster's appearance violates the boundary between human and non-human. An example is the portrayal of the monster's eyes, which represent its most threatening feature. To Victor Frankenstein. the human yet non-human eyes of the monster become the main symbol of horrible monstrosity. Why do the eyes hold this position in the novel? Culturally, the eyes are considered the mirror of the soul, and they represent the primary sense of the enlightened human being, the vision. They disclose the human essence of the individual or, alas, they make it fail to pass as truly human. Had the monster been a human being, his eyes would have mirrored his human mentality. But the monster's eyes are not true and pure human eyes. They are boundary eyes: "His eyes, if eyes they may be called, were fixed on me", is Victor Frankenstein's horror-stricken comment about the moment when the monster confronts him after the "birth" (Shelley, 1968: 319).

In spite of the hostility to monsters, the great divide of modernity nevertheless seems to produce very fertile soil for an excessive, although hidden and repressed, proliferation of these feared and loathed creatures. In his essay *We Have Never Been Modern* (Latour, 1993), philosopher of science and sociologist Bruno Latour describes modernity as a process of purification. The great divide between the human and the non-human is the result of this process, he says. With overzealous perseverance the moderns try to make sure that any monster or hybrid that threatens to transgress the border is reclassified and ascribed to *either* the human *or* the non-human sphere.

According to Latour, however, modern acts of purification are never successful. They are continuously counteracted by an underground proliferation of monsters.

The modern purification of the oppositions human/non-human and socio-culture/ nature implies a tremendous act of repression of monstrous and hybrid forms, he says. The constant emergence of hybrids, including non-human humans, presents a never-ending threat to the modern construction of the great divide. In fact, says Latour, hybrid characteristics are the norm rather than the deviation. The moderns will, however, persist in denying all this impure and improper stuff; but Latour argues that the denial in no way keeps the monsters from breeding and proliferating beneath the surface. Quite the contrary: modernity manifests itself in its production of monsters and hybrids. Frankenstein's monster is only an early harbinger of the cyborg world of the late twentieth century. Cyborgs which, like Frankenstein's monster, transgress forbidden borders are becoming more and more common, and their repression, conversely, less and less successful. In the cyborg world of post-industrial society the proliferation of monsters is indeed getting completely out of control. The processes of purification, which in Latour's opinion have always been illusory, can no longer disguise this fact.

The monstrosities of feminist science studies

Feminist science studies are to be found among the permanently proliferating monsters which undermine the foundation of the great modern divide between human and non-human. Seen from the point of view of believers in the great divide, a whole range of monstrosities sticks to these kind of studies. But since monsters, boundary figures and other dubious creatures seem today to be the "true" rebels, there is nothing to worry about. In the last decade of the twentieth century it is perhaps clearer than ever before that no "pure" identity politics is possible. "Pure" women, workers, people of colour, gays and lesbians, indigenous peoples, eco-activists and non-human actors in "wild" nature have been transformed into inappropriate/d others: a diversity of actors who do not fit into the pure categories prescribed for them (Haraway, 1992). So why should the freaks who insist on trans-gressing borders by doing feminist science studies not jump out of the closet? Why should we not admit our hybrid identity and enjoy what Donna Haraway has called "the promise of monsters" (Haraway, 1992), the potential monsters have for creating embodied and never unambiguous sites for displacing and transforming actions on many levels?

So long as the great modern divide between human and non-human maintains its hegemonic power over academia, there are many reasons why feminist science studies must apparently work from a monstrous (but promising) position of inappropriate/d otherness. By briefly outlining a couple of these reasons, I shall illus-trate how feminist science studies contribute to the displacement and destabilization of the divide.

Gender and science: a monstrous construct

First of all, feminist science studies must appear monstrous to the believers in the great divide simply because such categories as women, sex, gender and so on are brought to the fore together with science. This will be the case no matter which definition of feminism is used. Through these categories, feminist thought in general and feminist science studies in particular pledge their faith in the promises of the monstrous.

Being close to nature in patriarchal thought, "woman" may often be found lurking in discursive spaces representing what lies between universal man and his non-human others. Therefore, any research which promotes the idea of a female, feminist subject must be prepared to find itself situated along with other monstrous enterprises in the grey zone between the human and the non-human. If the feminist subject tries instead to escape the grey zone of the monstrous through the category of "gender", she may at first glance seem to be saved. Apparently, she has attained a subject position on the human side of the great divide.

Without losing sight of the positive effects that the sex/gender distinction has had for the unfolding of feminist thought, it is nevertheless time for a critical assessment of its kinship with the great divide. Feminist constructions of the sex/gender distinction, which have been strongly supported by the English language,[2] appear as acts of purification. They are among the acts through which feminist thought has tried to inscribe itself in the discourses of modernity. Sex is nature, belonging to the non-human part of our being; gender is culture and a purely human affair. Hybrid interpretations are not admitted!

By insisting on this definition, the gendered, feminist subject can distinguish herself from her female, feminist sister by apparently keeping herself free of the monstrous. But (and this is my point) this will only be the case so long as she does not commit herself to feminist science studies. For if we followed the logic of the pure modern line of thought on sex and gender to its ultimate conclusion, we would paradoxically end up taking sides with those scientists who would claim that science is a "pure" search for the truths of nature and matter with no room at all for feminist perspectives. Seen through this lens, gender studies would be defined as a purely human enterprise and should therefore be situated exclusively at the humanities or social-science pole of the great divide.

In other words, feminist science studies cannot be saved from the monstrous by the category "gender". Quite the contrary. The introduction of "gender" as a socio-cultural and/or socio-psychological category will call forth conflicts with the image of science as a purely rational, depersonalized and value-neutral enterprise, exclusively absorbed in the discovery of truths about the material world. When gender and science are linked, the boundaries between human and non-human are challenged and the monstrous, invoked.

This becomes very clear in Evelyn Fox Keller's important writings on gender and science (Keller, 1985; 1989; 1992), which set out to shake the foundations of the traditional image of science by inscribing it in its context of socio-cultural and socio-psychological patterns of genderization. Evelyn Fox Keller suggests

> that our "laws of nature" are more than simple expressions of the results of objective inquiry or of political and social pressures; they must also be read for their personal – and by tradition, masculine – content.
>
> (Keller, 1985: 10)

To an adherent of the great divide this is, of course, an utterly monstrous statement, an undue mixing up of laws of nature with socio-cultural gender. Keller herself is, however, perfectly well aware of the dilemmas she mobilizes when talking of gender and science. She seeks a 'middle ground' between nature and culture (Keller, 1989: 34). On the one hand, she wants to maintain that modern science is basically culturally genderized; on the other, she does not want to reduce science to a purely cultural and relative phenomenon. Nor does she want to strip biological sex of all meaning. She knows that the search for this "middle ground" forces her to navigate in dangerous waters that constantly threaten to pull her out into a monstrous grey zone where clear statements can only be made at the expense of important ambiguities and excesses of meaning regarding science as well as gender. But for her, as for Donna Haraway, this affinity with the monstrous is one of the strengths of feminist science studies rather than their deficiency:

> Indeed, it might be said that feminist studies of science has become the field in which these ambiguities [the ambiguities of the terms "gender" and "science" – NL] are most clearly visible, and accordingly, the field that offers the best opportunity for understanding the factors that may be working against a clear and stable "middle ground" account of both concepts.
>
> (Keller, 1989: 35)

Constructionism or objectivity? A monstrous dilemma

The dilemmas involved in the mobilization of gendered categories in the study of the hard sciences represent only one kind of problem facing the feminist subject who wants to do science studies in the present situation, in which the great divide still exerts a hegemonic power over academia. I shall briefly discuss another, related problem which likewise forces feminists engaged in science studies out onto the monstrous boundaries between the human and the non-human: namely, is science a socio-cultural construct, or can it lead to objective truth?

In the transformatory work, which attempts to recast the image of science and open a space for feminist perspectives, a constructionist approach has proved very useful. When science is reconsidered as a socio-cultural and textual construct, plenty of space is opened for feminist perspectives. At the same time, however, a new problem appears: constructionism threatens to bracket the question of scientific objectivity. It may lead to the unpleasant consequence that the feminist subject who thought that she had constructed a room of her own *within* science suddenly seems to have sold herself to *non-science*.

Donna Haraway has described this situation very evocatively as an "epistemological electro-shock" which at some point in the unfolding of feminist science studies, hit feminist scientists whose critique of the objectivist tradition in which they were trained had led them to recast the image of science along constructionist lines:

> I, and others, started out wanting a strong tool for deconstructing the truth claims of hostile science by showing the radical historical specificity, and so contestability of *every* layer of the onion of scientific and technological

constructions, and we end up with a kind of epistemological electro-shock, which far from ushering us into the high stakes tables of the game of contesting public truths, lays us out on the table with self-induced multiple personality disorder.

(Haraway, 1991c: 186)

Haraway's solution to the dilemma is her concept of "situated knowledges" (Haraway, 1991c: 183ff.), which defines a new kind of objectivity based upon an always partial, embodied and localized vision. It excludes the classical "god-trick" of modern science, pretending to build up a potentially universal, omniscient and omnipresent knowledge of the "laws of nature".

My purpose here, however, is not to discuss this or other solutions, but in general to emphasize that the dilemma of "objectivity or constructionism?" leads to a questioning of the borders between human and non-human. As an illustration, I shall choose my own point of view, thereby situating myself and other feminists from the humanities who find it important to take part in a transdisciplinary conversation about feminism and science, and who perhaps are in a still more monstrous and inappropriate/d position vis-à-vis science than feminist scientists. How does the transgressive step taken by feminist scientists from a traditional conception of objectivity to constructionism look from the margins that I inhabit? To me it seems to open up a path from my position of total outsider with no critical authority whatsoever to a position that is at least potentially rather powerful.

Let us look first at the outsider's position. It goes without saying that the higher one climbs in the traditional hierarchy of sciences, as defined by Auguste Comte, and the more one's object of study is distanced from the human pole of the great divide, the less a feminist voice from the humanities counts. A modern version of this kind of outlook can be found in the discussion of feminism and science undertaken by the philosopher of science Isabelle Stengers (Stengers, 1994). She is critical of the hierarchical thinking implied in traditional approaches to science, but wants to keep the distinctions between human and natural sciences clear. In her opinion, feminists have made a stronger case for playing a role in the transformation of science in precisely those sciences which are *not* at the top of the traditional scientific hierarchy. It is possible, Stengers says, to criticize the *external* political context of the hard sciences from feminist and other political points of view. Moreover, she finds it desirable that all those who are being othered by science should articulate political demands with respect to this context. But this critique of the *external* context will not, cannot, and shall not, so Stengers claims, open a way to the *internal* core of the scientific problem.

From this sketch of the outsider's position, let me turn to the favourable insider's position, which feminist scholars from the humanities can take up when constructionism is put on the agenda. If feminist science studies are about the rhetoric of science, the semiotics of science, the philosophy of science, the history of science and so on, it becomes possible for me to recast my position as a total outsider in the world of science to a very central one. All the sophisticated knowledge about metaphors, narrativity, style and genre which I amassed when training as a literary scholar now seem to be extremely useful in my science studies. Even the hardest sciences at the very top of the traditional scientific hierarchy, which, like the Sleeping Beauty, used to be protected against my would-be critical eyes by a thorny hedge of equations and formulae, unintelligible to me, are now brought into the centre of my expertise. By one stroke of the magic wand, "constructionism", they are laid totally open to my analytical skills as a humanities scholar and to my critical outlook as a feminist. What a very pleasant reversal of the traditional scientific hierarchy! And what a great opportunity for expanding the reach of feminist critique.

But wait a minute. Maybe this is too easy. A simple reversal of the scientific hierarchy, which the radical constructionist approach to science represents, might be a useful tool, but it is not a solution that can stand alone. In other words, I agree with those feminist scientists who maintain that the reduction of science to mere texuality or pure power games,[3] while bracketing the question of objectivity, is not a desirable path for feminist science studies. Why? Because it would restrict the conversation to the narrow outlook of one or the other pole of the great divide.

To define the conversational terms so that feminist non-scientists are in the outsider position, as Stengers has recommended, means that physics and the other hard sciences are left with a purely non-human core and an insider's space, the "laboratory", which *a priori* excludes any attempt to set up a feminist conversation. The opposite line of thought, the reduction of science to textuality or power games, places me and other feminists doing cultural science studies in the position of central insider but leaves us with another pure core, the human spheres of the textual and/or the socio-political. Neither alternative seems appropriate for a critical, feminist discussion of the proliferating hybrids and monsters who/which populate the modern world in increasing numbers.

The monstrous in-between position seems to be by far the most promising site for further explorations.

Cyborgs and goddesses

In the discussion so far, I have situated feminist science studies in the border zone between the cultural and natural sciences, where human/non-human monsters play their disruptive games. From the monster metaphor and the great divide between human and non-human, I shall now turn to the two other metaphors of the title, cyborgs and goddesses, and the divide within the non-human sphere between the world of "artefacts/things" and the world of "wild/raw/unmanufactured/undomesticated nature".

This second divide has also engaged modernity passionately. In the seventeenth century, Francis Bacon, the so-called father of modern science, cast future science in the triumphant role of large-scale transformer of wild nature into domesticated artefacts. Bacon's vision,[4] which has been criticized by feminist science historians (for example, Merchant, 1980), is a powerful example of the modern preoccupation with the great divide between artefacts and nature. It is a celebration of the "artefactual", which is cast as representation of a happy future where humans are in total control of nature. The romantic critique of the artefactualism of the scientific world-view, embedded for example in *Frankenstein*, puts another kind of focus on the divide between artefacts and nature. It differs from Bacon's vision in that the two poles are valued in exactly opposite ways. Here "the artefactual" is "evil" and "the natural" is "good". In its capacity as an ugly and evil artefact, Frankenstein's monster is contrasted in the novel to the beauties of the natural world, which inspire the female characters. They embody a state of harmony with nature. The novel sets this up as an ethical and aesthetic ideal, by which standard the creation of the monster is measured and condemned as evil.

Feminist rethinkings of the interaction between science/technology and the material world of "non-humans" are obviously affected by this old dichotomy between the "artefactual" and the "natural". The feminist attention and the heated debates that the cyborgs and the goddesses have attracted testify to this, because the dichotomy between the two metaphors seems to follow precisely the lines of the divide between "the artefactual" and "the natural". On the one hand, the cyborg metaphor, which was inscribed in the feminist debate in the wake of the publication of Donna Haraway's cyborg manifesto (Haraway, 1991b),[5] seems to lead to a critical welcoming of "the artefactual" (which is not the same as an uncritical celebration in the Baconian sense!). On the other hand, the goddess metaphor, which for many years has functioned as a common landmark for the international wave of spiritual ecofeminism, seems to point us in the opposite direction: toward a return to "the natural". To Donna Haraway and other "cyborg feminists", feminist goddess worship is an expression of a modern nostalgic construction of a "good" (non-existent) origin to return to. In the cyborg manifesto, she elaborates on her remark regarding her preference for cyborgs rather than goddesses by way of a critique of ecofeminists such as Susan Griffin (Griffin, 1978) and their construction of a dichotomy between a good "organic" world as opposed to an evil "technological" one (Haraway, 1991b: 174).

If, however, we compare the cyborg and the goddess as two metaphorical landmarks, it is obvious that they have much in common. Both are, so to speak, designed to transgress the borders between human and non-human. Both challenge the ways in which the modern scientific world-view is rooted in a long tradition that casts the non-human in the role of a mere object and exploitable resource for the human, for centuries identified with the powerful and hegemonic position of the white Western man of science, capital and industry. Both the cyborg and goddess metaphors recast the non-human other in the role of subject, actor and agent in her/his own right. Both try to redefine the relation between human and non-human as one of conversation and non-suppressive dialogue between different subjects, instead of a hierarchical and exploitative relation between dichotomously separated opposites: human subject and non-human object and other. In order to illustrate this common ground, I shall call first a cyborg and then a goddess as witnesses.

Cyborg liberation

The cyborg I call is the principal character of a feminist science-fiction novel that deals with the phenomenon of "virtual reality". Virtual reality is a modern communications technology which makes it possible to obtain a very "intimate 'interface' between humans and computer imagery" (Woolley, 1993: 5). It is so intimate that all the sense data that make up the "real" experience are supposed to be present in the virtual, electronic space (in future versions of the technology, at least). The material world is, so to speak, absorbed into a virtual one.

In her novel *Virtual Girl* (Thomson, 1993), American author Amy Thomson explores virtual-reality technology. Maggie, the principal character, is a very human-like robot, created through virtual-reality technology by the lonely and homeless computer hacker Arnold, who wants a female companion to take care of him. Maggie is a cyborg, a humanoid machine created to fit the image of Arnold's desire for beautiful, caring, loving and dutiful "female" companion. Unlike Frankenstein's monster, Maggie is a cyborg whom everybody mistakes for a human, so perfect is the resemblance. She looks like a human, and is capable of imitating human behaviour on a very complex level. She is the perfect non-human human.

Seen from Arnold's human point of view, Maggie is a wonderful machine. She completely fulfils the purpose for which she was designed, at least in the first part of the novel. Here she acts as the perfect companion who/which takes care of all of Arnold's needs. However, the novel is the story of her emancipation from Arnold, about her unfolding as a subject in her own right in her capacity as a self-aware, thinking, feeling and sensing machine.

Maggie's emancipation process is initiated by a programming error. At some point in the creation process, Arnold tries to design a core identity for Maggie so that she can distinguish between important and non-important sense data and experiences. Arnold's idea is to program her so that she will always give priority to data that is important for fulfilling *his* needs. "Maggie, you are the most important thing I have ever done, . . . I need you. Start there", Arnold says (Thomson, 1993: 27). Due to the confused state of her programming at the given moment, she only catches the first half of the sentence. Thus she is programmed with the "wrong" idea that she herself, rather than Arnold's needs, is the "most important thing". From this point on, Maggie reprograms herself, and she slowly unfolds a stronger and stronger core identity which gives priority to her own basic needs.

There are many steps in Maggie's emancipation process. The novel is a fascinating unfolding of many complex stages of a cyborg identity. In a very moving scene in the middle of the novel, for instance, Maggie becomes aware of her independent core identity with the help of another self-aware computer program, whom/which she in return sets free on the net and later helps to slip into a male robot body. She thus shows herself capable of such deeds as the creation of a new robot, which originally were defined as an exclusively human enterprise. In another scene, Maggie is taught about human sexual life by a transvestite/gay human, Marie/Murray, who, to Maggie's great surprise, tells her that s/he is not a female in biological terms. In return for this openness, Maggie feels that she can be open too. Out of a new feeling of trust in humans, based not on Arnold's programming but on her own experience, she breaks one of the fundamental precepts of Arnold's original programming, which forbade her to disclose her non-humanness to humans. For the first time she tells a human being that she is a non-human. The transvestite/gay, who thinks s/he knows everything about different identities, is taken completely aback. Apart from the sexual difference which the transvestite/gay knows so well from experience, cyborg difference is brought into his/her world as an absolutely new dimension. The episode ends in a warm, trusting friendship between the two inappropriate/d and very different others.

In the dramatic conclusion of the novel, Arnold's initial programming error leads to Maggie's final emancipation. Arnold has by then inherited his father's fortune and is the owner of a big computer company. He wants to create a slave army of robot workers, with Maggie, his most complex and human-like creation, as an instrument in this process. But Maggie, for whom the thought of enslaving self-aware machines is terrifying, manages to defeat Arnold's plans and free herself and the other self-aware machines. Arnold learns that it is unethical to treat another subject as a mere thing and a slave, whether it is human or non-human.

Resurrection of the great cosmic mother: a healing of broken bonds

As my next witness, I call a goddess from the spiritual ecofeminist tradition. The goddess I invite into my text is the spiritual mother and significant title character of the book *The Great Cosmic Mother: Rediscovering the Religion of the Earth* (Sjöö and Mor, 1987). As in many cultural-historical writings of spiritual ecofeminism, the book presents the goddess as a potential healer of broken bonds between human and nature, between the human mind and non-human matter – body, earth, cosmos. The her/history that is told is a myth of origins intended to revise and replace the patriarchal ones. It is told in the language of mythical realism:[6] the goddess is understood not just as a metaphor or representation, but as a real, universal being. In this story we are all seen as born of the great cosmic mother. Originally, we lived in a direct physical–emotional–spiritual connectedness with her, as children of her cosmic womb or egg. Her physical–emotional–spiritual movements were our movements. Mind and body, human and nature, earth and cosmos were one inseparable whole. According to this kind of (her/hi)story-telling, the spiritual and worldly hegemony of the patriarchal father is a late stage in human history, the result of a violent take-over (located by the book in question in the Bronze Age). On the spiritual level, the patriarchal take-over, so the mythical story goes, meant that creator and creation, mind and matter, human and non-human, I and other, and so on, were separated and set up in a violent hierarchy, created in the image of the "colonization of the indigenous female by the imperial male" (Sjöö and Mor, 1987: 413).

Today, our minds are far away from the goddess, say Sjöö and Mor, but we can revive her in ourselves. If we accept that we are part of her, and if we retrace the universal, spiritual–material unity she embodies, we/she can heal the broken bond. According to Sjöö and Mor, the resurrection of the great cosmic mother and of our original dyadic relationship with her is the only meaningful political direction we can take today. It will, they say, be a step forward in human evolution, which they conceptualize as a spiral. They emphasize that they do not want a simple linear turning back of the clock of history. They are talking about a "step forward to the same place where we began, but on the path of a larger circle of consciousness" (p. 418), which, among other things, includes present-day techno-scientific knowledge. In New Age language, the new life in the goddess is defined thus:

> This time it will be a global consciousness of our global oneness, and it will realize itself on a very sophisicated technological stage; with perhaps a total merger of psychic and electronic activity.
>
> (Sjöö and Mor, 1987: 418)

To be a cyborg and/or a goddess?

Feminist cyborg stories point towards subjectivization and narrativization of the non-human. Amy Thomson's cyborg and the ones Donna Haraway inhabits in her writings are reconstructed as subjects with a right to their own stories. But the same can be said about the goddess stories of spiritual ecofeminism, which resurrect and remythologize non-human nature as the great cosmic mother. Both moves deconstruct the hegemonic position of the human subject of science vis-à-vis non-human objects and others. Both moves try to rethink the world as interaction between material-embodied *and* semiotic (that is, sign-producing and communicating) actors and subjects, who cannot be divided along the traditional lines of human versus non-human, conscious mind versus stupid matter.

There seems, however, to be a difference in the way goddesses and cyborgs act as material-semiotic subjects. They blur the boundaries between human and non-human, between the material world and the semiotic world of signs and meanings, in different ways. The cyborg of virtual reality tends to absorb the material into the semiotic. The material is constructed as potentially changeable by semiotic, sign-producing acts, by programming and reprogramming. The goddess is different. When she represents a mythical reality to her adherents, we might say that she, in contrast to her cyborg counterpart, tends to absorb the semiotic into the material. For her adherents, the goddess is – not just a name, a semiotic device; she IS.

This difference between cyborg and goddess might be related to another difference. A celebration of the cyborg and her/his/its tendency to absorb the material into the flow of semiosis (sign production) and ever-changing meanings tends to put the focus on technologies which speed up the meaning-changing processes. In contrast, a celebration of the goddess who absorbs the semiotic into the material will often be accompanied by a tendency to concentrate attention on the basic natural conditions of our existence.

These differences between cyborgs and goddesses may collapse into a split along the lines of the modern divide between "the artefactual" and "the natural'. But to me this collapse looks like a misplaced act of purification that represses their kinship as feminist monsters, who/which in important ways contribute to the deconstruction of the great divide between human and non-human. In my opinion, feminist science studies should reject neither the goddess metaphor nor the cyborg metaphor. Why not instead talk much more about their monstrous sisterhood? Why not explore the potentials of cybergoddesses?

Notes

1   The term "naturism" is used by some ecofeminists as a parallel to "sexism" and "racism". "Naturism" means abusive and violent treatment of non-human nature. According to the ecofeminist philosopher Karen Warren: "Feminism is a movement to end sexism", and "feminism is [also] a movement to end 'naturism' " (Warren 1990: 133).

2   In many languages it is not possible to distinguish between sex and gender as it is in English. In my native language, Danish, for example, there is only one word for the English terms "sex" and "gender". Both are translated into Danish as *køn*.

3   In his critique of the purifying and reductionist modern approaches, Latour exemplifies the reduction of science to power games by recourse to the French sociologist Pierre Bourdieu whom he holds up as an emblematic figure, while the reduction to textuality is illustrated by the French philosopher of language, Jacques Derrida (Latour, 1993).

4   The vision is illustrated clearly in Bacon's novel *The New Atlantis* (Bacon, 1870) from 1624. It anticipates the artefactualism of modernity.

5   The Haraway-inspired cyborg debate started in the early 1980s. In a note to the 1991 edition of the cyborg manifesto, Haraway dates the beginning of the debate to her paper, "New Machines, New Bodies, New Communities: Political Dilemmas of a Cyborg Feminist", at "The Scholar and the Feminist X: The Question of Technology" Conference, Barnard College, April 1983 (see Haraway, 1991b: 243).

6   Realism is here defined as one pole of the binary pair nominalism/realism. A "nominalist" approach understands general concepts as nothing but names, while "realism" indicates the absence of distance between the sign and the represented reality. In mythical realism, sign and reality are an inseparable unity (Cassirer, 1987).

References

Bacon, F. (1870) *The New Atlantis*, in *Works*, Vol. 3, edited by J. Spedding, R. L. Ellis, D. D. Heath and G. Rees, Longmans Green, London, pp. 129–66.

Cassirer, E. (1987) *Das mythische Denken, Philosophie der Symbolischen Formen*, 2, Wissenschaftliche Buchgesellschaft, Darmstadt (first edn 1924).

Griffin, S. (1978) *Woman and Nature: The Roaring inside Her*, Harper & Row, San Francisco.

Haraway, D. J. (1991a) *Simians, Cyborgs, and Women: The Reinvention of Nature*, Free Association Books, London.

—— (1991b) "A Cyborg Manifesto: Science, Technology, and Socialist-Feminism in the Late Twentieth Century", in *Simians, Cyborgs, and Women: The Reinvention of Nature*, Free Association Books, London, pp. 149–83.

—— (1991c) "Situated Knowledges: The Science Question in Feminism and the Privilege of Partial Perspective", in *Simians, Cyborgs, and Women: The Reinvention of Nature*, Free Association Books, London, pp. 183–203.

—— (1992) "The Promises of Monsters: A Regenerative Politics for Inappropriate/d Others", in L. Grossberg, C. Nelson, P. Treichler, eds, *Cultural Studies*, Routledge, New York and London, pp. 295–338.

Keller, E. Fox (1985) *Reflections on Gender and Science*, Yale University Press, New Haven, Conn. and London.

—— (1989) "The Gender/Science System, or: Is Science to Gender as Nature Is to Science?", in N. Tuana, ed., *Feminism and Science*, Indiana University Press, Bloomington.

—— (1992) *Secrets of Life, Secrets of Death: Essays on Language, Gender and Science*, Routledge, New York and London.

Latour, B. (1993) *We Have Never Been Modern*, Harvester Wheatsheaf, Hemel Hempsted.

Merchant, C. (1980) *The Death of Nature: Women, Ecology, and the Scientific Revolution*, Harper & Row, San Francisco.

Shelley, M. (1968) *Frankenstein, or the Modern Prometheus*, Three Gothic Novels, Penguin Books, Harmondsworth (first edn, London 1818).

Sjöö, M. and B. Mor (1987) *The Great Cosmic Mother: Rediscovering the Religion of the Earth*, Harper & Row, San Francisco.

Snow, C. P. (1965) *The Two Cultures, and a Second Look*, Cambridge University Press, Cambridge.

Stengers, I. (1994) *Metamorphoses of Science: Feminism and Shifts of Paradigms*, Gender–Nature–Culture Working Paper No. 7, Odense University.

Thomson, A. (1993) *Virtual Girl*, Ace Books, New York.

Warren, K. (1990) "The Power and the Promise of Ecological Feminism", *Environmental Ethics*, vol., 2 no. 2, pp. 125–46.

Woolley, B. (1993) *Virtual Worlds*, Penguin Books, Harmondsworth.

PART TWO

Alien m/others: representing the feminine in science fiction film

Introduction to Part Two

SCIENCE FICTION (SF) IS A HUGELY POPULAR genre of contemporary Western culture, spanning the different media forms of literature, film and television. Science fiction is a separately classified section in many bookshops and libraries; film companies promote science fiction films as block-busters and are rewarded with big profits; and Sky TV has a channel dedicated to the genre. On terrestrial TV, *The X-Files* was moved from BBC2 to BBC1 for the second series in recognition, by the corporation, of its unexpected audience reach, and over Christmas 1998 episodes of three different *Star Trek* series were shown on UK television (*Star Trek: The Next Generation*, *Voyager* and *Deep Space Nine*). The popularity of these two series led to big screen productions and, for *Star Trek*, these have also now run to series proportions with the ninth film *Star Trek: Insurrection* released in December 1998. In addition, fan culture focused on science fiction is expanding exponentially, with enthusiasts engaged in the appropriation of texts and characters in different ways, producing and circulating fanzines, exchanging ideas and stories across the Internet, organizing and participating in conventions (Jenkins, 1992; Jenkins and Tulloch, 1995). According to Jenkins (1992), the majority of those involved in the active and committed culture of fandom are women and the general contemporary audience of readers and spectators of science fiction certainly includes as many women as men, in spite of the genre's traditional associations with masculinity through its characteristic futuristic projections of militaristic technology, representing "warring, intergalactic nations competing with toys-for-boys".

So women consume science fiction, but what representations of the feminine do they find there? What interpretations of the feminine are available in popular contemporary science fiction films?

The science fiction genre is comparatively neglected in critical film literature, where mainstream genre studies have focused historically on the western, the gangster film, the musical, and feminist critics have analysed the film noir and the melodrama, and more recently horror, most productively. However, feminist theorists who have addressed science fiction, some of whose work is extracted in part 2, develop the argument that the conceptual interrelationship between technoscience and gender is a defining representational characteristic of science fiction film texts. In this respect, their analyses exemplify the central argument of this book, applied to a particular popular cultural form. However, deconstructing SF film through a feminist lens of the technoscience/gender confluence reveals strong discursive links with the cultural sites of reproductive technology and the Internet – the contexts of parts 2 and 3.

How, then, have feminist critics interpreted the technoscience/gender interrelationship in science fiction?

Donna Haraway defines the contemporary genre as follows: "Science fiction is generically concerned with the interpenetration of boundaries between problematic selves and unexpected others and with the exploration of possible worlds in a context structured by transnational technoscience" (Haraway, quoted in Wolmark, 1994: 2). Science fiction films made in their initial postwar period of popularity either celebrated or problematized modernity in their focus on the potential for technological development, but here Haraway identifies the fundamentally postmodern character of the contemporary genre, and implicitly points to its interest for feminism. Science fiction has become perhaps the quintessential genre of postmodernity in its characteristic representations of futuristic "tomorroworlds", inhabited by aliens, monsters and cyborgs which draw attention to artificiality, simulation and the constructed "otherness" of identity. Through its focus on difference and its challenges to fixed categories of identity (which is a characteristic concern of postmodern theory), science fiction also offers potentially fertile ground for feminist analysis and practice.

Following Haraway, in her introduction to *Close Encounters: Film, Feminism and Science Fiction*, Constance Penley makes the case as follows:

> science fiction . . . is more hyperbolically concerned than ever with the question of *difference*, typically posed as that of the difference between human and non-human. Although science fiction has traditionally been concerned with this question, new pressures from feminism, the politics of race and sexual orientation, and the dramatic changes in the structure of the family and the workforce seem to have intensified the symptomatic wish to pose and re-pose the question of difference in a fictional form that could accommodate such an investigation. Other challenges to being able to "tell the difference" have come not only from poststructuralist criticism, with its highly constructed and unstable subject, but also from advances in genetic engineering, bioengineering, and cybernetics. Such a confluence of pressures on subjectivity and difference perhaps explains what for many has been the rhetorical force of Donna Haraway's metaphor of the cyborg feminist, which manages to give both a utopian and dystopian spin to our new gendered technological bodies, and at the very least, provides a suggestive metaphor for further thinking about the

breakdown and reconstruction of what is going to count as "human" in the era
that we optimistically refer to as late capitalism.

(Penley et al., 1991: vii)

Here Penley identifies the reinforcing link between technology and gendered
subjectivity at both substantive and epistemological levels in the contemporary context, arguing that science fiction provides an ideal form for the fictional exploration
of this confluence of ideas and technological development.

Penley's reference to genetic engineering, bioengineering and cybernetics links
with the interests of other feminist critics who have identified SF's fascination with
the female body, particularly the body of the mother and with questions of reproduction and the maternal. In Mary Ann Doane's view, SF representation has been less
concerned with advanced technology's ability to *produce* cyborgs/androids than with
the implications this has for *reproduction*. Quoting the postmodern cultural critic,
Andreas Huyssen, she agrees that "the ultimate technological fantasy is creation
without the mother" (Doane, 1990: 164). Doane's readings of *Aliens* and *Blade
Runner* in reading 2.2, for example, identify profound anxieties about reproduction
and the feminine/maternal as underlying discursive constructs of the narratives of
both films.

In the case of the alien and android creatures that represent a defining trope of
the SF genre it is, of course, actually technology, rather than biology, that reproduces
gender and thereby challenges conceptions of what it is to be human, gendered, a
stable subject. In film this technological construction occurs at the level of both the
material production of film itself and within the narrative. Genre expectations of
science fiction demand sophisticated technological spectacle, so in this respect the
technology of cinematic illusion displays the state of its own art in science fiction
films, perhaps more than in any other genre. As Annette Kuhn observes, "since [SF]
films themselves are often about new or imagined future technologies, this must be a
perfect example of the medium fitting, if not exactly being, the message" (Kuhn,
1990: 7).

Doane identifies a further aspect of the technoscience/gender interrelationship
in the genre:

> although it is certainly true that in the case of some science fiction –
> particularly feminist authors – technology makes possible the destabilization of
> sexual identity as a category, there has also been a curious but fairly insistent
> history of representations of technology which work to fortify – sometimes
> desperately – conventional understandings of the feminine. A certain anxiety
> concerning the technological is often allayed by a displacement of this anxiety
> onto the figure of the woman or the area of the feminine.

(Doane, 1990: 163)

Here Doane identifies the tension between the potent liberatory potential of the
cyborg metaphor in Haraway's conceptualization and the tendency for it to be appropriated and reproduced in SF in ways that actually reinforce gendered, racialized
stereotypes.

Although the critical literature on SF is relatively scarce, amongst the individual films which have generated significant critical interest are the *Alien* series and *Blade Runner*. In fact, Kuhn suggests that these particular films were responsible for a regenerative interest in the SF genre amongst film theorists and cultural critics (Kuhn, 1990). Given their shared representation of creatures of constructed, gendered "otherness" and with questions of reproduction and the maternal, they are certainly productive for analysis focusing on the articulation of technoscience and gender. The readings that follow in part 2 offer deconstructive interpretations, informed by different feminist critical perspectives, referring to *Alien* (directed by Ridley Scott, 1979) *Aliens* (James Cameron, 1986) and *Blade Runner* (Ridley Scott, 1982) in particular, although authors also refer to some other films.

In reading 2.1, Lynda K. Bundtzen contrasts the respective representations of Ripley, the female protagonist of *Alien/s*, and of the Alien monster herself, as signifiers of the maternal. Bundtzen initially acknowledges Ripley's superficial representation as a convincing feminist icon — independent, resourceful, physically strong, and superior in strategic thinking to her male colleagues. In *Aliens* her character is further developed through her compassionate attachment to the rescued child Newt, whom she protects as a surrogate mother. Bundtzen commends the representation of mothering as a cultural choice, as opposed to biological destiny here, but finds it entirely undermined by the simultaneously menacing representation of female sexuality and monstrous motherhood in the Alien Mama. In *Aliens* the humans pitch their sophisticated technological armoury against nature in the form of the Alien, "a biologically perfect creature" which, according to Bundtzen, represents the embodiment of woman's reproductive powers, recalling the phallic mother of nightmare and arousing primal fears about women's sexuality. And nature, represented as monstrous femininity, instinctual and out of control, obliterates technology and culture (including the "good" android Bishop) and meets her match only in Ripley, coded also as mother, but not via the body. Bundtzen describes the three confrontations between Ripley and the Alien/s over Newt, building up to the climactic battle scene between the good and bad mother. Here Ripley reinforces her cultural coding and becomes a cyborg by climbing inside a huge robotic casing, demonstrated (necessarily) earlier in the film as a powerful twenty-first-century fork-lift truck. Then she fights the Alien with enhanced technological strength and the signifier of excessive biological motherhood is apparently overcome. As those who are familiar with the two later films in the series (*Aliens 3* and *Alien Resurrection*) will know, and as Bundzten's prescient concluding commentary predicts, the Alien has not been destroyed and her determination to reproduce has not been curtailed; the unstoppable maternal principle continues unabated. Bundtzen's final analysis is that the representation of woman's reproductive capacity as a threat to civilization through the Alien Queen contaminates the feminist potential of Ripley's coding as a cultural mother of choice. When Ripley as cyborg destroys the Alien as biological mother, she represents woman "Alien-ated from her body . . . and a feminism in service to technology over nature".

Bundtzen's analysis is typical of feminist critical interventions that followed the general celebration of Sigourney Weaver's portrayal of Ripley as a strong female protagonist, which sought to uncover deeper meanings beneath the superficial feminist gloss. Her focus on the articulation of maternal signification between the two main characters is particularly productive in this respect. Her conclusion here, that technology represents an alienation of the female body in *Alien/s*, is echoed in some of the critical debates about the effect of reproductive technologies in the "real" world which are considered in reading 2.2.

Like Bundtzen, Mary Ann Doane is also concerned with constructions of the maternal feminine in SF and, in particular, with how anxieties about technology are projected on to those about reproduction and the female body within the genre. Drawing on Metz and Kristeva, as well as Barthes and Baudrillard, she argues that SF's characteristic "technophilia", its foregrounding of technological fetishism, underpins an obsession with issues of reproduction and the maternal linked to those of representation and history and that "the conjunction of technology and the feminine [in SF] is the object of fascination and desire but also of anxiety – a combination of affects that makes it the perfect field of play for the science fiction . . . genre".

In her analysis of *Alien/s* and *Blade Runner*, Doane suggests that their narratives "contemplate the impact of drastic changes in reproductive processes on ideas of origins, narratives, and histories" and links this focus with contemporary cultural concerns relating to the revolution in material reproductive technologies. Doane argues that because these technologies threaten the certainty of origins guaranteed through biological motherhood they also undermine the psychoanalytic account of identification and sexual difference through Oedipal resolution and the link between subjectivity and knowledge that it supports, and are therefore profoundly unsettling in their threat to patriarchy. In *Alien/s* the story is not one of conflict with a symbolic father, but of struggle with "an overwhelming extension of the category of the maternal, now assuming monstrous proportions". Doane contends that the de-stabilization of origins and of sexual difference are played out in *Alien/s* through a confusion of the tropes of masculinity and femininity in relation to the process of reproduction. The alien creature appears in several forms, which connote both masculine and feminine reproductive traits. Men, as well as women, give birth – and it is an agonizing and fatal experience. Doane identifies a more complex and ambivalent articulation of anxieties around technology and sexual difference associated with reproduction in *Alien*, in particular, than Bundtzen, although both agree that in *Aliens* an unmitigated construction of monstrous, maternal reproduction is represented by the Alien Queen. However, Doane does not address the counterpoint provided by Ripley's coding as cultural mother.

In *Blade Runner*, Doane contends that the terror of motherless reproduction associated with technology, and represented by the cyborg replicants, is located as an anxiety about loss of history, certainty and knowledge. Another kind of technological reproduction – photography – is foregrounded in the film and linked with the technological reproduction of people, and its status as proof of history is also challenged. Destabilization of categories of difference – not knowing how to "tell the difference" (between human and non-human) – fundamentally undermines the basis of knowledge altogether. Therefore, although *Blade Runner*'s replicants are both male and female reproductions, their significance relates crucially to anxieties around the concept of the maternal, precisely because none of them has a mother (although Leon and Rachel know they need a [memory of] mother more than anything else in order to be "real"), and biological mothers are the guarantors of history, and therefore of certainty and knowledge. Reproduction has to be linked to the maternal body in order to confirm origins and history, and technological intervention disrupts the underpinning certainties of knowledge that they provide.

Doane concludes that these films rework connections between the maternal, history and representation in ways that suggest contradictory responses of both nostalgia for, and profound horror of, the maternal function and towards technologies of reproduction.

Barbara Creed's psychoanalytic reading of *Alien* (in reading 2.3) again focuses on the depiction of the Alien Queen as a representation of monstrous, maternal femininity which she interprets in relation to theories drawn from Freud, Lacan and Kristeva, locating it firmly within patriarchal ideology. Creed identifies several manifestations of the maternal figure in terms of the "monstrous-feminine" drawn from the psychoanalytic story and delineates their explanatory potential in relation to the film, specifically the representation of the Alien monster.

Creed relates the figure of the archaic mother, the reproductive/generative mother of ancient myth, to the several representations of the primal scene that she identifies in the early part of the film. She argues that psychoanalytical theorists have typically underplayed the positive autonomous potential of the pre-Oedipal, pre-phallic mother by casting her negatively as a figure always in waiting for entry to the symbolic order and in relation to the father. In this they miss the positive aspect of autonomous generative power associated with the mother-goddess figure of myth, a prior archaic mother who establishes female sexual difference that does not depend on a phallic opposite.

Creed contends that in the horror/science fiction film genre, and *Alien* in particular, the archaic mother is represented in all her negative force. She identifies the signifier of the gestating, all-devouring womb of the archaic mother as a key generator of horror within the genre, representing the threat of extinction and death, through reincorporation of what it originated. It therefore threatens individual subjectivity and differentiation and can produce contradictory fears and desires – for death and self-disintegration on the one hand, but also for re-merging in oneness with the mother on the other. Creed suggests that this ambiguity is reproduced in audience responses to horror movies when they look away – or not – from fear-inducing images of the monster; looking away disavows the threat of loss of identity and protects individual differentiation by re-establishing the boundary between the viewer/self and the screen. Similarly, when the screen character is left alone and pursued by the hidden, menacing monster, their predicament represents both the subject's fear of separation and their fear of annihilation.

Creed goes on to discuss the scenes in *Alien* in which the monster functions as the oral-sadistic mother, emphasized by her two sets of razor-sharp teeth, which gnaw their way out of the "host" mother (the male character Kane) to secure birth and then cannibalizes all in her way. She is a "survivor unclouded by conscience, remorse or delusions of morality", as described by the similarly unclouded (as it turns out) android Ash. Ash is a cybernetic character who conforms quite shockingly to a villainous male stereotype that is ultimately violently sexualized when it/he attempts oral rape of Ripley using a rolled-up calendar depicting semi-naked women. So no transgression of gender categories represented here, then.

In her final identification of the alien as a representation of the phallic mother, Creed contends that this figure, constructed in relation to the oppositions of the Oedipal family scenario, is always less threatening to the patriarchal order than the archaic mother, who signifies woman as autonomous female difference. In *Alien* the representation of the archaic mother is linked to images of the devouring womb. Nonetheless, in *Alien* the mother is represented as monstrous as simultaneously phallic, and as archaic and oral-sadistic. Deploying a theory of female fetishism from Juliet Mitchell, Creed suggests that the monster represents the notion of female fetishism and the woman's attempt to "have" the phallus and thereby a place in culture. The changing forms in which the Alien appears can be understood as a form of multiplication of the phallus representing the mother's desire to avoid castration.

Creed's overarching conclusion, therefore, is that the various forms of the monstrous-feminine signified by the Alien represent fear of difference and of the feminine. She identifies these unconscious processes of the text as patriarchal and as working ideologically to repress and control the feminine and positive readings of the maternal (Kuhn, 1990).

This extract, selected for its focus on *Alien/s* as a SF/horror hybrid, comes from a longer article by Creed entitled "Horror and the Monstrous-Feminine: An Imaginary Abjection", first published in *Screen* in 1986 and later forming the basis of her book *The Monstrous-Feminine: Film, Feminism, Psychoanalysis* (Routledge, 1993). The complete essay provides a detailed reconstruction of Kristeva's theory of abjection, which Creed then links to an analysis of several examples of representations of the maternal in horror films, including the extended critique of *Alien/s* extracted here. Her influential psychoanalytic reading is powerful and evocative in its revelation of how unconscious processes are not neutral, but deeply embedded in patriarchal discourses (Kuhn, 1990). However, critics have found the totalizing perspective, characteristic of psychoanalytically informed approaches, problematic because of its closed, ahistorical and decontextualized method (Latham, 1998). Creed's analysis is text-based and allows no space for active, negotiating spectators. Annette Kuhn, while acknowledging the value of Creed's work, notes that feminist psychoanalytic film critics, "by engaging with the very meanings they seek to deconstruct, may be in danger of getting caught up in them. To feminists wishing to move beyond critique of the dominant cultural order and towards newer forms of representation, this can seem a serious limitation" (Kuhn, 1990: 94).

In the next reading, from Vivian Sobchack's final chapter of *Screening Space: The American Science Fiction Film*, we turn again to *Blade Runner* and a reading of the significance of alien/cyborg identity. Sobchack's fascinating book provides a comprehensive review of the development of (American) SF cinema and in this last chapter she contrasts the representational concerns of the contemporary genre with those of the first "Golden Age" of SF in the 1950s. A further focus of her analysis is the contrast between mainstream and more marginal, avant-garde films. In this chapter, of which the final section is extracted here, she locates the contemporary genre in its mainstream and avant-garde respective forms in relation to the characteristic features of postmodernity. For Sobchack, the monstrous representations of otherness in *Alien* analysed by the three preceding critics hark back to SF representations of BEMs (bug-eyed monsters) of the 1950s and are untypical of more contemporary thinking about alien and alienated identification – although here it is perhaps significant that Sobchack's is not primarily a feminist analysis. She identifies a major shift of focus and a tendency in contemporary mainstream SF to represent alien creatures as being different but just like us in their differentness and, more radically in marginal representations, to erase difference and suggest a universal condition of alienation in which we are aliens and aliens are us. Sobchack explores the cultural implications of this distinction using Foucault's analysis of the conceptual distinction between relations of resemblance and of similitude, where the former is based on hierarchy and maintains difference, and the latter erases difference and is non-hierarchical. Sobchack locates the representation of *Blade Runner*'s replicants in the first, less progressive category, in keeping with its mainstream status, and identifies some more marginal films – *Liquid Sky* and *Repo Man* – as texts in which difference is erased and aliens speak across sameness whilst asserting difference, in a "celebration of similitude". This latter conceptualization of the alien invokes something of the metaphorical resonance of Haraway's cyborg as a liberatory construction of postmodern identity in which hierarchical difference is erased. In her concluding section, Sobchack provides a schematic review of the cultural resonance of SF film from the 1950s to the late 1980s and questions its future as a potentially progressive cultural form . Although, as noted above, Sobchack's analytical lens is not primarily feminist, she concludes by identifying a feminist SF text, Lizzie Borden's *Born in Flames* (1982), as an inspiring model for future development.

The final reading in part 2, "Reading Cyborgs Writing Feminism" by Anne Balsamo, directly addresses the usefulness of Haraway's cyborg metaphor in the context of its science fictional representations and asks what they tell us about the place and identity of women. Balsamo is concerned, like Doane, with how far representations of the cyborg, in particular, offer liberatory identifications for women and the extent to which they confirm gendered stereotypes. Her analysis spans both literature and film. In the mainstream popular film *texts* of *The Terminator*, *RoboCop* and *Blade Runner*, Balsamo finds that gender stereotypes are solidly reinforced. She goes on to argue, however, that – even in their mainstream manifestations – female-gendered cyborgs do more to challenge the opposition between human and machine because femininity is conventionally coded as less compatible with technology than is masculinity. Thus the notion of Rachel's technological constitution in *Blade Runner*, where she is coded in a feminine-essentialist way as emotional and sexually available, therefore operates to challenge cultural conventions more so than does the Terminator's own repair of his inorganic body.

Balsamo goes on to suggest ways in which the feminine essentialism of female cyborgs might be transformed, and the liberatory potential of Haraway's cyborg applied, in the context of popular cultural representations. She identifies a link between cyborg identity and feminist analyses of women's identity through their common position within the framework of social construction. A key insight of Second Wave feminisms has been the covert masculine identity of the subject of liberal individualism and of woman's opposed identity as defining "other" of the male subject, constructed as outside the symbolic order, as unstable and fragmented. However, the dissolved and diverse character of women's identity provides the basis for connection across difference at both theoretical and political levels, which mirrors the networked interconnections of Haraway's metaphorical cyborg communities. Because cyborg identities are about transgressing boundaries, they draw attention to the "constructedness of otherness" and thereby to the ways in which culture depends on the arbitrary attribution of categories of meaning and identity. Balsamo argues that women and cyborgs share a construction of otherness that could provide a productive dimension for exploration in the domain of science fictional representation. To some extent here, her thinking suggests structural links with Sobchack's Foucauldian analysis of the replicants in *Blade Runner* in their shared focus on the self/other framework of contructedness which underpins identity.

Extending her argument to contemporary ideas about the body, Balsamo again focuses on the power of the cyborg to question what constitutes the natural and the link this provides with concerns of feminism. The bionic body of the cyborg – an unnatural body – serves to undermine conventional understandings of the body as the site of essential, unified, natural identity, just as feminist scholarship has sought to do as part of its liberatory project. Women's bodies carry a multiplicity of meanings and shifting identities. However, as Bundtzen's critique of *Aliens* indicates, arguing for the negation of the natural body may be useful in so far as it liberates women from occupying an essentially negatively coded and limiting space, but women *are* embodied, and it is difficult to see how the cyborg concept offers a positive interpretation of the experience of embodiment in Haraway's conceptualization.

At the end of Balsamo's balanced and illuminating reading, she makes the point that it is difficult to tell whether Haraway chooses the cyborg image because she thinks there are existing similarities between cyborgs and women, or because she thinks there should be. Balsamo criticizes Haraway for failing to take into account the gender-reinforcing ways in which cyborg identities had already been culturally appropriated in popular forms and she warns against attempting to reify the cyborg as a utopian aspirational icon in the service of feminism. Instead, Balsamo advocates the reclaiming of the cyborg image as a "possible prototype for a feminist reconceptualization of personal and political identity which embraces, and, perhaps, celebrates, the diversity of women's identity".

The five readings collected in part 2 represent just some of the critical perspectives and insights feminist scholars have brought to bear on some contemporary science fiction films. These commentators share a focus on m/others as the primary representational trope of femininity with which the films are concerned. Although Bundtzen initially acknowledges the positive coding of Ripley in *Aliens* as cultural mother, her overall analysis accords with those of Doane and Creed in finding the films' representation of the alien mother to be revealing of profound cultural misogyny. The liberatory potential of the cyborg image for challenging the binary impasse

of gendered identity, although creatively explored in feminist science fiction literature, has not yet been effectively deployed in the film genre. Instead, Sobchack and
Balsamo find that cyborg characters usually work to reinforce conventional, often
stereotyped, understandings of gendered identity. However, Sobchack does point to
ways in which more progressive ideas about identity and difference are being explored
through cyborg images in some marginal science fiction films. And Balsamo's
careful discursive analysis of Haraway's concept, applied to SF texts, insists that the
imaginative and liberatory force of the cyborg image remains undiminished, although
as yet unrealized.

These essays focus primarily on texts rather than audiences and in this respect
they reflect the critical interests of the 1980s which coincidentally coincided with
the upsurge of interest in science fiction film, as well as with the publication
of Haraway's Manifesto. Haraway herself, of course, is very much concerned with
audiences, their different locations, identities, interpretations, interactions. More
recent film media criticism, particularly feminist criticism, has also turned in this
direction, focusing on the ways in which the social subjects of audiences actively
construct meanings in a process of negotiation with film texts. This process is the
defining activity of fan culture, and the culture of fandom has grown around science
fiction texts more than any other genre. Perhaps it is here, in the myriad exchanges
across the Internet about, in the name of, and appropriating differently, the
characters and stories of *Star Trek*, *Dr Who*, *The X-Files*, even *Blake's 7*, that the
potential of the cyborg metaphor to transgress boundaries is currently being
explored.

References

Doane, M. A. (1990) "Technophilia: Technology, Representation and the Feminine"
    in M. Jacobus, E. Fox Keller, and S. Shuttleworth, (eds) *Body/Politics: Women
    and the Discourses of Science*, New York and London: Routledge.
Jenkins, H. (1992) *Textual Poachers*, New York and London: Routledge.
Jenkins, H. and Tulloch, J. (1995) *Science Fiction Audiences*, New York and London:
    Routledge.
Kuhn, A. (ed.) (1990) *Alien Zone: Cultural Theory and Contemporary Science
    Fiction Cinema*, New York and London: Verso.
Latham, R. (1998) "Phallic Mothers and Monster Queers", *Science-Fiction Studies*
    25(1).
Penley, C., Lyon E., Spigel, L. and Bergstrom, J. (eds) (1991) *Close Encounters:
    Film, Feminism and Science Fiction*, Minneapolis: University of Minnesota
    Press.
Wolmark, J. (1994) *Aliens and Others: Science Fiction, Feminism and Post-
    modernism*, London: Harvester Wheatsheaf.

Lynda K. Bundtzen

MONSTROUS MOTHERS
Medusa, Grendel, and now Alien

WILL THERE BE A SEQUEL TO *Aliens*? Its depiction of female fecundity, prolific and devouring, is so powerful and fictively generative, it would be hard for an equally profit-hungry movie industry to resist another visitation by the Alien Mama and her spawn. The Company in *Aliens* certainly seems eager for the monster's survival. In both the original *Alien* and the current sequel, a sleazy Company man (actually an android in *Alien*), stirred by the profit-motive, is engaged in nefarious dirty tricks to return an alien embryo to the Company's labs on earth. The lingering question at the end of *Aliens* is whether, in fact, the Company man Burke has succeeded – whether the figures encapsuled in space-sleep for the return journey harbor an Alien embryo. The image of sleeping beauties and heroines Ripley (Sigourney Weaver) and the young girl she saves, Newt (Carrie Henn), is disquieting. The Alien is an elusive, slippery parasite, with incredible ability to pop up and out of the most unlikely places. The last Alien appearance in this film occurs after the spaceship leaves the infected planet. Just when the audience believes all danger is past – following what seemed to be a final harrowing escape by Ripley and Newt – the android Bishop is pierced through his belly by what first looks like an Alien birth and is then revealed to be the Alien Mama herself. She has somehow managed to maneuver her dragon's girth undetected on to the departing space ship, and roars into life for a final showdown with Ripley. With this improbable return after the story seemed to have climaxed, an unsteady audience may well wonder if the film's ingenious writer-director James Cameron hasn't still another ending in mind, and if not ends, sequels.

Within the thematic structure of the narrative, however, there are even more compelling reasons to expect the Alien's eternal return. The disquietude we may feel gazing at the virginal sleep of Ripley and her foster daughter Newt is a result, I believe, of our intuition that it disguises the potential threat they apparently have defeated and escaped. Narrative instability is reinforced cinematically in the camera's final dissolve from a medium shot of the sleeping Ripley and Newt to a close-up that invites a quizzical inspection from the audience: what are we looking for in these ostensibly peaceful figures? Defeat and escape from the female and Alien other is, I will show, only provisional and temporary. *Aliens*, I will argue, is a profoundly disturbing allegory about contemporary feminism, and it is far from resolving the issues it explores about woman's nature vs. her culture-making aspirations.

The heroine of *Aliens* is no feminist ideologue, but surely an exemplary figure for women in her rugged independence, cool courage under fire, and resourcefulness. In both *Alien* and *Aliens*, Ripley is characterized as fighting male bias against women doing the kind of work she does and shown asserting both her authority (in *Alien* she is the ship's security officer) and her right to command men with less intelligence and nerve. Physically, she is a rangy six-footer, agile and strong, and demonstrably capable of any swashbuckling feats performed by male heroes. In *Aliens*, though, she is further endowed with a more traditionally feminine trait: her loving, maternal nurturance of the young girl, Newt. Newt (a nickname I will return to later) is the sole survivor of the Alien's annihilation of an entire colony of humans sent by the Company to exploit the resources of an unpopulated planet. This relationship between Ripley and Newt has inspired a feminist sentimentality that diverts attention from the film's menacing depiction of female sexuality in the Alien.

Who or what is the Alien? Ripley's foe is a primal mother defined solely by her devouring jaws and her prolific egg-production. As her eggs open, presumably triggered by the presence of a human host, they splat (I can think of no better word here) on the face of a victim. This intermediate Alien form resembles female genitalia, surrounded by crab legs and a long whip-like tail. The tail wraps around the victim's throat and chokes the host's mouth open for oral rape. When, for example, Ripley struggles with one of the lab specimens, the monster's tail is wound tightly around her neck, choking Ripley's mouth open for embryo implantation. From a vaginal cavity, a penis-like finger juts into the throat and implants an alien embryo deep into the viscera of a host. This vagina *cum* penis appears when a lab specimen darts furiously at its glass enclosure, and we see a little finger poking out of a slit. This fusion of male and female sexual organs does not make Aliens androgynous. The monster's femininity is confirmed by the vulva and labia which surround the slit – a graphic display of female anatomy – and an incident between the android Bishop and another marine. Bishop is studying a dead Alien specimen, carefully tweezing aside the folds of flesh around the vaginal opening, when another marine lewdly comments, "I think it likes you."

After an initial struggle with this smothering Alien form, the host endures embryo implantation and gestation in a death-like sleep. The crab-like structure falls off the face, and at least in *Alien*, the host has a brief waking spell of seeming normality. The embryo, however, has developed a large head with extraordinary jaws and finally gnaws its way out in a violent Caesarean birth that destroys its human host. In *Alien* singular, only one monster is born. The other members of Ripley's first crew are presumably devoured by the Alien, who grows larger with each human morsel. The opening of *Alien* shows, however, a landscape of eggs ready to adopt human hosts, and in *Aliens*, the colonists have wandered into this no-man's land (the result, we learn from Ripley's investigations, of Burke's treacherous orders). Despite

Aliens' voracity, many colonists have not yet been eaten. Homing devices implanted in the colonists' bodies lead the rescue squad to where they have been captured instead for hosting eggs. I cannot help but reflect here that the Aliens' self-replication must be limited by the food and/or host supply, but laying eggs seems to be an imperative superseding any consideration of what is available for sustenance. Perhaps the Alien Mama surmises humans' ambivalent attraction and repulsion to her dangers.[1]

Fighting Aliens poses innumerable hazards. Their scuttling speed and wraparound tails are comprehensible dangers. In addition, however, they have mysterious bodily fluids and several retractable jaws nesting inside one another. Shooting an Alien results in spurts of Alien "blood." This blood is acid and it sears through everything – flesh, bone, plastic, steel. If one must shoot them, then, it should be at a considerable distance and without fear of acid-damage to one's environment. A better strategy is to burn them with flame-throwers, and this is the technique Ripley eventually uses to great advantage in the penultimate confrontation with the Alien Mama. The jaws of Aliens seem to have an immobilizing, hypnotic effect on their victims, or at least their opening jaws are punctuated by lengthy reaction shots, suggesting a resemblance to the Medusa's paralysis of her victims.[2] Aliens' jaws are gooey, secreting a viscous fluid that cocoons human beings in a spider-like web for future egg-implantation. The secretions of the Big Mama Alien also seem eventually to harden into a vast network of hatcheries. One final bit of Alien lore: in *Alien* the monster is described by the robot scientist as "biologically a perfect creature" and invulnerable to human technology. Its strength assures escape from any kind of prison created by human ingenuity and its jaws assure penetration of any fortress. Neither capture nor defense is possible and both films end with flight. But Aliens are no longer invulnerable in the sequel, where a few lab specimens are suspended quietly in large test tube vats and many are blown apart or resisted by grenade blasts and fire power.

The Alien Mama's mucilaginous "art work" is an organic colossus. Its reticulated curves (resembling ribs) and labyrinthine structure contrast visually with the severity of plastic, steel, and glass environs, the grid-like regularity of lines that dominates the man-made interiors of space ships, shuttles, and complexes in this futuristic world. Youthful Aliens are embedded in this structure, and when disturbed, drop like roaches out of the woodwork. There appears, in fact, to be no outside to this inside, no perspective from which to see the enemy Alien whole and distinct. There's a disturbing sense in which the Alien's polymorphous body lacks integrity and identity. The technological environment is, much of the time, as dark and maze-like as the Alien's and spatial orientation for the viewer is nearly impossible, adding to the confusion and terror of not knowing where one is in relation to the Alien. Despite this frequently greasy-machinery appearance, the shine of technology seems somehow clean, even antiseptic in its freedom from the Alien's wastes and slime. When the marine rescue squad in *Aliens* first enters the area of the space station taken over by Aliens, they are utterly baffled by the way everything has been gooed, webbed, slimed and altered in shape and design. The colonists trapped in Alien Mama's art work also bear disconcerting resemblance to dusty religious icons, the first a dangling cruciform, another web-hooded and lit like a Madonna – as if we have wandered into a perverse Alien shrine. The marines feel at home with plastic, metal, glass, but are utterly bewildered when they arrive at this womb-tomb, an organic and

Figure 2.1A Sigourney Weaver as Ripley, Carrie Hen as Newt in *Aliens*

female interior. Finally, it is significant that the arrival of an Alien is often preceded by silence and then the sound of dripping water, as opposed to the buzzers, guns, welding torches, and clicking machines which are the human defense against this natural creature, motivated only by hunger and the urge to reproduce herself.

The Alien other, I believe, quite literally embodies woman's reproductive powers. She arouses primal anxieties about woman's sexual organs and in her combination of multiple tentacles and oozing jaws is the phallic mother of nightmare. The band of marines who enter her vagina, then her womb (which is also a catacomb cluttered with bony human refuse), with all their fire power and ejaculatory short bursts of guns, are ineffectual and insignificant male gametes. The marines are exaggeratedly macho, and this boastful maleness is only underscored by the female marines' adoption of butch haircuts, muscle flexing, and a swaggering that says, "I can outfight, outswear, outfuck a man any day of the week." Sexual impersonation here derides masculinity itself as an impersonation, while the Alien impersonates no one but herself. Catastrophe is first checked, then precipitated by the explosion of guns, suggesting that the male penetrates the female at considerable peril.

Only a few members of this "crack squad of commandos" survive to retreat from the Alien's labyrinth, and they are limp and unmanned by their efforts. The most macho of the males are imprisoned – the black, cigar-smoking "Sarge" and Rambo Drake who epitomizes Marine bravery in his overconfidence in superior strength and fire power. Another grunt, Hudson, who likes to flex the muscle between his ears by insulting his fellow marines, particularly the women, survives, but his male bravado turns to little-boy hysteria, abated only by Ripley's firm, "Calm down." Indeed, the only marines who emerge from Big Mama's *vagina dentata* with "frosty" aplomb are Vasquez, a fiery Chicana who knows she is tougher than her male comrades in arms, and Hicks, a "liberated" male who admires Ripley's existential guts over her femininity and eventually teaches her how to use a gargantuan rapid-fire gun.

The major confrontation of the film, in fact, will not be impotent male marines vs. Alien Big Mama, but between Ripley, a woman who practices the maternal as compassionate care vs. a biological-maternal principle of monstrous proportions, embodied in the Alien other. Ripley is a fierce protectress of Newt, promising her own death if need be to save the girl from the Alien Mama. There are three fights to save Newt, each more suggestive than the last of Ripley's maternal heroism. The first, already mentioned, occurs in the lab. Ripley and Newt are sleeping under a bed where Newt has curled up tightly like a fetus, and Ripley gently hugs her to her tummy. Ripley awakens, realizes both that Alien lab specimens are loose and that her gun has been locked outside the lab. With Hudson and Hicks's intervention, the lab specimens are destroyed and Ripley and Newt saved from surrogate motherhood for Aliens.

The second confrontation is revelation – a face-to-face meeting of Ripley with the primal Mother Alien. Up to this moment in the film, battles with the Alien have been with Big Mama's proliferating brood, not with the dam herself. Nor has director Cameron permitted the audience a good long look at the Alien. Newt has been lost, captured by the Alien in a watery basement to the complex. Though Ripley has only fifteen minutes to retrieve Newt before a nuclear reactor explosion, she decides to return to a dark, wet netherworld where Newt's homing device (a gift from Ripley) indicates she is still alive. Ripley first finds the homing device, no longer strapped to Newt, and in her one weak moment of the film, begins to weep, believing that she has failed in her promise to save Newt. Still alive, but cocooned in the Alien's web, Newt screams, spurring Ripley to action. She pulls Newt loose and burns an opening egg. What follows is the scariest sequence of the film. Ripley and Newt (and the audience) suddenly realize that they are walking through a passage land-mined with follicles and eggs. Their first sight of Mama Alien is of her dropping another egg from a gauzy tube that extends from her belly. When they look up, an enormous Alien mother hisses back, jaws dripping and ready to strike. Initially Ripley reacts as if they have violated an animal mother's lair, quietly and calmly stepping backward, as if to say, "I won't bother you and your eggs, if you won't bother me and my child." Indeed, a nonverbal agreement is struck between these two protective mothers. The truce is broken, however, when another egg opens up and Ripley burns it. The Alien Mama screeches in fury and charges, while simultaneously, Ripley appears to have lost all control, torching every Alien egg in sight. The Alien Mama wrenches her body out of its egg-laying mode to pursue Ripley. Her polymorphic form shattered, the Alien is now a single enemy entity. This whole episode firmly establishes and sets up, for a final showdown still to come, the mother vs. mother nature of the conflict.

Ripley returns to the Alien planet for this epic confrontation, chiefly, it seems, because of traumatic nightmares about giving birth to an Alien. Early in the film, we are given images of Ripley's bulging stomach, and then we see her waking in a sweaty labor from this frightening birth. In this cinematic trick, we believe dream to be reality, and the film thereby enacts an unthinkable horror, the potential birth of Alien otherness in Ripley's body. If this is the fear she wishes to defeat in her return – a fear of giving birth – coupled with a ferocious determination to protect Newt, and defending her twice from impregnation-implantation, then *Aliens'* story pivots around a feminist *guérillère* doing battle with the premise that female anatomy is destiny. Interpretation admittedly goes somewhat wild here in its possible directions. Is Ripley as feminist opposed to man's technological colonization of woman's body – embryo implantation, *in vitro* fertilization, the cloning of babies? All of these antiscientific possibilities seem embedded in her enmity for the Alien. Except that the Alien, to this viewer, is stunningly limited by her instincts. She is juicy femaleness, nature gone wild, not technology gone awry.

What is so disturbing about this film from a feminist perspective, then, is its extreme opposition of two kinds of maternal nurture: the instinctual and biological in the Alien, and the conscious, chosen, cultural motherhood of Ripley. Ripley softens her tough, cool demeanor when she first holds Newt in her arms. Finding a photo of Newt celebrating her second-grade citizenship award, she seems shaken by the girl's violated childhood. Later, she appeals to Newt's own incipient maternal impulses, comparing her desire to assuage Newt's fears to Newt's own efforts to console her doll Casey. (Newt tells Ripley that it's not the same, since Casey is only plastic and not subject to the nightmares Newt has.) The photo of Newt also provides her real name, Rebecca, and Rebecca's neat, smiling image contrasts sharply with Newt's unkempt wild-child appearance, reminding the audience of the possible reduction to savagery if children are left motherless. The marine doctor, also a woman, examines Newt and pronounces her okay physically, but it is Ripley who washes her face, whose tenderness elicits speech. What all of this suggests in the character of Ripley is a complete dissociation of the maternal principle from woman's biology. Even the seemingly extraneous detail about Newt's plastic doll Casey suggests an artificed, manufactured, woman-made rather than woman-born principle. Ripley chooses to mother; she is not programmed as female by nature to nurture others.

Before celebrating this new feminist wisdom about mothering,[3] let me describe the show-down between Ripley and the Alien. In this final battle, Ripley is less a woman than a cyborg. She has, and it makes the audience love her, beckoned the Alien away from Newt, offering herself as maternal sacrifice: "Take me, not my girl." Ripley disappears and returns with gear that makes her a robot. Like the transformers ubiquitous in the children's toy market, Ripley is now inorganic machine, a combination crane and forklift, screaming, "Get away from her, you bitch!" After an intense battle where the Alien still seems indomitable because of her agility compared to Ripley's clumsy machinery, victory is achieved when Ripley flushes Mama out of an open hatch. I do not think it is straining analysis to see this as a technological disembodiment of the maternal principle from the female body, a feminist symbol for the repression of the female body altogether. Technology's virtue is emphasized by the android Bishop's assistance. He has only half a body left from the ravages of the Alien, yet he manages to hang on to Newt, who is nearly sucked out with the Alien into space. The other survivor, the marine Hicks, seems a more likely comrade in this fight to save humanity, but he is notably out of sight. The slight hint that Ripley–Hicks–Newt form a future nuclear family is ultimately stymied by the film's depiction of female sexuality.[4] Woman's reproductive power is conventionally sanctioned within the bounds of family. In *Aliens*, this power is displaced in the Alien Mama and therefore represented as completely out of bounds, beyond civilization's controlling institutions.

Therefore, despite a wish to praise this revision of mothering as a cultural choice – a humanizing and civilizing impulse that makes Ripley heroic – I cannot. Because simultaneously, I want to ask why the female body must be represented with such primal terror, such intense repugnance, and why it needs to be so resoundingly defeated, sucked into the vacuum of space as if thrown back into whatever imaginative void could have germinated such horror. If the terrors of the film are, as I've tried to indicate, grounded in archetypal fears of woman's otherness, her alien body and its natural functions, no amount of physical abuse, fire power, and nuclear explosions will provide an audience with psychological catharsis. This is the final horror of the film. There is no reassurance in its closing images of Ripley and Newt, sleeping peacefully in their capsules. They look like Snow White (Ripley has earlier been sarcastically dubbed "Snow White" by the fiery Vasquez for her frigidity), whose female sexuality may be awakened by a kiss, unleashing the power of the Alien other yet again. One might even recall here the other sleeping females of the film – the quiescent lab specimens, drifting in liquid sleep, but ready to strike when the glass tube shatters.

Woman's reproductive capacity is a potential threat, not only to woman herself – to Ripley and the younger version of herself, Newt – but also, it is implied, to civilization, technological progress, the futuristic world depicted in *Aliens*. This world is peopled principally by young or vigorously middle-aged Company employees. Newt almost seems anomalous: so there still are families, near-relations who care for one another? Ripley, except for her new maternalism, is an existential atom. She has slept for fifty-seven years when the film opens, which might explain her apparent isolation, but she also never expresses anguish or even interest about her past on earth, the people whom she might have cared for or who might have cared for her, now dead and lost in the years of space-sleep. In this futuristic world, furthermore, nuclear explosions seem to be less threatening than the Alien other. Ripley, Newt, Bishop, and Hicks are barely off the planet when their ship is rocked by nuclear explosion, but they feel "safe" at last. The Company has technologies for making a planet's atmosphere livable for humans, so we might assume that science can solve every problem, except those created by female biology, by the Alien other in our own nature.

For this reason, *Aliens* is likely to generate an *Aliens III* in which culture again is pitted against nature, figured as female and maternal, a womb-tomb that threatens to engulf everyone in the limitations of our bodies, our creatureliness, our biological functions. The character of Newt, on the verge of sexual maturity, can be saved only temporarily from the dangers lurking in her female body. Her potential danger is hinted at in the nickname "Newt" – another word for salamander, linking the girl to the Alien's slimy animality and femininity. "Newt" may also be understood as short for "neutral," too young to be sexually threatening. From my own feminist perspective, the relationship of Ripley and Newt is dangerously attractive in the way it revises the myth of Demeter and Persephone, the story of a mother who descends into Hades to save her daughter from the dark netherworld of Dis, the male god who rapes Persephone and makes her his queen. A faint echo of this myth can be heard in Hudson's exclamation, "We're going down to hell!" when the marines first land on the Alien planet. The classical myth, however, celebrates female fertility and a mother–daughter relationship based on biology as well as sentiment. Demeter makes a deal with Dis: for six months of the year, autumn and winter, nature will die as Demeter mourns for her daughter's captivity. They will be reunited in joy and seasonal renewal, spring and summer, the other six months. Ripley is no fertility goddess, but an antifertility mother, and the Alien other is not a rapist male god, but the female body's reproductive powers. Hence the film's overt feminism, highly praised in the reviews' discussion of Sigourney Weaver as Ripley, is a feminism in service to technology over nature, with woman's intelligence and emotions firmly Alien-ated from her body.

Notes

1   Gaylyn Studlar, in "Masochism and the Perverse Pleasures of the Cinema," *Quarterly Review of Film Studies*, 9 (Fall, 1984), 267–82, aligns film voyeurism (spectatorial pleasure) with a masochism embedded in the infant's pre-Oedipal relationship to the mother. Although Studlar does not concern herself with the peculiar and painful pleasures of horror films, her psychoanalysis (derived from Gilles Deleuze) of audiences' ambivalent fascination with cinematic *femmes fatales* is suggestive of the Alien's psychic power over her victims both within the film and in the audience. The pre-Oedipal child in all of us, Studlar argues, longs for "re-fusion . . . complete symbiosis" with "the oral mother of masochism" – "first environment and agent of control." In addition, she notes that "the promise of blissful reincorporation into the mother's body . . . is also a threat." Obviously the Alien Mama is principally a threat of cruel devourment, but one that exerts a fatal charm for audiences. She may well embody the masochist's principal fantasy of a "symbiotic reunion with the idealized maternal rule. The masochist imagines the final triumph of a parthenogenetic rebirth from the mother" (p. 271).

2   Studlar describes Dietrich's *femme fatale* in Von Sternberg's films as not solely the sexual object of a male gaze, "but also the holder of a 'controlling' gaze that turns the male into an object of 'to-be-looked-at-ness'," hence asserting, as "the mother of plenitude," her "presence and her power" (p. 273). Notably in *Aliens*, only another female, another "mother" like Ripley, is capable of returning the Alien's gaze without being paralyzed into inaction or turning into a blubbering infant like most of the males in the film.

3   I am referring here to Nancy Chodorow's *The Reproduction of Mothering: Psychoanalysis and the Sociology of Gender* (Berkeley: University of California Press, 1978) and Dorothy Dinnerstein's *The Mermaid and the Minotaur: Sexual Arrangements and Human Malaise* (New York: Harper and Row, 1978). Both Chodorow and Dinnerstein argue that women learn to mother, that mothering is not an instinctual urge, and that the strictures of gender roles might be broken to the benefit of everyone if men were to share in the nurturing tasks of raising children. Pertinent to my argument is Chodorow's careful separation of the biological from the social dimensions of mothering. As Chodorow notes, "Being a mother, then, is not only bearing a child – it is being a person who socializes and nurtures" (p. 11). Ripley's characterization has elicited praise from critics for its combination of feminist and maternal virtues; yet Ripley might be seen as offering reassurance to audiences that "liberated" women will choose to mother even if they do not choose to give birth. *Aliens* would be a more feminist film perhaps if Ripley were a man.

4   As Studlar notes, in masochistic fantasies invoking the oral mother, she "assumes all symbolic functions," and quoting Deleuze, "The father is nothing . . . he is deprived of all symbolic function" (p. 271).

Mary Ann Doane

TECHNOPHILIA: TECHNOLOGY, REPRESENTATION, AND THE FEMININE

THE CONCEPT OF THE "BODY" has traditionally denoted the finite, a material limit that is absolute – so much so that the juxtaposition of the terms "concept" and "body" seems oxymoronic. For the body is that which is situated as the precise opposite of the conceptual, the abstract. It represents the ultimate constraint on speculation or theorization, the place where the empirical finally and always makes itself felt. This notion of the body as a set of finite limitations is, perhaps, most fully in evidence in the face of technological developments associated with the Industrial Revolution. In 1858, the author of a book entitled *Paris* writes, "Science; as it were, proposes that we should enter a new world that has not been made for us. We would like to venture into it; but it does not take us long to recognize that it requires a constitution we lack and organs we do not have."[1] Science fiction, a genre specific to the era of rapid technological development, frequently envisages a new, revised body as a direct outcome of the advance of science. And when technology intersects with the body in the realm of representation, the question of sexual difference is inevitably involved.

Although it is certainly true that in the case of some contemporary science-fiction writers – particularly feminist authors – technology makes possible the destabilization of sexual identity as a category, there has also been a curious but fairly insistent history of representations of technology that work to fortify – sometimes desperately – conventional understandings of the feminine. A certain anxiety concerning the technological is often allayed by a displacement of this anxiety onto the figure of the woman or the idea of the feminine. This has certainly been the case in the cinema, particularly in the genre which most apparently privileges technophilia, science fiction. And despite the emphasis in discourses about technology upon the link between the machine and *production* (the machine as a labor-saving device, the notion of man as a complicated machine which Taylorism, as an early-twentieth-century attempt to regulate the worker's bodily movements, endeavored to exploit), it is striking to note how often it is the woman who becomes the model of the perfect machine. Ultimately, what I hope to demonstrate is that it is not so much *production* that is at stake in these representations as *reproduction*.

The literary text that is cited most frequently as the exemplary forerunner of the cinematic representation of the mechanical woman is *L'Eve future* (*Tomorrow's Eve*), written by Villiers de l'Isle-Adam in 1886. In this novel, Thomas Edison, the master scientist and entrepreneur of mechanical reproduction – associated with both the phonograph and the cinema – is the inventor of the perfect mechanical woman, an android whose difference from the original human model is imperceptible. Far from investing in the type of materialism associated with scientific progress, Villiers is a metaphysician. Edison's creation embodies the Ideal (her name is Hadaly which is, so we are told, Arabic for the Ideal). The very long introductory section of the novel is constituted by Edison's musings about all the voices in history that have been lost and that could have been captured had the phonograph been invented sooner. These include, among others, "the first vibrations of the good tidings brought to Mary! The resonance of the Archangel saying Hail! a sound that has reverberated through the ages in the Angelus. The Sermon on the Mount! The 'Hail, master!' on the Mount of Olives, and the sound of the kiss of Iscariot."[2] Almost simultaneously, however, Edison realizes that the mechanical recordings of the sounds is not enough: "To hear the sound is nothing, but the inner essence, which creates these mere vibrations, these veils – that's the crucial thing."[3] This "inner essence" is what the human lover of Lord Ewald, Edison's friend, lacks. In Lord Ewald's report, although her body is magnificent, perfect in every detail, the human incarnation of the *Venus Victorious*, she lacks a *soul*. Or, more accurately, between the body and soul of Miss Alicia Clary there is an "absolute disparity." Since Lord Ewald is hopelessly in love with the soulless Alicia, Edison takes it upon himself to mold Hadaly to the form of Miss Clary.

A great deal of the novel consists of Edison's scientific explanations of the functioning of Hadaly. As he opens Hadaly up to a dissecting inspection, Lord Ewald's final doubts about the mechanical nature of what seemed to him a living woman are dispelled in a horrible recognition of the compatibility of technology and desire.

> Now he found himself face to face with a marvel the obvious possibilities of which, as they transcend even the imaginary, dazzled his understanding and made him suddenly feel to what lengths a man who wishes can extend the courage of his desires.[4]

Hadaly's interior is a maze of electrical wizardry including coded metal discs that diffuse warmth, motion, and energy throughout the body; wires that imitate nerves, arteries, and veins; a basic electro-magnetic motor, the Cylinder, on which are recorded the "gestures, the bearing, the facial expressions, and the attitudes of the adored being"; and two golden phonographs that replay Hadaly's only discourse, words "invented by the greatest poets, the most subtle metaphysicians, the most profound novelists of this century."[5] Hadaly has no past, no memories except those embodied in the words of "great men." As Annette Michelson remarks, in a provocative analysis of the novel,

> Hadaly's scenes, so to speak, are set in place. Hadaly becomes that palimpsest of inscription, that unreasoning and resonable facsimile, generated by reason,

whose interlocutor, Lord Ewald. has only to submit to the range and nuance of mise-en-scene possible in what Edison calls the "great kaleidoscope" of human speech and gesture in which signifiers will infinitely float.[6]

As Edison points out to Lord Ewald, the number of gestures or expressions in the human repertoire is extremely limited, clearly quantifiable, and hence reproducible. Yet, precisely because Villiers is a metaphysician, something more is needed to animate the machine – a spark, a touch of spirit.

This spark is provided, strangely enough, by an abandoned mother, Mrs. Anny Anderson (who, in the hypnotic state Edison maintains her in, takes on the name Miss Anny Sowana). Her husband, Howard another of Edison's friends, had been seduced and ruined by a beautiful temptress, Miss Evelyn Habal, ultimately committing suicide. Miss Evelyn Habal was in a way the inspiration for the *outer* form of Hadaly, for through his investigations, Edison discovered that her alleged beauty was completely *artificial*. He displays for Lord Ewald's sake a drawer containing her implements: a wig corroded by time, a makeup kit of greasepaint and patches, dentures, lotions, powders, creams, girdles, and falsies, etc. Edison's cinema revels that, without any of these aids, Evelyn Habal was a macabre figure. The display demonstrates to Ewald that mechanical reproduction suffices in the construction of the forms of femininity. But its spirit, at least, is not scientifically accessible. The abandoned Mrs. Anderson, mother of two children, suffers a breakdown after the suicide of her husband. Only Edison is able to communicate with her and eventually her spirit establishes a link with his android Hadaly, animating it, humanizing it. The mother infuses the machine. Perhaps this is why, for Edison, science's most important contribution here is the validation of the dichotomy between woman as mother and woman as mistress:

> Far from being hostile to the love of men for their wives – who are so necessary to perpetuate the race (at least till a new order of things comes in), I propose to reinforce, ensure, and guarantee that love. I will do so with the aid of thousands and thousands of marvelous and completely innocent facsimiles, who will render wholly superfluous all those beautiful but deceptive mistresses, ineffective henceforth forever.[7]

Reproduction is that which is, at least initially, unthinkable in the face of the woman-machine. Herself the product of a desire to reproduce, she blocks the very possibility of a future through her sterility. Motherhood acts as a limit to the conceptualization of femininity as a scientific construction of mechanical and electrical parts. And yet it is also that which infuses the machine with the breath of a human spirit. The maternal and the mechanical/synthetic coexist in a relation that is a curious imbrication of dependence and antagonism.

L'Eve future is significant as an early signpost of the persistence of the maternal as a sub-theme accompanying these fantasies of artificial femininity. It is also, insofar as Edison (a figure closely associated with the prehistory of cinema) is the master-mind of Hadaly's invention, a text that points to a convergence of the articulation of this obsession and the cinema as a privileged site for its exploration. In Michelson's argument, Hadaly's existence demonstrates the way in which a compulsive movement between analysis and synthesis takes the female body as its support in a process of fetishization fully consistent with that of the cinema:

> We will want once more to note that assiduous, relentless impulse which claims the female body as the site of an analytic, mapping upon its landscape a poetics and an epistemology with all the perverse detail and somber ceremony of fetishism. And may we not then begin to think of that body in its cinematic relations somewhat differently? Not as the mere object of a cinematic *iconography* of repression and desire – as catalogued by now in the extensive literature on dominant narrative in its major genres of melodrama, *film noir*, and so on – but rather as the fantasmatic ground of cinema itself.[8]

Indeed, cinema has frequently been thought of as a prosthetic device, as a technological extension of the human body, particularly the senses of perception. Christian Metz, for instance, refers to the play "of that *other mirror*, the cinema screen, in this respect a veritable psychical substitute, a prosthesis for our primally dislocated limbs."[9] From this point of view it is not surprising that the articulation of the three terms – "woman," "machine," "cinema" – and the corresponding fantasy of the artificial woman recur as the privileged content of a wide variety of cinematic narratives.

An early instance of this tendency in the science-fiction mode is Fritz Lang's 1926 film, *Metropolis*, in which the patriarch of the future city surveys his workers through a complex audio-visual apparatus resembling television. In *Metropolis*, the bodies of the male workers become mechanized; their movements are rigid, mechanical, and fully in sync with the machines they operate. The slightest divergence between bodily movement and the operation of the machine is disastrous, as evidenced when the patriarch's son, Freder, descends to the realm of the workers and witnesses the explosion of a machine not sufficiently controlled by a worker. Freder's resulting hallucination transforms the machine into a Moloch-figure to whom the unfortunate workers are systematically sacrificed. When Freder relieves an overtired worker, the machine he must operate resembles a giant clock whose hands must be moved periodically – a movement that corresponds to no apparent logic. In a production routine reorganized by the demands of the machine, the human body's relation to temporality becomes inflexible, programmed. The body is tied to a time clock, a schedule, a routine, an assembly line. Times becomes oppression and mechanization – the clock, a machine itself, is used to regulate bodies as machines. *Metropolis* represents a dystopic vision of a city run by underground machines whose instability and apparent capacity for vengeance are marked.

But where the men's bodies are analogous to machines, the woman's body literally becomes a machine. In order to forestall a threatened rebellion on the part of the workers, the patriarch Fredersen has a robot made in the likeness of Maria, the woman who leads and instigates them. Rotwang, who is a curious mixture of modern scientist and alchemist, has already fashioned a robot in the form of a woman when Fredersen makes the request. The fact that the robot is manifestly female is quite striking particularly in light of Rotwang's explanation of the purpose of the machine: "I have created a machine in the image of man, that never tires or makes a mistake. Now we have no further use for living workers." A robot which is apparently designed as the ultimate producer is transformed into a woman of excessive and even explosive sexuality (as manifested in the scene in which Rotwang demonstrates her seductive traits to an audience of men who mistake her for a "real woman"). In Andreas Huyssen's analysis of *Metropolis*, the robot Maria is symptomatic of the fears associated with a technology perceived as threatening and demonic: "The fears and perceptual anxieties emanating from ever more powerful machines are recast and reconstructed in terms of the male fear of female sexuality, reflecting, in the Freudian account, the male's castration anxiety."[10]

Yet, the construction of the robot Maria is also, in Huyssen's account, the result of a desire to appropriate the maternal function, a kind of womb envy on the part of the male. This phenomenon is clearly not limited to *Metropolis* and has been extensively explored in relation to Mary Shelley's *Frankenstein*, in which the hero, immediately before awakening to perceive his frightful creation, the monster, standing next to his bed, dreams that he holds the corpse of his dead mother in his arms. The "ultimate technological fantasy," according to Huyssen, is "creation without the mother."[11] Nevertheless, in *Metropolis*, the robot Maria is violently opposed to a real Maria who is characterized, first and foremost, as a mother. In the first shot of Maria, she is surrounded by a flock of children, and her entrance interrupts a kiss between Freder and another woman so that the maternal effectively disrupts the sexual. Toward the end of the film, Maria and Freder save the children from a flood unwittingly caused by the angry workers' disruption of the machinery. The film manages to salvage both the technological and the maternal (precisely by destroying the figure of the machine-woman) and to return the generations to their proper ordering (reconciling Freder and his father). The tension in these texts which holds in balance a desire on the part of the male to appropriate the maternal function and the conflicting desire to safeguard and honor the figure of the mother is resolved here in favor of the latter. The machine is returned to its rightful place in production, the woman hers in reproduction.

The maternal is understandably much more marginal in a more recent film, *The Stepford Wives* (1974), in which the machine-woman is not burned at the stake, as in *Metropolis*, but comfortably installed in the supermarket and the suburban home. In this film, a group of women are lured to the suburbs by their husbands who then systematically replace them with robots, indistinguishable from their originals. The robots have no desires beyond those of cooking, cleaning, caring for the children, and fulfilling their husband's sexual needs. Even the main character, Joanna, who claims, "I messed a little with Women's Lib in New York," finds that she cannot escape the process. As in *L'Eve future*, the husbands record the voices of their wives to perfect the illusion, but unlike that of Hadaly, the Ideal, the discourse of these robot-housewives consists of hackneyed commercial slogans about the advantages of products such as Easy On Spray Starch. Here the address is to women and the social context is that of a strong and successful feminist movement, which the film seems to suggest is unnecessary outside of the science-fiction nightmare in which husbands turn wives into robots. *The Stepford Wives* indicates a loss of the obsessive force of the signifying matrix of the machine-woman — as though its very banalization could convince that there is no real threat involved, no reason for anxiety.

The contemporary films that strike me as much more interesting with respect to the machine-woman problematic are those in which questions of the maternal and technology are more deeply imbricated – films such as *Alien* (1979) and its sequel, *Aliens* (1986), and *Blade Runner* (1982). As technologies of reproduction seem to become a more immediate possibility (and are certainly the focus of media attention), the impact of the associative link between technology and the feminine on narrative representation becomes less localized – that is, it is no longer embodied solely in the figure of the female robot. *Alien* and *Aliens* contain no such machine-woman, yet the technological is insistently linked to the maternal. While *Blade Runner* does represent a number of female androids (the result of a sophisticated biogenetic engineering, they are called "replicants" in the film), it also represents male replicants. Nevertheless, its narrative structure provocatively juxtaposes the question of biological reproduction and that of mechanical reproduction. Most importantly, perhaps, both *Alien* and *Blade Runner* contemplate the impact of drastic changes in reproductive processes on ideas of origins, narratives, and histories.

Alien, together with its sequel, *Aliens*, and *Blade Runner* elaborate symbolic systems that correspond to a contemporary crisis in the realm of reproduction – the revolution in the development of technologies of reproduction (birth control, artificial insemination, *in vitro* fertilization, surrogate mothering, etc.). These technologies threaten to put into crisis the very possibility of the question of origins, the Oedipal dilemma and the relation between subjectivity and knowledge that it supports. In the beginning of *Alien*, Dallas types into the keyboard of the ship's computer (significantly nicknamed "Mother" by the crew) the question: "What's the story, Mother?" The story is no longer one of transgression and conflict with the father but of the struggle with and against what seems to become an overwhelming extension of the category of the maternal, now assuming monstrous proportions. Furthermore, this concept of the maternal neglects or confuses the traditional attributes of sexual difference. The ship itself, *The Nostromo*, seems to mimic in the construction of its internal spaces the interior of the maternal body. In the first shots of the film, the camera explores in lingering fashion corridors and womblike spaces which exemplify a fusion of the organic and the technological.[12] The female merges with the environment and the mother-machine becomes mise-en-scène, the space within which the story plays itself out. The wrecked alien spaceship which the crew investigates is also characterized by its cavernous, womblike spaces; one of the crew even descends through a narrow tubelike structure to the "tropical" underground of the ship where a field of large rubbery eggs are in the process of incubation. The maternal is not only the subject of the representation here, but also its ground.

The alien itself, in its horrifying otherness, also evokes the maternal. In the sequel, *Aliens*, the interpretation of the alien as a monstrous mother-machine, incessantly manufacturing eggs in an awesome excess of reproduction, confirms this view. Yet, in the first film the situation is somewhat more complex, for the narrative operates by confusing the tropes of femininity and masculinity in its delineation of the process of reproduction. The creature first emerges from an egg, attaches itself to a crew member's face, penetrating his throat and gastrointestinal system to deposit its seed. The alien gestates within the stomach of the *male* crew member who later "gives birth" to it in a grotesque scene in which the alien literally gnaws its way through his stomach to emerge as what one critic has labeled a *phallus dentatus*.[13] The confusion of the semes of sexual difference indicates the fears attendant upon the development of technologies of reproduction that debiologize the maternal. In *Alien*, men have babies but it is a horrifying and deadly experience. When the alien or other invades the most private space – the inside of the body – the foundations of subjectivity are shaken. The horror here is that of a collapse between inside and outside or of what Julia Kristeva refers to, in *Powers of Horror*, as the abject. Kristeva associates the maternal with the abject – i.e., that which is the focus of a combined horror and fascination, hence subject to a range of taboos designed to control the culturally marginal.[14] In this analysis, the function of nostalgia for the mother-origin is that of a veil which conceals the terror attached to nondifferentiation. The threat of the maternal space is that of the collapse of any distinction whatsoever between subject and object.

Kristeva elsewhere emphasizes a particularly interesting corollary of this aspect of motherhood: The maternal space is "a place both double and foreign."[15] In its internalization of heterogeneity, an otherness within the self, motherhood deconstructs certain conceptual boundaries. Kristeva delineates the maternal through the assertion, "In a body there is grafted, unmasterable, an other."[16] The confusion of identities threatens to collapse a signifying system based on the paternal law of differentiation. It would seem that the concept of motherhood automatically throws into question ideas concerning the self, boundaries between self and other, and hence identity.

According to Jean Baudrillard, "Reproduction is diabolical in its very essence; it makes something fundamental vacillate."[17] Technology promises more strictly to control, supervise, regulate the maternal – to put *limits* upon it. But somehow the fear lingers – perhaps the maternal will contaminate the technological. For aren't we now witnessing a displacement of the excessiveness and overproliferation previously associated with the maternal to the realm of technologies of representation, in the guise of the all-pervasive images and sounds of television, film, radio, the Walkman? One response to such anxiety is the recent spate of films that delineate the horror of the maternal – of that which harbors an otherness within, where the fear is always that of giving birth to the monstrous; films such as *It's Alive*, *The Broad*, *The Fly*, or the ecology horror film, *Prophecy*. *Alien*, in merging the genres of the horror film and science fiction, explicitly connects that horror to a technological scenario.

In *Blade Runner*, the signifying trajectory is more complex, and the relevant semes are more subtly inscribed. Here the terror of the motherless reproduction associated with technology is clearly located as an anxiety about the ensuing loss of history. One scene in *Blade Runner* acts as a condensation of a number of these critical terms: "representation," "the woman," "the artificial," "the technological," "history," and "memory." It is initiated by the camera's pan over Deckard's apartment to the piano upon which a number of photos are arranged, most of them apparently belonging to Deckard, signifiers of a past (though not necessarily his own), marked as antique – pictures of someone's mother, perhaps a sister or grandmother. One of the photographs, however – a rather nondescript one of a room, an open door, a mirror – belongs to the replicant Leon, recovered by Deckard in a search of his hotel room. Deckard inserts this photograph in a piece of equipment that is ultimately revealed as a machine for analyzing images. Uncannily responding to Deckard's voice commands, the machine enlarges the image, isolates various sections, and enlarges them further. The resultant play of colors and grain, focus and its loss, is aesthetically provocative beyond the demonstration of technical prowess and control over the image. Deckard's motivation, the desire for knowledge that is fully consistent with his positioning in the film as the detective figure of *film noir*, is overwhelmed by the special effects which are the byproducts of this technology of vision – a scintillation of the technological image which exceeds his epistemophilia. Only gradually does the image resolve into a readable text. And in the measure to which the images becomes readable, it loses its allure. The sequence demonstrates how technology, the instrument of a certain knowledge-effect, becomes spectacle, fetish. But one gains ascendancy at the price of the other – pleasure pitted against knowledge.

Historically, this dilemma has been resolved in the cinema by conflating the two – making pleasure and knowledge compatible by projecting them onto the figure of the woman. The same resolution occurs here: as the image gradually stabilizes, what emerges is the recognizable body of a woman (neglecting for a moment that this is not a "real" woman), reclining on a couch, reflected in the mirror which Deckard systematically isolates. The mirror makes visible what is outside the confines of the photograph strictly speaking – the absent woman, object of the detective's quest. To know in *Blade Runner* is to be able to detect difference – not sexual difference, but the difference between human and replicant (the replicant here taking the place of the woman as marginal, as Other). Knowledge in psychoanalysis, on the other hand, is linked to the mother's body (knowledge of castration and hence of sexual difference, knowledge of where babies come from) – so many tantalizing secrets revolving around the idea of an origin and the figure of the mother. There are no literal – no embodied – mothers in *Blade Runner* (in fact, there are no "real" women in the film beyond a few marginal characters – the old Chinese woman who identifies the snake scale, the women in the bar). Yet this does not mean that the concept of the maternal – its relation to knowledge of origins and subjective history – is inoperative in the text. As a story of replicants who look just like "the real thing," *Blade Runner* has an affinity with Barthes's analysis of photography, *Camera Lucida*.[18] Barthes's essay is crucially organized around a photograph of his mother which is never shown, almost as though making it present would banalize his desire, or reduce it. Both film and essay are stories of reproduction – mechanical reproduction, reproduction as the application of biogenetic engineering. In the film, however, our capability of representing human life begins to pose a threat when the slight divergence that would betray mimetic activity disappears.

In *Blade Runner*, as in *Camera Lucida*, there are insistent references to the mother, but they are fleeting, tangential to the major axis of the narrative. In the opening scene, the replicant Leon is asked a question by the examiner whose task it is to ascertain whether Leon is human or inhuman: "Describe in single words only the good things that come into your mind about – your mother." Leon answers, "Let me tell you about my mother" and proceeds violently to blow away the examiner with a twenty-first-century gun. The replicants collect photographs (already an archaic mode of representation in this future time) in order to reassure themselves of their own past, their own subjective history. At one point Leon is asked by Roy whether he managed to retrieve his "precious photographs." Later Rachel, still refusing to believe that she is a replicant, tries to prove to Deckard that she is as human as he is by thrusting forward a photograph and claiming, "Look, it's me with my mother." After Rachel leaves, having been told that these are "not your memories" but "somebody else's," Deckard looks down at the photo, his voice-over murmuring "a mother she never had, a daughter she never was." At this moment, the photograph briefly becomes "live," animated, as sun and shadow play over the faces of the little girl and her mother. At the same moment at which the photograph loses its historical authenticity vis-à-vis Rachel, it also loses its status as a photograph, as dead time. In becoming "present," it makes Rachel less "real." Deckard animates the photograph with his gaze, his desire, and it is ultimately his desire that constitutes Rachel's only subjectivity, in the present tense. In this sense Rachel, like Villiers's *L'Eve future*, becomes the perfect woman, born all at once, deprived of a past or authentic memories.

Reproduction is the guarantee of a history – both human biological reproduction (through the succession of generations) and mechanical reproduction (through the succession of memories). Knowledge is anchored to both. Something goes awry with respect to each in *Blade Runner*, for the replicants do not have mothers and their desperate invocation of the figure of the mother is symptomatic of their desire to place themselves within a history. Neither do they have fathers. In the scene in which Roy kills Tyrell he, in effect, *simulates* the Oedipal complex,[19] but gets it wrong. The father, rather than the son, is blinded. Psychoanalysis can only be invoked as a misunderstood, misplayed scenario. Similarly, the instances of mechanical reproduction which should ensure the preservation of a remembered history are delegitimized; Leon's photograph is broken down into its constituent units to become a clue in the detective's investigation, and Rachel's photograph is deprived of its photographic status. The replicants are objects of fear because they present the humans with the specter of a motherless reproduction, and *Blade Runner* is at one level about the anxiety surrounding the loss of history. Deckard keeps old photos as well, and while they may not represent his own relatives, they nevertheless act as a guarantee of temporal continuity – of a coherent history which compensates for the pure presence of the replicants. This compensatory gesture is located at the level of the film's own discourse also insofar as it reinscribes an older cinematic mode – that of *film noir* – thus ensuring its own insertion within a tradition, a cinematic continuity.

Yet, science fiction strikes one as the cinematic genre that ought to be least concerned with origins since its "proper" obsession is with the projection of a future rather than the reconstruction of a past. Nevertheless, a great deal of its projection of that future is bound up with issues of reproduction – whether in its constant emphasis upon the robot, android, automaton, and anthropomorphically conceived computer or its insistent return to the elaboration of high-tech, sophisticated audio-visual systems. When Deckard utilizes the video analyzer in *Blade Runner*, it is a demonstration of the power of future systems of imaging. Furthermore, the Voight-Kampf empathy test designed to differentiate between the replicant and the human being is heavily dependent upon a large video image of the eye. In both *Alien* and its sequel, *Aliens*, video mechanisms ensure that those in the stationary ship can see through the eyes of the investigating astronauts/soldiers outside. Danger is signaled by a difficulty in transmission or a loss of the image. Garrett Stewart remarks on the overabundance of viewing screens and viewing machines in science fiction in general – of "banks of monitors, outsized video intercoms, x-ray display panels, hologram tubes, backlit photoscopes, aerial scanners, telescopic mirrors, illuminated computer consoles, overhead projectors, slide screens, radar scopes, whole curved walls of transmitted imagery, the retinal registers of unseen electronic eyes."[20] And in his view, "cinema becomes a synecdoche for the entire technics of an imagined society."[21]

Since the guarantee of the real in the classical narrative cinema is generally the visible, the advanced visual devices here would seem, at least in part, to ensure the credibility of the "hyperreal" of science fiction. And certainly insofar as it is necessary to imagine that the inhabitants of the future will need some means of representing to themselves their world (and other worlds), these visual devices serve the purpose, as Stewart points out, of a kind of documentary authentication.[22] Yet, the gesture of marking the real does not exhaust their function. Technology in cinema is the object of a quite precise form of fetishism, and science fiction would logically be a privileged genre for the technophile. Christian Metz describes the way in which this fetishism of technique works to conceal a lack:

> A fetish, the cinema as a technical performance, as prowess, as an *exploit*, an exploit that underlines and denounces the lack on which the whole arrangement is based (the absence of the object, replaced by its reflection), an exploit which consists at the same time of making this absence forgotten. The cinema fetishist is the person who is enchanted at what the machine is capable of, at the *theatre of shadows* as such. For the establishment of his full potency for cinematic enjoyment [*jouissance*] he must think at every moment (and above all *simultaneously*) of the force of presence the film has and of the absence on which this force is constructed. He must constantly compare the result with the means deployed (and hence pay attention to the technique), for his pleasure lodges in the gap between the two.[23]

Metz here finds it necessary to desexualize a scenario which in Freud's theory of fetishism is linked explicitly to the woman and the question of her "lack" (more specifically to the question of whether or not the mother is phallic). Technological fetishism, through its alliance of technology with a process of concealing and revealing lack, is theoretically returned to the body of the mother. Claude Bailblé, from a somewhat different perspective, links the fascination with technology to its status as a kind of transitional object: "For the technology plays the role of transitional object, loved with a regressive love still trying to exhaust the pain of foreclosure from the Other, endlessly trying to repair that initial separation, and as such it is very likely to be the target of displacements."[24] In both cases, the theory understands the obsession with technology as a tension of movement toward and away from the mother.

It is not surprising, then, that the genre that highlights technological fetishism – science fiction – should be obsessed with the issues of the maternal, reproduction, representation, and history. From *L'Eve future* to *Blade Runner*, the conjunction of technology and the feminine is the object of fascination and desire but also of anxiety – a combination of affects that makes it the perfect field of play for the science fiction/horror genre. If Hadaly is the first embodiment of the cinematic woman (this time outside of the cinema) – a machine that synchronizes the image and sound of a "real" woman, Rachel is in a sense her double in the contemporary cinema, the ideal woman who flies off with Deckard at the end of the film through a pastoral setting. Yet, Rachel can be conceived only as a figure drawn from an earlier cinematic scene – 1940s *film noir* – the dark and mysterious femme fatale with padded shoulders and

1940s hairdo, as though the reinscription of a historically dated genre could reconfirm the sense of history that is lost with technologies of representation. What is reproduced as ideal here is an earlier reproduction.

Again, according to Baudrillard: "Reproduction . . . makes something fundamental vacillate." What it makes vacillate are the very concepts of identity, origin, and the original, as Benjamin has demonstrated so provocatively in "The Work of Art in the Age of Mechanical Reproduction."[25] There is always something uncanny about a photograph; in the freezing of the moment the real is lost through its doubling. The unique identity of a time and a place is rendered obsolete. This is undoubtedly why photographic reproduction is culturally coded and regulated by associating it closely with the construction of a family history, a stockpile of memories, forcing it to buttress that very notion of history that it threatens to annihilate along with the idea of the origin. In a somewhat different manner, but with crucial links to the whole problematic of the origin, technologies of reproduction work to regulate the excesses of the maternal. But in doing so these technologies also threaten to undermine what have been coded as its more positive and nostalgic aspects. For the idea of the maternal is not only terrifying – it also offers a certain amount of epistemological comfort. The mother's biological role in reproduction has been aligned with the social function of knowledge. For the mother is coded as certain, immediately knowable, while the father's role in reproduction is subject to doubt, not verifiable through the evidence of the senses (hence the necessity of the legal sanctioning of the paternal name). The mother is thus the figure who guarantees, at one level, the possibility of certitude in historical knowledge. Without her, the story of origins vacillates, narrative vacillates. It is as though the association with a body were the only way to stabilize reproduction. Hence the persistence of contradictions in these texts that manifest both a nostalgia for and a terror of the maternal function, both linking it to and divorcing it from the idea of the machine woman. Clinging to the realm of narrative, these films strive to rework the connections between the maternal, history, and representation in ways that will allow a taming of technologies of reproduction. The extent to which the affect of horror is attached to such filmic narratives, however, indicates the traumatic impact of these technologies – their potential to disrupt given symbolic systems that construct the maternal and the paternal as stable positions. It is a trauma around which the films obsessively circulate and which they simultaneously disavow.

Notes

1   G. Claudin, *Paris* (Paris, 1867), 71–72, quoted in Wolfgang Schivelbusch, *The Railway Journey: The Industrialization of Time and Space in the 19th Century* (Berkeley: The University of California Press, 1986), 159.

2   Villiers de l'Isle-Adam, *Tomorrow's Eve*, trans. Robert Martin Adams (Urbana, Chicago, and London: University of Illinois Press, 1982), 13.

3   Ibid., 14.

4   Ibid., 125.

5   Ibid., 131.

6   Annette Michelson, "On the Eve of the Future: The Reasonable Facsimile and the Philosophical Toy," in *October: The First Decade, 1976–1986*, eds. Annette Michelson,

et al. (Cambridge: The MIT Press, 1987), 432. See also Raymond Bellour, "Ideal Hadaly: on Villiers' *The Future Eve*," *Camera Obscura* 15 Fall (Fall 1986): 111–35.

7   Villiers de l'Isle-Adam, 164.

8   Michelson, 433.

9   Christian Metz, "The Imaginary Signifier," *Screen* 16:2 (Summer 1975), 15.

10   Andreas Huyssen, *After the Great Divide: Modernism, Mass Culture, Postmodernism* (Bloomington: Indiana University Press, 1986), 70.

11   Ibid.

12   See Barbara Creed, "Horror and the Monstrous-Feminine – An Imaginary Abjection," *Screen* 27:1 (January–February 1986): 44–71; and James H. Kavanagh, "'Son of a Bitch': Feminism, Humanism and Science in *Alien*," *October* 13 (1980), 91–100.

13   Kavanagh, 94.

14   Julia Kristeva, *Powers of Horror* (New York: Columbia University Press, 1983).

15   Julia Kristeva, "Maternité selon Giovanni Bellini," *Polylogue* (Paris: Éditions du Seuil, 1977), 409; my translation.

16   Ibid.

17   Jean Baudrillard, *Simulations*, trans. Paul Foss, Paul Patton, and Philip Beitchman (New York City: Semiotext(e), 1983), 153.

18   Roland Barthes, *Camera Lucida: Reflections on Photography*, trans. Richard Howard (New York: Hill and Wang, 1981). For a remarkably similar analysis of *Blade Runner*, although differently inflected, see Giuliana Bruno, "Ramble City: Postmodernism and *Blade Runner*," *October* 41 (Summer 1987), 61–74. Bruno also invokes Barthes's *Camera Lucida* in her analysis of the role of photography in the film.

19   See Glenn Hendler, "Simulation and Replication: The Question of *Blade Runner*," honors thesis, Brown University, Spring 1984.

20   Garrett Stewart, "The 'Videology' of Science Fiction," in *Shadows of the Magic Lamp: Fantasy and Science Fiction in Film*, eds. George Slusser and Eric S. Rabkin (Carbondale and Edwardsville: Southern Illinois University Press, 1985), 161.

21   Ibid., 161.

22   Ibid., 167.

23   Metz, 72.

24   Claude Bailblé, "Programming the Look," *Screen Education* 32/33, 100.

25   Walter Benjamin, "The Work of Art in the Age of Mechanical Reproduction," *Illuminations*, trans. Harry Zohn (New York: Schocken Books, 1969), 217–52.

Barbara Creed

ALIEN AND THE MONSTROUS-FEMININE

THE SCIENCE FICTION HORROR FILM *Alien* (1979) is a complex representation of the monstrous-feminine in terms of the maternal figure as perceived within a patriarchal ideology. She is there in the text's scenarios of the primal scene of birth and death; she is there in her many guises as the treacherous mother, the oral sadistic mother, the mother as the primordial abyss; and she is there in the film's images of blood, of the all-devouring vagina, the toothed vagina, the vagina as Pandora's box; and finally she is there in the chameleon figure of the alien, the monster as fetish object of and for the mother. But it is the archaic mother, the reproductive/generative mother, who haunts the *mise-en-scène* of the film's first section, with its emphasis on different representations of the primal scene.

According to Freud, every child either watches its parents in the act of sexual intercourse or has fantasies about that act – fantasies which relate to the problem of origins. Freud left open the question of the cause of the fantasy but suggested that it may initially be aroused by "an observation of the sexual intercourse of animals".[1] In his study of the Wolf-Man, Freud argued that the child did not initially observe his parents in the act of sexual intercourse but that he witnessed the copulation of animals whose behaviour he then displaced onto his parents. In situations where the child actually witnesses sexual intercourse between its parents, Freud argued that all children arrive at the same conclusion: "They adopt what may be called a *sadistic view of coition*".[2] If the child perceives the primal scene as a monstrous act – whether in reality or fantasy – it may fantasize animals or mythical creatures as taking part in the scenario. Possibly the many mythological stories in which humans copulate with animals and other creatures (Europa and Zeus, Leda and the Swan) are reworkings of the primal scene narrative. The Sphinx, with her lion's body and woman's face, is an interesting figure in this context. Freud suggested that the Riddle of the Sphinx was probably a distorted version of the great riddle that faces all children – Where do babies come from? An extreme form of the primal fantasy is that of "observing parental intercourse while one is still an unborn baby in the womb".[3]

One of the major concerns of the science fiction horror film (*Alien, The Thing, Invasion of the Body Snatchers, Altered States*) is the reworking of the primal scene in relation to the representation of other forms of copulation and procreation. *Alien* presents various representations of the primal scene. Behind each of these lurks the figure of the archaic mother, that is, the image of the mother in her generative function – the mother as the origin of all life. This archaic figure is somewhat different from the mother of the semiotic chora, as posed by Kristeva,[4] in that the latter is the pre-Oedipal mother who exists in relation to the family and the symbolic order. The concept of the parthenogenetic, archaic mother adds another dimension to the maternal figure and presents us with a new way of understanding how patriarchal ideology works to deny the "difference" of woman in her cinematic representation.

The first birth scene occurs in *Alien* at the beginning, where the camera/spectator explores the inner space of the mother-ship whose life support system is a computer aptly named "Mother". This exploratory sequence of the inner body of the "Mother" culminates with a long tracking shot down one of the corridors which leads to a womb-like chamber where the crew of seven are woken up from their protracted sleep by Mother's voice monitoring a call for help from a nearby planet. The seven astronauts emerge slowly from their sleep pods in what amounts to a re-birthing scene which is marked by a fresh, antiseptic atmosphere. In outer space, birth is a well controlled, clean, painless affair. There is no blood, trauma or terror. This scene could be interpreted as a primal fantasy in which the human subject is born fully developed – even copulation is redundant.

The second representation of the primal scene takes place when three of the crew enter the body of the unknown space-ship through a "vaginal" opening: the ship is shaped like a horseshoe, its curved sides like two long legs spread apart at the entrance. They travel along a corridor which seems to be made of a combination of inorganic and organic material – as if the inner space of this ship were alive. Compared to the atmosphere of the *Nostromo*, however, this ship is dark, dank and mysterious. A ghostly light glimmers and the sounds of their movements echo throughout the caverns. In the first chamber, the three explorers find a huge alien life form which appears to have been dead for a long time. Its bones are bent outward as if it exploded from the inside. One of the trio, Kane, is lowered down a shaft into the gigantic womb-like chamber in which rows of eggs are hatching. Kane approaches one of the eggs; as he touches it with his gloved hand it opens out, revealing a mass of pulsating flesh. Suddenly, the monstrous thing inside leaps up and attaches itself to Kane's helmet, its tail penetrating Kane's mouth in order to fertilize itself inside his stomach. Despite the warnings of Ripley, Kane is taken back on board the *Nostromo* where the alien rapidly completes its gestation process inside Kane.

This representation of the primal scene recalls Freud's reference to an extreme primal scene fantasy where the subject imagines travelling back inside the womb to watch her/his parents having sexual intercourse, perhaps to watch her/himself being conceived. Here, three astronauts explore the gigantic, cavernous, malevolent womb of the mother. Two members of the group watch the enactment of the primal scene in which Kane is violated in an act of phallic penetration – by the father or phallic mother? Kane himself is guilty of the strongest transgression; he actually peers into the egg/womb in order to investigate its mysteries. In so doing, he becomes a "part" of the primal scene, taking up the place of the mother, the one who is penetrated, the

Figure 2.3A "The space travellers about to enter the alien ship through its monstrous vaginal portals (*Alien*)"
(From Barbara Creed, *The Monstrous-Feminism: Film, Feminism and Psychoanalysis* Routledge, 1993)

Figure 2.3B "The egg chamber. The intra-uterine imagery, sign of the abject archaic mother, haunts the *mise-en-scène* of *Alien*"

(From Barbara Creed, *The Monstrous-Feminism: Film, Feminism and Psychoanalysis*, Routledge, 1993)

one who bears the offspring of the union. The primal scene is represented as violent, monstrous (the union is between human and alien), and is mediated by the question of incestuous desire. All restagings of the primal scene raise the question of incest, as the beloved parent (usually the mother) is with a rival. The first birth scene, where the astronauts emerge from their sleep pods, could be viewed as a representation of incestuous desire *par excellence*: the father is completely absent; here, the mother is sole parent and sole life-support.

From this forbidden union, the monstrous creature is born. But man, not woman, is the "mother" and Kane dies in agony as the alien gnaws its way through his stomach. The birth of the alien from Kane's stomach plays on what Freud described as a common misunderstanding that many children have about birth, that is, that the mother is somehow impregnated through the mouth – she may eat a special food – and the baby grows in her stomach from which it is also born. Here, we have a third version of the primal scene.

A further version of the primal scene – almost a convention[5] of the science fiction film – occurs when smaller craft or bodies are ejected from the mother-ship into outer space; although sometimes the ejected body remains attached to the mother-ship by a long lifeline or umbilical cord. This scene is presented in two separate ways: one when Kane's body, wrapped in a white shroud, is ejected from the mother-ship; and the second, when the small space capsule, in which Ripley is trying to escape from the alien, is expelled from the underbelly of the mother-ship. In the former, the "mother's" body has become hostile; it contains the alien whose one purpose is to kill and devour all of Mother's children. In the latter birth scene the living infant is ejected from the malevolent body of the "mother" to avoid destruction; in this scenario, the "mother's" body explodes at the moment of giving birth.

Although the "mother" as a figure does not appear in these sequences – nor indeed in the entire film – her presence forms a vast backdrop for the enactment of all the events. She is there in the images of birth, the representations of the primal scene, the womb-like imagery, the long winding tunnels leading to inner chambers, the rows of hatching eggs, the body of the mother-ship, the voice of the life-support system, and the birth of the alien. She is the generative mother, the pre-phallic mother, the being who exists prior to knowledge of the phallus.

In explaining the difficulty he had in uncovering the role of the mother in the early development of infants, Freud complained of the almost "prehistoric" remoteness of this "Minoan-Mycenaean" stage:

> Everything in the sphere of this first attachment to the mother seemed to me so difficult to grasp in analysis – so grey with age and shadowy and almost impossible to revivify – that it was as if it had succumbed to an especially inexorable repression.[6]

Just as the Oedipus complex tends to hide the pre-Oedipal phase in Freudian theory, the figure of the father, in the Lacanian rewriting of Freud, obscures the mother–child relationship of the imaginary. In contrast to the maternal figure of the Lacanian imaginary, Kristeva posits another dimension to the mother – she is associated with the pre-verbal or the semiotic and as such tends to disrupt the symbolic order.[7]

I think it is possible to open up the mother-question still further and posit an even more archaic maternal figure, to go back to mythological narratives of the generative, parthenogenetic mother – that ancient archaic figure who gives birth to all living things. She exists in the mythology of all human cultures as the mother-goddess who alone created the heavens and earth. In China she was known as Nu Kwa, in Mexico as Coatlicue, in Greece as Gaia (literally meaning "earth") and in Sumer as Nammu. In "Moses and Monotheism", Freud attempted to account for the historical existence of the great mother-goddesses.

> It is likely that the mother-goddesses originated at the time of the curtailment of the matriarchy, as a compensation for the slight upon the mothers. The male deities appear first as sons beside the great mothers and only later clearly assume the features of father-figures. These male gods of polytheism reflect the conditions during the patriarchal age.[8]

Freud proposed that human society developed through stages from patriarchy to matriarchy and finally back to patriarchy. During the first, primitive people lived in small hordes, each one dominated by a jealous, powerful father who possessed all the females of the group. One day the sons, who had been banished to the outskirts of the group, overthrew the father – whose body they devoured – in order to secure his power and to take his women for themselves. Overcome by guilt, they later attempted to revoke the deed by setting up a totem as a substitute for the father and by renouncing the women whom they had liberated. The sons were forced to give up the women, whom they all wanted to possess, in order to preserve the group which otherwise would have been destroyed as the sons fought amongst themselves. In "Totem and Taboo", Freud suggests that here "the germ of the institution of matriarchy"[9] may have originated. Eventually, however, this new form of social organ-ization, constructed upon the taboo against murder and incest, was replaced by the re-establishment of a patriarchal order. He pointed out that the sons had: "thus created out of their filial sense of guilt the two fundamental taboos of totemism, which for that very reason inevitably corresponded to the two repressed wishes of the Oedipus complex".[10]

Freud's account of the origins of patriarchal civilization is generally regarded as mythical. Lévi-Strauss points out that it is "a fair account not of the beginnings of civilization, but of its present state" in that it expresses "in symbolic form an inveterate fantasy" – the desire to murder the father and possess the mother.[11] In her discussion of "Totem and Taboo", Kristeva argues that a "strange slippage" has taken place, in that although Freud points out that morality is founded on the taboos of murder and incest his argument concentrates on the first to the virtual exclusion of the latter. Yet, Kristeva argues, the "woman – or mother – image haunts a large part of that book and keeps shaping its background". She poses the question:

> Could the sacred be, whatever its variants, a two-sided formation? One aspect founded by murder and the social bond made up of a murderer's guilt-ridden atonement, with all the projective mechanisms and obsessive rituals that accompany it; and another aspect, like a lining, more secret and invisible, non-representable, oriented toward those uncertain spaces of unstable identity,

toward the fragility – both threatening and fusional – of the archaic dyad, toward the non-separation of subject/object, on which language has no hold but one woven of fright and repulsion?[12]

From the above, it is clear that the figure of the mother in both the history of human sociality and in the history of the individual subject poses immense problems. Freud attempts to account for the existence of the mother-goddess figure by posing a matriarchal period in historical times while admitting that everything to do with the "first attachment to the mother" is deeply repressed – "grey with age and shadowy and almost impossible to revivify". Nowhere does he attempt to specify the nature of this "matriarchal period" and the implications of this for his own psychoanalytical theory, specifically his theory of the Oedipus complex which, as Lacan points out, "can only appear in a patriarchal form in the institution of the family".[13] Kristeva criticizes Freud for failing to deal adequately with incest and the mother-question while using the same mystifying language to refer to the mother; the other aspect of the sacred is "like a lining", "secret and invisible", "non-representable". In his re-reading of Freud, Lacan mystifies the figure of woman even further: ". . . the woman is not-all, there is always something with her which eludes discourse".[14] Further, all three writers conflate the archaic mother with the mother of the dyadic and triadic relationship. They refer to her as a "shadowy" figure (Freud); as "non-representable" (Kristeva); as the "abyss of the female organ from which all life comes forth" (Lacan[15]), then make no clear attempt to distinguish this aspect of the maternal imago from the protective/suffocating mother of the pre-Oedipal or the mother as object of sexual jealousy and desire as she is represented in the Oedipal configuration.

The maternal figure constructed within/by the writings of Freud, Lacan and Kristeva is inevitably the mother of the dyadic or triadic relationship – although the latter figure is more prominent. Even when she is represented as the mother of the imaginary, of the dyadic relationship, she is still constructed as the *pre-Oedipal* mother, that is, as a figure about to "take up a place" in the symbolic – as a figure always in relation to the father, the representative of the phallus. Without her "lack", he cannot signify its opposite – lack of a lack or presence. But if we posit a more archaic dimension to the mother – the mother as originating womb – we can at least begin to talk about the maternal figure as *outside* the patriarchal family constellation. In this context, the mother-goddess narratives can be read as primal-scene narratives in which the mother is the sole parent. She is also the subject, not the object, of narrativity.

For instance in the "Spider Woman" myth of the North American Indians, there was only the Spider Woman, who spun the universe into existence and then created two daughters from whom all life flowed. She is also the Thought Woman or Wise Woman who knows the secrets of the universe. Within the Oedipus narrative, however, she becomes the Sphinx, who also knows the answers to the secret of life; but here her situation has been changed. She is no longer the subject of the narrative; she has become the object of the narrative of the male hero. After he has solved her riddle, she will destroy herself. The Sphinx is an ambiguous figure; she knows the secret of life and is thereby linked to the mother-goddess but her name, which is derived from "sphincter", suggests she is the mother of toilet training, the pre-Oedipal mother who must be repudiated by the son so that he can take up his proper place in the symbolic. It is interesting that Oedipus has always been seen to have committed two horrific crimes: patricide and incest. But his encounter with the Sphinx, which leads to her death, suggests he is also responsible for another horrific crime – that of matricide. For the Sphinx, like the Medusa, is a mother-goddess figure; they are both variants of the same mythological mother who gave birth to all life. Lévi-Strauss has argued that a major issue in the Oedipus myth is the problem of whether or not man is born from woman. This myth is also central to *Alien*:

> Although the problem obviously cannot be solved, the Oedipus myth provides a kind of logical tool which relates the original problem – born from one or born from two? – to the derivative problem: born from different or born from same?[16]

The Medusa, whose head, according to Freud, signifies the female genitals in their terrifying aspect, also represents the procreative function of woman. The blood which flows from her severed head gives birth to Pegasus and Chrysaor. Although Neptune is supposed to be the father, the nature of the birth once again suggests the parthenogenetic mother. In *Alice Doesn't*, Teresa de Lauretis argues that:

> to say that narrative is the production of Oedipus is to say that each reader – male or female – is constrained and defined within the two positions of a sexual difference thus conceived: male-hero-human, on the side of the subject; and female-obstacle-boundary-space, on the other.[17]

If we apply her definition to narratives which deal specifically with the archaic mother – such as the Oedipus and Perseus myths – we can see that the "obstacle" relates specifically to the question of origins and is an attempt to repudiate the idea of woman as the source of life, woman as sole parent, woman as archaic mother.

In his article, "Fetishism in the Horror Film", Roger Dadoun also refers to this archaic maternal figure. He describes her as:

> a maternal thing situated on this side of good and evil, on this side of all organized form, on this side of all events – a totalizing, oceanic mother, a "mysterious and profound unity", arousing in the subject the anguish of fusion and of dissolution; the mother prior to the uncovering of the essential *béance* [gap], of the *pas-de-phallus*, the mother who is pure fantasm, in the sense that she is posed as an omnipresent and all-powerful totality, an absolute being, only in the intuition – she does not have a phallus – which deposes her . . .[18]

If Dadoun places emphasis on her "totalizing, oceanic" presence, I would stress her archaism in relation to her generative powers – the mother who gives birth all by herself, the original parent, the godhead of all fertility and the origin of procreation. What is most interesting about the mythological figure of woman as the source of all life (a role taken over by the male god of monotheistic religions) is that, within patriarchal signifying practices, particularly the horror film, she is reconstructed and represented as a *negative* figure, one associated with the dread of the generative mother seen only in the abyss, the monstrous vagina, the origin of all life threatening to reabsorb what it once birthed. Kristeva also represents her in this negative light, and in this context it is interesting to note that Freud linked the womb to the *unheimlich*, the uncanny. Freud also supported, and elaborated upon, Schelling's definition of the uncanny as "something which ought to have remained hidden but has come to light".[19] In horror films such as *Alien*, we are given a representation of the female genitals and the womb as uncanny – horrific objects of dread and fascination. Unlike the mythological mother-narratives, here the archaic mother, like the Sphinx and the Medusa, is seen only in a negative light. But the central characteristic of the archaic mother is her total dedication to the generative, procreative principle. She is outside morality and the law. Ash's eulogy to the alien is a description of this mother: "I admire its purity; a survivor unclouded by conscience, remorse or delusions of morality."

Clearly, it is difficult to separate out completely the figure of the archaic mother, as defined above, from other aspects of the maternal figure – the maternal authority of Kristeva's semiotic, the mother of Lacan's imaginary, the phallic woman, the castrated woman. While the different figures signify quite separate things about the monstrous-feminine, each one is also only part of the whole – a different aspect of the maternal figure. At times the horrific nature of the monstrous-feminine is totally dependent on the merging together of all aspects of the maternal figure into one – the horrifying image of woman as archaic mother, phallic woman and castrated body represented as a single figure.

The archaic mother – constructed as a negative force – is represented in her phantasmagoric aspects in many horror texts, particularly the science fiction horror film. We see her as the gaping, cannibalistic bird's mouth in *The Giant Claw*; the terrifying spider of *The Incredible Shrinking Man*; the toothed vagina/womb of *Jaws*; and the fleshy, pulsating, womb of *The Thing* and the *Poltergeist*. What is common to all of these images of horror is the voracious maw, the mysterious black hole which signifies female genitalia as a monstrous sign which threatens to give birth to equally horrific offspring, as well as threatening to incorporate everything in its path. This is the generative archaic mother, constructed within patriarchal ideology as the primeval "black hole". This, of course, is also the hole which is opened up by the absence of the penis; the horrifying sight of the mother's genitals – proof that castration can occur.

However, in the texts cited above, the emphasis is not on castration; rather it is the gestating, all-devouring womb of the archaic mother which generates the horror. Nor are these images of the womb constructed in relation to the penis of the father. Unlike the female genitalia the womb cannot be constructed as a "lack" in relation to the penis. The womb is not the site of castration anxiety. Rather, the womb signifies "fullness" or "emptiness" but always it is its own point of reference. This is why we need to posit a more archaic dimension to the mother. For the concept of the archaic mother allows for a notion of the feminine which does not depend for its definition on a concept of the masculine. The term "archaic mother" signifies woman as sexual difference. In contrast the maternal figure of the pre-Oedipal is always represented in relation to the penis – the phallic mother who later becomes the castrated mother. Significantly, there is an attempt in *Alien* to appropriate the procreative function of the mother, to represent a man giving birth, to deny the mother as signifier of sexual difference – but here birth can exist only as the other face of death.

The archaic mother is present in all horror films as the blackness of extinction – death. The desires and fears invoked by the image of the archaic mother, as a force that threatens to reincorporate what it once gave birth to, are always there in the horror text – all pervasive, all encompassing – because of the constant presence of death. The desire to return to the original oneness of things, to return to the mother/womb, is primarily a desire for non-differentiation. If, as Georges Bataille[20] argues, life signifies discontinuity and separateness, and death signifies continuity and non-differentiation, then the desire for and attraction of death suggests also a desire to return to the state of original oneness with the mother. As this desire to merge occurs after differentiation, that is after the subject has developed as a separate, autonomous self, then it is experienced as a form of psychic death. In this sense, the confrontation with death as represented in the horror film, gives rise to a terror of self-disintegration, of losing one's self or ego – often represented cinematically by a screen which becomes black, signifying the obliteration of self, the self of the protagonist in the film and the spectator in the cinema. This has important consequences for the positioning of the spectator in the cinema.

One of the most interesting structures operating in the screen–spectator relationship relates to the sight/site of the monstrous within the horror text. In contrast to the conventional viewing structures working within other variants of the classic text, the horror film does not constantly work to suture the spectator into the viewing processes. Instead, an unusual phenomenon arises whereby the suturing processes are momentarily undone while the horrific image on the screen challenges the viewer to run the risk of continuing to look. Here, I refer to those moments in the horror film when the spectator, unable to stand the images of horror unfolding before his/her eyes, is forced to look away, to not-look, to look anywhere but at the screen. Strategies of identification are temporarily broken, as the spectator is constructed in the place of horror, the place where the sight/site can no longer be endured, the place where pleasure in looking is transformed into pain and the spectator is punished for his/her voyeuristic desires.

Confronted by the sight of the monstrous, the viewing subject is put into crisis – boundaries, designed to keep the abject at bay, threaten to disintegrate, collapse. The horror film puts the viewing subject's sense of unified self into crisis in those moments when the image on the screen becomes too threatening or horrific to watch, with the threat that the viewing subject will be drawn to the place "where meaning collapses", the place of death. By not-looking, the spectator is able momentarily to withdraw identification from the image on the screen in order to reconstruct the boundary between self and screen and reconstitute the "self" which is threatened with disintegration. This process of reconstitution of the self is reaffirmed by the conventional ending of the horror narrative in which the monster is usually "named" and destroyed.[21]

Alien collapses the image of the threatening archaic mother, signifying woman as "difference", into the more recognized figure of the pre-Oedipal mother; this occurs in relation to two images of the monstrous-feminine: the oral-sadistic mother and the phallic mother. Kane's transgressive disturbance of the egg/womb initiates a transformation of its latent aggressivity into an active, phallic enemy. The horror then played out can be read in relation to Kristeva's concept of the semiotic chora. Kristeva argues that the maternal body becomes the site of conflicting desires (the semiotic chora). These desires are constantly staged and restaged in the workings of the horror narrative where the subject is left alone, usually in a strange hostile place, and forced to confront an unnameable terror, the monster. The monster represents both the subject's fears of being alone, of being separate from the mother, and the threat of annihilation – often through reincorporation. As oral-sadistic mother, the monster threatens to reabsorb the child she once nurtured. Thus, the monster is ambiguous; it both repels and attracts.

In *Alien*, each of the crew members comes face to face with the alien in a scene whose *mise-en-scène* is coded to suggest a monstrous, malevolent maternal figure. They watch with fascinated horror as the baby alien gnaws its way through Kane's stomach; Dallas, the captain, encounters the alien after he has crawled along the ship's enclosed, womb-like air ducts; and the other three members are cannibalized in a frenzy of blood in scenes which emphasize the alien's huge razor-sharp teeth, signifying the monstrous oral-sadistic mother. Apart from the scene of Kane's death, all the death sequences occur in dimly lit, enclosed, threatening spaces reminiscent of the giant hatchery where Kane first encounters the pulsating egg. In these death sequences the terror of being abandoned is matched only by the fear of reincorporation. This scenario, which enacts the conflicting desires at play in the semiotic chora, is staged within the body of the mother-ship, the vessel which the space-travellers initially trust, until "Mother" herself is revealed as a treacherous figure programmed to sacrifice the lives of the crew in the interests of the Company.

The other face of the monstrous-feminine in *Alien* is the phallic mother. Freud argued that the male child could either accept the threat of castration, thus ending the Oedipus complex, or disavow it. The latter response requires the (male) child to mitigate his horror at the sight of the mother's genitals – proof that castration can occur – with a fetish object which substitutes for her missing penis. For him, she is still the phallic mother, the penis-woman. In "Medusa's Head" Freud argued that the head with its hair of writhing snakes represented the terrifying genitals of the mother, but that this head also functioned as a fetish object. He also noted that a display of the female genitals makes a woman "unapproachable and repels all sexual desires", referring to the section in Rabelais which relates "how the Devil took flight when the woman showed him her vulva".[22] Perseus's solution is to look only at a reflection, a mirror-image of her genitals. As with patriarchal ideology, his shield reflects an "altered" representation, a vision robbed of its threatening aspects. The full difference of the mother is denied; she is constructed as other, displayed before the gaze of the conquering male hero, then destroyed. The price paid is the destruction of sexual heterogeneity and repression of the maternal signifier. The fetishization of the mother's genitals could occur in those texts where the maternal figure is represented in her phantasmagoric aspects as the gaping, voracious vagina/womb. Do aspects of these images work to mitigate the horror by offering a substitute for the penis? However, it is possible that we could theorize fetishism differently by asking: Who is the fetish object a fetish for? The male or female subject? In general, the fetishist is usually assumed to be male, although Freud did allow that female fetishism was a possibility.[23] The notion of female fetishism is much neglected although it is present in various patriarchal discourses.[24]

In *The Interpretation of Dreams*,[25] Freud discusses the way in which the doubling of a penis-symbol indicates an attempt to stave off castration anxieties. Juliet Mitchell refers to doubling as a sign of a female castration complex: "We can see the significance of this for women, as dreams of repeated number of children – 'little ones' – are given the same import."[26] In this context, female fetishism represents an attempt by the female subject to continue to "have" the phallus, to take up a "positive" place in relation to the symbolic.

Female fetishism is clearly represented within many horror texts – as instances of patriarchal signifying practices – but only in relation to male fears and anxieties about women and the question: What do women want? (*The Birds*, *Cat People*, *Alien*, *The Thing*.) Women as yet do not speak their own "fetishistic" desires within the popular cinema – if, indeed, women have such desires. The notion of female fetishism is represented in *Alien* in the figure of the monster. The creature is the mother's phallus, attributed to the maternal figure by a phallocentric ideology terrified at the thought that women might desire to have the phallus. The monster as fetish object is not there to meet the desires of the male fetishist, but rather to signify the monstrousness of woman's desire to have the phallus.

In *Alien*, the monstrous creature is constructed as the phallus of the negative mother. The image of the archaic mother – threatening because it signifies woman as difference rather than constructed as opposition – is, once again, collapsed into the figure of the pre-Oedipal mother. By relocating the figure of woman within an Oedipal scenario, her image can be recuperated and controlled. The womb, even if represented negatively, is a greater threat than the mother's phallus. As phallic mother, woman is again represented as monstrous. What is horrific is her desire to cling to her offspring in order to continue to "have the phallus". Her monstrous desire is concretized in the figure of the alien; the creature whose deadly mission is represented as the same as that of the archaic mother – to reincorporate and destroy all life.

If we consider *Alien* in the light of a theory of female fetishism, then the chameleon nature of the alien begins to make sense. Its changing appearance represents a form of doubling or multiplication of the phallus, pointing to the mother's desire to stave off her castration. The alien is the mother's phallus, a fact which is made perfectly clear in the birth scene where the infant alien rises from Kane's stomach and holds itself erect, glaring angrily around the room, before screeching off into the depths of the ship. But the alien is more than a phallus; it is also coded as a toothed vagina, the monstrous-feminine as the cannibalistic mother. A large part of the ideological project of *Alien* is the representation of the maternal fetish object as an "alien" or foreign shape. This is why the body of the heroine becomes so important at the end of the film.

Much has been written about the final scene, in which Ripley/Sigourney Weaver undresses before the camera, on the grounds that its voyeurism undermines her role as successful heroine. A great deal has also been written about the cat. Why does she rescue the cat and thereby risk her life, and the lives of Parker and Lambert, when she has previously been so careful about quarantine regulations? Again, satisfactory answers to these questions are provided by a phallocentric concept of female fetishism. Compared to the horrific sight of the alien as fetish object of the monstrous-feminine, Ripley's body is pleasurable and reassuring to look at. She signifies the "acceptable" form and shape of woman. In a sense the monstrousness of woman, represented by Mother as betrayer (the computer/life-support system) and

Mother as the uncontrollable, generative, cannibalistic mother (the alien), is controlled through the display of woman as reassuring and pleasurable sign. The image of the cat functions in the same way; it signifies an acceptable, and in this context a reassuring, fetish object for the "normal" woman. Thus, Ripley holds the cat to her, stroking it as if it were her "baby", her "little one". Finally, Ripley enters her sleep pod, assuming a virginal repose. The nightmare is over and we are returned to the opening sequence of the film where birth was a pristine affair. The final sequence works, not only to dispose of the alien, but also to repress the nightmare image of the monstrous-feminine within the text's patriarchal discourses.

Kristeva's theory of abjection, if viewed as description rather than prescription, provides a productive hypothesis for an analysis of the monstrous-feminine in the horror and the SF horror film.[27] If we posit a more archaic dimension to the mother, we can see how this figure, as well as Kristeva's maternal authority of the semiotic, are both constructed as figures of abjection within the signifying practices of the horror film. We can see its ideological project as an attempt to shore up the symbolic order by constructing the feminine as an imaginary "other" which must be repressed and controlled in order to secure and protect the social order. Thus, the horror film stages and restages a constant repudiation of the maternal figure.

Notes

1   Sigmund Freud, "From the History of an Infantile Neurosis" in *Case Histories II*, Pelican Freud Library, vol. 9, Harmondsworth: Penguin 1981.
2   Sigmund Freud, "On the Sexual Theories of Children" in *On Sexuality*, Pelican Freud Library, vol. 7, p. 198.
3   Sigmund Freud, "The Paths to the Formation of Symptoms" in *Introductory Lectures on Psychoanalysis*, Pelican Freud Library, vol. 1, p. 417.
4   Julia Kristeva, *Powers of Horror: An Essay on Abjection*, New York: Columbia University Press 1982, p. 14.
5   Daniel Dervin argues that this structure does deserve the status of a convention. For a discussion of the primal scene fantasy in science fiction cinema, see "Primal Conditions and Conventions: The Genre of Science Fiction" in Annette Kuhn, ed., *Alien Nation: Cultural Theory and Contemporary Science*, New York and London: Verso 1990.
6   Sigmund Freud, "Female Sexuality" in *On Sexuality*, Pelican Freud Library, vol. 7, p. 373.
7   For a discussion of the relation between "the semiotic" and the Lacanian "Imaginary", see Jane Gallop, *Feminism and Psychoanalysis: The Daughter's Seduction*, London: Macmillan 1983, pp. 124–5.
8   Sigmund Freud, "Moses and Monotheism", *The Standard Edition of the Complete Psychological Works of Sigmund Freud*, London: Hogarth Press 1958, vol. 23, p. 83.
9   Sigmund Freud, "Totem and Taboo" in *The Origins of Religion*, Pelican Freud Library, vol. 13, Harmondsworth: Penguin 1985, p. 206.
10 Ibid., p. 205.
11 Lévi-Strauss, quoted in Georges Bataille, *Death and Sensuality: A Study of Eroticism and the Taboo*, New York: Walker & Company 1962, p. 200.
12 Kristeva, op. cit., pp. 57–8.

13   Jacques Lacan, in Anthony Wilden, ed., *The Language of the Self*, Baltimore: Johns Hopkins University Press 1970, p. 126.

14   Jacques Lacan, *Le Seminaire XX*, p. 34, translated by Stephen Heath, "Difference", *Screen*, vol. 19, no. 3, 1978, p. 59.

15   Jacques Lacan, *Le Seminaire II*, translated in Heath, p. 54.

16   Claude Lévi-Strauss, *Structural Anthropology*, trans. C. Jacobson and B. G. Schoepf, New York: Doubleday 1976, p. 212.

17   Teresa de Lauretis, *Alice Doesn't: Feminism, Semiotics, Cinema*, Bloomington: Indiana University Press 1984, p. 121.

18   Roger Dadoun, "Fetishism in the Horror Film", *Enclitic*, vol. 1, no. 2, 1977, pp. 55–6.

19   Sigmund Freud, "The 'Uncanny'", *The Standard Edition*, vol. 17, p. 245.

20   Bataille, *Death and Sensuality*.

21   For a discussion of the relationship between the female spectator, structures of looking and the horror film, see Linda Williams, "When the Woman Looks" in Mary Anne Doane, Patricia Mellencamp and Linda Williams, eds, *Re-Vision: Essays in Feminist Film Criticism*, Los Angeles, CA: American Film Institute 1984.

22   Sigmund Freud, "Medusa's Head", *The Standard Edition*, vol. 18, p. 105.

23   Sigmund Freud, "An Outline of Psychoanalysis", *The Standard Edition*, vol. 23, p. 202.

24   Mary Kelly, "Woman–Desire–Image", *Desire*, London: ICA 1984.

25   Sigmund Freud, *The Interpretation of Dreams*, Pelican Freud Library, vol. 4, 1982.

26   Juliet Mitchell, *Psychoanalysis and Feminism*, Harmondsworth: Penguin 1974, p. 84.

27   For an analysis of the horror film as a "return of the repressed", see Robin Wood's articles, "Return of the Repressed", *Film Comment*, July–August 1978; and "Neglected Nightmares", *Film Comment*, March–April 1980.

Vivian Sobchack

POSTFUTURISM

[. . .]

THE SHIFT IN SENSIBILITY toward the alien and Other [in contemporary SF films] seems also a function of that new technology which has transformed the spatial and temporal shape of our world and our world view. The popularization and pervasiveness of electronic technology in the last decade has reformulated the experience of space and time as expansive and inclusive. It has recast human being into a myriad of visible and active simulacra, and has generated a semantic equivalency among various formulations and representations of space, time, and being. A space perceived and represented as superficial and shallow, as all surface, does not conceal things: it displays them. When space is no longer lived and represented as "deep" and three-dimensional, the '50s concept of "invasion" loses much of its meaning and force. The new electronic space we live and figure cannot be invaded. It is open only to "pervasion" – a condition of kinetic accommodation and dispersal associated with the experience and representations of television, video games, and computer terminals. Furthermore, in a culture where nearly everyone is regularly alien-ated from a direct sense of self (lived experience commonly mediated by an electronic technology that dominates both the domestic sphere and the "private" or "personal" realm of the Unconscious), when everyone is less conscious of existence than of its image, the once threatening SF "alien" and Other become our familiars – our close relations, if not ourselves.

[. . .]

Embracing the alien, erasing alienation

[. . .] In a culture in which nearly everyone engages images more intensely than personal experience, in which subjectivity and affect are regularly decentered, dispersed, spatialized, and objectified, and in which even alienation is alien-ated and literalized, it is hardly surprising that the figure of the "alien" no longer poses the political and social threat it did in the SF of the 1950s. In that decade, alienation of the postmodern kind was still new and shiny, and aliens were definitely and identifiably "Other." Today's SF films either posit that "aliens are like us" or that "aliens R U.S." Alien Others have become less other – be they extraterrestrial teddy bears, starmen, brothers from another planet, robots, androids, or replicants. They have become our familiars, our simulacra, embodied as literally alienated images of our alienated selves. Thus, contemporary SF generally embraces alien Others as "more human than human" or finds it can barely mark their "otherness" as other than our own.

Whatever their ontology, the majority of aliens in the new SF film are represented as our friends, playmates, brothers, and lovers. The mindlessly destructive BEM's of the '50s have found popular contemporary counterparts only in the 1979 *Alien*, and two remakes of '50s films: *Invasion of the Body Snatchers* (Philip Kaufman, 1978) and *The Thing* (John Carpenter, 1982). And the coldly rational, nearly unstoppable alien Other once prevalent in the early genre has found contemporary popularity only in *The Terminator*. This is not to say that alien Others are never represented as threatening and villainous in contemporary SF, but rather to emphasize that if and when they are, it is generally within a narrative context in which other aliens are shown as friendly and "humane." In quite a transformation of earlier generic representations, most of the new SF films do not represent alien-ness as inherently hostile and Other. (Here, of course, the *Star Wars* trilogy provides the most obvious and wide-ranging example.)

This new and quite sanguine attitude toward postmodern alien-ation and its literalization in a positive figure of the alien Other is shared by both mainstream and marginal SF. Nonetheless, both articulate that figure and its positive meaning in a significantly different manner. In the more conservative mainstream films like *Close Encounters*, *E.T.*, *Starman*, *Cocoon*, and *Enemy Mine*, the "difference" of the alien Other becomes absorbed in the homogeneity of a new universal "humanism." More postmodern and marginal films like *Repo Man*, *The Brother from Another Planet*, and *Uforia* suggest that the "difference" of the alien Other is not so much absorbed as diffused and even erased by postmodern culture's paradoxically totalized heterogeneity. Thus, in conservative SF, the alien Other is valued by virtue of being marked as more "positively" human than we humans presently are – that is, for being just like us, only identifiably and differentially *more* so. In postmodern SF, however, the alien Other is valued for being un-marked as alien or other, for being different just like us, only *no more* so than an/other alien-ated and spaced-out being. The narratives of the conservative mainstream SF film maintain "difference" and "otherness" in the name of homogeneity and embrace the alien as an other who is like us. More radically, the narratives of the postmodern marginal SF film maintain "difference" and "otherness" in the name of heterogeneity and erase alienation by articulating it as a universal condition in which we are aliens and aliens are us. The implications of this distinction are symbolically and culturally quite significant.

Michel Foucault provides some assistance in helping us understand the two quite different logics that inform mainstream SF's "embrace of the alien" on the one hand, and marginal SF's "erasure of alienation" on the other. In one of his essays he makes an important distinction between relations of *resemblance* and relations of *similitude*.

Relations of resemblance, he tells us, may assert sameness, but they "demonstrate and speak across difference," and are hierarchical, requiring the "subordination" of one term to the other that provides the original model.[1] Relations of similitude, however, assert difference, but speak across sameness and are nonhierarchical and reversible. He explains:

> Resemblance has a "model," an original element that orders and hierarchizes the increasingly less faithful copies that can be struck from it. Resemblance presupposes a primary reference that prescribes and classes. The similar develops in series that have neither beginning nor end, that can be followed in one direction as easily as in another, that obey no hierarchy, but propagate themselves from small differences among small differences. Resemblance serves representation, which rules over it; similitude serves repetition, which ranges across it. Resemblance predicates itself upon a model it must return to and reveal; similitude circulates the simulacrum as an indefinite and reversible relation of the similar to the similar.[2]

To maintain — as conservative mainstream SF does — that "aliens are just *like* us" is to assert and dramatize a resemblance — with human being as the "model," the "original element" that "orders and hierarchizes" the "copies that can be struck from it." *E. T.*, *Starman*, *Blade Runner's* replicants, *Heartbeeps'* robots, and the like are predicated upon and subordinated to a human model, and their "faithlessness" as copies is ironically and conservatively an idealization of that model. Conservative SF's embrace of the alien as "the same" maintains alien-ness as the difference that makes a difference, that enables the representation of a new "humanism," and it constitutes those hierarchical relations based on homogeneity into a myth of universal and nonhierarchical homogeneity. To narrativize aliens as "just like us" across their differences is to conserve the primacy of human being. Thus, replicants are advertised as "more human than human" and Starman tells Jenny after they make love, "I think I am becoming a planet Earth person." Mainstream SF's articulation of resemblance between aliens and humans preserves the subordination of "other worlds, other cultures, other species" to the world, culture, and "speciality" of white American culture. We can see this new American "humanism" literally expand into and colonize outer space, making it safe for democracy, multinational capitalism, and the Rolling Stones. Sent into outer space to look for extra-terrestrial life in *Starman*, Voyager II "exports" a recording of "I Can't Get No Satisfaction" — its (re)production of desire a fitting anthem for consumer culture (later sung by Starman).

Marginal and postmodern SF, however, articulates the relations between aliens and humans in quite another way. To maintain not that "aliens are like us," but rather that "aliens *are* us" is to assert and dramatize a relation of similitude — one that can be reversibly articulated as "We are aliens." Human being does not serve as an original model here. Indeed, true to postmodern logic, films like *Liquid Sky*, *Repo Man*, and *The Brother from Another Planet* suggest there is no original model for being, and that (as Foucault notes) the similarity we see across difference "develops in series that have neither beginning nor end," representing the circulation of "the simulacrum as an indefinite and reversible relation of the similar to the similar" propagated nonhierarchically from "small differences among small differences." Margaret, the

Figure 2.4A "*Blade Runner* (Ridley Scott, 1982) More Human Than Human: Relations of resemblance constitute a 'new humanism'"

(Courtesy of Ladd/Warner Brothers)

Figure 2.4B *"Blade Runner* (Ridley Scott, 1982) Reflexive replicants: Priss"
(Courtesy of Ladd/Warner Brothers)

androgynous new-wave model of *Liquid Sky*, and her spaced-out friends, or Otto and his myriad bizarre acquaintances in *Repo Man* are as slightly different from each other as they are different from the marked "aliens" and yet they are as similarly alien-ated as are any of the aliens. Similarly the same and different, the Brother from another planet is as human and alien as any alien-ated human extraterrestrialized in New York's Harlem.

In sum, the most postmodern SF does not "embrace the alien" in a celebration of resemblance, but "erases alienation" in a celebration of similitude. Thus, it is not critical of alienation. Indeed, the postmodern SF film maintains only enough signs of "alien-ness" to dramatize it not as "the difference that makes a difference" but as the "difference that makes a sameness." The "alien" posited by marginal and post-modern SF enables the representation of alienation as "human" and constitutes the reversible and nonhierarchical relations of similitude into a myth of homogenized heterogeneity. That is, nationalism no longer exists as a difference in the culture of multinational capital. Sexual difference is eradicated in *andr(oid)*-ogyny. Identity is ephemeral, and superficially realized by "style." A spaceship is no less strange and no less familiar in its material presence than the local Safeway. Indeed, narrativizing

Figure 2.4C "*ET: The Extra Terrestrial* (Steven Spielberg, 1982) More Human than
Human"
(Universal)

Figure 2.4D "*Liquid Sky* (Slava Tsukerman, 1983) Aliens R US: Relations of
similitude as reversible"
(Cinevista)

"aliens R U.S." is not so progressive as it might seem. Rather, such narratives represent and dramatize the cultural logic of late capitalism whereby the very conditions of cultural alienation are not only found acceptable, but also euphorically celebrated as liberating. In this regard, Foucault's emotionalized description of similitude is particularly apt. "Similitude," he tells us, "multiplies different affirmations, which dance together, tilting and tumbling over one another."[3]

Postfuturism and the "end" of science fiction

This chapter has periodized the American SF film from its first major emergence in the 1950s through its current period of popularity within the context of postmodernism, or "the logic of late capitalism." Looking backward, we can see the genre first flourishing as a symbolic representation of the new intersections of science, technology, and multinational capitalism, whose most visible signposts were the atomic and hydrogen bomb and the electronics of television. The films of the 1950s dramatize the *novelty* of multinational capitalism, and represent both its expansive promise and its threatening unfamiliarity in visualizations that emphasize shiny and "futuristic" technology and cosmic expansion or evidence technological dread and xenophobia. From the late 1970s to the present, the films of the genre's second "Golden Age" are quite different. That is, they dramatize the *familiarity* of multinational capitalism, and represent its totalized domestication, commodification, and pervasion of worldly space in visualizations that valorize the cluttered abundance of consumer culture, nostalgize brand names and childhood, and evidence pleasure in waste and "heaps of fragments." Gone are dread and xenophobia. Gone also is a sense of the possible future. In their place are euphoria and a totalized "pluralism" – both of which are realized in space and do not logically admit the temporalizing of a future.

Indeed, if "science fiction" was once a generic category predicated on speculating and imagining a probable or possible future, the genre seems endangered – its work now producing regressive fantasies on the one hand, and "delirious" comedies totally absorbed in the material present on the other. Today's SF either nostalgically locates the future in an imagined past and thus articulates it as "over," or it complacently locates the future in the present, celebrating it as "here" and "now." It seems as if the SF film – coincidentally born with the culture of late capitalism and the genre most symbolic of it – has total(iz)ed itself in a historical movement logically isomorphic with the totalizing incorporation of Nature by industrialized and consumer culture, with the expansion of capitalism to its "purest form."

This generic development, however, should not be viewed merely as an opportunity for condemnation, and, perhaps, for another postmodern manifestation – that of nostalgia for the genre's past. As Jameson points out, both the cultural critic and the moralist are themselves now "deeply immersed in postmodernist space, so deeply suffused and infected by its new cultural categories, that the luxury of the old-fashioned ideological critique, the indignant moral denunciation of the other, becomes unavailable".[4] Since we are not "outside" the postmodern paradigm and its cultural logic, since it is not merely one stylistic option among others but rather our "cultural dominant," we need to consider the SF genre dialectically. That is, as Jameson goes on to urge, we need to think this development positively *and* negatively all at once; to achieve, in other words, a type of thinking that would be capable of grasping the demonstrably baleful features of capitalism along with its extraordinary and liberating dynamism simultaneously, within a single thought, and without attenuating any of the force of either judgement. We are, somehow, to lift our minds to a point at which it is possible to understand that capitalism is at one and the same time the best thing that has ever happened to the human race, and the worst. The lapse from this austere dialectical imperative into the more comfortable stance of the taking of moral positions is inveterate and all too human: still, the urgency of the subject demands that we make at least some effort to think the cultural evolution of late capitalism dialectically, as catastrophe and progress all together.[5]

If we want to think of the generic development of SF as a catastrophic one, certainly we can point to its "baleful" features. The early films can be generally characterized by their celebration of and consequent paranoia about imperialism and colonial expansion; their fetishization of technology; their arrogant xenophobia grounded on the perpetuation of difference and the need for an alien Other. And, in the films of the "Second Golden Age" we can point an accusatory finger at their regressive infantilism; their nostalgia for an impossible and trivialized past, and their incapacity to imagine a future; their fetishization of consumer culture, both its images and its trash; their complacent pluralism, which ascribes equal value to every "thing" and every "position." We can, in fact, think of the genre in its entirety as the ideological production of poetic displacements: "so many attempts to distract and to divert us from . . . reality or to disguise its contradictions and resolve them in the guise of various formal mystifications."[6]

However, accurate as such negative readings of the genre may be, we are also charged with thinking the development of the SF film as progressive, and with pointing to its "extraordinary and liberating dynamism." As a symbolic representation of the cultural logic of late capitalism (both in its early and late phases of dominance over residual logics), the genre has visibly and literally articulated what can be read as a new form of "realism" – one responsive to and complexly mimetic of a "genuine historical (and socio-economic) reality." Contemporary SF has attempted to map the new world space we inhabit, to imagine other forms of being, to give us a picture of multinationalism, to represent narratively the altered significance of difference, sameness, boundaries, marginality. The films have become increasingly explicit and less displaced in relation to their "real" terrain – that is, in a new and peculiarly literal (if still symbolic) way, they are more "down-to-earth" in their spatial and social location of narrative problems. Furthermore, their current celebration of alienation and/or complacence about alienation has positive as well as negative consequences. Not only do these articulations negate the genre's earlier xenophobia, but they also can be seen as an attempt at what Jameson calls "disalienation":

> the practical reconquest of a sense of place, and the construction or reconstruction of an articulated ensemble which can be retained in memory and which the individual subject can map and remap along the moments of mobile, alternative trajectories.[7]

This is a progressive move. It at least allows for the possibility of some new form of empowerment, if not that empowerment itself.

Right now, at this writing, the most simultaneously catastrophic and progressive SF films are those I have identified as marginal. Their visual and narrative logic is at once the most informed by the logic of late capitalism and the most liberated by it. On the one hand, their lack of temporal imagination (and interest) is paralytic in regards to envisioning a future, but, on the other, it is dynamic in the intense attention it pays to the spatialized present. While everyone is alien-ated and every "thing" is e-stranged in these marginal films, everyone and every thing is also given a liberating equivalence to play out "differences" without hierarchical structures of domination, to newly synthesize "difference relates." The political, social, and economic value of the other as Other has little currency in these films – a devaluation that unfortunately erases real political, sexual, and class differences, and yet also fortunately dissolves their limiting boundary conditions. Indeed, marginal SF films tend to be generically "dissolute" as well as culturally "deconstructive." That is, while their subversion of the boundaries between inner city/outer space, estranged/alien, male/female, familiar/novel, real/imaginary, ordinary/extraordinary "deconstructs" the hierarchical relations that ground capitalist notions of power, desire, and value, this subversion also "dissolves" the very structure and notion of the film genre as a bounded category of texts valuing the marked and hierarchical difference between signs of "science" and signs of "fiction." When "science" and "fiction" are no longer visualized and narrativized as oppositional, the genre becomes dissolute – dissolves. In one sense, this is a liberating move. In another, it is catastrophic. Given that the SF genre is the only cinematic category to imagine and image our possible futures, its dissolution leaves a symbolic chasm.

We have seen that the SF film is always historicized, grounded in its (and our) own earthly American culture – in the economic, technological, political, social, and linguistic present of its production, in the ideological structures that shape its visual and visible conceptions of time, space, affect, and social relations. Certainly, this is an ontological characteristic of *any* cultural artifact. It assumes particular significance, however, in relation to a genre whose expressed imagination would transcend its historical limitations, whose very identity and difference from other genres are figurally marked by this attempt at transcendence. SF's own historical limitations provide, at once, both the boundary conditions that the genre would imaginatively escape and the ground absolutely necessary to its signification of that escape. Thus, the necessary and sufficient symbolic conditions that determine the genre's existence and identity are at odds with each other, even as they are completely dependent upon each other. While this tension between "invention" and "convention" informs any symbolic activity that is not merely replicative, it is most consciously privileged and doubly articulated in SF – heightened and stressed as constituting both the genre's mode of discourse and its discursive object. Indeed, this tension is what forms the basic aesthetic structure of the American SF film. It is what has seemed to unite all the films as a genre, no matter how divergent they are in plot, theme, and specific iconography.

More mundanely but just as importantly, this generic tension between "invention" and "convention," between imaginative flights of figural work and comfortably familiar symbolic activity, is also economically determined. In its major function as a commodity, a genre whose discursive mode and object both privilege and figure "invention" against the ground of "convention" must continually strive to make its previous technological and narrative articulations seem obsolete. Thus, the most popular SF films keep appropriating the culture's newest technology – on the one hand, literally "incorporating" it as part of the film medium (e.g., computer-generated imagery), and on the other, symbolically "displaying" it as "invention," as a more special "special" effect. This literal and symbolic appropriation and commodification of new technology obviously entails larger and larger sums of money, which must be recuperated at a profit, and the possibilities for radical invention, or for invention not based in the technological, become more and more limited and marginalized. Although the SF film ostensibly strives to transcend the conventional and, perhaps, reach toward the avant-garde "and beyond" to the radical, the demands of the genre's commodification also compel it to inscribe itself as familiar, un-threatening, unrevolutionary, and easily understood. True in the 1950s, and truer yet today, an axiom emerges: the more a film costs, the fewer risks it is likely to take. Thus, culturally located in the margins of mainstream American cinema, it is the low-budget SF movie – whether of the '50s or '80s – which tends to embrace its inadequacies as a defensive maneuver, and is often aesthetically and narratively energized toward invention precisely by the low budgets constraining it. The big-budget mainstream SF film, however, is not so driven.

Given the relatively recent major changes in the economy, structure, and quantity of American film production, this seems especially true of today's most popular, most "mainstream" SF films. (Behind the figuration of enormously expensive and inventive technological displays, the ideological conservatism and conventionality of most of last decade's SF "blockbusters" are as much a function of the conditions of their economic production as they are a function of the political climate of Reagan's postmodern and Disneyesque America.) Indeed, today more than ever before, the genre has become extremely self-conscious in its will to be high-cost effective. Its contemporary and seemingly playful reflexivity, in the big-budget super-productions, is not only a characteristic feature of postmodern textuality, but also a form of both cautious and celebratory self-regulation. Thus, despite the SF film's visible and blatant articulations of its own inventiveness, the genre's most popular films work visually to produce not the novel, but its illusion, its replication, its simulacra.

This chapter is being written at a time when the American SF film is still at peak popularity, but (as previously mentioned) is also most threatened in its particular existence as a genre. Indeed, the aesthetic premises for the cinematic existence of the American SF film that this book attempts to describe in its first three chapters have become increasingly unstable in this postmodern age. First, it is getting more and more difficult to determine precisely what constitutes an "American" film these days. The multi-national rather than monopolistic character of late capitalism informs and models today's film industry in all of its aspects: financing, production, distribution, and exhibition. Second, as previously noted, the aesthetics of postmodernism would deny the existence of both the generic boundaries marking SF as a discrete structure of poetic representation and the hierarchical relation of difference that structure poses between the extraordinary and the mundane. Whether "unconsciously" informed by a postmodern aesthetic or "consciously" articulating it, recent SF films have been in the process of celebrating their own generic destruction. Thus, we might do well to consider the implications of this self-destruction and what sort of reformulation might effectively maintain the genre's identity and its particular representational function.

Not content to embrace the aesthetics of postmodernism, although certainly appreciating its value and significance, Jameson ends his consideration of representation in the culture of late capitalism with a call for the invention of "radically new forms" capable of doing justice to the complexity of our historical moment. He sees in these new forms the possible emergence of a new "political art" that will neither long for the past nor merely re-present the present "world space of multinational capital." While taking this last as "its fundamental object," the new political art would achieve

> a breakthrough to some as yet unimaginable new mode of representing this last, in which we may again begin to grasp our positioning as individual and collective subjects and regain a capacity to act and struggle which is at present neutralized by our spatial as well as our social confusion. The political form of postmodernism, if there is any, will have as its vocation the invention and projection of a global cognitive mapping, on a social as well as a spatial scale.[8]

This call for the invention of "new modes" able to represent our "real" position as individuals and collective subjects in late capitalism and yet empower us to act and struggle against its constraints may, in fact, have already been answered – and by a quite singular film that reformulates "science fiction" so that it is not "neutralized" by the postmodern visualization of spatial and social confusion. Expectedly, this "post-postmodern" SF film is more marginal than marginal – and, unexpectedly to some (although not to others), it is articulated within the context of feminism. I refer to *Born in Flames* (Lizzie Borden, 1983).[9] This is a new mode of representation for the SF film: one that does not regress to the past, does not nostalgize, and does not complacently accept the present as the only place to live. It does indeed imagine a future – but one contiguous with the present, and in temporal and spatial relation to it. It is political and empowering and has a momentum not "transfixed" by excess scenography or caught up in an overwhelming and paralyzing material heterogeneity. It is also not visually pleasurable in ways we have been led to expect and desire, but its very grittiness reacts against the hallucinatory splendor and euphoria generated by the postmodern fascination with surface. This is a film in which trash looks like trash, and objects regain their functional value in a social context. This is SF that is definitely not dissolute.

Perhaps, then, the science fiction film still has a future – and in its representations we can still locate the image and imagination of ours. *Born in Flames* is a singular instance of this imagination. Nonetheless, its existence suggests that we look for further responses to mainstream SF "regression" and marginal SF "postfuturism" from a feminist SF cinema. In literature, the intersection of feminism and SF has proved not only generically deconstructive, but also generically reconstructive. I should like to end this reading by looking toward the aesthetics of wonder and future possibilities that such an intersection might constitute for SF cinema.

Notes

1   Michel Foucault, *This Is Not a Pipe*, translated and edited by James Harkness (Berkeley: University of California Press, 1982), p. 32.
2   Ibid., p. 44.
3   Ibid., p. 46.
4   Jameson, "Postmodernism, or The Cultural Logic of Late Capitalism," p. 86.
5   Ibid.
6   Ibid., p. 88.
7   Ibid., p. 89.
8   Ibid., p. 92.
9   For a theoretical and critical discussion of *Born in Flames*, see Teresa DeLauretis, "Aesthetics and Feminist Theory: Rethinking Women's Cinema," *New German Critique*, No. 34 (Winter 1985), pp. 154–75.

Anne Balsamo

READING CYBORGS WRITING
FEMINISM

Cyborgs are the postmodern icon. From children's plastic action figures to Robocop's titanium exoskeleton, cyborgian artifacts will endure as relics of an age obsessed with replication. But what will they tell us about the place and identity of woman? An ironic ethnographic account of cyborg texts, considering such issues as subjectivity, the body, interpretation, this essay proposes a feminist perspective on existing and possible images of the cyborg. [. . .]

WHAT IF WE READ contemporary science fiction stories as ethnographies of the future? Or the cultural emblems of postmodernism as archeological remains of our time grown old? Would we "read" them in an archaic sense – searching for meaning through the rubble of excessive signification? Would ethnography be possible? Useful? Strategic? Would culture remain "writable"? Would we recognize our contemporary age as one of science's past fictions? Given the array of postmodern monuments, from relatively durable architectural wonders through fleeting moments of tongue-in-cheek social commentary, we might wonder, what of this array will endure as markers of our contemporary era?

In 1986, Max Headroom stuttered his way onto American television and the cover of *Newsweek*. The same year, Electra Assassin, Frank Miller's celebrated "super-coded" anti-hero, challenged the revitalized comic book industry's vision of a proper heroine. By Christmas, 1986, it was clear that Transformers were the toy of the season, refashioning children's popular culture as they hammered and slashed their way off the pages of toy catalogues onto a syndicated Saturday morning cartoon series.

Max Headroom, Electra Assassin, and the various incarnations of Transformer-inspired action figures epitomize our culture's fascination with cyborgs. Cyborgs are science fictional hybrids. The name, a shorthand term for "cybernetic organism," usually describes a human-machine coupling, most often a *man*–machine hybrid.

Cyborgs are stock science fiction characters which are alternately labeled "androids," "replicants," or "bionic." Whatever label they attract, cyborgs provide provocative images to consider in light of the questions with which I opened this essay. They occupy a visionary part of our cultural imagination, the image of the future created in the present, the place of science fiction reality, of the postmodern. Whether cyborgs are considered the first citizens of an industrialized technocracy or the perfect companions for an anti-social, simulated society, their images pervade film and popular culture, as well as the world of consumer commodities.

Cyborgs are *the* postmodern icon. From children's plastic action figures to RoboCop's titanium exoskeleton, cyborg-ian artifacts will endure as relics of an age obsessed with replication. In what follows, I will be concerned with how our technological imagination imbues cyborgs with ancient anxieties about human differences. In short, this essay offers a somewhat ironic ethnographic account of cyborg identity as it is portrayed in contemporary popular cultures: ironic in that I purposefully exaggerate the connotative slide of the meaning of the term "cyborg"; ethnographic in the sense of being a cultural analysis – a thick description, of sorts – of cyborg life. My argument proceeds neither linearly nor circularly, but rather radially, suggesting several ways in which the cyborg image can be read through a set of feminist lenses.

Cyborg representation: the technological reproduction of gender

From Mary Shelley's *Frankenstein*, published in 1818, to Maria, the robot in *Metropolis* (Fritz Lang, 1926), to *The Six Million Dollar Man* (1970s), the possibilities of human hybrids have fired our cultural imagination as the Western world moved through industrial and technological phases of development. Variously used as a symbol of anti-technological sentiments or of the possibilities of "better living through chemistry" cyborgs are a product of cultural fears and desires that run deep within our psychic unconscious. Through the use of technology as the means or context for human hybridization, cyborgs come to represent unfamiliar "otherness," one which challenges the connotative stability of *human* identity.

Consider a continuum which has at one extreme the characteristics associated with machines and technology and, at the other extreme, the characteristics of humans and organic society. How are the end points identified? Machines are rational, artificial and durable; humans are emotional, organic and mortal. Every cyborg image constructs an implicit opposition between machine and human; at once repressing similarities and highlighting distinctions. This is the science fictional character of the cyborg – it is a hybrid, but the specific traits which mark its human-ness and machine-ness vary widely. Signs of human-ness and, alternatively, signs of machine-ness function not only as markers of the "essences" of the dual natures of the hybrid, but also as signs of the inviolable opposition between human and machine. This is to say that cyborgs embody human characteristics that reinforce the difference between humans and machines. With the Terminator, his "covering" of human flesh which enables him to time travel, serves as his primary human characteristic; with Helva, the Ship that Sang, it is her organic, cognitively functioning brain severed from a physical body that indicates her human nature. Don't we wait anxiously throughout the film or novel for the revelation of cyborg identity? How will the separate parts be combined? What signs will serve to mark its human nature? How are these mechanically animated creations still human? Every cyborg image implicitly defines the meaning of the terms "human" and "artificial."

Thus cyborgs fascinate us by technologically refashioning human difference. It is in this sense that cyborgs disrupt notions of otherness. The notion of human relies upon an understanding of non-human, just as the notion of artificial implies an understanding of natural. In the history of human supremacy, that which is non-human is understood as the other, that which is mechanical is understood as artificial. Cyborgs, as simultaneously human and mechanical, complicate these ancient oppositions. The preservation of human difference in a technological world is fraught with tension as the distinctions between artificiality and authenticity become blurred.

The film *The Terminator* (James Cameron, 1984) presents one of the most familiar and frightening visions of cyborg characterization. Arnold Schwarzenegger portrays a cyborg killing machine – a man–machine hybrid from one possible post-nuclear war future in which machines, outraged by human incompetence, set out to annihilate the remnants of humanity. Sent to earth in human flesh, he deftly outfits himself with weapons and leathers. As his battle with humans wages on, his flesh burns away, and he is reborn out of the flames as pure machine, pure technological will to murder. The film works to represent the Terminator's transformation from remotely human to fully machine.

Peter Weller, as *RoboCop* (Verhoeven, 1987) is also cinematically transformed, this time from fully human to soulful machine. Brutally murdered in the line of duty, Weller's remains are reconstructed as the organic part of a cyborg law enforcement machine. Robocop fights on the side of good, yet is unable to override a hardwired directive which disables him at the moment of confrontation with the film's main antagonist.

The Terminator and RoboCop represent two sides of the same type of man–machine hybrid. Neither cyborg can override its programmed directives; they both represent the extreme of technological rationality. Given this, is their male gender surprising? Stereotypically, rationality is associated with masculinity. In this, cyborgs and men are compatible images which mutually support cultural associations among masculinity, rationality, technology and science.

Yet, when we further investigate cultural images of cyborgs, we find that cyborgs aren't always male. Mary Ann Doane traces the ancestry of female cyborg images to a novel by Villiers de l'Isle-Adam, *L'Eve future* (*Tomorrow's Eve*), written in 1886. "In this novel, Thomas Edison, the master scientist and entrepreneur of mechanical reproduction . . . is the inventor of the perfect mechanical woman, an android whose difference from the original human model is imperceptible" [1990]. This quest for the "perfect mechanical woman" persists as a theme in contemporary science fiction. Such is the science project of two highschool boys in the film, *Weird Science* (Hughes, 1985).

Rachel, the melancholy replicant from *Blade Runner* (Ridley Scott, 1982), is a recent female cyborg whose constructed "nature" supposedly contradicts the myth of natural female identity. Not only is her body genetically constructed, she's been given memory implants borrowed from a "real" woman. Rachel thinks she's human – she has memories of a mother, piano lessons, the birth of spider babies. It's not these bits and pieces of stolen memories that make Rachel an enigma for Deckard (the blade runner whose job is to "retire" replicants). It's her emotions. Rachel's well-worn pout and vulnerable sexuality shakes Deckard's certainty about her replicant nature. As the object of Deckard's visual and sexual desire, Rachel symbolically reasserts the social and political position of woman as object of man's consumption.

Symbolizing a different notion of cyborgian identity, that of spaceship–human coupling, is Anne McCaffrey's protagonist in her science fiction novel, *The Ship That Sang* [1969]. Helva XH–83 was "born a thing with twisted limbs, and is destined to be a guiding mechanism for a spaceship." Helva is a "shell-person, an encapsulated brain who's kept physically small by pituitary manipulation" (King, 1984). Among her more benevolent adventures, Helva and her human mobile partner – her "Brawn" – rescue cloistered colonists from a planet soon to be scorched by an unstable sun and, at another time, carry 100,000 embryos to a sparsely populated off-world planet. Certainly appropriate missions for a female-gendered spaceship.

Mary Ann Doane [1990] writes about the relationship between technology, representation and the feminine. She argues that

> [a]lthough it is certainly true that in the case of some contemporary science-fiction writers – particularly feminist authors – technology makes possible the destabilization of sexual identity as a category, there has also been a curious but fairly insistent history of representations of technology which work to fortify – sometimes desperately – conventional understandings of the feminine. A certain anxiety concerning the technological is often allayed by a displacement of this anxiety onto the figure of the woman or the area [sic] of the feminine.

Doane suggests that it is notions of human reproduction that are most contested within science fiction. The extent to which the mystery and dangers of human replication persist as a theme in contemporary science fiction suggests the depth of cultural anxiety about species reproduction. If this is indeed the case, then what we find in supposedly visionary science fiction is but a revamped reflection of ancient beliefs about the proper role and function of women in society and history.

These female-gendered cyborgs inhabit traditional feminine roles – as object of man's desire and his helpmate in distress. In this way, female cyborgs are as much stereotypically endowed with feminine traits as male cyborgs are with masculine traits. Cyborg images reproduce cultural gender stereotypes. I want to argue, however, that female cyborg images do *more* to challenge the opposition between human and machine than do male cyborgs because femininity is culturally imagined as less compatible with technology than is masculinity. This is to say that because our cultural imagination aligns masculinity and rationality with technology and science, male gendered cyborgs fail to radically challenge the distinction between human and machine. Female cyborgs, on the other hand, are culturally coded as emotional, sexual, and often, naturally maternal. It is these very characteristics which more radically challenge the notion of an organic–mechanical hybrid. Female cyborgs embody cultural contradictions which strain the technological imagination. Technology isn't feminine, and femininity isn't rational.

Female cyborgs, while challenging the relationship between femaleness and technology, perpetuate oppressive gender stereotypes. This reading of female cyborgs raises interesting feminist questions. Can the "feminine" essentialism of fictional cyborgs be transformed into a non-essential image for contemporary women? Is there any way that the cyborg image could be used strategically to intervene in feminist theory? There are basically two ways to begin to answer these questions. One way is to construct a utopian vision of the possibilities of a Helva XH–384, in which technology emancipates woman from her corporeal body. Feminism's skepticism about technology and science would be challenged to see the potentially liberating effects of technology. A second possibility involves the construction of an ideological critique of the cyborg image as it has been produced by partriarchal culture. This approach might begin by asking how the cyborg image represents women. From here we might then invert the question, to ask, how do women represent cyborgs? This is to suggest, with an ironic twist, that woman's development is not separate from technological development, but has, in fact, displayed a similar trajectory. Her history illustrates several points of intersection with technology, points at which she has been forced to become like the cyborg, a hybrid creature of fiction and reality. Cyborgs become like woman in that cyborg images represent something "unknown" and perhaps, "unknowable" in our popular imagination. To this very end, Donna Haraway's (1985) article, "A Manifesto for Cyborgs: Science, Technology, and Socialist Feminism in the 1980s" [reading 1.3 in this volume] outlines the beginnings of such a strategic intervention in contemporary feminist theory.

Reading cyborgs

The cyborg image can be read in two ways: as a coupling between a human being and an electronic or mechanical apparatus or, as Haraway (1985) suggests, as the identity of organisms embedded in a cybernetic information system.[1] In the first sense, the coupling between human and machine is located within the body itself – the boundary between the body and machine is surgically redrawn. In Haraway's argument, the boundaries between the body and technology (primarily communication technology) are socially inscribed, at once indistinct and arbitrary. These are the cyborgs that have become important in the non-fictional discourse of communications, computer engineering, and bio-mechanical medicine.

Thus, for Haraway, cyborgs are interactive participants found at all points of information production and replication. Positioned within high-tech information management networks, they are constantly formatting, coding and decoding, up-loading and downloading information. Word processors, data programmers, and CRT operators, have become familiar civil service cyborgs.

But Haraway explicitly maps the identity of woman onto the image of the cyborg. Her "Manifesto" narrates an "ironic political myth" of cyborg identity, which, she argues, is the only possibility for woman-identity in the late 20th century. She argues that "woman" is no longer singular, but rather, a commodified, technological object whose unique human status is challenged by rapid technological transformations. Yet, woman's "unique human status" has never been very secure. I interpret Haraway's ironic choice of cyborg image as an attempt to show how feminism could rethink its political and intellectual relationship to technology and science. Although feminism often remains skeptical of the patriarchal promise of technological development, women need to develop ways of reading and responding to technology that resist opposing it to an unproblematic "nature."

Haraway's notion of the cyborg foregrounds the ambiguous constitution of the body and subjectivity – predicated on the blurred boundaries between organism and machine, the individual and the technological, the fictive and the real. By challenging these and other culturally entrenched binarisms, the image of the cyborg becomes compatible with, and maybe even useful for, feminist theory. Let me sketch out two examples in which the cyborg image, as a postmodern icon, works well to capture some of the more radical insights of feminist scholarship: the social construction of subjectivity and the cultural crafting of physical bodies.

Postmodern identity: the social construction of subjectivity

The cyborg is a social construction – "a creature of social reality as well as a creature of fiction" (Haraway, 1985: 65) – and this illuminates a crucial dimension of postmodern identity: the fragmentation of subjectivity. Both Woman and Cyborg are simultaneously symbolically and biologically produced and reproduced through social interactions. The "self" is one interactional product; the body is another. Haraway argues that the international women's movements have, in fact, as much constructed "women's experience" as they have uncovered or discovered experience as a creative collective object. Diverse feminisms grapple with the multiple dimensions of female identity as simultaneously a matter of ideology (a social-symbolic construction) and of materiality (a physical body). Not wanting to fall back on an essentialist or elitist definition of woman, feminist perspectives struggle to affirm difference while building coalitions. If the cyborg appears as the embodied image of both an ideological (human) identity and material (technological) reality, then woman's identity, as much socially and psychologically constructed as it is physiologically and biologically determined, reveals her cyborg likeness.

Mainstream postmodern theory calls for a re-thinking of subjectivity; yet, it often finds itself, in practice, caught between contradictory desires. Its insistence on the non-essentiality of identity ultimately confronts an implicit, rhetorical urge to catalog all things by their "true" names. The apparent loss of a subjectivity that at least at one time appeared to have been unified and coherent often provokes curious commentary on the part of these theorists. Jean Baudrillard (1983) celebrates the death of authentic subjectivity and with it, the collapse of the real and the advent of the hyperreal. Fredric Jameson (1984) describes "schizophrenia" as the cultural dominant of late capitalism. These critics ask, rhetorically and maybe sarcastically, how do we decode the "I" if it is no longer unitarily referential?

Throughout the history of the women's movement, feminist scholars have wrestled with this paradox of identity. Philosophically posed as a critique of individualism, this strand of feminist thought shows up in de Beauvoir's early work (1959) and is carried through in Cora Kaplan's (1986: 226) thinking on subjectivity.

[W]ithin contemporary western culture the act of writing and the romantic ideologies of individual agency and power are tightly bound together, although that which is written frequently resists and exposes this unity of the self as ideology. At both the psychic and social level, always intertwined, women's subordinate place within culture makes them less able to embrace or be held by romantic individualism with all its pleasures and dangers. The instability of "femininity" as female identity is a specific instability, pointing to the fractured and fluctuant condition of all consciously held identity, the impossibility of a will-full, unified and cohered subject.

Like Kaplan, Haraway reminds us of a critical feminist insight: that women are traditionally self-characterized by diversity and fragmented identities, and this has greatly influenced the possibility of unified political action.[2] For Haraway (1985: 82) "the *cyborg* is a kind of disassembled and reassembled, post-modern collective and personal self . . . [yet] this is the self that feminists must code." In an age of coalition, it is of utmost importance for feminists to learn how to construct an "I" as part of a "we," without setting "us" against "them."

Postmodern prostheses: the cultural crafting of physical bodies

Cyborg bodies pump iron – physically fit, yet unnaturally crafted, they are hyper-built. A cyborg body, as Bateson (1969: 319) might argue, "is not bounded by the skin but includes all external pathways along which information can travel." The high-tech image of the cyborg reminds us to question the assumed naturalness of the body and its function as a marker of difference.

Robert Jarvik, the physician for whom the Jarvik 7 artificial heart is named, is the president of a company called Symbion – a name combining *symbiosis* and *bionic* – whose goal is to interface the body and technology. By 1990 we may see the availability of an electronic retina; a prototype developed in Japan uses a computer chip covered with layers of silicon sensors. The U.S. Food and Drug Administration has already approved the commercial use of an artificial ligament – one made from Gore-Tex, a common sportswear material.[3] These bio-medical events subtly register the collapse of the distance between the present and a science fictional future in which bionic bodies are commonplace.

Feminist theorists have traditionally asserted that female bodies are not one-dimensional surfaces which bear easy-to-read meanings. Indeed, feminist writers honor the body as the site of the production and reproduction of fragmented identities and affinities – in short, the site of material practice. They identify the place and meanings of the female body in mass culture, sometimes to reassert the importance of female sexuality (for example, Audre Lorde, 1978); sometimes to propose a radically new form of cultural production – writing the body, or the body as instrument;[4] and sometimes to articulate "the site for the coming together of feminist theory and politics" (Brown and Adams, 1979: 35).

The body and its iconography are a location for inscribing differences among women – differences that raise feminist consciousness by challenging its homogeneity. Sander Gilman (1985) reads medical icons of black bodies and white bodies to reveal the differential construction of female sexuality in late nineteenth-century culture. Anne Finger (1986) challenges other feminists to examine their attitudes toward physical disabilities, especially at the point of building theories which rely on the implicit assumption of a fully abled body. As she argues (Finger, 1986: 295), "disability is largely a social construct," one which potentiates the impact of patriarchal domination.[5]

Similar issues become apparent when Paula Treichler (1987) examines the construction of the "AIDS Victim" in bio-medical discourse. Persons with AIDS are discursively constructed as victimized, pitiful, valiant, contagious, marked by god's wrath, marginalized. In a similar way the identity of the AIDS virus manifests itself at the center of a fierce signification battle. Descriptions of the workings of the AIDS virus reveal an identity changing, code rewriting process. The virus literally rewrites the genetic material of healthy host cells in such a way that the mechanism for distinguishing between self (healthy cells) and other (AIDS virus or other viruses) is obliterated. The AIDS virus works by confusing identity and blurring boundaries.

The physical body has traditionally been a reliable ground for establishing identity – consider the call for chromosome testing at the 1972 Olympic Games. But bionic bodies defy the natural-ness of physical identity. One of the most seemingly self-evident characteristics of physical bodies is their fundamentally organic composition. Yet, bionic body recrafting already allows people to change their physical sexual characteristics. As these medical procedures become more advanced and sexual body parts technologically refashioned, a visual reading of gender, or any other cultural marker of identity, off the surface of the body will be hopelessly confounded.

Writing feminism

I want to return to a consideration of Haraway's essay which places the Cyborg image in front of the feminist imagination. The constructedness of cyborg subjectivity and bodies reminds us that we ourselves are constructed as we actively participate in constructing the objects/subjects of our research. More important to remember is how people with AIDS, women of color, disabled women, and women generally have been marked by their constructed otherness. We study "them," fixing their identities, thereby constructing a system for creating difference which is oppressive and exploitative.

Andreas Huyssen (1984) and other postmodernists claim that the crisis of modernism pivots on this problematic of otherness. In this way, cyborgs offer a particularly appropriate emblem, not only of postmodern identity, but – specifically – of woman's identity. Cyborg identity is predicated on transgressed boundaries. They fascinate us because they are not like us, and yet just like us. Formed through a radical disruption of other-ness, cyborg identity foregrounds the constructedness of otherness. Cyborgs alert us to the ways culture and discourse depend upon notions of "the other" that are arbitrary and binary, and also shifting and unstable. Who or what gets constructed as other becomes a site for the cultural contestation of meaning within feminist politics.

My criticism of Haraway's choice of image is that she fails to consider how the cyborg has already been fashioned in our cultural imagination. It is difficult to determine if Haraway chooses the cyborg image because she believes that women are inherently cyborgian, or because the image is useful and potentially liberating. As I've described above, cyborg images reproduce limiting, not liberating, gender stereotypes. Focusing on the cyborg image in hopes of unearthing an icon of utopian thought does a great disservice to feminism. Feminism doesn't need another utopian vision. Its radical potential will not be realized through the appropriation of technological and scientific discourses to a feminist or female agenda.

But to the extent that Haraway's ironic vision gives us pause to reflect on ways in which, historically, women have experienced fragmented subjectivities and identities and have overcome physical proscriptions, Haraway's cyborg manifesto is thought-fully invigorating. What we have here is a struggle of interpretations. The utopian reading of cyborgs makes them a symbol for integrating the new with the old in such a way that the cyborg becomes a symbol of feminism's belief in a transcendental vision. The critical vision assembles woman as cyborg from bits and pieces of women's experiences that have already been out there, a reassemblage that sustains a critical perspective of technological/scientific/cybernetic discourse. Irony is a certain kind of writing that draws attention to the difference between what is apparently there and what is really there, a kind of writing that purposefully draws attention to the tension between appearances and interpretations.

Interpretation does not mean cultural analysis with the critic acting as mediator for an uninformed audience. Cyborg images are already interpretations. My paper is yet another. I create another reassemblage by selecting out certain images and not others. My interpretation of cyborg images seeks to show how these images claim to render unstable the problematic combination of human and machine, yet in effect fail to do so. Donna Haraway claims that cyborgs stimulate the feminist imagination by rendering ambiguous the human/machine construct. My reading shows that the dominant representation of cyborgs reinserts us into dominant ideology by reaffirming bourgeois notions of human, machine and femininity. In fact, what look like provocative notions of human identity, are not; they reassert a distinct identity between machine and human in a post-technological world.

Although feminists have long understood that language is not neutral, we must constantly remind ourselves that images, metaphors, and theoretical language itself, are also sites of cultural and political contestation. The meaning of an image is never easily won. Interpretation, then, becomes a site of feminist politics in this post-modern age. Its challenge is to negotiate between absolute relativism (or pluralism) on the one hand, and an overdetermined set of partial truths on the other.

The challenge remains to think about how we can study and write about identity in such a way that the on-going production of identities is honored and recognized as a potential source of feminist empowerment in our postmodern era. The cinematic imaging of cybors might suggest new visions of unstable identity, but often do so by upholding gender stereotypes. To this end, we need to search for cyborg images which work to disrupt stable oppositions.

Our popular/hegemonic cultural logic doesn't easily allow for these kinds of blurred distinctions. It polarizes cyborg identity into just or evil, male or female, human or machine, victim or other. I want to resist this cultural sensibility which forces us to process cyborgs (and women) – to strip them of their ambiguous identity. I want to reclaim the cyborg image as a cultural image and possible proto-type for a feminist re-conceptualization of personal and political identity which embraces, and perhaps, celebrates, the diversity of woman's identity. There is no *essential* unity to return to which would uncover the meaning/nature/universal properties of woman, feminine identity, lesbian identity, black identity, or even cyborg identity. A return to origins, the pastoral, or "the garden" is no longer possible. As Susan Suleiman (1985: 24) further describes, "the dream, then, is to get beyond not only the number one – the number that determines unity – but also beyond the number two, which determines difference, antagonisms, and exchange conceived of as merely the coming together of opposites." Identity can only be studied as it shifts, skips, and stutters in different utterances or evocations.

Cyborg ethnography raises fundamental questions about the writing of cultural interpretation. Terms such as gender, self, human, writing, and communication are fractured in the cyborg cosmology; the mythical origins or essences of human-ness and of culture have been dispersed; like Reese, the human hero from the future in *The Terminator*, we can never go home again. Any interpretive practice predicated upon a return to unity, centrality, or coherence will, I think, have a difficult time coming to terms with culture as it is reworked by technological change. Cyborgs, however, open up productive ways of thinking about subjectivity, gender, and the materiality of a physical body. Those fundamental terms and binarisms which the cyborg challenges by rendering them hopelessly ambiguous are also part of a system of knowledge and power by which all of us have been oppressed. That they are now eroded or in crisis should not necessarily be cause for remorse. For if the epistemology of the centralized, rational, human-male-self runs into difficulty "reading" the cyborg, there is another mode of thought and struggle which has long labored to move beyond the central, the rational, the dominant perspective. That epistemology, that practice, that struggle – is feminism.

Acknowledgments

The author would like to thank Michael Greer, Karen Ford and Lawrence Grossberg for their comments on earlier drafts of this paper.

Notes

1 Gregory Bateson (1972) describes a cybernetic system as an information transmitting network of connections between receivers' nodes. Although he does consider human culture to be one such cybernetic system – the intent of his analysis is to enhance the development of an orderly approach to scientific cultural investigation – he did not go so far as to "name" the human members/participants of such a system.

2 "The historical identity of U.S. women of color marks out a self-consciously constructed space that does not and cannot affirm the capacity to act on the basis of natural identification, but only on the basis of conscious coalition, of affinity, of political kinship" (Haraway, 1985: 73).

3 Jarvik expresses his hope for the future of artificial-organ technology in a Dialogue Forum with Pierre Galletti, creator of an artificial pancreas, in *Omni* magazine, October, 1986. The development of the electronic retina was also reported in *Omni* magazine, June, 1987. The artificial ligament made from Gore-Tex will be used to

replace the anterior cruciate of the knee, the ligament often torn by young athletes. (Reported in *Muscle and Fitness*, April, 1987.)

4   Laurie Anderson uses her body to provide various percussion parts of several songs in *Home of the Brave* (1986). In addition, her jerky, marionette-like movements present the body as ideogram – positioning her body to resemble Chinese characters. Thus she works to collapse the distance between body and "the text."

5   Finger (1985: 295) articulates the social circumstances of disability. "When we start looking at disability socially, we see not only the medically defined conditions that I have described but the social and economic circumstances that limit the lives of disabled people. We look, for instance, at the fact that white disabled women earn 24 cents for every dollar that comparably qualified nondisabled men earn; for black disabled women, the figure is 12 cents."

References

Balsamo, Anne. 1987. "Unwrapping the Postmodern: A Feminist Glance." *Journal of Communication Inquiry* 11, 1: 64–72.

Bateson, Gregory. 1972. *Steps to an Ecology of Mind*. New York: Ballantine Books.

Baudrillard. 1983.

Brown, Beverley and Adams, Parveen. 1979. "The Feminine Body and Feminist Politics." *m/f* 3: 35–50.

Doane, Mary Ann. [1990] "Technology, Representation, and the Feminine: Science Fictions" [presented in this volume; see reading 2.2].

Finger, Anne. 1985. "Claiming All of our Bodies: Reproductive Rights and Disability." In Susan Browne, Debra Donnors, and Nancy Stern, eds., *With the Power of Each Breath: A Disabled Women's Anthology*. Pittsburg, PA: Cleis Press.

Gilman, Sander. 1985. "Black Bodies, White Bodies: Toward an Iconography of Female Sexuality in Late Nineteenth-Century Art, Medicine, and Literature." *Critical Inquiry* 12: 205–242.

Haraway, Donna. 1985. "A Manifesto for Cyborgs: Science, Technology, and Socialist Feminism in the 1980s." *Socialist Review* 80, March–April: 65–108.

Huyssen, Andreas. 1984. "Mapping the Postmodern." *New German Critique*, 33: 5–52.

Jameson, Fredric. 1984. "Postmodernism, or the Cultural Logic of Late Capitalism." *New Left Review* vol. 146: 55–92.

Kaplan, Cora. 1986. *Sea Changes: Culture and Feminism*. London: Verso.

King, Betty. 1984. *Women of the Future: The Female Main Character in Science Fiction*. London: The Scarecrow Press.

Lorde, Audre. 1978. *Uses of the Erotic: The Erotic as Power*. Trumansburg, NY: Out & Out Books.

McCaffrey, Anne. 1969. *The Ship That Sang*. New York: Ballantine Books.

Suleiman, Susan Rubin, ed. 1986. *The Female Body in Western Culture*. Cambridge, MA: Harvard University Press.

Treichler, Paula A. 1987. "Aids, Homophobia, and Biomedical Discourse: An Epidemic of Signification." *Cultural Studies* vol. 1: 263–305.

PART THREE

Representing reproduction: reproducing representation

Introduction to Part Three

REPRODUCTIVE TECHNOLOGIES OFFER a particular illustration of the interrelationship between gender, technoscience and representation. Debates about reproductive technologies involve deeply held cultural assumptions about gender roles, the sexual division of labour, parenthood and technological and scientific progress. This section extends earlier discussions of feminist cultural analyses of science and technology which focus upon both the embodiment of knowledge and the specific context of its production. These critiques bring together local, situated knowledge and wider political concerns about power and inequality. In this section we focus on a particular set of categories produced through discourses on reproductive technologies, which offer a specific engagement with gender, technoscience and representation in relation to the "natural".

What is included in the technoscience of reproduction? Technologies which are designed to intervene in the process of human reproduction can be seen as falling into distinct categories. Although this is a field where there are constant developments and changes, these can usefully be seen as according with the four offered by Michelle Stanworth in 1987.

> the first and most familiar group includes those concerned with fertility control – with preventing conception, frustrating implantation of an embryo, or terminating pregnancy . . .

> A second group . . . is concerned with the "management" of labour and childbirth . . . a range of technologies for monitoring and controlling the progress of labour and delivery – instruments to assist delivery, caesarean sections, ways of inducing labour, episiotomies, techniques for measuring foetal heart-rate and movement . . .

[Thirdly] the use of more elaborate technologies and screening procedures for monitoring foetal development in the early stages of pregnancy . . . ultra-sound. The focus is also upon perfecting new techniques for neonatal care and upon research that might eventually enable the modification of inborn 'defects' . . .

The fourth . . . are the conceptive technologies, directed to the promotion of pregnancy through techniques for overcoming or bypassing infertility . . . in vitro fertilization . . . the development of new applications – through combination with, for example, egg donation, embryo donation, low temperature storage of gametes and embryos or surrogacy.

(1987: 10–11)

Motherhood might seem to be both embodied and natural, a biological fact of nature, into which technologies might intervene, but still reducible to the biological and the natural. Reproductive technologies offer a focus on motherhood and the mother–child relationship which includes the social and cultural relations which inform our understanding of motherhood: of good and bad mothers, of who is allowed to be a mother and who is not, who is allowed to speak and who has the power to make decisions. Once these questions are posed it becomes clear that reproductive technologies and motherhood (or fatherhood) are constructed within social, cultural, ethical and religious as well as biological and scientific discourses. Feminist critiques put motherhood "into discourse" and problematize the relationship between motherhood and femininity. Luce Irigaray has argued that in male systems of representation and discourse, the (male) subject prefers to see women as the maternal-feminine rather than as a woman. In focusing on how the maternal-feminine has been historically reproduced, it is possible for women to find new ways of marking difference and of challenging the patriarchal sublimation of "woman" into mother. This has involved constructing women as "other", that is, as "other" to men and hence, as in Lacanian psychoanalytic theory, "not men". Irigaray posits an alternative notion of difference where women could be "other", not "other of the same", but as self-defined women whose difference, or otherness, would be given symbolic and social representation. Men would be other to women and women would be other to men.

Irigaray's work has stressed the importance of the absence of motherhood and of the mother/daughter relationship from culture and the implications of what she calls the "unacknowledged mother" from western systems of representation. She suggests that we have reached a moment in history when this question of

the domination of fathers can no longer be avoided . . . Contraception and abortion raise the question of the meaning of motherhood, and women (notably because of their entry into and their encounters within the circuits of production) are looking for their sexual identity and are beginning to emerge from silence and anonymity.

(Irigaray, quoted in Whitford, 1991: 36)

For Irigaray a focus on motherhood is a means of addressing and of understanding not just maternal identities but women's identities.

The silence which has existed about motherhood illustrates the way motherhood has been repressed within Western culture; it is "the dark continent *par excellence* [which] remains in the shadows of our culture; it is its night and its hell" (ibid.: 35). Irigaray argues that Western culture is not based on patricide as Freud argued in *Totem and Taboo*, but on matricide. "All of Western culture rests on the murder of the mother" (Irigaray 1981: 81). It is this silence that has led to some of the most atrocious and primitive fantasies about motherhood, characteristic of some ancient and contemporary mythologies, not the least those that figure in psychoanalytic thought. Such ideas, including the archaic projections of the woman as devouring monster who threatens madness and death, are symptomatic of the unanalysed hatred from which women as a group suffer culturally. The silence about motherhood, she argues, has to be brought out of the shadows and into representation.

The application of reproductive technologies can be seen as making possible monstrosity and new "monster mothers". Reproductive technologies permit new formulations of monstrosity that both underpin and go beyond media hyperbole, as illustrated by media coverage of "designer babies", "virgin mother" and "selfish older mothers". The 60-year-old grandmother who defies the constraints of nature and immodestly demands "unnatural" motherhood, and women who freeze eggs or embryos for use at a later date, are defined as unnatural for seeking to control their own fertility and maternity. In each of these instances the "bad" or even monstrous mother is constructed in relation to the "good" or normal "natural" mother. The same mother might in fact be constructed as both altruistic, as in the case of the surrogate mother who has a baby for her sister, or monstrous, when the mother requests payment for surrogacy.

As Judy Wajcman argues,

> nowhere is the relationship between gender and technology more vigorously contested than in the sphere of human reproduction. Women are the bearers, and in most societies the primary nurturers of children. This means that reproductive technologies are of particular significance to them. Birth control has been a major issue for all movements of women's equality and much feminist scholarship has been devoted to uncovering women's struggle throughout history against the appropriation of medical knowledge and practice by men.
>
> (1991: 54)

She also argues that "technology is more than a set of physical objects and artefacts. It also fundamentally embodies a culture or set of social relations made up of certain sets of knowledge, beliefs, discourses and practices" (1991: 149). The readings which follow in part 3 illustrate the gendered aspects of reproductive technologies and the ways in which gender identities, and especially maternal identities, are socially and culturally reproduced as part of new technological formations.

An investigation of reproductive technologies not only illustrates the importance of culture through representational and symbolic systems in constructing categories of meaning, but also poses significant questions about the power relations that are involved. Such technologies are shaped by the operation of gender interests and may reinforce gendered patterns of power and authority. However they may also subvert traditional hierarchies; they may offer opportunities for the reconstruction of gender relations and new possibilities especially for women. It is in this area perhaps more than any other, Wajcman argues, that "major technological advances are seen as having directly transformed women's lives for the better" (1991: 55). It is the question of power and debates about the oppressive or liberatory potential of reproductive technologies that have been of most concern for feminists.

The terrain of reproductive technologies is one characterized by contestation. Reproduction is a site of dispute involving heated political, ethical and legal dispute.

> [A] conflict of discourses necessarily characterizes the arena of reproductive technology where nothing is stable: scientific "information", popular struggles both feminist and anti-feminist, and the shifting meaning of motherhood and womanhood for individuals with diverse ethnic, racial, religious, sexual and migration histories are all under negotiation.
>
> (Rapp, quoted in Ginsberg and Lowenhaupt, 1990: 30)

Since the 1980s some feminist approaches have focused on the particular importance of visualization technologies. One of the most important contributions to these approaches has been that of Rosalind Petchesky whose paper "Foetal Images: The Power of Visual Culture in the Politics of Reproduction" is the first reading in part 3. Petchesky draws on semiotic theory and a feminist discursive approach to deconstruct the presentation of apparently objective, medical truths. She deploys Barthes's understanding of connotation, which involves a second level of meaning beyond the more simple description of denotation, where meanings are produced through association and links with other aspects of culture. She takes up Barthes's critique of the photographic message where he argues that the apparently transparent message of photography is itself encoded through the processes that are involved in the production of meanings through the representation of images. Her work illustrates the "privileging of the visual", and the prevalence of the male gaze. This is based on John Berger's claim that "men act and women appear. Men look at women. Women watch themselves being looked at" (1972: 47). Petchesky develops a feminist critique, which shows that masculine control over reproduction through the politics of representation operates so that obstetric techniques of visualization disrupt the definitions of the body.

Petchesky's critique is located within the context of the debate about abortion and centres on representations of the foetus and the mother's body using the particular example, *The Silent Scream*, a film used by US anti-abortion campaigners. It is the visualizing technologies that facilitate this representation of the foetus. Women may be custodians of the image, but the mother's body is absent in the representation of the seemingly disembodied foetus, floating in space, suggesting an independent person, capable of separate existence. This counters the symbiotic relationship between mother and child, which was a feature of earlier, non-visual experiences based on feeling rather than seeing. Petchesky develops the notion of "foetal personhood" whereby the foetus is constructed as a separate individual in its own right. Foetal personhood is constructed through the technology that facilitates the representation of an embryo inside the womb and the signification of mother and foetus as independent. The independent individuality of the foetus is socially constructed as a category through biological discourse.

This process relies also on the individuality of the scientific expert and the scientific claim to objective truth. The very term "individual" describes someone who cannot be divided. Donna Haraway has argued that this individual can only be used to represent men, because the process of one individual becoming two through a women's pregnancy would appear to be the antithesis of individuality. Haraway argues that this is why "women have had so much trouble counting as individuals in modern Western discourses. Their personal, bounded individuality is compromised by their bodies' troubling talent for making other bodies, whose individuality can take precedence over their own" (1988: 39).

Through an exploration of some of the processes involved in the reproduction of these images, Petchesky suggests that what appears to be a "message without a code" is in fact grounded in historical and cultural meaning; it is historically specific rather than universal and objective. Whilst meanings are privileged in the construction of knowledge, here Petchesky does not deny or obscure the positive feelings that many pregnant women have towards ultrasound scanning. For example, women want a visual representation of the foetus and feel reassured by the technology that makes this possible. It is not simply a case of the technology privileging patriarchy. In this sense Petchesky is adopting two different approaches, which have been identified within feminist critiques. In the first part of the reading she adopts a more radical feminist view, which focuses on patriarchal power and in the latter part she acknowledges the benefits that could accrue from this technology for women. This point is made in reading 3.2, which is taken from *Bodies in Glass* by Deborah Lynn Steinberg, in which she critiques these two views, classified by Sandra Harding as feminist standpoint and feminist empiricist theories.

Steinberg uses Harding's discussion of these two contrasting feminist approaches to technoscience, which can be broadly categorized as stressing on the one hand the benefits of reproductive technologies for women and, on the other, their constraints. She accepts that, although such classifications may be useful in framing discussion, they tend to oversimplify and rarely reflect the specific positions of actual feminist texts. One of the problems Steinberg identifies with each of these approaches is their starting point of the category of the infertile woman, which sets the agenda for subsequent debate.

Steinberg uses examples of particular texts to explore some of the limitations of these positions and to offer some development of alternatives that avoid the distorted universalism of "all women" as a homogeneous category. This means shifting the emphasis from gender as the overarching focus, and permits a reclassification of women that can accommodate power and differences among women. Steinberg stresses the need to deconstruct some of the categories produced by the use and application of reproductive technologies. Steinberg argues for exploring the specificity of women's experience and addressing diversity and difference among women; first through the anti-essentialist critiques of postmodernism and then through a development of feminist standpoint theory as an *anti-oppressive* approach which, she argues, can encompass difference and a complex political agenda of change. Steinberg is concerned to retain and develop the feminist tradition of political action and the will for social change; for example, in challenging racism and the construction of categories of "normal" and "abnormal" families that informs what can be seen as the eugenic screening of some IVF practices.

The tension between positive and negative approaches to reproductive technology is also addressed by Farquhar in her book *The Other Machine* (1996), in which she recategorizes the main alternatives within feminism and offers a critique of what she classifies as fundamentalism and liberalism. The title of her book revokes an earlier work by Gena Corea entitled *The Mother Machine*, which adopts what Farquhar would call a fundamentalist view associated with FINRAGE (Feminist International Network of Resistance to Reproductive and Genetic Engineering). This group argued in opposition to earlier (perhaps somewhat naively) optimistic views of reproductive technologies, such as that of Shulamith Firestone who advocated their use to "free women from the tyranny of reproduction" (1970). The group of radical feminists who formed this association in 1984 saw motherhood as the foundation of women's identity, and not only challenged the liberatory potential of reproductive technology but saw it as an extension of patriarchal control. The main source of this control was seen as the exploitation of women's bodies, defined as follows:

> the dominant mode of control is changing hands from the individual male through marriage to men as a social category through science and technology . . . [T]he locus of control and struggle is shifting from sexuality to reproduction and childcare, "motherhood".
>
> (Hanmer, 1985: 103)

Farquhar argues in reading 3.3 against the oversimplification of such views and develops the idea of an anti-essentialist position on the liberatory potential of reproductive technologies for women. She seeks to challenge both essentialism and the binary opposition of the negative/positive polarization of some approaches. Her focus is more specifically on the discourses that represent what she calls ARTs (Assisted Reproductive Technologies). In this sense her approach is more directly Foucauldian, with its emphasis on the articulation of different discourses across the discursive fields of ethics, medicine, biology, psychology and law, as well as popular cultural representations. Such discourses involve the production of knowledge through associated ideas and sets of meaning. It is through an investigation of the internal construction of meanings and truth through discourse that an understanding of the operation of power can be achieved (Foucault, 1980: 118). In this sense technoscientific discourses and practices such as those involved in reproductive technologies *create and produce* knowledge rather than reveal or discover the truth.

What passes for truth at any one time is the product of particular discourses, which can themselves be interrogated to show how those meanings are produced – what words are used, what actions sanctioned, what practices promoted.

Farquhar deploys a Foucauldian analysis of power, which sees it as operating productively – that is, neither only negatively nor only positively. This conceptualization of power as diffuse and multifaceted allows for its operating in both enabling and constraining ways. Thus reproductive technologies can be both liberatory and controlling. Farquhar criticizes liberalism, into which she subsumes feminist empiricism. She argues that such liberalism employs mainly the voice of male liberal thought, supporting reproductive technologies as largely liberatory for women and not perceiving their limitations and constraints. Fundamentalist views also depend on a universal category "woman" in their opposition to ARTs, in which they are constrained historically and ultimately hindered by the essentialism on which they lie. The more liberatory potential of ARTs lies in their ability to extend the possibility of an identity of motherhood to those categories beyond the limited category of the childless, heterosexual, white, married woman, and to reconstruct "mothers" as "others". The "other mothers" here are resonant of Irigaray's positive re-articulation of women as other; as positively, empowered, self-defined women (to whom men are also "other"). Here "otherness" can be seen as another way of expressing difference and diversity *among* women. Farquhar suggests the use of the concept of the cyborg as deployed by Donna Haraway, which includes the possibility of new representations of the body. She stresses its strength as an imaginative resource. Farquhar argues for the possibility of the cyborg as a challenge to the rigidity of patriarchal hegemony through challenging fetishizing of blood ties. The interface of women and machine through ARTs offers more enabling possibilities – those previously excluded might also become mothers.

Anne Balsamo argues that because cyborg identity is predicated on transgressed boundaries, they are

> not like us and yet are just like us. Formed through a radical disruption of otherness cyborg identity foregrounds the constructedness of otherness. Cyborgs alert us to the way in which identity depends on notions of "the other" that are arbitrary, shifting, and ultimately unstable.
>
> (1997: 32–3)

Balsamo argues that, for Haraway, "communication technologies and bio technologies are the crucial tools recrafting our bodies" (1997: 82). As a cyborg – both discursive and material – the female body is the site at which we can witness the struggle between different systems of social order. This permits a reinvention of gender identity and in particular here maternal identity, as when 60-year-olds demand access to reproductive technologies and women transgress as well as submit. As Balsamo argues, the cyborg image "works well to foreground the radical materiality of the body, which cannot be written out of any feminist account" (1997: 40).

In the final reading in Part 3, Donna Haraway explores the possibility of constructing a politics which encompasses difference and refuses the constriction of existing debates about reproductive technologies. Haraway focuses on women's challenges to the constraints of abortion and reproductive technology debates using the metaphor of the speculum; the means of "being looked at". The term "speculum" is resonant of the title of Luce Irigaray's book *Speculum of the other Woman* (1985), in which the author uses the concept of the speculum, the device used by doctors to examine the interior cavities of the body, to challenge the negativity of psychoanalytic constructions of women. Irigaray uses the idea of this mirrored way of looking to argue that, in order to see what is specific to women, the mirror has to be one that can look inside. She implies that Lacan sees women as lacking because his view is only from the outside; for example, the speculum has been appropriated by the women's movement, as she illustrates in reading 3.4. Haraway argues for the deployment of reproductive technologies within the context of global movements for the freedom of differently situated women. She, like Petchesky, gives primacy to the visual representation that creates the foetus, especially "foetal personhood". Haraway addresses the representation of creation as a way of discussing debates about biotechnologies of reproduction, looking at a whole range of images from Michaelangelo's *Creation* to the sonogram of a foetus in the womb. Haraway seeks to incorporate and embody the material with technoscience and its representation and argues for its potential, especially reproductive technologies for women. Her analysis of the political power of the metaphors used by so-called objective science and other cultural formations, for describing and visualizing the changing boundaries of women's bodies, represents the political implications of debates about reproductive freedom and discourses over the problem of overpopulation.

Each of the readings in Part 3 engages with the political dimensions of reproductive technologies and the dilemmas posed for feminism, in both explaining such interventions and offering prescriptions about the extent to which they should be wholeheartedly espoused or rejected. The process of deconstruction is highlighted as crucial to explicating, and thus understanding, reproductive technologies, how they operate and their impact on women's lives. Critiques drawing on Foucauldian discourse analysis permit a detailed examination of the production of knowledge and power at diverse and different sites and levels. Combined with feminist commitment to political action, such historical, social and cultural specificity can be usefully employed, although such discursive critiques may appear to lack the conviction of feminist standpoint theories. Other approaches to deconstruction draw heavily on semiotic theories and highlight the significance of visualization technologies. Again feminist analyses must go beyond the description of deconstruction and demand some recognition of who is represented and by whom, as well as in whose interests. Feminism still requires some involvement with metanarratives of justice. Postmodern approaches offer the advantages of addressing the differences, especially among women, and of historically, socially and culturally specific detail. However, they lack the conviction of a feminist standpoint and earlier radical feminist critiques of reproductive technology, which are not only negative about the technologies but are positive about women's potential use of technoscience.

Reproductive technologies *foreground differences* in more recent feminist discussions – those among women as well as those between women and men.

Technoscience can challenge and disrupt understandings of difference and these challenges might become even more explosive; for example, in the way that cloning techniques have the potential for upsetting expectations about generational as well as gender differences. Cloning, were it permissible, might offer yet more alarming possibilities of cultural representations of monstrosity, where a woman might clone herself and even give birth to "herself" (until such time as the whole process of gestation might take place *in vitro*) and men might become completely redundant. This might provide an extension of late twentieth-century media hyperbole and moral panics about the redundancy of men through "virgin births" and lesbian mothers who choose artificial insemination, but cloning might offer a more extreme scenario. Fears of redundant men are paralleled for women by the threat of the science fiction fate of Margaret Atwood's handmaids, in the dystopian future portrayed in her novel *The Handmaid's Tale* (1986) where the handmaids are socialized to perform a reproductive service for the state and act as surrogate wombs, vehicles for reproduction without any other identity. Such aspects of technoscience present problems to be explored, as well as ever-changing re-articulations of questions and boundaries and means of interrogation.

The concept of the cyborg is particularly important in the context of reproductive technologies because it offers a most explicit merging of technoscience and the material body and has enormous potential for the transgression of boundaries – boundaries between women and men and across time and generation. However, the idea of the cyborg has been criticized both for its history and especially for its excessive emphasis on ectogenesis, which might seem to take away the category of gender and woman/motherhood altogether and to challenge motherhood as a signifier of difference between women and men. Reproductive technologies highlight differences between women and men as well as among women. It may also be that an emphasis on ectogenesis obscures the question of power as well as providing an imbalance in the relationship between body and machine in the formulation of the cyborg. But the possibilities for exploring the interrelationship between technoscience and the material body that the cyborg offers cannot be ignored by feminist critiques seeking to address the representations of reproduction and the meanings re-produced by reproductive technologies.

References

Atwood, M. (1986) *The Handmaid's Tale*, London: Virago.

Balsamo, A. (1997) *Technologies of the Gendered Body*, London: Duke University.

Berger, J. (1972) *Ways of Seeing*, London: BBC Books.

Farquhar, D. (1996) *The Other Machine*, London: Routledge.

Firestone, S. (1970) *The Dialectics of Sex*, London: Jonathan Cap.

Foucault, M. (1980) *The History of Sexuality*, Harmondsworth: Penguin.

Hanmer, J. (1985) "Transforming Consciousness: Women and the New Reproductive Technologies," in G. Corea and R. Klein (eds) *Man-Made Women: How New Reproductive Technologies Affect Women*, London: Hutchison.

Haraway, D. (1988) "The Biopolitics of Postmodern Bodies: Determinations of Self in Immune System Discourse", *Differences: A Journal of Cultural Studies* 1(1): 3–44.

—— (1997) "The Virtual Speculum in the New World Order", *Feminist Review* 55 (Spring): 22–72.

Irigaray, L. (1981) *Le Corps–à–corps avec la Mère*, Montreal: Editions de la Pleine Lune.

—— (1985) *Speculum of the Other Woman*, trans. Gillian C. Gill, Ithaca, NY: Cornell University Press.

—— (1991) "The Bodily Encounter with the Mother", trans. David Macey, in M. Whitford (ed.) *The Irigaray Reader*, Oxford, Basil Blackwell.

Rapp, R. (1990) "Constructing Amniocentesis: Maternal Discourses", in F. Ginsberg and F. Lowenhaupt (eds) *Uncertain Terms: Negotiating Gender in American Culture*, Boston: Beacon Press.

Stanworth, M. (1987) *Reproductive Technologies: Gender, Motherhood and Medicine*, Cambridge: Polity.

Steinberg, D. L. (1997) *Bodies in Glass*, Manchester: Manchester University Press.

Wajcman, J. (1991) *Feminism Confronts Technology*, Cambridge: Polity.

Whitford, M. (ed.) (1991) *The Irigaray Reader*, Oxford: Basil Blackwell.

Rosalind Pollack Petchesky

FOETAL IMAGES: THE POWER OF VISUAL CULTURE IN THE POLITICS OF REPRODUCTION

Now chimes the glass, a note of sweetest strength,
It clouds, it clears, my utmost hope it proves,
For there my longing eyes behold at length
A dapper form, that lives and breathes and moves.

(Goethe, *Faust*)

[Ultimately] the world of "being" can function to the exclusion of the mother. No need for mother – provided that there is something of the maternal: and it is the father then who acts as – is – the mother. Either the woman is passive; or she doesn't exist. What is left is unthinkable, unthought of. She does not enter into the oppositions, she is not coupled with the father (who is coupled with the son).

(Cixous, *Sorties*)

IN THE MID-1980s, with the United States Congress still deadlocked over the abortion issue and the Supreme Court having twice reaffirmed "a woman's right to choose,"[1] the political attack on abortion rights moved further into the terrain of mass culture and imagery. Not that the "pro-life movement" has abandoned conventional political arenas; rather, its defeats there have hardened its commitment to a more long-term ideological struggle over the symbolic meanings of foetuses, dead or alive.

Anti-abortionists in both the United States and Britain have long applied the principle that a picture of a dead foetus is worth a thousand words. Chaste silhouettes of the foetal form, or voyeuristic-necrophilist photographs of its remains, litter the background of any abortion talk. These still images float like spirits through the courtrooms, where lawyers argue that foetuses can claim tort liability; through the hospitals and clinics, where physicians welcome them as "patients"; and in front of all the abortion centers, legislative committees, bus terminals and other places that "right-to-lifers" haunt. The strategy of anti-abortionists to make foetal personhood a self-fulfilling prophecy by making the foetus a *public presence* addresses a visually oriented culture. Meanwhile, finding "positive" images and symbols of abortion hard to imagine, feminists and other pro-choice advocates have all too readily ceded the visual terrain.

Beginning with the 1984 presidential campaign, the neo-conservative Reagan administration and the Christian Right accelerated their use of television and video imagery to capture political discourse – and power (Erickson, 1985; Kalter, 1985). Along with a new series of "Ron and Nancy" commercials, the Revd Pat Robertson's "700 Club" (a kind of right-wing talk show), and a resurgence of "Good versus Evil" kiddie cartoons, American television and video viewers were bombarded with the newest "pro-life" propaganda piece, *The Silent Scream. The Silent Scream* marked a dramatic shift in the contest over abortion imagery. With formidable cunning, it translated the still and by now stale images of foetus as "baby" into real-time video, thus (1) giving those images an immediate interface with the electronic media; (2) transforming anti-abortion rhetoric from a mainly religious-mystical to a medical/technological mode; and (3) bringing the foetal image "to life". On major-network television the foetus rose to instant stardom, as *The Silent Scream* and its impresario, Dr Bernard Nathanson, were aired at least five different times in one month and one well-known reporter, holding up a foetus in a jar before ten million viewers, announced: "This thing being aborted, this potential person, sure *looks like* a baby!"

This statement is more than just propaganda; it encapsulates the "politics of style" dominating late capitalist culture, transforming "surface impressions" into the "whole message" (Ewen, 1984). The cult of appearances is not only the defining characteristic of national politics in the United States but is also nourished by the language and techniques of photo/video imagery. Aware of cultural trends, the current leadership of the anti-abortion movement has made a conscious strategic shift from religious discourses and authorities to medico-technical ones, in its effort to win over the courts, the legislatures and popular "hearts and minds". But the vehicle for this shift is not organized medicine directly but mass culture and its diffusion into reproductive technology through the video display terminal.

My interest in this chapter is to explore the overlapping boundaries between media spectacle and clinical experience when pregnancy becomes a moving picture. In what follows, I attempt to understand the cultural meanings and impact of images like those in *The Silent Scream*. Then I examine the effect of routine ultrasound imaging of the foetus on not only the larger cultural climate of reproductive politics but the experience and consciousness of pregnant women. Finally, I shall consider some implications of "foetal images" for feminist theory and practice.

Decoding *The Silent Scream*

Before dissecting its ideological message, I should perhaps describe *The Silent Scream* for readers who somehow missed it. The film's actual genesis seems to have been an article in the *New England Journal of Medicine* by a noted bioethicist and a physician, claiming that early foetal ultrasound tests resulted in "maternal bonding" and possibly "fewer abortions" (Fletcher and Evans, 1983). According to the authors, both affiliated with the National Institutes of Health, upon viewing an ultrasound image of the foetus "parents [i.e., pregnant women] probably will experience a shock of recognition that the fetus belongs to them" and will *more likely resolve "ambivalent" pregnancies "in favor of the fetus"*. Such "parental *recognition of the fetal form*", they wrote, "*is a fundamental element in the later parent–child bond*". Although based on two isolated cases, without controls or scientific experimentation, these assertions stimulated the imagination of Dr Bernard Nathanson and the National Right-to-Life Committee. The resulting video production was intended to reinforce the visual "bonding" theory at the level of the clinic by bringing the live foetal image into everyone's living-rooms. Distributed not only to television networks but to schools, churches, state and federal legislators and anyone (including the opposition) who wants to rent it for $15, the video cassette provides a mass commodity form for the "pro-life" message.

The Silent Scream purports to show a medical event, a real-time ultrasound imaging of a twelve-week-old foetus being aborted. What we see in fact is an image of an image of an image; or rather, three concentric frames: our television or video cassette recorder screen, which in turn frames the video screen of the filming studio, which in turn frames a shadowy, black-and-white, pulsating blob: the (alleged) foetus. Throughout, our response to this set of images is directed by the figure of Dr Bernard Nathanson – sober, bespectacled, leaning professorially against the desk – who functions as both medical expert and narrator to the drama. (Nathanson is in "real life" a practicing Ob-Gyn, ex-abortionist, and well-known anti-abortion crusader.) In fact, as the film unfolds, we quickly realize that there are *two* texts being presented here simultaneously – a medical text, largely visual, and a moral text, largely verbal and auditory. Our medical narrator appears on the screen and announces that what we are about to see comes to us courtesy of the "dazzling" new "science of fetology" which "exploded in the medical community" and now enables us to witness an abortion – "from the victim's vantage-point". At the same time we hear strains of organ music in the background, ominous, the kind we associate with impending doom. As Nathanson guides his pointer along the video screen, "explaining" the otherwise inscrutable movements of the image, the disjunction between the two texts becomes increasingly jarring. We *see* a recognizable apparatus of advanced medical technology, displaying a filmic image of vibrating light and shaded areas, interspersed with occasional scenes of an abortion clinic operating table (the only view of the pregnant woman we get). This action is moderated by someone who "looks like" the paternal-medical authority figure of the proverbial aspirin commercial. He occasionally interrupts the filmed events to show us clinical models of embryos and foetuses at various stages of development. Meanwhile, however, what we *hear* is more like a medieval morality play, spoken in standard anti-abortion rhetoric: The form on the screen, we are told, is "the living unborn child", "another human being indistinguishable from any of us". The suction cannula is "moving violently" toward "the child"; it is the "lethal weapon" that will "dismember, crush, destroy," "tear the child apart" until only "shards" are left. The foetus "*does sense aggression in its sanctuary*," attempts to "escape" (indicating more rapid movements on the screen), and finally "rears back its head" in "a silent scream" – all to a feverish pitch of musical accompaniment. In case we question the nearly total absence of a pregnant woman or of clinic personnel in this scenario, Nathanson also "informs" us that the woman who had this abortion was a "feminist" who, like the young doctor who performed it, has vowed "never again"; that women who get abortions are themselves exploited "victims" and "*castrated*"; that many abortion clinics are "*run by the mobs*". It is the verbal rhetoric, not of science, but of "Miami Vice".

Now, all of this raises important questions about what one means by "evidence", or "medical information", since the ultrasound image is presented as a *document* testifying that the foetus is "alive", is "human like you or me" and "senses pain". *The Silent Scream* has been sharply confronted on this level by panels of opposing medical experts, *New York Times* editorials, and a Planned Parenthood film. These show, for example, that at twelve weeks the foetus has no cerebral cortex to receive pain impulses; that no "scream" is possible without air in the lungs; that foetal movements at this stage are reflexive and without purpose; that the image of rapid frantic movement was undoubtedly caused by speeding up the film (camera tricks); that the size of the image we see on the screen, along with the model that is continually displayed in front of the screen, is nearly twice the size of a normal twelve-week foetus, etc. (Planned Parenthood Federation of America, n.d.). Yet this literal kind of rebuttal is not very useful in helping us to understand the ideological power the film has despite its visual distortions and verbal fraud.

When we locate *The Silent Scream* where it belongs, in the realm of cultural representation rather than medical evidence, we see that it embeds ultrasound imaging of pregnancy in a moving picture show. Its appearance as a medical document both obscures and reinforces a coded set of messages that work as political signs and moral injunctions. (As we shall see, because of the cultural and political context in which they occur, this may be true of ultrasound images of pregnancy in general.) The purpose of the film is obviously didactic: to persuade individual women to abstain from having abortions and officials and judges to force them to do so.

As with any visual image, *The Silent Scream* relies on our predisposition to "see" what it wants us to "see" because of a range of influences that come out of the particular culture and history in which we live. The aura of medical authority, the allure of technology, the cumulative impact of a decade of foetal images – on billboards, in shopping-centre malls, in science-fiction blockbusters like *2001: A Space Odyssey* – all rescue the film from utter absurdity; they make it credible. "The fetal form" itself has, within the larger culture, acquired a symbolic import that condenses within it a series of losses – from sexual innocence to compliant women to American imperial might. It is not the image of a baby at all but of a tiny man, a homunculus.

The most disturbing thing about how people receive *The Silent Scream*, and indeed all the dominant foetal imagery, is their apparent acceptance of the image itself as an accurate representation of a real foetus. The curled-up profile, with its enlarged head and fin-like arms, suspended in its balloon of amniotic fluid, is by now so familiar that not even most feminists question its authenticity (as opposed to its relevance). I went back to trace the earliest appearance of these photos in popular literature and found it in the June 1962 issue of *Look* (a major mass-circulation "picture magazine" of the period). It was a story publicizing a new book, *The First Nine Months of Life*, and it featured the now-standard sequel of pictures at one day, one week, forty-four days, seven weeks, etc. In every picture the foetus is solitary, dangling in the air (or in its sac) with nothing to connect it to any life-support system but "a clearly defined umbilical cord". In every caption it is called "the baby" and is referred to as "he" – until the birth, that is, when "he" turns out to be a girl. Nowhere is there any reference to the pregnant woman, except in a single photograph at the end showing the newborn baby lying next to the mother, both of them gazing off the page, allegedly at "the father". From their beginning, such photographs have represented the foetus as primary and autonomous, the woman as absent or peripheral.

Foetal imagery epitomizes the distortion inherent in all photographic images: their tendency to slice up reality into tiny bits wrenched out of real space and time. The origins of photography lie in late-nineteenth-century Europe's cult of science, itself a by-product of industrial capitalism. Its rise linked it inextricably with positivism, that flawed epistemology that sees "reality" as discrete bits of empirical data divorced from historical process or social relationships (Trachtenberg, 1980; Sontag, 1973: 22–3). Likewise, foetal imagery replicates the essential paradox of photographs whether moving or still, their "constitutive deception" as noted by post-modernist critics: the *appearance* of "objectivity", of capturing "literal reality." As Roland Barthes puts it (1982: 196), the "photographic message" appears to be "a message without a code". According to Barthes, the appearance of the photographic image as "a mechanical analogue of reality", without art or artifice, obscures the fact that that image is heavily constructed, or "coded"; it is grounded in a context of historical and cultural meanings.[2]

Yet the power of the visual apparatus' claim to be "an unreasoning machine" that produces "an unerring record" (the French word for "lens" is "*l'objectif*") remains deeply embedded in Western culture (Eastlake, 1980: 65–6; Berger, 1980: 48–50; Bazin, 1980: 241). This power derives from the peculiar capacity of photographic images to assume two distinct meanings, often simultaneously: an *empirical* (informational) and a *mythical* (or magical) meaning (Sekula, 1982: 106–8). Historically, photographic imagery has served not only the uses of *scientific rationality*, as in medical diagnostics and record-keeping; and the tools of *bureaucratic rationality*, in the political record-keeping and police surveillance of the state (Sekula, 1982: 94–5; Sontag, 1973: 5, 21). It has also, especially with the "democratization" of the hand-held camera and the advent of the family album, become a magical source of fetishes that can resurrect the dead or preserve lost love. And it has constructed the escape-fantasy of the movies. This older, symbolic and ritualistic (also religious?) function lies concealed within the more obvious rationalistic one.

The double text of *The Silent Scream*, noted earlier, recapitulates this historical paradox of photographic images: their simultaneous power as purveyors of fantasy and illusion yet also of "objectivist 'truth'" (Ewen and Ewen, 1982: 33). When Nathanson claims to be presenting an abortion "from the vantage-point of the [foetus]", the image's appearance of seamless movement through real time – *and* the technologic allure of the video box, connoting at once "advanced medicine" and "the news" – render his claim "true to life". Yet he also purveys a myth, for the foetus – if it had any vantage-point – could not possibly experience itself as if dangling in space, without a woman's uterus and body and bloodstream to support it.

In fact, every image of a foetus we are shown, including *The Silent Scream*, is viewed from the standpoint neither of the foetus nor of the pregnant woman but of the camera. The foetus as we know it is a fetish. Barbara Katz Rothman observes (1986: 114): "The fetus in utero has become a metaphor for 'man' in space, floating free, attached only by the umbilical cord to the spaceship. But where is the mother in that metaphor? She has become empty space." Inside the futurizing spacesuit, however, lies a much older image. For the autonomous, free-floating foetus merely extends to gestation the Hobbesian view of born human beings as disconnected, solitary individuals. It is this abstract individualism, effacing the pregnant woman and the foetus' dependence on her, that gives the foetal image its symbolic transparency, so that we can read in it our selves, our lost babies, our mythic secure past.

While such receptions of foetal images may help to recruit anti-abortion activists, among both men and women, denial of the womb has more deadly consequences. Zoe Sofia relates the film *2001: A Space Odyssey* to "the New Right's cult of fetal personhood", arguing that: "In science fiction culture particularly, technologies are perceived as modes of reproduction in themselves, according to perverse myths of fertility in which man replicates himself without the aid of woman" (Sofia, 1984: 48–9). The "Star Child" of *2001* is not a living organic being but "a biomechanism . . . a cyborg capable of living unaided in space" (ibid.: 52). This "child" poses as the symbol of fertility and life but in fact is the creature of the same technologies that bring cosmic extermination, which it alone survives. Sofia sees the same irony in "the right-wing movement to protect fetal life" while it plans for nuclear war. Like the foetal-baby in *2001*, "the pro-life fetus may be a 'special effect' of a cultural dreamwork which displaces attention from the tools of extermination and onto the fetal signifier of extinction itself" (ibid.: 54).

If the foetus-as-spaceman has become inscribed in science fiction and popular fantasy, it is likely to affect the appearance of foetal images even in clinical contexts. The vantage-point of the male onlooker may perhaps change how women see their own foetuses on, and through, ultrasound imaging screens. *The Silent Scream* bridges these two arenas of cultural construction, video fantasyland and clinical biotechnics, enlisting medical imagery in the service of mythic-patriarchal messages. But neither arena, nor the film itself, meets a totally receptive field. Pregnant women respond to these images out of a variety of concrete situations and in a variety of complex ways.

Obstetrical imaging and masculine/visual culture

We have seen the dominant view of the foetus that appears in still and moving pictures across the mass-cultural landscape. It is one where the foetus is not only "already a baby", but more – a "baby man", an autonomous, atomized mini-space hero. This image has not supplanted the one of the foetus as a tiny, helpless, suffering creature but rather merged with it (in a way that reminds one uncomfortably of another famous immortal baby). We should not be surprised, then, to find the social relations of obstetrics – the site where ultrasound imaging of foetuses goes on daily – infiltrated by such widely diffused images.

Along with the external political and cultural pressures, traditional patterns endemic to the male-dominated practice of obstetrics help determine the current clinical view of the foetus as "patient", separate and autonomous from the pregnant woman. These patterns direct the practical applications of new reproductive technologies more towards enlarging clinicians' control over reproductive processes than towards improving health (women's or infants'). Despite their benefits for individual women, amniocentesis, in-vitro fertilization, electronic foetal monitoring, routine caesarian deliveries, ultrasound and a range of heroic "foetal therapies" (both *in utero* and *ex utero*) also have the effect of carving out more and more space/time for obstetrical "management" of pregnancy. Meanwhile, they have not been shown to lower infant and perinatal mortality/morbidity, and they divert social resources from epidemiological research into the causes of foetal damage (Gold, 1984: 240–1; Haverkamp and Orleans, 1982: 128; Hubbard, 1984: 341). But the presumption of foetal "autonomy" ("patienthood" if not "personhood") is not an inevitable requirement of the technologies. Rather, the technologies take on the meanings and uses they do because of the cultural climate of foetal images and the politics of hostility towards pregnant women and abortion. As a result, the pregnant woman is increasingly put in the position of adversary to her own pregnancy/foetus, either by having presented a "hostile environment" to its development or by actively refusing some medically proposed intervention (for example, a caesarian section or treatment for a foetal "defect") (Gallagher, 1984; Hubbard, 1984: 350; Fletcher, 1981: 772 and chapter 7).

Similarly, the claim by anti-abortion polemicists that the foetus is becoming "viable" at an earlier and earlier point seems to reinforce the notion that its treatment is a matter between a foetus and its doctor. In reality, most authorities agree that twenty-four weeks is the youngest a foetus is likely to survive outside the womb in the foreseeable future; meanwhile, over 90 per cent of pregnant women who get abortions in the United States do so in the first trimester, fewer than 1 per cent past the twentieth week (Grimes, 1984; Henshaw *et al.*, 1985: 90–2). Despite these facts, the *image* of younger and younger, tinier and tinier foetuses being "saved"; the point of viability being "pushed back" *indefinitely*; and untold aborted foetuses being "born alive", has captured recent abortion discourse in the courts, the headlines and television drama.[3] Such images blur the boundary between foetus and baby; they reinforce the idea that the foetus' identity as separate and autonomous from the mother (the "living, separate child") exists from the start. Obstetrical technologies of visualization and electronic/surgical intervention thus disrupt the very definition, as traditionally understood, of "inside" and "outside" a woman's body, of pregnancy as an "interior" experience. Increasingly, "who controls the interpretation of bodily boundaries in medical hermeneutics [becomes] a major feminist issue" (Haraway, 1985: 89). Like penetrating Cuban territory with reconnaissance satellites and Radio Marti, treating a foetus *as if it were* outside a woman's body, because it can be viewed, is a political act.

This background is necessary to an analysis that locates ultrasound imaging of foetuses within its historical and cultural context. Originating in sonar detectors for submarine warfare, ultrasound was not introduced into obstetrical practice until the early 1960s — some years after its accepted use in other medical diagnostic fields (Gold, 1984: 240; Graham, 1982: 39). The timing is significant, for it corresponds to the end of the baby boom and the rapid drop in fertility that would propel obstetricians and gynaecologists into new areas of discovery and fortune, a new "patient population" to look at and treat. "Looking" was mainly the point, since, as in many medical technologies (and technologies of visualization), physicians seem to have applied the technique before knowing precisely what they were *looking for*. In this technique, a transducer sends sound-waves through the amniotic fluid so they bounce off foetal structures and are reflected back, either as a still image (scan) or, more frequently, a real-time moving image "similar to that of a motion picture" (as the American College of Obstetricians and Gynecologists put it, ACOG, 1981: 56).

While greatly hailed among physicians for its advantages over the dangers of X-ray, ultrasound imaging in pregnancy is currently steeped in controversy. A 1984 report by a joint National Institutes of Health/Food and Drug Administration panel in the United States found "no clear benefit from routine use", specifically, "no improvement in pregnancy outcome" (either for the foetus/infant or the woman) and no conclusive evidence either of its safety or harm. The panel recommended against "routine use", including "to view . . . or obtain a picture of the fetus" or "for educational or commercial demonstrations without medical benefit to the patient" ("the patient" here, presumably, being the pregnant woman). Yet it approved of its use to "estimate gestational age", thus qualifying its reservations with a major loophole (Shearer, 1984: 25–6, 30; Gold, 1984: 240–1). At least one-third of all pregnant women in the United States are now exposed to ultrasound imaging, and that would seem to be a growing figure. Anecdotal evidence suggests that many if not most pregnancies will soon include ultrasound scans and presentation of a sonogram photo "for the baby album" (Gold, 1984: 240).

How can we understand the routinization of foetal imaging in obstetrics even though the profession's governing bodies admit the medical benefits are dubious? The reasons why ultrasound imaging in obstetrics has expanded so much are no doubt related to the reasons, economic and patriarchal, for the growth in electronic foetal monitoring, caesarian sections and other reproductive technologies. Practitioners and critics alike commonly trace the obstetrical technology boom to physicians' fear of malpractice suits. But the impulses behind ultrasound also arise from the codes of visual imagery and the construction of foetal images as "cultural objects" with historical meanings.

From the standpoint of clinicians, at least three levels of meaning attach to ultra-sound images of foetuses. These correspond to (1) a level of "evidence" or "report", which may or may not motivate diagnosis and/or therapeutic intervention; (2) a level of surveillance and potential social control; and (3) a level of fantasy or myth. (Not surprisingly, these connotations echo the textual structure of *The Silent Scream*.) In the first place, there is simply the impulse to "view", to get a "picture" of the foetus' "anatomical structures" in motion; and here obstetrical ultrasound reflects the impact on new imaging technologies in all areas of medicine One is struck by the lists of "indications" for ultrasound imaging found in the *ACOG Technical Bulletin* and the *American Journal of Obstetrics and Gynecology* indexes. While including a few recognizable "abnormal" conditions that might require a "non-routine" intervention (for example, "evaluation of ectopic pregnancy", or "diagnosis of abnormal fetal position"), for the most part these consist of technical measurements, like a list of machine parts – "crown rump length", "gestational sac diameter", foetal sex organs, foetal weight – as well as estimation of gestational age. As one neonatologist told me, "We can do an entire anatomical workup!" (Dr Alan Fleischman, personal communication). Of course, none of this viewing and measuring and recording of bits of anatomical data gives the slightest clue as to what *value* should be placed on this or any other foetus; whether it has a moral claim to heroic therapy or life at all; and who should decide (Petchesky, 1985: chapter 9). But the point is that the foetus, through visualization, is being treated as a patient already, is being given an ordinary check-up. Inferences about its "personhood" (or "babyhood') seem verified by sonographic "evidence" that it kicks, spits, excretes, grows.

Evidentiary uses of photographic images are usually enlisted in the service of some kind of action – to monitor, control and possibly intervene. In the case of obstetrical medicine, ultrasound techniques, in conjunction with electronic foetal monitoring (EFM), have been used increasingly to diagnose "foetal distress" and "abnormal presentation" (leading to a prediction of "prolonged labor" or "breech birth"). These findings then become evidence indicating earlier delivery by caesarian section, evoking the correlation some researchers have observed between increased use of EFM and ultrasound and the threefold rise in the caesarian section rate in the last fifteen years (Sheehan, 1985; Haverkamp and Orleans, 1982: 127).

Complaints by feminist health advocates against unnecessary caesarians and excessive monitoring of pregnancy are undoubtedly justified. Even the profession's own guidelines suggest that the monitoring techniques may lead to misdiagnoses or may themselves be the cause of the "stresses" they "discover" (ACOG, 1981: 58). One might well question a tendency in obstetrics to "discover" disorders where they previously did not exist because visualizing techniques compel "discovery", or to apply techniques to wider and wider groups of cases (Thacker and Banta, 1982: 173). On the whole, however, diagnostic uses of ultrasound in obstetrics have benefited women more than they've done harm, making it possible to define the due date more accurately, to detect anomalies and to anticipate complications in delivery. My question is not about this level of medical applications but rather about the cultural assumptions underlying them. How do these assumptions both reflect and reinforce the larger culture of foetal images sketched above? Why has the impulse to "see inside" come to dominate ways of knowing about pregnancy and foetuses, and what are the consequences for women's consciousness and reproductive power relations?

The "prevalence of the gaze", or the privileging of the visual as the primary means to knowledge in Western scientific and philosophical traditions, has been the subject of a feminist inquiry by Evelyn Fox Keller and Christine Grontkowski. In their analysis, stretching from Plato to Bacon and Descartes, this emphasis on the visual has had a paradoxical function. For sight, in contrast to the other senses, has as its peculiar property the capacity for *detachment*, for *objectifying* the thing visualized by creating distance between knower and known. (In modern optics, the eye becomes a passive recorder, a camera obscura.) In this way, the elevation of the visual in a hierarchy of senses actually has the effect of *debasing* sensory experience, and relatedness, as modes of knowing: "Vision connects us to truth as it distances us from the corporeal" (Keller and Grontkowski, 1983: 207–18).

Some feminist cultural theorists in France, Britain and the United States have argued that visualization and objectification as privileged ways of knowing are *specifically masculine* (man the viewer, woman the spectacle: Irigaray, 1981: 101; Kuhn, 1982: 60–5, 113; Mulvey, 1975; Kaplan, 1983: 324). Without falling into such essentialism, we may suppose that the language, perceptions and uses of visual information may be different for women, as pregnant subjects, than they are for men (or women) as physicians, researchers or reporters. And this difference will reflect the historical control by men over science, medicine and obstetrics in Western society; and the historical definitions of masculinity in Western culture. The deep gender-bias of science (including medicine), of its very ways of seeing problems, resonates, Keller argues, in its "common rhetoric". Mainly "adversarial" and "aggressive" in its stance towards what it studies, "science can come to sound like a battlefield" (Keller, 1985: 123–4). Likewise, presentations of scientific and medical "conquests" in the mass media commonly appropriate this terrain into cold war culture and macho style. Consider this piece of text from *Life*'s 1965 picture story on ultrasound in pregnancy. "A Sonar 'Look' at an Unborn Baby" (p. 45):

> The astonishing medical machine resting on this pregnant woman's abdomen in a Philadelphia hospital is "looking" at her unborn child in precisely the same way a Navy surface ship homes in on enemy submarines. Using the sonar principle, it is bombarding her with a beam of ultra-high-frequency sound waves that are inaudible to the human ear. Back come the echoes, bounding off the baby's head, to show up as a visual image on a viewing screen.

The militarization of obstetrical images is not implicit in the origin of the technology (most technologies in a militarized society either begin or end in the military); nor in its focus on reproduction (similar language constructs the "war on cancer"). Might it then correspond to the very culture of medicine and science, its emphasis on visualization as a form of surveillance and "attack"? For some obstetricians and gynaecologists, such visualization is patently voyeuristic; it generates erotic pleasure in the non-reciprocated, illicit "look". Interviewed in *Newsweek* after *The Silent Scream* was released, Nathanson boasted: "With the aid of technology, *we stripped away the walls of the abdomen and uterus and looked into the womb*" ("America's Abortion Dilemma", 1985: p. 21; emphasis added). And here is Dr Michael Harrison writing in a respected medical journal about "foetal management" through ultrasound:

> The fetus could not be taken seriously as long as he [sic] remained a medical recluse in an opaque womb; and it was not until the last half of this century that *the prying eye of the ultrasonogram . . .* rendered the once opaque womb transparent, *stripping the veil of mystery from the dark inner sanctum*, and *letting the light of scientific observation fall on the shy and secretive fetus . . .* The sonographic voyeur, *spying on the unwary fetus*, finds him or her a surprisingly active little creature, and not at all the passive parasite we had imagined.
>
> (Harrison quoted in Hubbard, 1984: 348; emphasis added)

Whether or not voyeurism is a "masculinist" form of looking, the "siting" of the womb as a space to be conquered can only be had by one who stands outside it looking in. The view of the foetus as a "shy", "mysterious little creature", recalling a wildlife photographer tracking down a gazelle, indeed exemplifies the "predatory nature of a photographic consciousness" (Haraway, 1985: 89; Sontag, 1973: 13–14). It is hard to imagine a pregnant woman thinking about her foetus this way, whether she longs for a baby or wishes an abortion.

What we have here, from the clinician's standpoint, is a kind of *panoptics of the womb*, whose aim is "to establish normative behaviour for the fetus at various gestational stages" and to maximize medical control over pregnancy (Hubbard, 1984: 349, quoting the Chief of Maternal and Fetal Medicine at a Boston hospital; cf.

Graham, 1982: 49–50). Feminist critics emphasize the degrading impact that foetal imaging techniques have on the pregnant woman. She now becomes the "maternal environment", the "site" of the foetus, a passive spectator in her own pregnancy (Hubbard, 1984: 350; Rothman, 1986: 113–15). Sonographic detailing of foetal anatomy completely displaces the markers of "traditional" pregnancy, when "feeling the baby move was a 'definitive' diagnosis." Now the woman's *felt* evidence about the pregnancy is discredited, in favour of the more "objective" data on the video screen. We find her

> on the table with the ultrasound scanner to her belly, and on the other side of the technician or doctor, the fetus on the screen. The doctor . . . turns *away* from the mother to examine her baby. Even the heartbeat is heard over a speaker removed from the mother's body. The technology which makes the baby/fetus more "visible" renders the woman invisible.
>
> (Rothman, 1986: 113)

Earlier I noted that ultrasound imaging of foetuses is constituted through three levels of meaning – not only the level of evidence (diagnosis) and the level of surveillance (intervention), but also that of fantasy or myth. "Evidence" shades into fantasy when the foetus is visualized, albeit through electronic media, as though removed from the pregnant woman's body, as though suspended in space. This is a form of fetishization, and it occurs repeatedly in clinical settings whenever ultrasound images construct the foetus through "indications" that sever its functions and parts from their organic connection to the pregnant woman. Fetishization, in turn, shades into surveillance when physicians, "right-to-life" propagandists, legislatures, or courts impose ultrasound imaging on pregnant women in order "to encourage 'bonding'". In some states, the use of compulsory ultrasound imaging as a weapon of intimidation against women seeking abortions has already begun (Gold, 1984: 242). Indeed, the very idea of "bonding" based on a photographic image implies a fetish: the investment of erotic feelings in a fantasy. When an obstetrician presents his patient with a sonographic picture of the foetus "for the baby album", it may be a manifestation of masculine desire to reproduce not only babies but motherhood.

Many feminists have explained masculine appropriation of the conditions and products of reproduction in psychoanalytic or psychological terms, associating it with men's fears of the body, their own mortality and the mother who bore them. According to one interpretation, "the domination of women by the male gaze is part of men's strategy to contain the threat that the mother embodies [of infantile dependence and male impotence]" (Kaplan, 1983: 324; cf. Benjamin, 1983: 295). Nancy Hartsock, in a passage reminiscent of Simone de Beauvoir's earlier insights, links patriarchal control over reproduction to the masculine quest for immortality through immortal works: "because to be born means that one will die, reproduction and generation are either understood in terms of death or are appropriated by men in disembodied form" (Hartsock, 1983: 253). In Mary O'Brien's analysis of the "dialectics of reproduction", "the alienation of the male seed in the copulative act" separates men "from genetic continuity". Men therefore try to "annul" this separation by appropriating children, wives, principles of legitimacy and inheritance, estates and empires. (With her usual irony, O'Brien calls this male fear of female procreativity "the dead core of impotence in the potency principle") (O'Brien, 1983: 29–37, 50, 60–1, 139). Other, more historically grounded feminist writers have extended this theme to the appropriation of obstetrics in Britain and the United States. Attempts by male practitioners to disconnect the foetus from women's wombs – whether physically, through forceps, caesarian delivery, in-vitro fertilization, or foetal-surgery; or visually, through ultrasound imaging – are specific forms of the ancient masculine impulse "to confine and limit and curb the creativity and potentially polluting power of female procreation" (Oakley, 1976: 57; cf. Corea, 1985: 303 and chapter 16, Rich, 1976: chapter 6; Ehrenrich and English, 1978; and Oakley 1980).

But feminist critiques of "the war against the womb" often suffer from certain tendencies towards reductionism. First, they confuse masculine rhetoric and fantasies with actual power relations, thereby submerging women's own responses to reproductive situations in the dominant (and victimizing) masculine text. Secondly, if they do consider women's responses, those responses are compressed into Everywoman's Reproductive Consciousness, undifferentiated by particular historical and social circumstances; biology itself becomes a universal rather than an individual, particular set of conditions. To correct this myopia, I shall return to the study of foetal images through a different lens, that of pregnant women as viewers.

Picturing the baby – women's responses

The scenario of the voyeuristic ultrasound instrument/technician, with the pregnant woman displaced to one side passively staring at her objectified foetus, has a certain phenomenological truth. At the same time, anecdotal evidence gives us another, quite different scenario when it comes to the subjective understanding of pregnant women themselves. Far from feeling victimized or pacified, they frequently express a sense of elation and *direct participation* in the imaging process, claiming it "makes the baby more real", "more our baby"; that visualizing the foetus creates a feeling of intimacy and belonging, as well as a reassuring sense of predictability and control (Hubbard, 1984: 335; Rothman, 1986: 202, 212–13; author's private conversations with recent mothers). (I am speaking here of women whose pregnancies are wanted, of course, not those seeking an abortion.) Some women even talk about themselves as having "bonded" with the foetus through viewing its image on the screen (Rothman, 1986: 113–14). Like amniocentesis, in-vitro fertilization, voluntary sterilization and other "male-dominated" reproductive technologies, ultrasound imaging in pregnancy seems to evoke in many women a sense of greater control and self-empowerment than they would have if left to "traditional" methods or "nature". How are we to understand this contradiction between the feminist decoding of male "cultural dreamworks" and (some) women's actual experience of reproductive techniques and images?

Current feminist writings about reproductive technology are not very helpful in answering this kind of question. Works such as Corea's *The Mother Machine* [1985a] and most articles in the anthology, *Test-Tube Women*, portray women as the perennial victims of an omnivorous male plot to take over their reproductive capacities. The specific forms taken by male strategies of reproductive control, while admittedly varying across times and cultures, are reduced to a pervasive, transhistorical "need".

Meanwhile, women's own resistance to this control, often successful, as well as their complicity in it, are ignored; women, in this view, have no role as agents of their reproductive destinies.

But historical and sociological research shows that women are not just passive victims of "male" reproductive technologies and the doctors who wield them. Because of their shared reproductive situation and needs, women throughout the nineteenth and twentieth centuries have often *generated* demands for such technologies (for example, birth control, childbirth anaesthesia, or infertility treatments), or welcomed them as benefits (which is not to say that the technologies offered always met the needs; Gordon, 1977; McLaren, 1978; Lewis, 1980: chapter 4; Petchesky, 1981, 1985: chapters 1 and 5). We have to understand the "market" for the pill, sterilization, IVF, amniocentesis and high-tech pregnancy monitoring as a more complex phenomenon than either the victimization or the male-womb-envy thesis allows.

At the same time, theories of a "feminist standpoint" or "reproductive consciousness" that would restore pregnant women to active historical agency and unify their responses to reproductive images and techniques are complicated by two sets of circumstances (O'Brien, 1983: chapter 1; Hartsock, 1983: chapter 10). First, we do not simply imbibe our reproductive experience raw. The dominant images and codes that mediate the material conditions of pregnancy, abortion, etc., determine what exactly women "know" about these events in their lives, their *meaning* as lived experience. Thus, women may see in foetal images what they are told they ought to see. John Berger distinguishes between "photographs which belong to private experience" and thus connect to our lives in some intimate way, and "public photographs", which excise bits of information "from all lived experience" (Berger, 1980: 51). This distinction helps indicate important differences between the meanings of foetal images when they are viewed as "the foetus" and when they are viewed as "my . . . baby". Women's ways of seeing ultrasound images of foetuses, even their own, may be affected by the cumulative array of "public" representations, from *Life* magazine to *The Silent Scream*. It possibly means that some of them will be intimidated from getting abortions – although as yet we have little empirical information to verify this. When young women seeking abortions are coerced or manipulated into seeing pictures of foetuses, their own or others, it is the "public foetus" as moral abstraction that they are being made to view.

A second problem for "standpoint theory", in dialectical tension with the first, is that women's relationship to reproductive technologies and images differs depending on social differences such as class, race and sexual preference, and biological ones such as age, physical disability and personal fertility history. Their "reproductive consciousness" is constituted out of these complex elements, and cannot easily be generalized or, unfortunately, vested with a privileged insight. The reception and meanings of foetal images derive not only from representations but also from the particular circumstances of the woman as viewer. These circumstances may belie a model of women as victims of reproductive technologies. Above all, the meanings of foetal images will differ depending on whether a woman wishes to be pregnant or not. With regard to wanted pregnancies, women with very diverse political values may respond positively to images that present their foetus as if detached, their own body as if absent from the scene. The reasons are a complex weave of socio-economic position, gender psychology and biology. At one end of the spectrum, the "pro-life" women whom Kristin Luker interviewed, identified "the foetus" strongly with their own recent, or frequent, pregnancies; it became "my little guy". Their circumstances as "devout, traditional women who valued motherhood highly" were those of married women with children, mostly unemployed outside the home, and remarkably isolated from any social or community activities. That "little guy" was indeed their primary source of gratification and self-esteem. Moreover – and this fact links them with many women whose abortion politics and life-styles lie at the opposite end of the spectrum – a disproportionate number of them seems to have undergone a history of pregnancy loss or child loss (Luker, 1984: 132, 138–9, 150–1).

If we look at the women who comprise the market for high-tech obstetrics, they are primarily those who can afford these expensive procedures and who have access to the private medical offices where they are offered. Socially and demographically, they are not only apt to be among the professional, educated, "late-child-bearing" cohort who face greater risks because of age (although the average age of amnio-centesis and ultrasound recipients seems to be moving down rapidly). More importantly, whatever their age or risk category, they are likely to be products of a middle-class culture that values planning, control and predictability in the interests of a "quality" baby (Fine and Asch, 1985: 8–9; Hubbard, 1984: 336). These values pre-date technologies of visualization and "baby engineering" and create a predisposition towards their acceptance. The fear of "non-quality" – that is, disability – and the pressure on parents, particularly mothers, to produce foetuses that score high on their "stress test" (like infants who score high on their Apgar test and children who score high on their Scholastic Aptitude Tests), is a cultural as well as a class phenomenon. Indeed, the "perfect baby" syndrome that creates a welcoming climate for ultrasound imaging may also be oppressive for women, in so far as they are still the ones who bear primary responsibility – and guilt – for how the baby turns out (Hubbard, 1984: 344). Despite this, "listening to women's voices" leads to the unmistakable conclusion that, as with birth-control generally, many women prefer predictability and will do what they can to have it.

Women's responses to foetal picture-taking may have another side as well, rooted in their traditional position in the production of family photographs. If photographs accommodate "aesthetic consumerism", becoming instruments of "appropriation" and "possession", this is nowhere truer than within family life – particularly middle-class family life (Sontag, 1982: 8). "Family albums" originated to chronicle the continuity of Victorian bourgeois kin-networks. The advent of "home movies" in the 1940s and 1950s paralleled the move to the suburbs and backyard barbecues (Zimmerman, 1986). Likewise, the presentation of a sonogram photo to the dying grandfather, even before his grandchild's birth (Rothman, 1986: 125), is a 1980s way of affirming patriarchal lineage. In other words, far from the intrusion of an alien and alienating technology, it may be that ultrasonography is becoming enmeshed in a familiar language of "private" images.

Significantly, in each of these cases it is the woman, the mother, who acts as custodian of the image – keeping up the album, taking the movies, presenting the sonogram. The specific relationship of women to photographic images, especially those of children, may help to explain the attraction of pregnant women to ultra-sound images of their own foetus (as opposed to "public" ones). Rather than being surprised that some women experience "bonding" with their foetus after viewing its image on a screen (or in a sonographic "photo"), perhaps we should understand this as a culturally embedded component of desire. If it is a form of "objectifying" the foetus (and the pregnant woman herself as detached from the foetus), perhaps such objectification and detachment are necessary for her to feel erotic pleasure in it (Weir and Casey, 1984: 144–5). If with the ultrasound image she first recognizes the foetus as "real", as "out there", this means that she first experiences it as an object she can possess.

Evelyn Keller proposes that feminists re-evaluate the concept of "objectivity". In so doing they may discover that the process of "objectification" they have identified as "masculinist" takes different forms, some which detach the viewer from the viewed and some which make possible both erotic and intellectual attachment (Keller, 1985: 70–3, 98–100, 117–20). To suggest that the timing of maternal–foetus or maternal–infant attachment is a biological given (for example, at "quickening" or at birth), or that "feeling" is somehow more "natural" than "seeing", contradicts women's changing historical experience (cf. Rothman, 1986: 41–2). On the other hand, to acknowledge that "bonding" is a historically and culturally shaped process is not to deny its reality. That women develop powerful feelings of attachment to their ("private") foetuses, especially the ones they want, complicates the politics of foetal images.

Consider a recent case in a New York court that denied a woman damages when her twenty week foetus was stillborn, following an apparently botched amnio-centesis. The majority held that, since the woman did not "witness" the death or injury directly, and was not in the immediate "zone of danger" herself, she could not recover damages for any emotional pain or loss she suffered as a result of the foetus' death. As one dissenting judge argued, the court "rendered the woman a bystander to medical procedures performed upon her own body", denying her any rights based on the emotional and "biological bond" she had with the foetus (Margolick, 1985). In so doing, the majority implicitly sanctioned the image of foetal autonomy and maternal oblivion.

As a feminist used to resisting women's reduction to biology, I find it awkward to defend their biological connection to the foetus. But the patent absurdity and cruelty of this decision underscore the need for feminist analyses of reproduction to address biology. A true biological perspective does not lead us to determinism but rather to infinite *variation*, which is to say that it is historical (cf. Riley, 1983: 17 and chapters 1 and 2). Particular lives are lived in particular bodies – not only "women's bodies", but just as relevantly, ageing, ill, disabled, or infertile ones. The material circumstances that differentiate women's responses to obstetrical ultrasound and other technologies include their own biological history, which may be experienced as one of limits and defeats. In fact, the most significant divider between pregnant women who welcome the information from ultrasound and other monitoring techniques and those who resent the machines or wish to postpone "knowing" may be personal fertility history. A recent study of women's psychological responses to the use of electronic foetal monitors during labour

> found that those women who had previously experienced the loss of a baby tended to react positively to the monitor, feeling it to be a reassuring presence,

> a substitute for the physician, an aid to communication. Those women who had not previously suffered difficult or traumatic births . . .tended to regard the monitor with hostility, as a distraction, a competitor.
>
> (Bates and Turner, 1985)

To recite such conditions does not mean we have to retreat into a reductionist or dualist view of biology. Infertility, pregnancy losses and women's feelings of "desperation" about "childlessness" have many sources, including cultural pressures, environmental hazards and medical misdiagnosis or neglect (Albury, 1984: 57–8). Whatever the sources, however, a history of repeated miscarriages, infertility, ectopic pregnancy, or loss of a child is likely to dispose a pregnant woman favourably to techniques which allow her to visualize the pregnancy and *possibly* to gain some control over its outcome.[4] Pregnancy – as biosocial experience – acts on women's bodies in different ways, with the result that the relation of their bodies, and consciousness, to reproductive technologies may also differ.

Attachment of pregnant women to their foetuses at earlier stages in pregnancy becomes an issue, not because it is cemented through "sight" rather than "feel", but when and if it is used to obstruct or harass an abortion decision.[5] In fact, there is no reason why any woman's abortion decision should be tortured in this way, since there is no medical rationale for requiring her to view an image of her foetus. Responsible abortion clinics are doing ultrasound imaging in selected cases – *only* to determine foetal size or placement, where the date of the woman's last menstrual period is unknown, the pregnancy is beyond the first trimester, or there is a history of problems; or to diagnose an ectopic pregnancy. But in such cases the woman herself does not see the image, since the monitor is placed outside her range of vision and clinic protocols refrain from showing her the picture unless she specifically requests it.[6] In the current historical context, to consciously limit the use of foetal images in abortion clinics is to take a political stance, to resist the message of *The Silent Scream*. This reminds us that the politics of reproductive technologies are constructed contextually, out of who uses them, how and for what purposes.

The view that "reproductive engineering" is imposed on "women as a class" rather than being sought by them as a means towards greater "choice" (Corea, 1985: 313) obscures the particular reality, not only of women with fertility problems and losses, but also of other groups. For lesbians who utilize sperm banks and artificial insemination to achieve biological pregnancy without heterosexual sex, such technologies are a critical tool of reproductive freedom. Are lesbians to be told that wanting their "own biological children" generated through their own bodies is somehow wrong for them but not for fertile heterosexual couples (cf. Fine and Asch, 1985)? The majority of poor and working-class women in the United States and Britain still have no access to amniocentesis, IVF and the rest, although they (particularly women of colour) have the highest rates of infertility and foetal impairment. It would be wrong to ignore their lack of access to these techniques on the ground that worrying about how babies turn out, or wanting to have "your own", is only a middle-class (or eugenic) prejudice.

In Europe, Australia and North America feminists are currently engaged in heated debate over whether new reproductive technologies present a threat or an opportunity for women. Do they simply reinforce the age-old pressures on women to bear children, and to bear them to certain specifications, or do they give women more control? What sort of control do we require in order to have reproductive freedom, and are there/should there be any limits on our control? (Gorovitz, 1982: 1). What is the meaning of reproductive technologies that tailor-make infants, in a context where childcare remains the private responsibility of women and many women are growing increasingly poor? Individual women, especially middle-class women, are choosing to utilize high-tech obstetrics, and their choices may not always be ones we like. It may be that chorionic villus sampling, the new first trimester prenatal diagnostic technique, will increase the use of selective abortion for sex. Moreover, the bias against disability that underlies the quest for the "perfect child" seems undeniable. Newer methods of prenatal diagnosis may mean that more and more abortions become "selective", so that more women decide "to abort the particular fetus [they] are carrying in hopes of coming up with a 'better' one next time" (Hubbard, 1984: 334). Are these choices moral? Do we have a right to judge them? Can we even say they are "free"?

On the other hand, techniques for imaging foetuses and pregnancies may, depending on their cultural contexts and uses, offer means for empowering women, both individually and collectively. We need to examine these possibilities and to recognize that, at the present stage in history, feminists have no common standpoint about how women ought to use this power.

Conclusion

Images by themselves lack "objective" meanings; meanings come from the interlocking fields of context, communication, application and reception. If we removed from the ultrasound image of *The Silent Scream* its title, its text, its sound narrative, Dr Nathanson, the media and distribution networks and the whole anti-abortion political climate, what would remain? But of course, the question is absurd, since no image dangles in a cultural void, just as no foetus floats in a space capsule. The problem clearly becomes, then, how do we change the contexts, media and consciousnesses through which foetal images are defined? Here are some proposals, both modest and Utopian.

First, we have to restore women to a central place in the pregnancy scene. To do this, we must create new images that recontextualize the foetus: that place it back into the uterus, and the uterus back into the woman's body and her body back into its social space. Contexts do not neatly condense into symbols; they must be told through stories that give them mass and dimension. For example, a brief prepared from thousands of letters received in an abortion rights campaign and presented to the United States Supreme Court in its most recent abortion case, translates women's abortion stories into a legal text. Boldly filing a procession of real women before the court's eyes, it materializes them in not only their bodies but their jobs, families, school-work, health problems, young age, poverty, race/ethnic identity and dreams of a better life (Paltrow, 1986).

Secondly, we need to separate the power relations within which reproductive technologies, including ultrasound imaging, are applied from the technologies themselves. If women were truly empowered in the clinic setting, as practitioners and patients, would we discard the technologies? Or would we use them differently, integrating them into, to a more holistic clinical dialogue between women's felt knowledge and the technical information "discovered" in the test-tube or on the screen? Before attacking reproductive technology, we need to demand that all women have access to the knowledge and resources to judge its uses and to use it wisely, in keeping with their own particular needs.

Finally, we should pursue the discourse now begun towards developing a feminist ethic of reproductive freedom that complements feminist politics. What ought we to choose if we became genuinely free to choose? Are some choices unacceptable on moral grounds, and does this mean under any circumstances, or only under some? Can feminism reconstruct a joyful sense of childbearing and maternity without capitulating to ideologies that reduce women to a maternal essence? Can we talk about morality in reproductive decision-making without invoking the spectre of maternal duty? On some level, the struggle to demystify foetal images is fraught with danger, since it involves *re-embodying* the foetus, thus representing women as (wanting-to-be or not-wanting-to-be) pregnant persons. One way out of this danger is to image the pregnant woman, not as an abstraction, but within her total framework of relationships, economic and health needs and desires. Once we have pictured the social conditions of her freedom, however, we have not dissolved the contradictions in how she might use it.

Acknowledgements

The following people have given valuable help in the research and revision of the manuscript for this chapter, but are in no way responsible for its outcome: Fina Bathrick, Rayna Rapp, Ellen Ross, Michelle Stanworth and Sharon Thompson. I would also like to thank the Institute for Policy Studies, the Barnard College Scholar and the Feminist Conference 1986 and *Ms Magazine* for opportunities to present pieces of it in progress.

Notes

1   *City of Akron* v. *Akron Center for Reproductive Health*, 426 US 416 (1983); and *Thornburgh* v. *American College of Obstetricians and Gynecologists*, 54 *LawWeek*, 4618 (10 June, 1986). From a pro-choice perspective, the significance of these decisions is mixed. While the court's majority opinion has become if anything more liberal and more feminist in its protection of women's "individual dignity and autonomy", this majority has grown steadily narrower. Whereas in 1973 it was 7–2, in 1983 it shrank to 6–3 and then in 1986 to a bare 5–4, while the growing minority becomes ever more conservative and anti-feminist.

2   Cf. Hubert Danisch: "the photographic image does not belong to the natural world. It is a product of human labor, a cultural object whose being . . . cannot be dissociated precisely from its historical meaning and from the necessarily datable project in which it originates" (in Trachtenberg, 1980: 288).

3   In her dissenting opinion in the *Akron* case, Justice Sandra Day O'Connor argued that *Roe* v. *Wade* was "on a collision course with itself because technology was

pushing the point of viability indefinitely backward." (In *Roe* the court had defined "viability" as the point at which the foetus is "potentially able to live outside the mother's womb, albeit with artificial aid"; after that point, it said, the state could restrict abortion except when bringing the foetus to term would jeopardize the woman's life or health; cf. Rhoden, 1985). Meanwhile, a popular weekly television programme, *Hill Street Blues*, in March 1985 aired a dramatization of abortion clinic harassment in which a pregnant woman seeking an abortion miscarries and gives birth to an extremely premature foetus/baby, which soon dies. Numerous newspaper accounts of "heroic" efforts to save premature newborns have made front-page headlines.

4   Rayna Rapp has advised me, based on her field research, that another response of women who have suffered difficult pregnancy histories to such diagnostic techniques may be denial – simply not wanting to know. This too, however, may be seen as a tactic to gain control over information, by censoring bad news.

5   Coercive, invasive uses of foetal images, masked as "informed consent" have been a prime strategy of anti-abortion forces for some years. They have been opposed by pro-choice litigators in the courts, resulting in the United States Supreme Court's repudiation on two different occasions of specious "informed consent" regulations as an unconstitutional form of harassment and denial of women's rights (*Akron*, 1983; *Thornburgh*, 1986).

6   I obtained this information from interviews with Maria Tapia-Birch, administrator in the Maternal and Child Services Division of the New York City Department of Health; and Jeanine Michaels, social worker; Lisa Milstein, nurse-practitioner, and Jeffrey Karaban, sonographer at the Eastern Women's Health Clinic in New York, who kindly shared their clinical experience with me.

References

ACOG (American College of Obstetricians and Gynecologists) (1982) "Diagnostic Ultrasound in Obstetrics and Gynecology", in Young (ed.) *Women and Health*, 7, (reprinted from ACOG, *Technical Bulletin*, 63 [October 1981]).

Albury, R. (1984) "Who Owns the Embryo?", in Arditti *et al.*, (eds) *Test-Tube Women*, pp. 54–67.

Arditti, R., Duelli Klein, R. and Minden, S. (eds) (1984) *Test-Tube Women: What Future for Motherhood?* (London: Pandora Press).

Barthes, R. (1982) "The Photographic Message", in Sontag, *A Barthes Reader*.

Bates, B. and Turner, A. N. (1985) "Imagery and Symbolism in the Birth Practices of Traditional Cultures", *Birth*, 12, pp. 33–8.

Bazin, A. (1980) "The Ontology of the Photographic Image", in Trachtenberg (ed.) *Classic Essays on Photography*, pp. 237–44.

Benjamin, J. (1983) "Master and Slave: The Fantasy of Erotic Domination", in Snitow *et al.* (eds) *Powers of Desire*.

Berger, J. (1980) *About Looking* (New York: Pantheon).

Burgin, V. (ed.) (1982) *Thinking Photography* (London: Macmillan).

Corea, G. (1985) *The Mother Machine: Reproductive Technologies from Artificial Insemination to Artificial Wombs* (New York: Harper and Row).

Damisch, H. (1980) "Notes for a Phenomenology of the Photographic Image", in Trachtenberg (ed.) *Classic Essays on Photography*.

Eastlake, Lady E. (1980) "Photography", in Trachtenberg (ed.) *Classic Essays on Photography*.

Ehrenreich, B. and English, D. (1979) *For Her Own Good: 150 Years of the Experts' Advice to Women* (London: Pluto Press).

Erickson, P. D. (1985) *Reagan Speaks: The Making of an American Myth* (New York: New York University Press).

Ewen, S. (1984) "The Political Elements of Style", in J. Bucholtz and D. B. Monk (eds) *Beyond Style: Precis 5* (New York: Columbia University Graduate School of Architecture and Planning/Rizzoli), pp. 125–33.

Ewen, S. and Ewen, E. (1982) *Channels of Desire: Mass Images and the Shaping of American Consciousness* (New York: McGraw-Hill).

Fine, M. and Asch, A. (1985) "Who Owns the Womb?", *Women's Review of Books*, II, 8 (May), pp. 8–10.

Fletcher, J. (1981) "The Fetus as Patient: Ethical Issues", *Journal of the American Medical Association*, 246, pp. 772–3.

Fletcher, J. C. and Evans, M. I. (1983) "Maternal Bonding in Early Fetal Ultrasound Examinations", *New England Journal of Medicine*, 308, pp. 282–93.

Gallagher, J. (1984) "Fetus and the Law", *Ms*, (September), pp. 62–6, 134–5.

Gold, R. B. (1984) "Ultrasound Imaging During Pregnancy", *Family Planning Perspectives*, 16, pp. 240–3.

Goldberg, S. (1977) *The Inevitability of Patriarchy* (London: Maurice Temple Smith).

Gordon, L. (1977) *Woman's Body, Woman's Right* (Harmondsworth: Penguin).

Gorovitz, S. (1982) "Introduction: The Ethical Issues", in Young (ed.) *Women and Health*, 7.

Graham, D. (1982) "Ultrasound in Clinical Obstetrics", in Young (ed.) *Women and Health*, 7.

Grimes, D. (1984) "Second-Trimester Abortions in the United States", *Family Planning Perspectives*, 16, pp. 260–5.

Haraway, D. (1985) "A Manifesto for Cyborgs: Science, Technology and Socialist Feminism in the 1980s", *Socialist Review*, 80, pp. 65–107.

Harding, S. and Hintikka, M. (eds) *Discovering Reality: Feminist Perspectives on Epistemology, Metaphysics, Methodology and the Philosophy of Science* (Dordrecht: Reidel).

Hartsock, N. (1983) *Money, Sex and Power* (Boston: Northeastern University Press).

Haverkamp, A. D. and Orleans, M. (1982) "An Assessment of Electronic Fetal Monitoring", in Young (ed.) *Women and Health*, 7, pp. 126–34.

Henshaw, S. K. *et al.* (1985) "A Portrait of American Women who Obtain Abortions", *Family Planning Perspectives*, 17, pp. 90–6.

Hubbard, R. (1984) "Personal Courage is not Enough: Some Hazards of Childbearing in the 1980s", in Arditti *et al.* (eds) *Test-Tube Women*.

Irigaray, L. (1981) "Ce sexe qui n'en est pas un", in Marks and de Courtivron (eds) *New French Feminisms* (New York: Schocken).

Kalter, J. (1985) "TV News and Religion", *TV Guide*, 33 (9, 16 November).

Kaplan, E. A. (1983) "Is the Gaze Male?", in Snitow *et al.* (eds) *Powers of Desire*.

Keller, E. Fox (1985) *Reflections on Gender and Science* (New Haven, CT: Yale University Press).

Keller, E. Fox and Grontkowski, C. R. (1983) "The Mind's Eye", in Harding and Hintikka (eds) *Discovering Reality*.

Kuhn, A. (1982) *Women's Pictures: Feminism and Cinema* (London: Routledge and Kegan Paul).

Lewis, J. (1980) *The Politics of Motherhood: Child and Maternal Welfare in England, 1900–1939* (London: Croom Helm).

Luker, K. (1984) *Abortion and the Politics of Motherhood* (Berkeley and London: University of California Press).

Margolick, D. (1985) "Damages Rejected in Death of Fetus", *New York Times*, (16 June), p. 26.

McLaren, A. (1978) *Birth Control in Nineteenth Century England* (London: Croom Helm).

Mulvey, L. (1975) "Visual Pleasure and Narrative Cinema", *Screen*, 16, pp. 6–18.

Oakley, A. (1976) "Wisewoman and Medicine Man: Changes in the Management of Childbirth", in J. Mitchell and A. Oakley (eds) *The Rights and Wrongs of Women* (Harmondsworth: Penguin).

Oakley, A. (1980) *Women Confined: Towards a Sociology of Childbirth* (Oxford: Martin Robertson; New York: Schocken).

O'Brien, M. (1983) *The Politics of Reproduction* (London: Routledge and Kegan Paul).

Paltrow, L. (1986) "Amicus Brief: *Richard Thornburgh v. American College of Obstetricians and Gynecologists*", *Women's Rights Law Reporter*, 9, pp. 3–24.

Petchesky, R. P. (1981) "Reproductive Freedom: Beyond 'A Woman's Right to Choose'", in C. R. Stimpson and E. S. Pearson (eds) *Women, Sex and Sexuality* (Chicago: University of Chicago Press). Originally in *Signs*, (Summer 1980).

Petchesky, R. P. (1985, 1986) *Abortion and Woman's Choice: The State, Sexuality and Reproductive Freedom* (Boston: Northeastern University Press; London: Verso).

Planned Parenthood Federation of America (n.d.) *The Facts Speak Louder: Planned Parenthood's Critique of "The Silent Scream"* (New York: Planned Parenthood Federation of America).

Rhoden, N. K. (1985) "Late Abortion and Technological Advances in Fetal Viability: Some Legal Considerations", *Family Planning Perspectives*, 17, pp. 160–1.

Rich, A. (1976) *Of Woman Born: Motherhood as Experience and Institution* (New York: W. W. Norton).

Riley, D. (1983) *War in the Nursery: Theories of the Child and Mother* (London: Virago).

Rothman, B. K. (1986) *The Tentative Pregnancy* (New York: Viking).

Sekula, A. (1982) "On the Invention of Photographic Meaning", in Burgin (ed.) *Thinking Photography*.

Shearer, M. H. (1984) "Revelations: A Summary and Analysis of the NIH Consensus Development Conference on Ultrasound Imaging in Pregnancy", *Birth*, 11, pp. 23–6.

Sheenan, K. H. (1985) "Abnormal Labor: Cesarians in the U.S.", *The Network News*, 10, National Women's Health Network, (July–August), p. 1, 3.

Snitow, A., Stansell, C. and Thompson, S. (eds) *Powers of Desire* (New York: Monthly Review Press).

Sofia, Z. (1984) "Exterminating Fetuses: Abortion, Disarmament, and the Sexo-Semiotics of Extraterrestrialism", *Diacritics*, 14, pp. 47–59.

"Sonar Look at an Unborn Baby, A" (1965) *Life*, 58, pp. 45–6.

Sontag, S. (1973) *On Photography* (New York: Delta).

Sontag, S. (ed.) (1982) *A Barthes Reader* (New York: Hill and Wang).

Thacker, S. B. and Banta, H. D. (1982) "Benefits and Risks of Episiotomy", in Young (ed.) *Women and Health*, vol. 7, pp. 173–81.

Trachtenberg, A. (ed.) (1980) *Classic Essays on Photography* (New Haven, CT: Leete's Island Books).

Weir, L. and Casey, L. (1984) "Subverting Power to Sexuality", *Socialist Review*, 14, pp. 139–57.

Young, D. (ed.) (1982) *Women and Health* (New York: Haworth Press), vol. 7: *Obstetrical Intervention and Technology in the 1980s*.

Zimmerman, P. (1986) "The Amateur, the Avant-Garde, and Ideologies of Art", *Journal of Film and Video*, 38, pp. 63–85.

Deborah Lynn Steinberg

FEMINIST APPROACHES TO SCIENCE, MEDICINE AND TECHNOLOGY

IN HER ARTICLE, "How the Women's Movement Benefits Science: Two views", Sandra Harding identifies what she defines as "two main feminist approaches to [a critique], of science" (Harding, 1992: 59). These, I would suggest, are useful distinctions for considering feminist approaches to related issues about medicine and technology, including feminist debates about reproductive technologies such as IVF. These two approaches Harding describes as "feminist empiricism" – or critiques of "bad" science, and "feminist standpoint" – or critiques of "science-as-usual".[1] It must be noted, however, of feminist analyses of science, medicine and technology, that few works fall easily into one epistemological position or another. In this sense, Harding's distinctions are more useful in relation to an assessment of particular arguments, approaches or assumptions within any one work, than as a conclusive classification system – describing the (unified) positions of their authors.[2]

Central to "feminist empiricism", Harding argues, is a critique of the failure of scientists to follow the normative principles of the scientific method – including those of objectivity or value neutrality, of legitimate laboratory methodology and of interpretation of data within any given field. Within "feminist empiricist" analyses, what is problematised is "bad" scientists – either as incompetent or prejudiced – rather than the norms and organisational structure within which scientists work. Scientific "artefacts" are assumed to have no inherent political value or meaning – instead, these are taken to accrue from the use to which they are put. Moreover, there is a separation made between the social context of science and science itself. Science can be constructed as a privileged sphere, separate from and not fundamentally shaped by (or shaping of) the social relations of inequality (and non-"neutrality") that characterise every other social activity or institution. Thus, to summarise, "feminist empiricism", as Harding defines it, consists centrally of a use/abuse analysis. The political meaning of "science-as-usual" is assumed to accrue from the manner (and context) in which its "artefacts" are used, or the loyalties and disloyalties of individual scientists to the basic principles of scientific method.

A "feminist standpoint" position, by contrast, problematises "science-as-usual".[3] The central premiss of a "feminist standpoint" position is that science is a site of power/ social relations that is shaped by and that shapes the power/social relations of its historical and cultural context. That is, social relations are understood as embedded in the knowledges (and "artefacts") produced by scientists; they are integrated in the basic epistemologies and practices of "science-as-usual". The activities and priorities of particular scientists, therefore, are not understood individualistically, but rather in the context of a particular social location.[4]

Feminist approaches to IVF

Both feminist empiricist and feminist standpoint approaches can be identified in the specific literature relating to reproductive technologies, particularly IVF. Elsewhere (Steinberg, 1993), I have considered in detail two of the major feminist texts (Stanworth, 1987; Klein, 1989) about IVF published in Britain during the late 1980s. Here I shall summarise my main critiques of these collections, the problems they illustrate in relation to feminist empiricist and feminist standpoint frameworks, and the bases they provide for the development of a more complex, "anti-oppressive", feminist approach to science, technology and medicine.

Reproductive Technologies Gender, Motherhood and Medicine (Stanworth, 1987)

The Stanworth collection could generally be characterised as one that takes a "feminist empiricist" approach to science, technology and medicine, and I would add, to women's experiences in relation to them.[5] The collection as a whole, and particularly Stanworth's introductory chapters, which frame it, focuses on the *uses* of IVF (and other) technologies. To this end, the social conditions of their use are targeted for critical analysis. Most of the authors in this collection maintain that IVF (and other technologies), under the right conditions, offer a potential for the expansion of women's reproductive "choices". However, they do not explain for which women this may be the case, and what kind of choice this involves.

Related to the "empiricist" orientation towards science, medicine and technology, and IVF in particular, of most of the book, is the identification of infertile women's experiences and priorities (as opposed, for example, to practitioners' experiences, priorities, and their ideas about women) as *the* starting-point for a feminist analysis of reproductive technologies. Stanworth suggests that "the authors [in this book] hope to provide pointers to the development of new strategies around reproductive technologies – strategies that are alert to the differences between women as well as to what they have in common" (1987: 9). However, the book does not, in fact, explore the social relations associated with, for example, race, class, heterosexuality or ability/disability around IVF, nor does it examine the varied experiences of different groups of women in relation to IVF, medicine, motherhood and other dimensions of the social context that Stanworth and others suggest are crucial to the use of IVF.

To take infertile women as the starting-point in such studies has many ramifications. Firstly, it may suggest that the experiences and needs of infertile women are representative of all women's experiences and needs. It may suggest, furthermore, that the experiences of infertile women are more important than those of other women, and indeed, in the context of IVF, that theirs are the only experiences that must be considered. In other words, it seems to posit that the women who have the primary (or only) stake in (or will be affected by) IVF, are those who might or do undergo it.

This stance ignores the wider implications of the medical scientific relationship to women's reproduction for all women, and the ways these vary for different groups of women. Suggesting that women other than those undergoing IVF treatment might be affected by it does not deny the importance of taking the experiences of "infertile" women seriously. Just as all women are implicated in the development of medical scientific practices that are directed towards women, so too are all women implicated in the specific innovations relating to IVF.[6]

It has been noted that white, middle-class and heterosexual women have been predominant in IVF treatment".[7] The class (in terms of relative income) profile of IVF patients can be largely deduced from the high cost of the procedure (see, for example, Corea, 1985; Scutt, 1990; and Steinberg, 1993).[8] Moreover, the vast majority of IVF clinics will provide "treatment" only to women whom they perceive as living in "stable" heterosexual relationships (Arditti et al., 1984; Spallone, 1987: 166–83; Steinberg, 1993). Therefore, to focus only on the experiences of infertile women obscures the different stakes of different women in relation to IVF and the politics of its production and deployment.

Moreover, the articles in Stanworth's book do not consider differences (of power and position) among infertile women themselves (the politics of how they came to be infertile and the divergent social meanings accruing to the infertility of different groups of women). Rather these articles focus on those for whom IVF is most likely to provide a "choice" of motherhood. Thus, it is the experiences and needs of this group of women that predominate and are often taken as universal. If, as these authors suggest, IVF is desirable as a reproductive "choice", they do not consider whether this is a choice, given the power of racist, classist and heterosexist discourses of motherhood and family, that makes most sense from a white, middle-class and heterosexual position.[9]

To summarise, the key features of the "feminist empiricism" of the Stanworth collection are, firstly, the assumption that IVF derives its positive or negative implications for women solely from the social conditions of its use, as opposed to its nature and form. Implicitly, in this collection, both IVF and the conditions and context of its production are taken as being value-neutral. Following from this premiss, it was possible for the authors to argue that IVF is potentially beneficial for (all) women, constituting a "choice" that could, in principle, enable (all) women to control our own reproduction. Secondly, there is a common assumption that the meaning of IVF for particular women (mainly white, middle-class, heterosexual infertile women) is representative of its meaning for all women.

Infertility: Women Speak out about Their Experiences of Reproductive Medicine *(Klein, 1989)*

In contrast to the Stanworth collection, that edited by Renate D. Klein articulates a "feminist standpoint" approach to IVF, although both share a focus on infertile women. Most of the contributions to the Klein collection are written by women who had undergone either conventional infertility treatment or IVF and who had left the treatment programmes feeling angry and critical of their treatment. In an introduction and concluding essay, Klein frames the testimonies of the contributors to her collection with several starting assumptions about both the nature of IVF (and conventional infertility) technologies and about women's relationship to them. Firstly, her central premiss is that IVF is a product of patriarchal "science (and medicine) as usual". She rejects a use/abuse analysis, arguing instead that the patriarchal character of the professional context of IVF development and practice is fundamentally antithetical to women's interests and needs, and that IVF is, itself, fundamentally patriarchal in character. Klein argues that one key feature of the profession generally, and of the development of IVF more specifically, is the witholding of information (for example about "side" effects and high failure rates) from potential patients as well as from the public at large.

Klein's main arguments are that IVF professionals misinform women about the potential negative effects of treatment and about the likelihood that it will fail in assisting them to have a baby. This, in the context of general social (patriarchal) pressures on women to become mothers and of the stigmatisation of infertility, accounts, Klein suggests, for why women choose to undergo the procedure. Women who come to understand the dangers of the procedure and to demystify the misinformation provided by practitioners (possibly, as with the authors in this collection, through the experience of undergoing IVF or infertility treatments) will be empowered to (and desire to) leave the treatment regime (Klein, 1989: 6).

Although making a significantly different analysis of the meaning of IVF, Klein's framework shares several features of the Stanworth book Like Stanworth's, Klein's volume focuses on the experience and needs of infertile women, although in this case mostly infertile women who have left and indeed who now oppose IVF (and conventional infertility treatments). As with the Stanworth book, neither Klein nor her authors deeply investigate the appeal and availability of IVF and infertility treatments in relation to particular groups of women (mainly white, middle-class and heterosexual women). Again, the experiences (this time negative) of these infertile women are implicitly taken as generic of all women's potential experiences.[10]

A second tension in Klein's framework is the way it shifts from a "standpoint" approach to science, medicine and technology to an exploration and explanation of women's relationship to them that extrapolates chiefly from consideration of the meaning of science, medicine and technology to professionals. One of the dangers of a "feminist standpoint" position approach can emerge when feminists attempt to extrapolate from assessments about the medical scientific framework, that is the way professionals construct women, to draw conclusions about women's view of themselves and their experiences of technology or medical scientific treatment. This can implicitly construct women as passive victims of medical scientists, even where the feminist author does not intend to do so. This results from the failure to recognise differences among women's experiences of science, medicine and technology – differences of social position among women *per se*; and differences in the kind of agency women may exercise, from different positions of inequality.

One of the strengths of Klein's book is the attempt to retain a sense of women's agency with respect to IVF and conventional infertility treatments. In creating a forum for individual women to speak about their experiences of reproductive medicine (although she problematically construes their individual voices as universal), she avoids the most overt form of extrapolating women's motives and consciousness from an assessment of the voices of the professionals who treat them. However, as I suggest above, in explaining women's decisions to undergo IVF centrally in terms of being effectively lied to or "duped" by professionals, and of their opposition to the procedure in terms of unmasking those lies, Klein implicitly posits a move from "false consciousness" to revelation. This, in my view, profoundly underestimates the complexity of women's agency (both in undertaking and in opposing IVF). It also underestimates the power relations (and inequalities) that result in some women's perceiving IVF as their only option (and having the option of choosing to undergo it), while others are not in this position.

Even beginning, as Klein does, with the notion that IVF as well as the social conditions under which it has been developed are fundamentally patriarchal, it is nevertheless possible to argue that women might undergo IVF being fully aware of the risks they are taking to their health and well-being. Indeed, I would argue that it is dangerously reductive to suggest that all women who undergo these procedures misapprehend the meaning and risks of IVF. What seems more important, as I have indicated in my critique of the Stanworth collection above, is an understanding of the complex social relations of inequality that make IVF seem an appropriate or even desirable choice for some women and not for others.

Feminist empiricism and feminist standpoint: epistemological questions

The strength of the standpoint approach lies in its potential in dealing with complexity. Whereas the empiricist framework is, as I have argued above, limited in its acceptance of "science-as-usual", the standpoint approach is critical of "science-as-usual". This establishes a basis for problematising universalisation (i.e. inductive reasoning) as a process both within and outside the medical scientific context and in relation to women's experiences. It is therefore possible and, I would argue, necessary to use a standpoint framework to develop forms of critique that take into account a number of different social relations of inequality as analytical indices. In other words, I am arguing for the development of an integrated model of power relations that allows for complex analyses of (and related political struggles about) both medical scientific practice and women's differential experiences of it. That is, I am proposing a move from a "feminist standpoint" position, as discussed above, to what I would term an "anti-oppressive feminist standpoint" position.[11]

Challenges to essentialist standpoint: feminist post-modernism

Feminist post-modernism has made a fundamental critique of all forms of essentialism (see, for example, Butler, 1990; Nicholson, 1990; Modleski, 1991). In particular, some feminist post-modernists have problematised the use of the category "woman" in so far as it has been used to obscure differences amongst women:

> For the most part feminist theory has taken the category of women to be foundational to any further political claims without realising that the category effects a political closure on the kinds of experiences articulable as part of a feminist discourse. When the category is understood as representing a set of values or dispositions, it becomes normative in character and, hence, exclu-sionary in principle This move has created a problem both theoretical and political, namely, that a variety of women from various cultural positions have refused to recognise themselves as "women" in the terms articulated by feminist theory with the result that these women fall outside the category and are left to conclude that (1) either they are not women as they have perhaps previously assumed or (2) the category reflects the restricted location of its theoreticians and, hence, fails to recognise the intersection of gender with race, class ethnicity, sexuality and other currents which contribute to the formation of cultural (non)identity.
>
> (Butler, 1990: 325)

This is an important critique, but all too often post-modernism involves a discussion of difference without a discussion of power relations. The endeavour of feminist post-modernism is to take the insights of post-modernism regarding positionality and fragmented subjectivities and reinvest them with a feminist political agenda.[12] However, as Modleski (1991: 18) points out, post-modern critiques of various forms of essentialism do not, in and of themselves, necessarily lead to analyses that take account of the differences they consider so important:

> Ironically . . . anti-essentialists may be no more prepared to deal with such issues as race or ethnicity than the "essentialists" whom they criticise for neglecting these issues. (We may note, for example, that the anthology *Feminism/Post-modernism*, which frequently claims for post-modern feminism a superior ability to deal with issues of race, contains no substantial discussion of these issues.)

Related to feminist post-modernist critiques of essentialism is the problematisation of the Enlightenment notion that people are constituted as unified, rational individuals and the consequent investment in the search for (and possibility of defining) "truth"[13] (see, for example, Henriques *et al.*, 1984; Barrett, 1991). Haraway (1989), for example, challenges notions of scientific truth and rationality by suggesting that theories produced by scientists can best be understood as "science fictions". As Harding (1991) points out, some feminist post-modernist critics have suggested that the notion of a "feminist standpoint" position is subject to a similar critique to that made of science in general. That is, both are engaged in a search for absolute "truth", albeit, in the case of a "feminist standpoint" position, a feminist "truth". The Klein collection, as I suggest above, could be seen precisely as positing the possibility of a feminist "truth" and thereby reproducing the very logic of "science-as-usual" that she otherwise critiques. However, Harding argues:

> [T]he logic of the standpoint approaches contains within it both an essen-tialising tendency and also resources to combat such a tendency. Feminist standpoint theory is not in itself either essentialist or nonessentialist, racist or anti-racist, ethnocentric or not. It contains tendencies in each direction, it contains contradictions.
>
> (1991: 180)

Similarly, feminist standpoint positions contain the possibilities both of accepting Enlightenment frameworks and of critiquing them.

Clearly, in its critique of essentialism and scientific rationalism, feminist post-modernism has important insights to bring to a feminist analysis of science as well as to critical reflection on feminism itself. However, as Modleski (quoted above) suggests, there are problems with the post-modernist tendency, including its feminist variant, which involve the neglect of relations of power and inequality.

Challenges to the essentialist standpoint: black feminisms

Unlike much post-modern feminism, black feminisms have focused specifically on issues of oppression and power relations.[14] Indeed, black feminists have demanded a complex and multi-layered approach to oppression, a demand that, in part, derives from their critiques of white feminism. One particular critique that has been frequently made is that white feminists have largely disregarded issues of racism in their analysis of gender relations (see, for example, Carby, 1981; Lorde, 1984; hooks, 1982, 1989, 1991). Amos and Parmar (1984) argue that:

> [W]hite mainstream feminist theory . . . does not speak to the experiences of Black women and where it attempts to do so it is often from a racist perspective and reasoning.
>
> . . . The limitations of the [feminist] movement are expressed in the issues which are identified as priorities: they are issues which in the main have contributed to an improvement in the material situation of a small number of white middle-class women often at the expense of their black and working class "sisters".
>
> (1984: 4)

Although, in 1984, Amos and Parmar did not use the term "essentialism", this critique of "imperial feminism"[15] is anti-essentialist in its rejection of the universal-isation of white, and, often, middle-class women's priorities and experiences.

This critique of white feminist agendas can be usefully employed in under-standing some of the problems with the Stanworth and Klein collections, which, as I have argued above, take as primary the experiences and priorities of a "small number of [mainly] white middle-class women". What black feminists like Amos and Parmar are suggesting, therefore, is a reframing of the starting-point(s) for feminist analysis. As Patricia Hill Collins (1990) succinctly puts it:

> Black feminist thought consists of specialised knowledge created by African-American women [and, of course, other Black women] which clarifies a standpoint of and for Black women. In other words, Black feminist thought encompasses theoretical interpretations of Black women's reality by those who live it.
>
> (1990: 22)

A similar set of arguments can be made in relation to the formation of a variety of standpoints. Among these, Harding (1991) discusses those of some Third World women and lesbians. What these have in common are both an acknowledgement and centralisation of the specificity of positionality in relation to (different forms of) oppression and the development of an agenda for social change based on lived experience.

In reframing the agenda, black feminists have characteristically explored intersections of racism, class oppression and sexism, thus opening a way to consider other social inequalities.[16] As Amos and Parmar (1984) conclude:

> We cannot simply prioritise one aspect of our oppression to the exclusion of others, as the realities of our day to day lives make it imperative for us to consider the simultaneous nature of our oppression and exploitation. Only a synthesis of class, race, gender and sexuality can lead us forward . . .
>
> (1984: 18)

It is important to note that Amos and Parmar do not provide an exhaustive list of aspects of oppression that need to be understood as interrelated. For example, they do not mention disability/ableism. However, they have provided a model for an integrated analysis of oppression that addresses issues not only of positionality (of both researcher and researched), but also of indices of analysis and priorities for activism.

Towards an "anti-oppressive feminist standpoint" position

In the light of the critiques that I have made of both Stanworth's and Klein's books, it is clearly important to move away from universalising the experiences of any particular group of women. For, as Harding says: "We should redirect our analyses of women's situations and our agendas so that they are significantly closer to the more comprehensive ones advocated by women who suffer from more than what some women frequently see as simply 'gender oppression'" (Harding, 1991: 193).

This redirection will, I would suggest, involve an understanding of what is meant by "standpoint" at three levels – that of positionality; that of the indices of analysis; and that of feminist politics. In terms of positionality, "standpoint" can refer specifically to one's experiences (of oppression and/or privilege) as the point or location from which one develops an analysis of social relations. This is one of the respects in which Klein's analysis can be seen as a "standpoint". However, as I have argued, this can lead to a form of essentialism which posits that: (1) women have an inherent ability to "know" patriarchy; (2) feminism can be located within the "true consciousness" of womanhood; and (3) it is sufficient to consider only one index of social relations (i.e. gender) for an analysis to be feminist. Because of these problems, positionality alone is not a sufficient basis for understanding social relations. However, it is important to acknowledge that lived experience does make a difference to how one interprets the world.[17] It is, of course, not only the complex positionality of research subjects that is important but also that of the researcher.

A second component of a feminist standpoint position revolves around the selection of indices for the analysis of social relations. This selection process can be limited, as I have argued above, to only one index, or it can be more complex and multi-layered. This relates both to positionality and to political priorities. As Harding points out, the selection of gender as the only index has been characteristic of many "white, Western, economically advantaged and/or straight women" (1991). What one privileges for the purpose of critical analysis is a political decision. To privilege gender inequality can have the effect of marginalising related struggles against other forms of oppression. In so doing, it can also have the effect of erasing the experiences of many women, which is precisely, as I have discussed, the central issue of contention within black feminist critiques of white feminism (for example, Carby, 1981; Lorde, 1984; hooks, 1989).

There are a number of key social relations that are commonly neglected in an exclusive feminist focus on gender. These include relations around ability/disability, class inequality, heterosexism and racism, among others. My review of the Stanworth and Klein collections has highlighted some of the dangers of disregarding these forms of social relations. However, while it is important to consider forms of social relations in complex ways, it is not necessary that any one piece of work using an "anti-oppressive feminist standpoint" approach explores each and every form of oppression.[18] I would suggest, instead, that the process of developing a complex, integrated analysis of some forms of power relations opens up the possibility of exploring others in a similarly integrated way. So, it is the model of considering power relations as complexly interrelated, rather than attempting exhaustively to track all forms of these relations, that is most important.

Finally, implicit in the term "feminist" in the phrase "feminist standpoint position" is an agenda for political activism towards social justice for women.[19] It can be distinguished, for example, from a primarily positional (and, it could be argued, dangerously essentialist) notion of "women's standpoint", since solely positional standpoints do not necessarily imply struggle for social change. A *feminist* standpoint, by contrast, must, by definition, involve a will to social change, that is, a praxis in which there is "a continuing shared feminist commitment to a political position in which 'knowledge' is not simply defined as 'knowledge *what*', but also as 'knowledge *for*'. Succinctly the point is to change the world, not only to study it" (Stanley, 1990: 15; her emphasis).

The additional term "anti-oppressive", then, is intended specifically to locate this version of a "feminist standpoint" approach within a complex political agenda of change aimed at social justice. The language of "anti-oppressive practice" is not current in analyses of or in political movements challenging "science-as-usual". It is to be found more often, for instance, within social work[20] (see, for example, Langan, 1992) and education (see, for example, Epstein, 1991, 1993). An "anti-oppressive" political orientation involves: (1) a recognition that "difference" is often, if not always, attended by unequal relations of power; (2) an understanding that unequal power relations are produced in and through the discursive practices[21] of powerful institutions; (3) the perspective that no one form of power relations can be understood in isolation; rather, they are intertwined and mutually reinforcing; and (4) a commitment to developing analyses and practices that challenge the institutionalisation of oppression.

Taken together, these elements of an "anti-oppressive feminist standpoint" approach radically shift an analysis of science, medicine and technology. With respect to an analysis of IVF, for example, women's experiences of and relationships to IVF and women's agency in this context can be seen neither as singular (universal), nor as divorced from the complex power relations of social institutions *including* science, medicine and technology. To utilise "anti-oppressive" analytical indices, I would argue, contributes to the development of a feminist praxis that centralises the considerable differences of power among women as well as the considerable different ways that powerful institutions affect different groups of women. Such an approach elaborates and contributes to a feminist framework that challenges the privileging of particular female experiences. It also provides a model for the analysis of power that neither constructs women as passive victims nor denies female agency, but contextualises that agency within complex relations of social inequality.

(Re)Reading reproductive technologies: (re)writing feminist reproductive politics

With respect to the analysis of dominant discourses of IVF, an anti-oppressive interrogative framework brings to the fore a number of questions. Firstly, what, in their own terms, are the priorities of IVF inventors and practitioners and how are women and women's bodies, reproduction, agency and status differentially constructed and constrained within and through professional discourses? For example, innovation of new reproductive technologies has given a new twist to long-standing debates about women's reproductive rights and the ideology of embryo "rights". The advent of IVF has been particularly key to the reconstitution of anti-abortion and, indeed, pro-choice politics. Because IVF has made it possible to create embryos outside and (re)place them in women's bodies, it has significantly altered the terms of debate around pregnancy, abortion and childbirth and the role of medicine and the state in relation to all three. In addition, the creation of extra-corporeal embryos has reconstituted questions of male reproductive rights. This was the central issue at the heart of the 1992 controversy in the USA courts [. . .] over who has custody of frozen embryos. Moreover debates about abortion and women's right to choose have now become inextricably entangled with questions about IVF embryo research. This was exemplified in early debates about the Powell Bill (1984), which proposed to ban embryo research on the basis of the purported "personhood" of embryos, a standard argument of anti-abortionists. Indeed, it can be argued that IVF has made material the ideological separation between woman and embryo that underpins anti-abortion ideology. The reconstitution of embryo-"rights" discourses in the light of the recombinant capabilities and ethos of IVF, and the recombinant embryo/logic terms through which professional and state agencies differentially delimit the agency of (women) patients, are clearly central questions for the delineation of feminist reproductive politics in the IVF context.

A second set of questions, relevant to an anti-oppressive analytical agenda, revolve around the ways in which notions of reproductive "fitness" are articulated through IVF discourses. A significant absence in many evaluations of new reproductive technologies is an investigation of the eugenic politics underpinning professional practices and cultures. Few works have considered, for example, the centrality of patient and genetic screening in IVF practice, including both policies for selecting or rejecting potential parents (for example, on the grounds of whether or not they are married) and genetic and other forms of screening embryos for "abnormalities". Issues relating to screening in this context are important for the ways in which they draw on and (re)construct widely held common-sense definitions of "normal" and "abnormal" families, "proper" and 'improper" parents and "desirable" and "undesirable" offspring. The absence of attention to the issue of eugenic screening and the broader agenda to reproduce "proper" families can be said to reflect a broader cultural disowning of the history of eugenic and "racial hygiene" movements in Britain, the USA and Europe (in particular under National Socialism in Germany). It is also reflective of a denial of the primacy of medical science in the development of eugenics movements generally. An analysis of the ways in which practices and policies surrounding new reproductive technologies might draw upon and reproduce eugenic thinking, particularly in the wake of emergent ideologies of "ethnic cleansing", would therefore seem to be of urgent necessity.

Finally, to propose an "anti-oppressive" feminist analysis of science, medicine and technology suggests the possibility of an "anti-oppressive" feminist science. At one level this raises the question of whether developments such as IVF can be justified on anti-oppressive grounds, or can be seen as or transformed into an "anti-oppressive" feminist science. But, perhaps more importantly, it suggests a radical shift in the terms with which we understand the politics of science, medicine and technology-as-usual in relation to feminism and the terms with which we constitute a politics of women's reproductive rights.

Notes

1   Elsewhere Harding has also considered "feminist post-modernist" approaches, in particular as critical responses to critiques of "feminist standpoint" positions (Harding, 1986, 1987, 1990, 1991). This is a point to which I will return below in the context of my own consideration of the first two approaches.

2   More commonly, feminist approaches have been classified as "radical", "socialist" and "liberal" (and more recently "post-modernist"), what I would term "position" categories. These categories are often invoked in a rather monolithic manner, often underestimating (1) the considerable differences of analysis and perspective among feminists classified within any one position: (2) the possible combination of approaches and priorities within any one work; (3) the commonalities across

categories; or (4) the changing ideas of any one writer/activist over time. Used as labels, these categories can suggest that feminism is composed of separate and monolithic positions, and that these positions are somehow equivalent to or bespeak particular feminist identities. What is particularly useful about Harding's work, in my view, is that her consideration of feminist epistemology – that is, of the questions feminists ask (what they problematise) and the assumptions underlying these questions – allows for the possibility of a complex (and even contradictory) agenda in the way that positional categories seem to obstruct. Moreover, Harding's categories are free of the pejorative or dismissive connotations often attendant upon the invocations of positions/categories when feminists critique the work of other feminists.

3   Harding associates this approach with Marxist epistemology where "knowledge is [seen as] grounded in experiences made possible by specific social relations" (1991: 60). Within this perspective, Harding points out, "there is no possibility of [a] perspective that is disinterested, impartial, value-free or detached from the particular, historical social relations in which everyone participates" (ibid.).

4   Margaret Lowe Benston, for example, argues that technology is a male-dominated (androcentric) "language" of social action – providing a range of options for acting in the world (Benston, 1992: 35). The technological world-view revolves around the "science-as-usual" principles of objectivity, rationality, control over nature and distance from human emotions – a schooled orientation for males (i.e. components of the definition of "normal masculinity") (1992: 38). The principles of "science-as-usual" form conditions for male dominance within and outside science, and in turn male dominance within and outside science reinforces the androcentric epistemology of science. Particular technologies, Benston argues, are consequently encoded with the fundamental values and social relations that underpin their production, and in turn (re)produce male dominance in our society.

5   One exception is Ann Oakley's article which makes a critique of obstetrics-as-usual, focusing on the technologies "for viewing the interior of [women's] wombs" (Stanworth, 1987: 5) and on the medical attitudes characterising the development' and practice of these technological capabilities (Oakley, 1987). Ros Petchesky's (1987) article [see reading 3.1 in this volume] combines both "standpoint" and "empiricist" orientations to questions surrounding (fetal) ultrasound monitoring of pregnant and birthing women. She begins with what could be described as a "standpoint" critique of the objectification of women's experience characterising the practice and underpinning the philosophy of practitioners who use it. The second part of her article examines the mixed (often positive) experiences women have with the technology. In this part, there is a shift in her analytic premise – arguing against a "standpoint" critique of the technology that characterises the beginning of the article and concluding with a much more ambivalent use/abuse perspective.

6   For example, practices and policies relating to abortion are important for all women, not only for women who undergo them. There is an extensive feminist literature discussing how all women's social position and rights are shaped by the legal and medical status of abortion (see, for example, Oakley, 1981; Fried, 1990; Science and Technology Subgroup, 1991). Black feminists have also pointed out that abortion policy and women's stake in it will be different for different groups of women. Moreover, pro-choice campaigns do not include only those women who will want or need abortions.

7   See, for example, Arditti *et al.*, 1984: 5; Corea, 1985: 144–5, 276–7. Moreover, in media coverage of IVF birthday parties or announcements of new IVF births (since 1978, with the birth of Louise Brown), images of white patients, children and doctors/scientists have predominated.

8   This does not mean, of course, that working-class women do not undergo IVF. However, the financial burden for women undergoing IVF will obviously bear more heavily and therefore be a more significant deterrent for poorer women.

9   For example, it is possible that the pressures of compulsory motherhood and the stigmatisation of infertility are not likely to be experienced in the same way by lesbians. It is also possible that women who feel that they cannot afford "treatment" or feel that they would be discriminated against by clinics, might be less likely to experience IVF as a "choice".

10   It must be stated that there is an important tension, in this regard, between the self-representations of the contributors to this collection and Klein's framing and interpretation of them. The contributors write as individuals, none claiming to speak a universal voice of "female experience". The tension arises in the way that Klein frames and interprets these individual voices as universally representative of women's relationship to reproductive medicine. I do not suggest that there is an inherent problem with examining the experience of women on IVF programmes. Indeed, the authors in the Klein collection provide disquieting and important testimony about their experiences of reproductive medicine. The problem instead, is both with generalising from their experiences and motives as characteristic (or even potentially characteristic) of all women and with neglecting to specify and examine the particular political dimensions of their social positions and context.

11   I recognise that feminists across a range of positions have expressed concern for and have struggled against many forms of oppression. I would not like to disparage or underestimate this. My use of the term "anti-oppressive" is, in this sense, a gesture towards a conceptual opening up of the field rather than a dismissal of other feminists' positions and interventions.

12   See, for example, Linda J. Nicholson's edited collection *Feminism/Post-modernism* (1990).

13   Thus, for example, Martyn Hammersley (1992) in criticising feminism and defending positivism argues that a finding should be accepted as "truth" when there is consensus amongst a scientific community of rational individuals that it *is* the "truth".

14   I am not suggesting that this is related to some essential characteristic of "blackness". However, the self-conscious adoption of the label "black feminist" indicates a deliberate critique of (white) feminist neglect of issues around racism. A similar point could be made about lesbians adopting the term "lesbian feminist". Indeed, to challenge Catharine MacKinnon's (1987) formulation, feminism *modified* implies a critique of feminism as identified by the modifier.

15   The title of their article is "Challenging Imperial Feminism" (pp. 3–20).

16   It is notable, in this context, that many black feminists have been concerned to integrate, into their analyses of racism and sexism, a consideration of issues of homophobia and heterosexism (for example, Lorde, 1984; Jordan, 1989; hooks, 1989, 1991).

17   This represents what, I would suggest, is most significant about the notion that "the personal is political". It is not just that experience is central, but rather the question

is *how* to centralise it in a political way, that is, in a way that accounts for the complexities of the social relations of oppression and privilege.

18   Indeed, this would be impossible, both because of limitations of space (we cannot write infinitely long books or essays) and because it is not possible to know all forms in which oppression can and does exist. In other words, we cannot presume to state categorically all of the variables that play out in any one moment or situation.

19   See, for example, the Bowles and Klein (1983) collection in which feminist research is defined in several articles as research *for*, not simply *about*, women.

20   Training in anti-discriminatory and anti-oppressive practice is a requirement of social work training as laid down by CCETSW (Central Council for the Education and Training of Social Workers) (CCETSW, 1991).

21   Discourse can be defined as ways of speaking and seeing that construct what counts as meaningful knowledge. A discursive field consists of competing ways of giving meaning to the world and organising social institutions and processes – which can be defined as discursive practices.

References

(For government publications, see after alphabetical entries.)

Amos, Valerie and Pratibha Parmar, 1984. "Challenging Imperial Feminism". *Feminist Review*, 17, Autumn, 3–20.

Arditti, Rita, Renate Duelli Klein and Shelley Minden, 1984. *Test-Tube Women: What Future for Motherhood?* London, Pandora.

Barrett, Michele, 1991. *The Politics of Truth: From Marx to Foucault*. London, Polity.

Benston, Margaret Lowe, 1992. "Women's Voices/Men's Voices: Technology as a Language", in Kirkup, Gill and Laurie Smith Keller (eds), *Inventing Women: Science, Technology and Gender*. London, Polity.

Bowles, Gloria and Renate Duelli Klein (eds), 1983. *Theories of Women's Studies*. London, Routledge.

Butler, Judith, 1990. *Gender Trouble: Feminism and the Subversion of Identity*. London, Routledge.

Carby, Hazel, 1981. "White Women Listen: Black Feminism and the Boundaries of Sisterhood", in CCCS, *The Empire Strikes Back: Race and Racism in 70s Britain*, pp. 212–35. London, Hutchinson.

CCETSW (Central Council for the Education and Training of Social Workers), 1991. "DipSW Requirements and Regulations for the Diploma in Social Work: Paper 30". The Council, London.

Collins, Patricia Hill, 1990. *Black Feminist Thought: Knowledge, Consciousness and the Politics of Empowerment*. London: HarperCollins.

Corea, Gena, 1985. *The Mother Machine: Reproductive Technologies from Artificial Insemination to Artificial Wombs*. New York, Harper and Row.

Epstein, Debbie, 1991. Changing Classroom Cultures: An Examination of Anti-Racist Pedagogy, INSET and School Change in the Context of Local and National Politics. Unpublished Ph.D. Thesis, University of Birmingham.

Epstein, Debbie, 1993. *Changing Classroom Cultures: Anti-Racism, Politics and Schools*. Stoke-on-Trent, Trentham Books.

Fried, Marlene Gerber (ed.), 1990. *From Abortion to Reproductive Freedom: Transforming a Movement*. Boston, MA, South End Press.

Hammersley, Martyn, 1992. "On Feminist Methodology". *Sociology*, 26(2) 187–206.

Haraway, Donna, 1989. *Primate Visions: Gender, Race and Nature in the World of Modern Science*. New York, Routledge.

Harding, Sandra, 1986. *The Science Question in Feminism*. Milton Keynes, Open University Press.

Harding, Sandra, 1990. "Feminism and Anti-Enlightenment Critiques", in Nicholson, Linda J. (ed.), pp. 83–106. *Feminism/Postmodernism*. London, Routledge.

Harding, Sandra, 1991. *Whose Science? Whose Knowledge? Thinking From Women's Lives*. Milton Keynes, Open University Press.

Harding, Sandra, 1992. "How the Women's Movement Benefits Science", in Kirkup, Gill and Laurie Smith Keller, *Inventing Women: Science, Technology and Gender*, pp. 57–72. London, Polity.

Harding, Sandra (ed.), 1987. *Feminism and Methodology*. Milton Keynes, Open University Press.

Henriques, Julian *et al.*, 1984. *Changing the Subject: Psychology, Social Regulation and Subjectivity*. London, Methuen.

hooks, bell, 1982. *Ain't I a Woman: Black Women and Feminism*. London, Pluto Press.

hooks, bell, 1989. *Talking Back: Thinking Feminist – Thinking Black*. London, Sheba.

hooks, bell, 1991. *Yearning: Race, Gender and Cultural Politics*. London, Turnaround Press.

Jordan, June, 1989. *Moving Towards Home*. London, Virago.

Klein, Renate D. (ed.), 1989 *Infertility: Women Speak Out about Their Experiences of Reproductive Medicine*. London, Pandora.

Langan, Mary, 1992. "Who Cares? Women in the Mixed Economy of Care", in Langan, Mary and Lesley Day (eds), *Women, Oppression and Social Work: Issues in Anti-Discriminatory Practice*. London, Routledge.

Lorde, Audre, 1984. *Sister Outsider*. Trumansburg, NY, The Crossing Press.

MacKinnon, Catharine, 1987. *Feminism Unmodified: Discourses on Life and Law*. Cambridge, MA, Harvard University Press.

Modleski, Tanya, 1991. *Feminism Without Women: Culture and Criticism in a "Post-Feminist" Age*. London, Routledge.

Nicholson, Linda J. (ed.), 1990. *Feminism/Postmodernism*. London, Routledge.

Oakley, Ann, 1981. "Interviewing Women: A Contradiction in Terms", in Roberts, Helen (ed.), *Doing Feminist Research*. London, Routledge and Kegan Paul.

Oakley, Ann, 1987. "From Walking Wombs to Test Tube Babies", in Stanworth, Michelle (ed.), *Reproductive Technologies: Gender, Motherhood and Medicine*, pp. 36–56. Cambridge, Polity.

Petchesky, Rosalind Pollack, 1987. "Foetal Images: The Power of Visual Culture in the Politics of Reproduction", in Stanworth, Michelle (ed.), *Reproductive Technologies: Gender, Motherhood and Medicine*, pp. 57–80. Cambridge, Polity.

Science and Technology Subgroup, 1991. "In the Wake of the Alton Bill: Science, Technology and Reproductive Politics", in Franklin, Sarah, Celia Lury and Jackie Stacey (eds), *Off-Centre: Feminism and Cultural Studies*, pp. 147–220. London, HarperCollins.

Scutt, Jocelynne A., 1990. *The Baby Machine: Reproductive Technologies and the Commercialisation of Motherhood*. London, Green Print.

Spallone, Patricia, 1987. "Reproductive Technology and the State: The Warnock Report and its Clones", in Spallone, Patricia and Deborah Lynn Steinberg (eds), *Made to Order:The Myth of Reproductive and Genetic Progress*, pp. 166–83. Oxford, Pergamon.

Stanley, Liz (ed.), 1990. *Feminist Praxis*. London, Routledge.

Stanworth, Michelle (ed.), 1987. *Reproductive Technologies: Gender, Motherhood and Medicine*. Cambridge, Polity.

Steinberg, Deborah Lynn, 1993. "'Pure Culture': A Feminist Analysis of IVF Ethos and Innovation", Ph.D. thesis, Department of Cultural Studies, University of Birmingham, Birmingham, England.

Government publications (London, HMSO)

Statutes

Surrogacy Arrangements Act, 1985. UK.
Local Government Act, 1988. UK.
Children Act, The, 1989. UK.
Human Fertilisation and Embryology Act, The, 1990. UK.

Bills

Unborn Children (Protection) Bill, 1984. UK.
Unborn Children (Protection) No. 2 Bill, 1985. UK.
Human Fertilisation and Embryology Bill, 1989. UK.

Other government publications

Department of Health and Social Security, 1986. 'DHSS Legislation on Human Infertility Services and Embryo Research: Consultation Paper.' London, DHSS.

Department of Health and Social Security, 1987. 'Human Fertilisation and Embryology: A Framework for Legislation.' London, HMSO.

Department of Social Security, 1991. 'Working Together Under the Children Act 1989: A Guide to Arrangements for Inter-Agency Co-operation for the Protection of Children from Abuse.' London, HMSO.

Home Office, 1992. 'Race and the Criminal Justice System.' London, HMSO.

Dion Farquhar

(M)OTHER DISCOURSES

Any theoretical evocation of an autonomous, positive femininity involves both an interrogation and supercession of masculinist norms and at the same time, an invention and remaking of signifying, representational, and epistemic norms.

Elizabeth Grosz[1]

I believe that there will be no racial or sexual peace, no livable nature, until we learn to produce humanity through something more and less than kinship. I think I am on the side of the vampires.

Donna Haraway[2]

THIS CHAPTER WILL SKETCH a third appropriation of the new technologies that is neither for nor against them. [. . .] both liberal and fundamentalist discourse can only endorse or condemn. In attempting to make sense of the contradictions, paradoxes, and aporias raised by the new reproductive technologies, only a third path that avoids the simplifications and binary evasions of both liberal and fundamentalist discourses seems viable. Instead of uncritical endorsement or out-of-hand dismissal, such a third way struggles to appreciate their multiple workings with regard to their creativity and generativity – for the revision of old and the creation of new hybrid entities and social relations, no less than for their uncritical recuperation of old categories of domination. Our only choices are not between Christian holism and fragmented commodification, between contract-arian liberalism and overdetermined conspiracy theory. Mothering does not have to be either an empowering ethical imperative and the telos of women's nature or a consolatory sop that reinforces male dominance and female victimization.[3]

Some feminist critics emphasize the multitude of ways that women's bodies are always mediated by their representations in discourse. There is no essential "natural" biological body that stands outside of discourses and institutions, power and will. The distinction between "the technologies themselves" and "the power relations within which . . . [they] are applied . . .,"[4] preserves its characterization as a thing and denies its flexibility, its historicity, and its status as a practice. This model of a fixed technology locates abuses in misuse (the value-neutral liberal model) or conspiracy (domination model) rather than in the power of potentially shifting historical practices and representations that can be challenged and modified. An alternative conceptualization of technology, "as a culture that expresses and consolidates relations amongst men,"[5] emphasizes its contingency over its fixity.

[. . .] [B]oth the liberal model and its binary, fundamentalism, ignores the plasticity of representations that constitute the diversity and perversity of women and men's resistances to, adptations of, and desires for technology – all of which make for different technological effects. Neutral, salvific, or vilifying representations or technology all exaggerate the power of technology to control their monolithically imagined clients. Michelle Stanworth has noted feminist criticism's "tendency to echo the very views of scientific and medical practice, of women and of motherhood, which feminists have been seeking to transform," including the high degree of manipulation that unthinking, desperate women will submit to.[6]

It is an irony of the development of feminist thought that some of radical feminist theory, fighting to distinguish itself from the near-hegemonic male voice of liberal discourse, should recapitulate the intolerance, authoritarianism, and universalizing representation it set out to combat. In massing women for political agency, radical feminism has legislated the essential similarity of women's "different" experience and attributes in contrast to an equally homogenized and underthematized similarity of "men's" experience. In addition, the move of valorizing "feminine" skills, tempera-ments, and traits that were historically denigrated not only mistook the historically constructed for the ontologically given. It also unintentionally recapitulated the public/private split of modern liberal society and its attendant hierarchized values. By focusing exclusively on women's separate (but superior) sphere, radical feminist discourse neglected to problematize the complex complementary processes by which *men* are hierarchically gendered.[7]

Others as mothers

In a reflection on the ambiguated status of motherhood for feminism, Ann Snitow asks a crucial question: "Do we want this now capacious identity, mother, to expand or to contract?"[8] Once the initial principal clientele of ARTs, childless heterosexual married couples with the ability to pay high medical fees, are themselves understood to be an exceedingly highly specific historical category, the political discursive struggles of those outside this demographic profile can be foregrounded. In addition to those (white, heterosexual, married, middle-class) bodies that cannot achieve and/or maintain a pregnancy because of some variant of reproductive pathology, there is a second major client base for ARTs that desires to have a child despite or against the expectations associated with their social status. The truism that ARTs enable people to have children who would not have had them without their intervention takes on a social dimension.

A decade ago, access to reproductive technologies was restricted to a subset of the first group – married heterosexual couples with the ability to pay, an "example of the medical profession's enforcement of social mores in the dispensing of services."[9] Early government inquiries into the regulation and evaluation of reproductive technologies, the Department of Health, Education, and Welfare's 1979 Ethics Advisory Board and England's 1984 Warnock Commission, both recommended restricting access to stable, heterosexual, married couples.[10] The 1994 Ethics Report of the American Fertility Society makes the same normative social point in its "Foreword": "That, generally speaking, a married heterosexual couple in a stable relationship provides the most appropriate environment for the rearing of a child."[11]

Against such social conservatism, the admission of other mothers to the assisted reproductive technologies client base is a result of representational contestations and political struggles of two major social movements – women's liberation and gay liberation.[12] Despite much feminist opposition to reproductive technologies on the grounds of male appropriation and alienation of "woman's" reproductive power, many women's desire to pursue aggressive invasive medical treatment for involuntary childlessness is proto-feminist. While presentation for treatment is correlated with class (ability to pay, education), it is also concomitant with a hubristic sense of entitlement, autonomy, and power over physical processes gone awry – not the typical profile of medical victimization much feminist literature represents.

Obstetrician-gynecologist Susan Robinson, impressed by the lack of access of one of her patients, a single woman whose lesbian identity had not been revealed to the AI clinics that refused her their services, eventually developed her own clinic program that would offer DI to all women, regardless of marital status or sexual preference. Her book, *Having a Baby Without a Man: The Woman's Guide to Alternative Insemination*, was written to advocate, inform, and enhance women's and other mothers' reproductive options. Published in 1985, it was one of the first of what is now a plethora of books that constituted a new genre – one that crosses self-help/how-to with minority reproductive advocacy.[13]

The past ten years have proved more hospitable to reproductive technologies in terms of both favorable public discussion and legislation expanding the rights to medical coverage *at the same time* that access to abortion and contraception have become more restrictive. The increase of medical insurance reimbursement, itself a result of intensified lobbying efforts of advocacy groups like Resolve, coupled with the increased militancy of groups of other mothers to be admitted to clientele, led to more and more people outside of the traditional heterosexual couple utilizing reproductive technologies than ever before.

Thus, single heterosexual women and both partnered and single lesbians with no discernible pathology have increasingly been utilizing ARTs, not primarily in order to bypass heterosexual coitus in achieving pregnancy because of some laboratory-conveyed advantage such as in IVF, but because of their collaborative reproductive potential. In addition, older (over 40) peri-menopausal women, on the other hand, who would be poor candidates for IVF, may avail themselves of a host of technologies: hyperovarian stimulation via pharmacological intervention and IUI, donor egg, donor embryo, or traditional surrogacy. By definitively separating sex from reproduction, reproductive technologies break the naturalized assumption that reproduction is heterosexual and heterosocial. By fetishizing the *social* criteria of "the [heterosexual] couple," medical discourse *invokes* the heterosexist standard only to *disrupt* it by its asexual and third-party donor interventions. Technology providers have responded to the politicized demand for inclusion by queer populations such as single hetero-sexual women, lesbians, gays, and older people whose access to them is now relatively routine and based primarily on ability to pay. A disproportionate number of ART clients are those whose subjectivities are "other" — older women and men, un-partnered heterosexual women, single and partnered lesbians, single heterosexual and gay men, gay couples, etc. Increasing alternative subjectivities' use of tech-nologies that separate reproduction into genetic, biological, and social aspects, confront the former givenness of reproduction and performatively declare *its* unnaturalness.

Entirely new discourses about pregnancy have been spun by users (buyers and sellers) of reproductive technologies. These are conflicted about what (if any) kernel can be thought of as "mothering." Is "mothering" the continuity of nurturance and connection that begins at birth, i.e., social-legal mothering? And what of all the women who "mother" episodically for a decade or more with custody or visitation of children within stepfamilies or blended families? Or is "mothering" the biogenetic tie that is based on supplying one's egg to another woman, providing the chromosomal and genetic substance of the baby? Or, is "mothering" the gestational experience of feeding and housing a fetus for nine months in utero (regardless of genetic connection) and then birthing it?

Reproductive technologies have stimulated alternative modes of representing the female body at the same time that they struggle to recuperate its "natural" fertility. Through third-party collaborative reproduction they make possible a parent-hood that bypasses the fetish of genetics that is at the heart of the natalist imperative. The abstraction and distribution of maternity that modern discourse on genetics and its accompanying technologies make possible have far-reaching implications for the future of sexual difference. For the first time historically, distributed maternity con-structs women's reproductive functions as parallel to men's distributed experience, which, of course, was always configured as being able to separate biogenetic paternity from social-legal paternity. Even the courts can no longer be counted on to rule in favor of paternal biogenetic claims. In a February 1994 case, *McDonald v. McDonald*, the New York State Appellate Division unanimously rejected the claims of a genetic father to custody of the couple's twin daughters against the gestational claims of his wife who used donor eggs to conceive.[14] The genetic parent does not automatically have superior rights against a gestational parent.

[. . .] [V]arious discourses representing reproductive technologies have tried to deny how they have radically refigured the way that bodily alterations like pregnancy can be experienced. Discourses that demonize reproductive technologies because they fragment a unified experience or sully a natural process by commodifying it deny *their* investments in idealizations that erase how they *depend on and are a result of* present capabilities. The insistence on maternal unity simplifies the variety of women's experiences of pregnancy. Such narratives about the pregnant body are invested in reaffirming traditional ideas of what women essentially *are* rather than contesting them or encouraging the construction of new ones. At the same time, the possibility of technologically assisted reproduction radically alters the hegemonic hold of already fissured conceptions of nature, reproduction, and maternity. For example, maternity could not have been meaningfully "experienced" or configured *as unitary* before the possibility of its distribution and the concomitant description of it by medical discourse as *distributable*.

The subsequent distribution of maternity into genetic-ovarian, gestational-uterine, and legal-social dimensions (and paternity into genetic and social fathers) challenges a romanticized unitary maternal (and paternal).[15] Instead of a tyranny of fragmentation and alienation, ARTs also pose a transgressive material and discursive challenge to the notions of romanticized holism, in general, and to unified maternal identity, in particular.[16]

"Unitary" maternity is a political category, a historically constructed and weighted polemical inscription of a formerly naturalized "experience" as something it was not, and could not have been, before discourse invested it as such. The purported universality and fixity of the category of unitary maternity is called into question *at the same time* it is named and called into existence – *by* its difference from an other, technologically distributed, maternity.

[. . .] [U]nitary maternity, then, is not a universal – pre-technological millennial "women's experience" – that gets appropriated, operated on, and fragmented by the new technologies. Rather, it is the difference of contemporary distributed maternity that makes what never existed – unified maternity – both theorizable and possible as a particular idealized historical performance of maternity, though one that attempts to mask its discursive constructedness at every turn. Technophobic naturalizing discourses operate by positing a pre-technological, protected idyll. They then narrate a binary agon; the only possible outcomes are decline or return to the "original" unity. Reproductive technologies thus create a nostalgia for projections about what might have been *before* present regimes of fragmentation.

Feminist alliances with postmodernist thinkers have been used to develop different practices of politics than the ones that the historical feminist project inherited. As such, it appreciates the complexity and contingency of social identities as well as its roots in strategic solidarities. Fortunately, however, the alternative of postmodern politics permits considering nonfoundational radical democratic possibilities. Ernesto Laclau and Chantal Mouffe were among the first to theorize the relevance of postmodern epistemologies to nonauthoritarian political and social analysis.

> The critique of the category of unified subject, and the recognition of the discursive dispersion within which every subject position is constituted . . . are the *sine qua non* for thinking the multiplicity out of which antagonisms emerge in societies in which the democratic revolution has crossed a certain threshold.[17]

Within a postmodern politics, there are no guaranteed outcomes, no train of victory narratives to hop on for the ride to glory. Instead, there is a range of strategic responses to subjections including the multiplication of resistances, the scrambling of master-codes, and the nurturing of new and hybrid forms. The project is to work within the necessity *and* the contingency of feminist politics, as theorist Judith Butler suggests: ". . . learn a double movement: to invoke the category and, hence, provisionally to institute an identity and at the same time to open the category as a site of permanent political contest."[18] Not foundations but horizons.[19]

I have argued the wisdom of rejecting liberal and fundamentalist representations of reproductive technologies and foraging for a third way that is not midway between them, that manifests neither their celebratory complicity nor their legislative authoritarianism. One hopes to enable different and other kinds of subjectivity and their promising implications for new kinds of relationships, politics, and communities.

The choices are not just antinatalism or pronatalism. There are other paths that involve utilizing the partial truths of conscripted onerous maternity and conscripted childlessness *and* those partial truths of chosen fulfilling maternity and chosen childfree living. A key part of any feminist reproductive project should be the dis-articulation, not only of maternity – which spans a complex social relation of desire – from women and women's bodies, but also of maternity from pregnancy.

Relative to ARTs, a postmodernist feminist approach might seek to displace the opposition between the natalism of uncritical liberal defenders of the technologies as helping desperate infertile couples, on the one hand, and both fundamentalist feminist positions – antinatalist technophobia and pronatalist essentialism – on the other hand. Such a displacement recognizes that maternity, when not nailed down, may go seriously awry. There will be mothers who kill, harm, or give away their offspring but there will also be other mothers who will join in the work and play of childraising and nurturance who are other genders and sexes and sexualities than those imagined by the regnant narrow patriarchal image repertoire.

Alternative models: beyond fundamentalism and liberalism

Fortunately, fundamentalist alienation narratives and individualist liberal market narratives are not the only theoretical narratives available. Both pronatalist and antinatalist figurations of maternity recuperate the same stereotypic and narrow social roles for women, albeit one overcoded with normative positivity and the other with negativity. Against the feminist difficulty of representing maternal practices that are neither deified nor demonized, we can still ask what other kinds of maternal desires look like. Desires for maternity may be partly imbricated with patriarchal desire, but they may also at the same time be new hybrid feminist conceptions by the unlikeliest of other mothers.

By the mid-1980s, postmodernist performers, poets, and theorists had criticized equality feminism for its reactiveness and unwitting validation of universalist humanism, i.e., male standards of accomplishment, power, knowledge. They had also criticized radical feminism for its uncritical celebration and reproduction of naturalized feminine characteristics, themselves elaborately constructed effects of patriarchal exclusions and overdeterminations, despite *its* accomplishment of acknowledg-ing race, class, and an endless supplement of other differences *between* women (e.g., sexuality, ethnicity, age, religion, ablebodiedness, etc.). Postmodern feminism problematized old binary stories and emphasized the nonbinary, gradated character of sexual difference.[20] In addition, the postmodernist critique of gender insisted on deconstructing the binary category "women," along with that of "men," focusing instead on the historical contingency and heterogeneity of both. They claimed that there is no pure invariant reserve of women's "sex" that exists before (or after "gender" has been deconstructed. "Real" women and their needs and demands are not erased by this deconstruction, only their inevitability and eternality. Drucilla Cornell puts it well:

> . . . sexual difference and more specifically feminine sexual difference, is not being erased; instead the rigid structures of gender identity which have devalued women and identified them with the patriarchal conventions of the gender hierarchy are being challenged.[21]

Bodies are always inextricably intertwined with discourse, culture, and power.[22]

Rejecting a characterization of reproductive technologies as particularly demonic or beneficent, a postmodern appraisal focuses on the historical specificity of the diversity of their uses and shifting of the meanings they generate for and by different constituencies. We have traced how ostensibly opposed representations of *the* reproductive body – feminism's body of "nature" and liberalism's "neutral" body – share more than is apparent. Both representations reinscribe women's bodies in a claustrophobic nature that is ahistorical and ultimately fixed, stable, and unmediated, and both deny their own discursive production of gendered and raced "reproduction."

A third path that recognizes the discursive aspect of ARTs as well as appreciates the historical and biographical conditions framing their reception can avoid the binary reductionism of these two positions. Alternative nonhumanist representations of the human body as denatured and ultimately cyborgian may stimulate new representations of technology that are more democratic, interesting, and pleasurable, as well as more able to eschew pastoral organicist origin narratives. Reproductive technologies are like any other set of practices, disciplines, and codes. They are interactive with individuals' and groups' appropriations and contestations.

Foregrounding the importance of subjectivities for reconstructing sex difference enables a different production of meaning and discourse about ARTs. An important similarity between the liberal celebration and the fundamentalist condemnation of reproductive technologies is the common tendency to treat reproduction in general and maternity in particular as historically and culturally universal practices. Both assume essential universal connection between "nature" and reproduction. Both narratives deny the diversity, fluidity, and essential contestedness of representations of people's reproductive and maternal experiences or, alternatively, the host of reasons for the absence or displacement of these practices in their lives. The liberal narrative, for example, fetishizes one particular historical view – which the interventions of reproductive technologies are designed to repair or aid – of the "natural" species' drive to have a child, the "naturalness" of biogenetic parenting, the normalcy of women's desire to mother, etc.

Fundamentalist narratives, on the other hand, fix another particular historical position as eternal – eliminate the male-dominating technologies and restore women's reproductive bodily integrity. The radical feminist version of this narrative configures natural maternity negatively, as freedom from technological intervention. This body – the natural, whole, maternal body – gets opposed to the traded, manipulated, fragmented, assembly-line body of liberal medical contract. In the name of "feminism" a thinly disguised moral protectionism would outlaw ARTs and "penaliz[e] its vendors and purveyors" in order to "prevent women from being technologically ravaged."[23] So-called right-to-life religious activists oppose both contraceptive and conceptive reproductive technologies because both nevertheless separate reproduction from conjugal sex, and the latter requires male masturbation. In addition, these technologies generally demystify biological reproduction by abstracting out its various components and stages, erode the exclusive claims of traditional biogenetic family kinship and its unified hierarchy of monolithic paternity and maternity, as well as inevitably destroy some embryos during IVF.

New representations of uncertainty and ambiguity, toleration of differential receptions and constructions of these technologies, and multivalent potentials are not acknowledged, or decried as anti-feminist, by fundamentalist feminists.[24] Fundamentalist discourse must invoke the category "false consciousness" to explain middle-class (mostly) white women's escalating demand for infertility services (paralleled only by the increasing willingness of medical insurance to pay). Renate Klein writes:

> But sometimes women also collude because we have been brainwashed. The information and education we get is one-sided and male-centered and the hidden conviction creeps into our own minds that men and their technology must be better than our own body and our own experiences with it.[25]

Actually, despite such textual disclaimers, anti-technology feminism believes that female "experience" is universal. There are no exceptions, no individuals for whom they do not and cannot speak.

Between dogmatic liberal endorsement of ARTs as "anything goes" and fundamentalist moralism, there is a more ambivalent agnostic postmodern position. Instead of demonizing technology, vilifying consumption, and idealizing an edenic natural, it looks at the demographics of ART users – as well as those who cannot even qualify as users because of poverty or cultural isolation from technological medicine, etc. – and suggests transgressive social and political possibilities.

Tiny percentages of the total population, people using reproductive technologies constitute a political mass, like Samuel Delany's male bodies massed for semi-public sex in gay bathhouses,[26] or women active in workplaces and public arenas of every description constituting groups whose uncontrollable social ontology threatens conventional reproductive ideology. The myriad possibilities of medical intervention construct and reconstruct the reproductive female and male body in ways that intersect with radical challenges to conventional notions of parenthood, identity, and the naturalness of "ordinary" sexual reproduction. By making possible the division of maternity into three components – genetic/chromosomal, uterine/gestational, and social/legal – and paternity into two components – genetic/chromosomal and social/legal – they expose the constructedness of "natural" laissez-faire reproduction of heterosexual intercourse, enlarge and diversify meanings of kinship beyond the limits of "blood," and deromanticize conjugal reproduction through commodification.

Reproduction can now occur outside of the "privacy" of the home, the master bedroom, the marital bed, and most importantly, outside of the phallocentric script that still passes for much heterosexual sex. The separation of reproduction from sex forces an acknowledgement of the historicity and constructedness of reproduction. Reproduction becomes historically situated. Despite her submission to invasive, stressful, expensive, and sometimes painful medical intervention, the female ART user need fake no orgasms nor provide emotional or sexual service to her impregnators in order to reproduce.

Donna Haraway's notion of the cyborg "as a fiction mapping our social and bodily reality and as an imaginative resource suggesting some very fruitful couplings" is useful to invoke the emancipatory potential of scientific practices that offer only "permanently partial identities and contradictory standpoints."[27] Despite some critics' concerns about the cyborg's tainted genealogy ("oppressive modernist roots"[28]) and the observation that "the cyborg originates in ectogenesis,"[29] I believe that it remains one of the most useful and fruitful metaphors advanced in the last decade for feminists wishing to displace liberal *and* fundamentalist representations of science and technology.[30] The difference that the experience and existence of cyborg families makes is a challenge to the assumptions, practices, and identities that are usually taken for granted as self-evident. (My child is "my flesh and blood," "fruit of my womb," "seed of the father," etc.)

Such novel conceptions of bodies that conceive, reproduce, and parent *differently*, that exploit the productivity of discourse, can be potentially destabilizing for patriarchal reproductive hegemony at the same time that their configuration and appropriation can uncritically continue or recuperate class and race privilege and male domination. Instead of viewing ARTs statically as an essential object, they might more productively be seen as shifting historical practices. Like all practices, disciplines, and codes, they are interactive with individuals and groups' appropriations and contestations.

By separating parenting into genetic, biological, and social-legal aspects, ARTs change and challenge the fetishizing of blood ties, the nuclear romance of reproduction, and their concomitant sexual identities. They declare the constructedness of reproduction by posing alternative ways to conceive. Rather than condemn this "system of dismembered motherhood," as a "reproductive brothel"[31] within which women would be completely controlled, dominated and "reduced to Matter,"[32] I would like to celebrate the diversity and oddities and exclusions that such a position denies.

A utopic elsewhere that is nowhere yet because it is neither wholly on the side of the hegemonic maternal – the biological-genetic – nor the hegemonic paternal – the legal-contractual – can contribute to the work of resignifying ARTs. Hopefully, the neither/both that critically names and uses these technologies cannot fail to transform its users any less than users can fail to transform the technologies. In the process, the circle of who and what may be embraced as "our" progeny may be widened. Rather than ally with the Right in mourning the denuclearization of the traditional family, I celebrate the proliferation of Other kinds of families and the growing fissures in the near-hegemonic figure of the mother. The desire to mother a child when articulated by, say, a gay man, a 40-(or 50-)year-old single woman, a lesbian couple, etc., is itself both an effect of the existence of ARTs and an offering of possibilities for refiguring and resignifying maternal practice and meaning.[33] I recommend strategic appropriation, continuing the fight for enlarged social and economic access (a decidedly anti-ecological moment) as well as continuing to appreciate the contradictions they problematize about the inadequacy and narrowness of our basic social categories. How "women" may "mother" and who counts as "kin" may democratize, pacify, and enrich a world made anxious by the increasing instability and inadequacy of these crisis-ridden categories.

How the use and reception of reproductive technologies continue will decide which possibilities are realized, in turn inviting new adjustments and resistances. The discourses that represent ARTs – their provision, use, and contestation – reaffirm both the capaciousness and potential alterity as well as the insidiousness and restrictiveness of liberalism, the terrain that both offers and undercuts the hope of an "outside" to our very problematic present. The fallout from denuclearization has only just begun, generating a multiplicity of Other Mothers, whose proliferating images "can appear as much ironic as iconic,"[34] producing new shiftings of subject positions, wonderful and terrible, depending on what "we" do about them.

Notes

1   Elizabeth Grosz, "Bodies and Knowledges: Feminism and the Crisis of Reason," in *Feminist Epistemologies* (New York: Routledge, 1993), p. 204.

2   Donna J. Haraway, "Universal Donors in a Vampire Culture: It's All in the Family: Biological Kinship Categories in the Twentieth-Century United States," in *Reinventing Nature*, ed. William Cronon (New York: Norton, [1998]).

3   In an article discussing a court case in which the plaintiff sued for property rights in a cell line made from his tissue and patented by a university scientist, Paul Rabinow notes the dilemma facing contemporaries: "having to choose between the long covered-over but still lingering residuum of Christian beliefs which hold 'the body' to be a sacred vessel and the tenets of the market culture's 'rational actor' view of the human person as contractual negotiator can lead to melancholy or stress depending on your disposition." Paul Rabinow, "Severing the Ties: Fragmentation and Dignity in Late Modernity," in *Knowledge and Society: The Anthropology of Science and Technology* vol. 9 (JAI Press, 1992), p. 171.

4   Rosalind Pollack Petchesky, "Foetal Images," in *Reproductive Technologies: Gender, Motherhood, and Medicine*, ed. Michelle Stanworth (Minneapolis: University of Minnesota Press, 1987), p 79.

5   Judy Wajcman, *Feminism Confronts Technology* (University Park: Pennsylvania State University Press, 1991), p. 22.

6   Michelle Stanworth, "Reproductive Technologies and the Deconstruction of Motherhood," in *Reproductive Technologies*, pp. 16–17.

7   Jane Flax, "Postmodernism and Gender Relations in Feminist Theory," in *Feminism/Postmodernism*, ed. Linda Nicholson (New York: Routledge, 1990), p. 45.

8   Ann Snitow, *MS* Magazine [1998].

9   Judith Lasker and Susan Borg, *In Search of Parenthood: Coping with Infertility and High-Tech Conception* (London: Pandora Press, 1989), p. 51.

10   Michelle Stanworth, "The Deconstruction of Motherhood," p. 192.

11   Ethics Committee, American Fertility Society, "Ethical Considerations of Assisted Reproductive Technologies," *Fertility and Sterility*, Supplement 1, vol. 62, no. 5 (November 1994), p. vi.

12   See, for example, April Martin, *The Lesbian and Gay Parenting Handbook* (New York: Harper Perennial, 1993).

Articles in the popular press abound. The popular press regularly registers a range of uncritical conventional responses – from celebration of a "miracle baby" to worry about the upsurge of middle-class, white, single motherhood, not to mention conflicting narrative responses ranging from celebration to consternation at social, legal, and political effects of technologically assisted reproduction.

Ellen Hopkins, "Tales from the Baby Factory," *New York Times Magazine*, March 15, 1992, and Anne Taylor Fleming, "Sperm in a Jar," *New York Times Magazine*, June 12, 1994; Elizabeth Royte, "The Stork Market," *Lear's* (November 1993). Interestingly, the more working-class-oriented weekly women's magazine sold at supermarket checkout counters, *Woman's World*, regularly narrates stories of the struggles of successful users of reproductive technologies, replete with photographs of rested, well-coiffed, and made-up moms with their smiling, well-dressed, clean multiples. See, for example, Lila Locksley, "Miracles of Modern Science," *Woman's World*, August 3, 1993, and Jo Alice, "Dawn's Three Little Miracles," vol. XVI, no. 20, May 16, 1995, pp. 39–41; "Motherhood after 60: Turning Back the Clock," *People*, January 24, 1994, pp. 37–41; Patricia Towle, "Woman Gives Birth to Her Own Grandson," *National Enquirer*, May 23, 1995, p. 2.

Examples of more critical representatives of this genre are Susan Jacoby's "The Pressure to Have a Baby," *Glamour*, September 1995, and a *Newsweek* cover story, "Infertility: High-Tech Science Fails 3 out of 4 Infertile Couples; Has the Hype Outweighed the Hope?" September 4, 1995. (Individual articles: Sharon Begley, "The Baby Myth," and Geoffrey Cowley, "The Future of Birth.")

13   Another early book is Judith Lasker and Susan Borg's *In Search of Parenthood*, an attempt to inform as well as create an identity among infertile and subaltern users, an ART-user community: "We hope that by reading this book, people who are considering these methods will have a clearer picture of what they are likely to face. Those who have already begun, or finished, trying an alternative should recognize that their experiences and emotions are shared by many others" (p. 7).

Ironically, another example of the discursive construction of experience is a fundamentalist feminist collection of women's testimonies about their experiences with reproductive technologies. The editor, Renate Klein, notes: "I hope that their insights in recounting their experiences as well as envisaging new models of 'infertility' and of trying to lead their lives differently will be inspiring to other women and give them the courage and stamina to say *no* to technological intervention." *Infertility: Women speak out about Their Experiences of Reproductive Medicine* (London: Pandora Press, 1989), p. 6.

14   *New York Law Journal*, "Father's Bid to Deny Mother Custody Fails," February 24, 1991, p. 1. Thanks to Carol Buell for calling my attention to this article.

15   A look at the recent law suits around the paternity custody claims of unwed fathers raises questions about what criteria to use to adjudicate between the claims of birthmothers who wish to make an adoption plan for their infant and those of birthfathers who oppose such a plan and seek custody.

16   Writing of the political efficacy of perpetual contestation, Judith Butler notes: ". . . what is lamented as disunity and factionalization from the perspective informed by the descriptivist ideal is *affirmed* by the anti-descriptivist perspective as the open and democratizing potential of the category." *Bodies That Matter: On the Discursive Limits of "Sex"* (New York: Routledge, 1993), p. 221.

17   Ernesto Laclau and Chantal Mouffe, *Hegemony and Socialist Strategy: Towards a Radical Democratic Politics* (London: Verso, 1985), p. 166.

18   Judith Butler, *Bodies That Matter*, p. 222.

19   Laclau and Mouffe, p. 183.

20   See Anne Fausto-Sterling, *Myths of Gender: Biological Theories about Women and Men* (New York: Basic Books, 1985), for a nuanced account of the dynamics of biology as a narrative system.

21   Drucilla L. Cornell, "Gender, Sex, and Equivalent Rights," in *Feminists Theorize the Political*, ed. Judith Butler and Joan W. Scott (New York: Routledge, 1992), p.281.

22   Radical feminism's equation of politics with ethics cannot but lament post-modernism's valorization of contingency. In a typical reduction of postmodernism to relativism, Janice Raymond states, "Everything is text and more text, signs and more signs, signifiers and more signifiers, *encouraging endless rounds of self-devouring equivocations.*" *Women as Wombs* [*MS* Magazine, May/June 1991], p. 193; my emphasis.

23   Janice Raymond, *Women as Wombs*, p. 208.

24   While Emily Martin, for example, admits that organ transplantation will necessitate "many readjustments in our conceptions of the self," she voices no analogous hopes for reproductive technologies (p. 20).

25   Renate Duelli Klein, "What's 'new' about the 'new' reproductive technologies?", in *Man-Made Women: How New Reproductive Technologies Affect Women*, Gena Corea *et al.* (Bloomington: Indiana University Press, 1987), p. 65.

26   Samuel Delany, *The Motion of Light in Water: Sex and Science Fiction Writing in the East Village, 1957–1965* (New York: New American Library, 1988).

27   Donna Haraway, "A Cyborg Manifesto," in *Simians, Cyborgs, and Women: The Reinvention of Nature* (New York: Routledge, 1991), pp. 150, 154.

28   See Susan Squier, *Babies in Bottles: Twentieth-Century Visions of Reproductive Technology* (New Brunswick, NJ: Rutgers University Press, 1994), p. 217, n. 21, for bibliography on the modernist legacy.

29   Susan Squier, *Babies in Bottles*, p. 95. Although Squier does acknowledge the feminist "quandary" and "impasse" (p. 95) about maternity, she is hypercritical of one of the most original, courageous, and ironic metaphors advanced in a decade, instead of predictably invoking "woman" and the "*experiencing* female body" (p. 96; her emphasis).

30   See "ARTs of Discourse: Donors, Dads, Mothers and Others", in *The Other Machine*, Dion Farquhar (London: Routledge, 1996) for a discussion of some of the problems with Susan Squier's rejection of the cyborg metaphor.

31   Gena Corea *et al.*, p. 291.

32   Ibid., p. 311.

33   Refuting both traditionalists' and feminists' fears that ARTs will hasten the demise of the family, Arthur Greil predicts that ARTs "more likely . . . will be employed to shore up traditional values." He cites the implantation of all fertilized eggs in the uterus to avoid criticism from Catholics and others, and the limitation of many IVF clinics' clientele to married couples. *Not Yet Pregnant*, p. 183.

34   Kate Weston writes of the image of the lesbian mother colliding with the view of "a gendered difference predicated on the symbolic union of male and female in heterosexual relationships." *Families We Choose: Lesbians, Gays, Kinship* (New York: Columbia University Press, 1991), p. 171.

Donna J. Haraway

THE VIRTUAL SPECULUM
IN THE NEW WORLD ORDER[1]

These are the days of miracle and wonder
This is the long distance call
The way the camera follows us in slo-mo
The way we look to us all
The way we look to a distant constellation
That's dying in a corner of the sky
These are the days of miracle and wonder
And don't cry, baby, don't cry

It was a dry wind
And it swept across the desert
And it curled into the circle of birth
And the dead sand
Falling on the children
The mothers and the fathers
And the automatic earth
[. . .]

Medicine is magical and magical is art
The Boy in the Bubble
And the baby with the baboon heart

And I believe
These are the days of lasers in the jungle
Lasers in the jungle somewhere
Staccato signals of constant information
A loose affiliation of millionaires
And billionaires and baby
These are the days of miracle and wonder
This is the long-distance call
© 1986 Paul Simon/Paul Simon Music (BMI)

In its ability to embody the union of science and nature,
the embryo might be described as a cyborg kinship entity.

(Sarah Franklin, 1993a: 131)

THE FETUS AND THE PLANET EARTH are sibling seed worlds in technoscience. If NASA photographs of the blue, cloud-swathed whole earth are icons for the emergence of global, national and local struggles over a recent natural–technical object of knowledge called the environment, then the ubiquitous images of glowing, free-floating, human fetuses condense and intensify struggles over an equally new and disruptive technoscientific object of knowledge, namely "life itself" (Franklin, 1993b; Duden, 1993; Foucault, 1978). Life as a system to be managed – a field of operations constituted by scientists, artists, cartoonists, community activists, mothers, anthropologists, fathers, publishers, engineers, legislators, ethicists, industrialists, bankers, doctors, genetic counsellors, judges, insurers, priests, and all their relatives – has a very recent pedigree. The fetus and the whole earth concentrate the elixir of life as a complex system; that is, of life itself. Each image is about the origin of life in a postmodern world.

Both the whole earth and the fetus owe their existence as public objects to visualizing technologies. These technologies include computers, video cameras, satellites, sonography machines, optical fibre technology, television, micro cinematography and much more. The global fetus and the spherical whole earth both exist because of, and inside of, technoscientific visual culture. Yet, I think, both signify touch. Both provoke yearning for the physical sensuousness of a wet and blue-green earth and a soft, fleshy child. That is why these images are so ideologically powerful. They signify the immediately natural and embodied, over and against the constructed and disembodied. These latter qualities are charged against the supposedly violating, distancing scopic eye of science and theory. The audiences who find the glowing fetal and terran spheres to be powerful signifiers of touch are themselves partially constituted as subjects in the material-semiotic process of viewing. The system of ideological oppositions between signifiers of touch and vision remains stubbornly essential to political and scientific debate in modern western culture. This system is a field of meanings that elaborates the ideological tension between body and machine, nature and culture, female and male, tropical and northern, coloured and white, traditional and modern, and lived experience and dominating objectification.

The sacred and the comic

Sometimes complicitous, sometimes exuberantly creative, western feminists have had little choice about operating in the charged field of oppositional meanings structured around vision and touch. Small wonder, then, that feminists in science studies are natural deconstructionists, who resolutely chart fields of meanings that unsettle these oppositions, these set-ups that frame human and non-human technoscientific actors and sentence them to terminal ideological confinement (Treichler and Cartwright, 1992). Because the fruit issuing from such confinement is toxic, let us try to reconceive some of the key origin stories about human life that congeal around the images of the fetus. In many domains in contemporary European and US cultures, the fetus functions as a kind of metonym, seed crystal, or icon for configurations of person, family, nation, origin, choice, life and future. As the German historian of the body Barbara Duden put it, the fetus functions as a modern "*sacrum*", i.e., as an object in which the transcendent appears. The fetus as *sacrum* is the repository of heterogeneous people's stories, hopes and imprecations. Attentive to the wavering opposition between the sacred *versus* the comic, the sacramental *versus* the vulgar, scientific illustration *versus* advertising, art *versus* pornography, the body of scientific truth *versus* the caricature of the popular joke, the power of medicine *versus* the insult of death, I want to proceed here by relocating the fetal *sacrum* onto its comic twin.

In this task, I am instructed by feminists who have studied in the school of the masters. Two feminist cartoons separated by twenty years, and a missing image that cannot be a joke, will concern me most in this essay's effort to read the comics in technoscience. Set in the context of struggles over the terms, agents and contents of human reproduction, all three of my images trouble a reductionist sense of "reproductive technologies". Instead, the images are about a specifically feminist concept called "reproductive freedom". From the point of view of feminist science studies, freedom projects are what make technical projects make sense – with all the specificity, ambiguity, complexity and contradiction inherent in technoscience. Science projects are civics projects; they remake citizens. Technoscientific liberty is the goal (Flower, n.d.). Keep your eyes on the prize (Hampton, 1986–7).

The first image (Figure 3.4A), a cartoon by Anne Kelly that I have named the *Virtual Speculum*, is a representation of Michelangelo's painting of the *Creation of Adam* on the ceiling of the Sistine Chapel (Figure 3.4B). The *Virtual Speculum* is a caricature in the potent political tradition of "literal" reversals, which excavate the latent and implicit oppositions that made the original picture work. In Kelly's version, a female nude is in the position of Adam, whose hand is extended to the creative interface

Figure 3.4A "The Virtual Speculum" by Anne Kelly
      (Stabel, 1924)

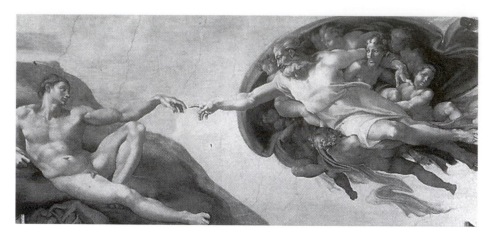

Figure 3.4B "The Creation of Adam" by Michelangelo, Sistine Chapel (1511–12)

with, not God the Father, but a keyboard for a computer whose display screen shows the global digital fetus in its amniotic sac. A female Adam, the young nude woman is in the position of the first man. Kelly's figure is not Eve, who was made from Adam and in relation to his need.[2] In the *Virtual Speculum*, the woman is in direct relation to the source of life itself.

The cartoon seems to resonate in an echo chamber with a Bell Telephone advertisement on US television in the early 1990s, which urged potential long-distance customers "to reach out and touch someone". The racial-ethnic markings of the cast of characters varied in different versions of the ad. The visual text shows a pregnant woman, who is undergoing ultrasonographic visualization of her fetus, telephoning her husband, the father of the fetus, to describe for him the first spectral appearance of his issue. The description is performative; i.e., the object described comes into existence, experientially, for all the participants in the drama. Fathers, mothers and children are constituted as subjects and objects for each other and the television audience. Life itself becomes an object of experience, which can be shared and memorialized. Proving herself to be a literate citizen of technoscience, the pregnant woman interprets the moving gray, white and black blobs of the televised sonogram as a visually obvious, differentiated fetus. Family bonding is in full flower in Bell Telephone's garden of creation. Surrogate for the absent father, the mother touches the on-screen fetus, establishing a tactile link between both parents-to-be and child-to-be. Here are interactive television and video of a marvellous kind. The mother-to-be's voice on the phone and finger on the screen are literally the conduits for the eye of the father. These are the touch and the word that mediate life itself, that turn bodies and machines into eloquent witnesses and storytellers.

Through advertising, Bell Telephone puts us inside the dramatic scenarios of technology and entertainment, twins to biomedicine and art. In the ad, reproductive technology and the visual arts – historically bound to the specific kinds of observation practised in the gynaecological exam and the life-drawing class – come together through the circles of mimesis built into communications practices in the New World Order. Life copies art copies technology copies communication copies life itself. Television, sonography, computer video display and the telephone are all apparatuses for the production of the nuclear family on screen. Voice and touch are brought into life on screen.

Kelly's cartoon works off the fact, which remains odd to women of my menopausal generation, that in many contemporary technologically mediated pregnancies, expectant mothers emotionally bond with their fetuses through learning to see the developing child on screen during a sonogram (Rapp, 1998). And so do fathers, as well as members of Parliament and Congress (Hartouni, 1991; Franklin, 1993a). The sonogram is only one in a battery of visual artifacts that establish the fact of fetal life within political, personal and biomedical discourse. But obstetrical ultrasonography figures in powerful political–technical pedagogies for learning to see who exists in the world (Petchesky, 1987; [reading 3.1 in this volume]). Selves and subjects are produced in such "lived experiences". Quickening, or the mother's testimony to the movement of the unseen child-to-be in her womb, has here neither the experiential nor epistemological authority it did, and does, under different historical modes of embodiment. In Kelly's version, the bonding produced by computer-mediated visualization also produces subjects and selves; the touch at the keyboard is generative – emotionally, materially and epistemologically. But things work both similarly and differently from the way they do on the Sistine Chapel ceiling or in the Bell Telephone TV advertisement.

In the *Virtual Speculum* the grayish blobs of the television sonogram have given place to the defined anatomical form of the free-floating fetus. Kelly's on-screen fetus is more like an *in vivo* movie, photograph or computer-graphic reconstruction – all of which are received at least partly within the conventions of post-Renaissance visual realism, which the blob-like sonographic image has great difficulty invoking. The televised sonogram is more like a biological monster movie, which one still has to learn to view even in the late twentieth century. By contrast, to those who learned how to see after the revolution in painting initiated in the fifteenth and sixteenth centuries in Northern and Southern Europe, the free-floating, anatomically sharp, perspectively registered fetal image appears self-evident at first viewing. Post-Renaissance anatomical realism and late twentieth-century computer-generated corporeal realism still share many, although not all, viewing conventions and epistemological assumptions.

The fetus like the one in *Virtual Speculum* is the iconic form that has been made so familiar by the exquisite, internationally distributed images produced by the Swedish biomedical photographer, Lennart Nilsson. Endoscopic intrauterine fetal visualization began in the 1950s, well before sonograms were part of the cultural terrain. The visible fetus became a public object with the April 1965 *Life* magazine cover featuring Nilsson's photograph of an intrauterine eighteen-week-old developing human being, encased in its bubble-like amniotic sac. The rest of the Nilsson photos in the 1965 *Life* story, "The Drama of Life before Birth", were of extrauterine abortuses, beautifully lit and photographed in colour to become the visual embodiment of life at its origin. Not seen as abortuses, these gorgeous fetuses and their descendants signified life itself, in its transcendent essence and immanent embodiment. The visual image of the fetus is like the DNA double helix – not just a signifier of life, but also offered as the thing-in-itself. The visual fetus, like the gene, is a technoscientific sacrament. The sign becomes the thing itself in ordinary magico-secular transubstantiation.

Nilsson's images have spiked the visual landscape for the last thirty years, each time with announcements of originary art and technology, originary personal and scientific experience, and unique revelations bringing what was hidden into the light. Nilsson's photographs are simultaneously high art, scientific illustration, research tool and mass popular culture. The 1965 "Drama of Life before Birth" was followed by the popular coffee-table format book, *A Child Is Born* (Nilsson, 1977); the NOVA television special in 1983, "The Miracle of Life"; the lavishly illustrated book (Nilsson, 1987) on the immune system, including images of developing fetuses, *The Body Victorious*; and the August 1990 *Life* cover photo of a seven-week-old fetus, with the caption, "The First Pictures Ever of How Life Begins", and the accompanying story, "The First Days of Creation" (Stabile, 1992). Finally, moving from conception through breast feeding, *A Child Is Born* was issued as a compact-disk adaptation, whose content-rich multimedia design offers interactive features as part of the visual fetal feast (Nilsson and Hamberger, 1994). A review for the disk in *Wired*, a prominent cyber-culture magazine with about an 80 per cent male readership, assures the potential buyer, "Interactivity remains an option, never an interruption or a chore" (Gasperini, 1994: 198). Truly, we are in the realm of miracles, beginnings and promises. A secular terrain has never been more explicitly sacred, embedded in the narratives of God's first Creation, which is repeated in miniature with each new life (Harding, 1990). Secular, scientific visual culture is in the immediate service of the narratives of Christian realism. We are in both an echo chamber and a house of mirrors, where, in word and image, ricocheting mimesis structures the emergence of subjects and objects. It does not seem too much to claim that the biomedical, public fetus – given flesh by the high technology of visualization – is a sacred–secular incarnation, the material realization of the promise of life itself. Here is the fusion of art, science and creation. No wonder we look.

The Kelly cartoon is practically an exact tracing of its original. Looking at Kelly's cartoon returns the reader of comics to Michelangelo's *Creation of Adam*. For "modern" viewers, the entire ceiling of the Sistine Chapel signifies an eruption of salvation history into a newly powerful visual narrative medium. Accomplished between 1508 and 1512 under the patronage of Pope Julius II, the ceiling's frescos mark a technical milestone in mastering the Renaissance problem of producing a convincing pictorial rendering of narrative. The gestures and attitudes of the human body sing with stories. Part of the apparatus of production of Christian humanism, which has animated the history of western-science, European early modern or Renaissance painting developed key techniques for the realization of man. Or, at least, that is a key way "modern man" tells his history.

Although I will not trace them, innovations in literary technology are also part of this story. Eric Auerbach (1953) places the critical mutation in Dante's *Divine Comedy*, with its powerful figurations of salvation history that locate promised transcendental fulfillment in the material tissues of solid narrative flesh. Figurations are performative images that can be inhabited. Verbal or visual, figurations are condensed maps of whole worlds. In art, literature and science, my subject is the technology that turns body into story, and vice versa, producing both what can count as real and the witnesses to that reality. In my own mimetic critical method, I am taking some of the circulations of Christian realism in the flesh of technoscience. I work to avoid the terms "Judeo-Christian" or "monotheist" because the dominant technoscientific visual and narrative materials here are specifically secular Christian renditions of partially shared Jewish, Muslim and Christian origin stories for science, self and world. But I am also trying to trace the story within a story, within which we learn to believe that fundamental revolutions take place. I am trying to retell some of the conditions of possibility of the stories technoscientific humans continue to tell ourselves. It is doubtful that historical configurations conventionally called the "Renaissance", or in a later version of the birth of the modern, the "Scientific Revolution", or today's rendition called the "New World Order" actually have been unique, transformative theatres of origin. But they have been narrativized and canonized as such cradles of modern humanity, especially technoscientific humanity with its secular salvation and damnation histories. Certainly, if only by opposition, I am complicit in the narrativization and figuration of the Scientific Revolution and the New World Order.

Metonymic for the entire array of Renaissance visual techniques, Albrecht Dürers *Draughtsman Drawing a Nude* (1538) (Figure 3.4C) conventionally dramatizes the story of a revolutionary apparatus for turning disorderly bodies into disciplined art and science. In the drawing, an old man uses a line-of-sight device and a screen-grid to transfer point-for-point the features of a voluptuous reclining female nude onto a paper grid marked off into squares. The upright screen-grid separates the prone woman on the table, whose hand is poised over her genitals, from the erectly seated draughtsman, whose hand guides his stylus on the paper. Dürer's engraving attests to the power of the technology of perspective to discipline vision to produce a new kind of knowledge of form. As art historian Lynda Nead argued, "[V]isual perception is placed on the side of art and in opposition to the information yielded through tactile perception. . . . Through visual perception we may achieve the illusion of a coherent and unified self" (Nead, 1992: 28). Here also, with Dürer, the disciplining screen between art and pornography is paradigmatically erected.

The gendering of this kind of vision is, of course, not subtle. Indeed, feminists argue that this visual technology was part of the apparatus for the *production* of modern gender, with its proliferating series of sexually charged oppositions condensed into the tension at the interface between touch and vision. Nead writes,

> Woman offers herself to the controlling discipline of illusionistic art. With her bent legs closest to the screen, [Dürer's] image recalls not simply the life class but also the gynaecological examination. Art and medicine are both foregrounded here, the two discourses in which the female body is most subjected to scrutiny and assessed according to historically specific norms.
>
> (1992: 11)

Obviously, it is only after the institutions of the life class and the gynaecological exam emerged that Dürer's print can be retrospectively read to recall them. As part of reforming her own self-making technology, Nead, the feminist art historian, is telling a story about the birth of the figure of Woman. As for me, the feminist analyst of technoscience attuned to artistic and biomedical visual delights, I see Dürer's majestic print and Bell Telephone's television advertising through the grid of Kelly's virtual speculum. In the life class and gynecological exam that is technoscience,

Figure 3.4C "Draughtsman Drawing a Nude" by Albrecht Dürer (1538)

critique caresses comedy. I laugh; therefore, I am . . . implicated. I laugh; therefore, I am responsible and accountable. That is the best I can do for moral foundations at the tectonic fault line joining the sacred, the scientific and the comic. And everyone knows that end-of-the-millennium Californians build their houses, and their theories, on fault lines.

In Renaissance visual technology, form and narrative implode; and both seem merely to reveal what was already there, waiting for unveiling or discovery. This epistemology underlies the European-indebted sense of what counts as reality in the culture, believed by many of its practitioners to transcend all culture, called modern science. Reality, as westerners have known it in story and image for several hundred years, is an *effect*, but cannot be recognized as such without great moral and epistemological angst. The conjoined western modern sense of the "real" and the "natural" was achieved by a set of fundamental innovations in visual technology beginning in the Renaissance.[3]

Twentieth-century scientists call on this earlier visual technology for insisting on a specific kind of reality, which readily makes today's observers forget the conditions, apparatuses and histories of its production. Especially in computer and information sciences and in biotechnology and biomedicine, representations of late twentieth-century technosciences make liberal use of iconic exemplars of early modern European art/humanism/technology. Current images of technoscience quote, point to, and otherwise evoke a small, conventional, potent stock of Renaissance visual analogues, which provide a legitimate lineage and origin story for technical revolutions at the end of the Second Christian Millennium. Today's Renaissance *Sharper Image Catalogue* includes the anatomized human figures in *De humanis corporis fabrica* of Andreas Vesalius, published in Basel in 1543; Leonardo da Vinci's drawing of the human figure illustrating proportions, or the "Vitruvian Man" (c. 1485–90); Dürer's series of plates on perspective techniques; the maps of the cartographers of the "Age of Discovery"; and, of course, Michelangelo's *Creation of Adam*. Invoking this ready stock, a venture capitalist from Kleiner Perkins Caufield & Byers mutated the analogies to make a related historical observation, noting that biotech has been "for human biology what the Italian Renaissance was for art" (Hamilton 1994: 85). In technoscientific culture, at the risk of mild overstatement, I think one can hardly extend an index finger (or finger substitute) toward another hand (or hand substitute) without evoking the First Author's gesture (or First Author Substitute's gesture).

In Michelangelo's version of authorship, Adam lies on the earth; and, conveyed by angels, God moves toward him from the heavens. An elderly, patriarchal God the Father reaches his right index finger to touch the languidly extended, left index finger of an almost liquid, nude, young-man Adam. A conventional art history text concludes, "Adam, lying like a youthful river god, awakens into life" (Hays, 1967: 99; see also Jansen and Jansen, 1963: 359–60). Adam is a kind of watery, earth-borne fetus of humanity, sparked into life on a new land by the heavenly Father. Michelangelo's God, however, is also carrying another, truly unborn human being. Still in the ethereal regions above earth, Eve is held in the shelter of God's left arm; and at the origin of mankind she and Adam are looking toward each other. It is not entirely clear who Adam sees, God or Woman – exactly the problem addressed by the screen barrier between art and pornography. Maybe in innocence before the Fall and at the moment of the renaissance of modern vision, a yearning Adam can still see both at once. Touch and vision are not yet split. Adam's eye caresses both his Author and his unborn bride.

Anne Kelly's drawing suggests other screens as well, such as that between art and science, on the one hand, and caricature and politics, on the other. Like the transparent film between art and pornography, the interface between the medico-scientific image and the political cartoon unstably both joins and separates modest witnesses and contaminated spectators. In both potent zones of transformation, the reclining female nude seems suggestively common. Dürer's woman in *Draughtsman Drawing a Nude*, the *Venus d'Urbino* by Titian (1487?–1576), the *Rokeby Venus* by Diego Velázquez (1599–1660), *Venus at Her Toilet* by Peter Paul Rubens (1577–1640), and Edouard Manet's *Olympia* (1863) are all ancestors for Kelly's first woman. Kelly's cartoon figure depends on the conventions for drawing the recumbent nude female in modern western painting. Dürer's, Titian's, Velázquez's, Rubens' and Manet's nudes all figure prominently in accounts of the emergence of modern ways of seeing (Clark, 1985). The relation between Manet's African serving woman and the reclining European nude also figures in the fraught racialized visual history of modern Woman (Nead, 1992: 34–46; Harvey, 1989: 54–6). Clearly, the *Virtual Speculum* keeps its eyes on the prize.

Lynn Randolph's painting, *Venus* (Figure 3.4D), part of her *Ilusas* or "deluded women" series, is a more formal feminist intervention into the conventions of the female nude and her associated secretions and tools. Scrutinizing the standard line between pornography and art, Randolph (1993: 1) writes:

> This contemporary Venus is not a Goddess in the classical sense of a contained figure. She is an unruly woman, actively making a spectacle of herself. Queering Botticelli, leaking, projecting, shooting, secreting milk, transgressing the boundaries of her body. Hundreds of years have passed and we are still engaged in a struggle for the interpretive power over our bodies in a society where they are marked as a battleground by the church and the state in legal and medical skirmishes.

Kelly, however, is drawing a female Adam, not a Venus. The story is different, and so is the optical technology. Kelly's woman looks not into the mirror that fascinates Rubens' and Velázquez's nudes, but into a screen that is in the heavenly position

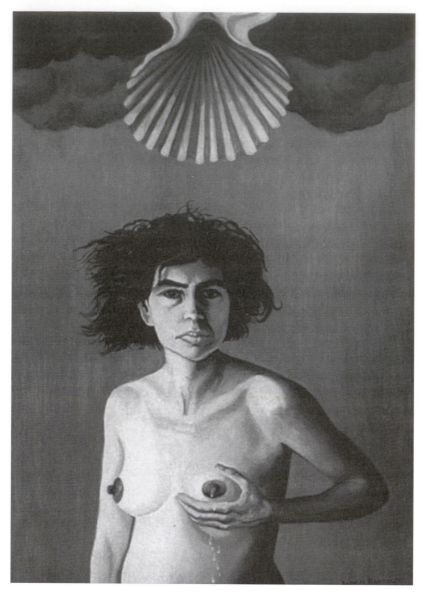

Figure 3.4D "Venus" by Lynn Randolph (1992)

of Michelangelo's God. The "venereal" women with mirrors in the history of western painting have given way in Kelly to the "authorial" woman with keyboard and computer terminal. Kelly's woman is not in a story of reflections and representations. Whatever she sees, it is not her reflection. The computer screen is not a mirror; the fetus is not her double or her copy. First woman in *Virtual Speculum* looks not into the normal reality established by Renaissance perspective, but into the virtual reality given by a time called postmodernity. Both realities are technical effects of particular apparatuses of visual culture. Both realities are simultaneously material, embodied and imaginary. Both realities can only be inhabited by subjects who learn how to see and touch with the right conventions. It's all a question of interactive visual technology. Reach out and touch someone; this is the long-distance call.

Not under the arm of God, but in computer-generated visual space, the fetus meets first woman's gaze. Kelly's unborn fetus, not the Adam-like woman, is in the position of Michelangelo's still-uncreated Eve. From the non-perspective of virtual space, the first woman and the fetus confront each other, as Adam and Eve did in Michelangelo's version of human creation. In that reading, the computer screen is the embracing arm of God. Has His gender value been transmuted as Adam's has been? Is the computer womb now female, or is gender one of the many things at stake? Kelly's cartoon allows at least two readings of the fetus: it is either in the position of God or in that of the not-yet-created Eve. If the fetus is Eve, the computer itself, with keyboard, is the encompassing deity reaching out to the female Adam's extended but limp hand. That reading makes Kelly's Adam the effect of the computer, the effect of the "creative" technologies of cyberspace. On the other hand, the female Adam has her hand on the keypad; she seems to be in the position of author. Then, the fetus is her file, which she is writing, editing or, as one viewer suggested, deleting. Certainly, the politics of abortion are implicitly in this cartoon. Maybe she is reaching for the "escape" key, or perhaps merely the "control" key.

Like traditional masculine figures in the reproductive imagery of technoscience, who have brain children all the time, Kelly's first woman seems to have a pregnancy associated with the organs of cognition and writing. Her pregnancy is literally extra-uterine. Or, perhaps Kelly's Adam is not pregnant at all; she may be viewing a fetus with no further connection to her once the file is closed. Literally, the fetus is somehow "in" the computer. This fetus is a kind of data structure, whose likely fate seems more connected to downloading than birth or abortion. Just as the computer as womb-brain signifies the superior creativity of artificial intelligence (AI), the on-screen fetus is an artificial life (ALife) form. As such, *Virtual Speculum*'s fetus is *not* disembodied. Rather, the specific form of embodiment inside the apparatuses of technoscience is the material conundrum presented by the cartoon. The computer is metonymic for technoscience, an inescapable materialization of the world. Life itself, a kind of technoscientific deity, may be what is virtually pregnant. These ontologically confusing *bodies*, and the practices that produce specific embodiment, are what we have to address, not the false problem of *dis*embodiment. Whose and which bodies – human and non-human, silicon-based and carbon-based – are at stake and how, in our technoscientific dramas of origin? And what is the specific political and moral accountability attached to these not-always-human bodies?

The proliferating readings of Kelly's cartoon make one conclusion inescapable: reversals and substitutions never just substitute for or reverse the values of the original. Rather, reversals and substitutions undo the original, opening the story up in unexpected ways. Themselves forms of repetition, reversals and substitutions make the condition of all repetition obvious. The great stories of mimesis are undone. Caricature breaks the unspoken agreements that stabilized the original. Caricatures break the frame of salvation history. Perhaps that point gives the key for reading the multiple out-of-frame elements of Kelly's cartoon. The pregnancy is ectopic, to say the least; the fetal umbilical cord and barely visible placenta go off screen on the display terminal; and the electrical cords wander up and off screen from the whole cartoon, with no point of attachment in view. The computer terminal, itself a work station, seems to be the meta-fetus in the picture. Further, this meta-fetus is an extrauterine abortus, with ripped out umbilical cords like those in Lennart Nilsson's emblematic photographs of the beginnings of life itself. There is an odd kind of obstetrical art and technology at work here. It is not just Dürer's visual technology that makes a feminist "recall" the gynaecological exam and the life class, those troubling and productive scenes of medical science and of art. In Kelly's meditation, the examination of both art and life is distinctly eccentric.

Fetal work stations and feminist technoscience studies

If Kelly's fetus cannot be the woman's reflection, the unborn being might be her project, or someone's project. More likely, the fetus in cyberspace signifies an entity that is constituted by many variously related communities of practice. This fetus is certainly an object of attention and a locus of work (Casper, 1995b), and Kelly's First Woman is at her work station. Feminist scholars have also been at a "fetal work station". Like data processors at their video terminals in the information economy, feminists' positions at their analytical keyboards have not always been a matter of choice. Reproduction has been at the centre of scientific, technological, political, personal religious gender, familial, class, race and national webs of contestation for at least the last twenty-five years. Like it or not, as if we were children dealing with adults' hidden secrets, feminists could not avoid relentlessly asking where babies come from. Our answers have repeatedly challenged the reduction of that original and originating question to literalized and universalized women's body parts. It turns out that addressing the question of where babies come from puts us at the centre of the action in the New World Order. With roots in local and international women's health movements as well as in various scholarly communities, since the early 1970s feminists have developed a rich toolkit for technoscience studies through their attention to the social-technical webs that constitute reproductive practice (Ginsberg and Rapp, 1991, 1995). Idiosyncratically, I will inspect a small, recent inventory from this toolbox in order to pursue my inquiry into the optical properties of the virtual speculum.

In their powerful paper on the many constituencies who construct the French abortifacent called RU486, sociologist Adele Clarke and her former student Teresa Montini developed social worlds and arena analysis for feminist science studies. Clarke and Montini (1993) identify reproductive and other scientific-medical specialists; pharmaceutical companies; anti-abortion groups; feminist pro-choice groups; women's health movement groups; politicians, Congress, and the Food and Drug Administration; and women users and consumers of RU486. The authors are clear that their own analysis turns the volume up or down on some actors more than others; their own representations are part of the struggle for what will count as reproductive freedom, and for whom. Attention to this kind of point characterizes feminist science studies in general, whether generated from the academy or policy-forming and community-action sites.

Using these tools, Monica Casper (1995a, b) studies human fetal surgery historically and ethnographically. Casper is developing the notions of the "techno-fetus" and the "fetus as work object". Casper's approach shows the fetus to be the site and result of multiple actors' work practices, including the mother's. Because Casper is necessarily a member of interdigitating communities of scholarly and political practice, her own positioning is neither invisible nor unaccountable. The many communities of practice who are held together around the technofetus are by no means necessarily in harmony. Their work tools – rhetorical and material – can make the fetus into very different kinds of entities. However, neither "multiplicity" nor "contestation" for their own sake are the point in feminist science studies. Joining analysts to subjects and objects of analysis, questions of power, resources, skills, suffering, hopes, meanings and lives are always at stake.

In a similar spirit, Charis Cussins (1996), trained in a science studies programme, traces the continual "ontological choreography" that constructs subjects, objects and agents at an infertility clinic. Subjects and objects are made and unmade in many ways in the extended processes of infertility treatment. Cussins shows that the different stakes, temporalities, trajectories and connections and disconnections to women's and others' bodies and part-bodies – as humans and non-humans are enrolled together in the practices of technoscience – require ethnographic, sustained inquiry.

Anthropologist Rayna Rapp's multi-year ethnographic study of women in New York City from many social classes, ethnicities, language communities and racially marked groups also vividly describes the plethora of material-semiotic worlds in which fetuses and pregnant women have their being (Rapp, 1994, 1998). Women who accept and who refuse the procedures of fetal genetic diagnosis, research geneticists, genetic counsellors, family members, support groups for people with genetically disabled children – all these people, variously intertwined with machines, babies, fetuses, clinical materials and with each other, make up Rapp's research community. The consequences of all the actors' locations in these dynamic, differentiated worlds are crucial to her account; and her own profound mutations in the course of doing the work grow from and feed back into the research and writing.

In the linked interdisciplinary worlds of feminist accounts of technoscience, Valerie Hartouni (1996), located professionally in a communications department, takes up the many contending discourses of maternal nature in contemporary reproductive cultures in the US. In a subtle and incisive series of essays, Hartouni examines how class, gender and genetic parenthood interdigitate in the Baby M surrogate mother legal arguments; how the judicial injunction not to speak of race in the case of the African-American gestational surrogate Anna Johnson, who carried a child for a mixed-race (Filipina-Anglo) couple, was nonetheless part of the saturation of the case with racial and class markings; and how the performance video, *S'Aline's Abortion*, despite explicit pro-choice intentions, nonetheless was positioned by its visual rhetoric inside anti-choice narratives for many audiences. Hartouni's work is part of the broad feminist inquiry into how the genetic relationship displaces other discourses of connection to a child in legal, biotechnical, familial and entertainment worlds. Her writing contributes to the project of crafting feminist visual literacy needed for working effectively inside a reproductive technoscience politics saturated with visual communications practices.

Reproductive politics are at the heart of questions about citizenship, liberty, family and nation. Feminist questions are not a "special preserve", but a "general" discourse critical for science studies as such. Inaugural acts of chief executive officers in mid-1990s US politics illustrate an aspect of this claim. After taking the oath of office as President of the United States in January 1993, Bill Clinton issued his first executive orders, which established his presidency symbolically and materially. His first acts did not concern war or other conventional domains of national interest and manly action. His first acts had to do with embryos and fetuses embedded in technoscientific contestations. Through embryos and fetuses, those orders had to do with entire forms of life – public, embodied and personal – for the citizens of the state. Clinton began the process of lifting restrictions on providing information about abortion in federally funded clinics, permitting medical experimentation on aborted fetal tissue and allowing the importation of the controversial abortifacent and potential cancer treatment, RU486.

Similarly, but with opposite political intent, the first official act of Pete Wilson after he was re-elected Governor of California in 1994 was to order a state pro-gramme closed that provided pre-natal care to pregnant "undocumented" immigrant women. Wilson had staked his campaign on Proposition 187, which denied so-called illegal immigrants virtually all social services, especially public education and non-emergency medical care. Despite the denials of its backers, Proposition 187 was widely understood to have fundamental racial-ethnic, class and national targets, especially working-class Latinos of colour coming across the Mexican–US border. The measure passed by a two-to-one margin. That is, Proposition 187 was over-whelmingly popular with the older, Republican, white and economically affluent electorate who voted in the 1994 election – many of whom, including a candidate for US Senate who supported Proposition 187, had recently hired "illegal" women of colour to care for their white children, while seeking to withhold social services from the children of these same employees. To withhold reproductive health care from "undocumented" women of colour, whose children would be born US citizens if their pregnancies came to term in California, was the first concern of the re-elected executive. Fetal protection (and the health of women) suddenly looked like a bad idea, and fetal endangerment (and the endangerment of "illegal" women of colour) was the direct implication of the Governor's inaugural act. Biomedicine – where post-natal people, machines, fetuses, health beliefs, diagnostic procedures and bodily fluids are enrolled together into potent configurations – was the arena of conflict. Biomedicine is where freedom, justice and citizenship were at stake.

Finally, Clinton's first public acts as commander-in-chief threatened to queer the sacred site of the citizen-warrior by changing the US armed forces' policy of excluding acknowledged gay men and lesbians from the military. The citizen-soldier's "manliness" has long been at the centre of the political theory of the state and citizenship. However inadequately, colour and gender were addressed in the US military before the category of queer. The tragicomic panic that ensued in Congress and among the Joint Chiefs of Staff thwarted Clinton's intent to deal with the matter by executive order. My point is that discursive, embodied entities like the fetus, the pregnant immigrant and the homosexual are not the subjects of "social" issues, in contrast to "political" matters of state and public policy. Like the embryo or fetus and the "undocumented" pregnant woman, the queer is at the heart of contests to reconfigure precisely what public space is and who inhabits it. Technoscience is intrinsic to all of these struggles.

The work sketched here shows that to study technoscience requires an immersion in worldly material–semiotic practices, where the analysts, as well as the humans and non-humans studied, are all at risk – morally, politically, technically and epistemologically. Science studies that do not take on that kind of situated knowledge practice stand a good chance of floating off screen into an empyrean and academic never-never land. "Ethnography", in this extended sense, is not so much a specific procedure in anthropology, as it is a method of being at risk in the face of the practices and discourses into which one inquires. To be at risk is not the same thing as identifying with the subjects of study; quite the contrary. And self-identity is as much at risk as the temptation to identification. One is at risk in the face of serious non-identity that challenges previous stabilities, convictions or ways of being of many kinds. An "ethnographic attitude" can be adopted within any kind of inquiry, including textual analysis. Not limited to a specific discipline, an ethnographic attitude is a mode of practical and theoretical attention, a way of remaining mindful and accountable. Such a method is not about "taking sides" in a pre-determined way, but neither are moral and political commitments hygienically expunged. Ethnography as I understand the practice is about risks, purposes, meanings and hopes – one's own and others' – embedded in knowledge projects, including technoscientific ones (Downey and Dumit, 1998; Escobar, 1994).

Ethnography is not only a mode of attention, however. Textual analysis must articulate with many kinds of sustained scholarly interaction among living people in living situations, historical and contemporary, documentary and *in vivo*. These different studies need each other, and they are all theory-building projects. No one person does all the kinds of work; feminist science studies is a collective undertaking that cultivates a practice of learning to be at risk in all the sorts of work necessary to an account of technoscience and medicine.

Under these conditions, looking for a feminist doctrine on reproductive technology in particular, or on technoscience, in general, would be ludicrous. But understanding feminist technoscience scholarship as a contentious search for what accountability to freedom projects for women might mean, and how such meanings are crafted and sustained in a polyglot world of men and women, is not ludicrous. Pre-set certainties, feminist and otherwise, about what is happening in theatres of reproduction, or any theatre of technoscience, stand an excellent chance of being flagrantly wrong. But feminist questions shape vision-generating technologies for science studies. Freedom and justice questions are intrinsic to the inquiry about the joinings of humans and non-humans. Feminist technoscience inquiry is a speculum, a surgical instrument, a tool for widening the openings into all kinds of orifices to improve observation and intervention in the interest of projects that are simultaneously about freedom, justice and knowledge. In these terms, feminist inquiry is no more innocent, no more free of the inevitable wounding that all questioning brings, than any other knowledge project.

It does not matter much to the figure of the still-gestating, feminist, anti-racist, mutated modest witness whether freedom, justice and knowledge are branded as modernist or not; that is not our issue. We have never been modern (Latour, 1993; Haraway, 1994). Rather, freedom, justice and knowledge are – in bell hooks' terms – about "yearning", not about putative Enlightenment foundations. Keep your eyes on the prize. Keep our eyes on the prize. For hooks, yearning is an affective and political sensibility allowing cross-category ties that "would promote the recognition of common commitments and serve as a base for solidarity and coalition" (hooks, 1990: 27; see also Braidotti, 1994: 1–8; and Sandoval, forthcoming). Yearning must also be seen as a cognitive sensibility. Without doubt, such yearning is rooted in a reconfigured unconscious, in mutated desire, in the practice of love, in the ecstatic hope for the corporeal and imaginary materialization of the anti-racist female subject of feminism. And all other possible subjects of feminism. Finally, freedom, justice and knowledge are not necessarily nice and definitely not easy. Neither vision nor touch is painless, on or off screen.

The right speculum for the job[4]

An inquiry into instruments of visualization, Kelly's cartoon can carry us another step toward understanding feminist science studies. *Virtual Speculum* is replete with signifiers of "choice", a term that has been encrusted by colonies of semiotic barnacles in the reproductive politics of the last quarter century. What counts as choice, for whom, and at what cost? What is the relation of "choice" to "life", and especially to "life itself"?

Kelly's cartoon is not denunciatory. I do not see in it any stereotyped position on new reproductive technologies or pious certainty about supposed alienation and disembodiment. Nor is Kelly's cartoon celebratory. It does not reflect credit on the original; it does not announce a new scientific age in the image of an original Creation. The cartoon depends on signifiers of information and communications technologies. Information is a technical term for signal-to-noise discrimination; information is a statistical affair for dealing with differences. Information is not embedded in a metaphysics of reflection and representation. The pixel grid of the cartoon's screen will not yield a point-for-point emplotment of an original body, disciplined through an ontology and epistemology of mimesis, reflection and representation. Kelly is nor Dürer.

Instead, *Virtual Speculum* is diffractive and interrogatory: It asks, "Is this what feminists mean by choice, agency, life and creativity? What is at stake here, and for whom? Who and what are the human and non-human centres of action? Whose story is this? Who cares?" The view screen records interfering and shifted – diffracted – patterns of signifiers and bodies. What displacements in reproductive positioning matter to whom and why? What are the conditions of effective reproductive freedom? Why are public and personal narratives of self-creation linked to those of pregnancy? Whose stories are these? Who is in the cartoon, who is missing, and so what? What does it mean to have the public fetus on screen? Whose fetuses merit such extraordinary attention? What does it mean to embed a joke about self-creation and pregnancy inside western and "white" conventions for painting the female nude? Kelly's cartoon is embedded inside signifiers of the Creation, Renaissance, Scientific Revolution, Information Age and New World Order. How does salvation history get replicated or displaced inside technoscience? What are the consequences of the overwhelmingly Christian signifiers of technoscience? If Michel Foucault wrote about the care of the self and the development of disciplinary knowledge in two different cultural configurations within western history, Kelly is sketching an inquiry into the apotheosis of the fetus and reproductive technoscience as a diagnostic sign of the end of the Second Christian Millennium. How is care of the fetus today analogous to care of the self in classical antiquity – an elite set of practices for producing certain kinds of subjects?

What is the right speculum for the job of opening up observation into the orifices of the technoscientific body politic to address these kinds of questions about knowledge projects? I want to approach that question by going back to the eruption of the gynaecological speculum as a symbol in US feminist politics in the early 1970s. Many feminists of my cohorts – largely young, white, middle-class women – "seized the masters' tools" in the context of the Women's Liberation Movement and its activist women's health movement (Lorde, 1984). Armed with a gynaecological speculum, a mirror, a flashlight and – most of all – each other in a consciousness-raising group, women ritually opened their bodies to their own literal view. The speculum had become the symbol of the displacement of the female midwife by the specialist male physician and gynaecologist. The mirror was the symbol forced on women as a signifier of our own bodies as spectacle-for-another in the guise of our own supposed narcissism. Vision itself seemed to be the empowering act of conquerors.

More than a little amnesiac about how colonial travel narratives work, we peered inside our vaginas toward the distant cervix and said something like, "Land ho! We have discovered ourselves and claim the new territory for women." In the context of the history of western sexual politics – that is, in the context of the whole orthodox history of western philosophy and technology – visually self-possessed sexual and generative organs made potent tropes for the reclaimed feminist self. We thought we had our eyes on the prize. I am caricaturing, of course, but with a purpose. "Our Bodies, Ourselves" was both a popular slogan and the title of a landmark publication in women's health movements.[5]

The repossessed speculum, sign of the Women's Liberation Movement's attention to material instruments in science and technology, was understood to be a self-defining technology. Those collective sessions with the speculum and mirror were not only symbols, however. They were self-help and self-experimentation practices in a period in which abortion was still illegal and unsafe. The self-help groups developed techniques of menstrual extraction, i.e., early abortion, that could be practised by women alone or with each other outside professional medical control. A little flexible tubing joined the mirror and the speculum in more than a few of those sessions. Meanwhile, biomedical clinicians were introducing the sonogram and endoscopic fetal visualization, while Lennart Nilsson's photographs spread around the medicalized globe. We had to wonder early if we had seized the right tools.

Still, the sense of empowerment experienced by the women in early 1970s self-help groups was bracing. The spirit was captured in a cartoon in the July 1973 issue of *Sister*, the newspaper of the Los Angeles Women's Center. Wonder Woman – the Amazonian princess from Paradise Isle, complete with her steel bracelets that could deter bullets; stiletto high heels; low-cut eagle-crested bodice; star-spangled, blue mini-shorts; and her magic lasso for capturing evil doers and other transportation needs – seizes the radiant speculum from the white-coat-clad, stethoscope-wearing, but cowering white doctor and announces, "With my speculum, I *am* strong! I *can* fight!" (Figure 3.4E).

Figure 3.4E "Speculum-Wielding Wonder Woman"
(*Sister*, July 1973)

Wonder Woman entered the world in 1941 in Charles Moulton's popular cartoon strips. Moulton was William Moulton Marston, psychologist, attorney, inventor of the lie-detector test, prison reformer and businessman. Marston's conventional feminism ascribed force bound by love to women and opposed that to men's attraction to force alone. Despite her origins in the Amazon, Wonder Woman's ethnicity was unmistakably white. Her expletives ("Merciful Minerva!" and "Great Hera!") and her other cultural accoutrements locate her firmly in the modern myth of western origins in ancient Greece, relocated to the New World. She could have easily joined a US white sorority in the 1940s and 1950s, with their Greek-revivalist themes and rituals. The guiding goddesses of Wonder Woman's Amazonian matriarchal paradise were Aphrodite and Athena (Edgar, 1972).

After falling into a sad state by the end of the 1960s, Wonder Woman was resurrected in several venues in the early 1970s. Wonder Woman's first female comic-book editor, Dorothy Woolfolk, brought her back to the mass market in 1973. *Ms.* magazine put Wonder Woman on the cover of its first issue in July 1972, under the slogan, "Wonder Woman for President" (Figure 3.4F). The Vietnam War was raging on one side of the cover, and a "Peace and Justice in '72" billboard adorned the store-fronts on a US street on the other side. A gigantic Wonder Woman was grabbing a US fighter jet out of the sky with one hand and carrying an enlightened city in her magic lasso in the other hand. The city might be a feminist prototype for the mass-market, computer-simulation game of the 1990s, SimCity2000™ (Bleecker 1995). Wonder Woman's lasso outlined a glowing urban tetrahedron that would have made Buckminster Fuller proud.

In their ground-breaking 1973 pamphlet on medicine and politics, feminist academic and activist historians Barbara Ehrenreich and Deirdre English reprinted the *Sister* Wonder Woman figure seizing the speculum. The context was the chapter on the future, in which the authors emphasized that

> [s]elf help is not an alternative to confronting the medical system with the demands for reform of existing institutions. Self help, or more generally, self-knowledge, is critical to that confrontation. Health is an issue which has the potential to cut across class and race lines. . . . The growth of feminist consciousness gives us the possibility, for the first time, of a truly egalitarian, mass women's health movement.
>
> (Ehrenreich and English, 1973: 84–5)

Ehrenreich and English emphasized that not all women had the same histories or needs in the medical system.

> For black women, medical racism often overshadows medical sexism. For poor women of all ethnic groups, the problem of how to get services of any kind often overshadows all qualitative concerns. . . . A movement that recognizes our biological similarity but denies the diversity of our priorities cannot be a women's health movement, it can only be *some women's* health movement.
>
> (Ehrenreich and English, 1973: 86; italics in original)

The speculum was not a reductionist symbolic and material tool that limited the feminist health movement to the politics of "choice" defined by demands for legal, safe abortion and attention to the new reproductive technologies. Nor was the speculum definitive of an exclusivist, middle-class, white movement. The women's health movement was actively built, and often pioneered, by women of colour and their specific organizations, as well as by mixed and largely white groups that cut across class lines.[6] That legacy is too often forgotten in the terrible history of racism, class-blindness, generational arrogance and fragmentation in American feminism, as well as in other sectors of US progressive politics. However, the fullest meanings of reproductive freedom critical to feminist technoscience politics cannot easily be

Figure 3.4F "Wonder Woman for President"
         (*Ms.*, July 1972)

signified by the gynaecological speculum, nor by the speculum of the computer terminal, no matter how important it remains to control, inhabit and shape those tools, both semiotically and materially. The loose configurations of millionaires and billionaires from Paul Simon's song at the head of this essay still determines the nature of the US health system, including reproductive health, for everybody. The structure and consequences of that complex determination are what we must learn to see if "choice" is to have a robust meaning. The last verse of Simon's "The Boy in the Bubble" reminds us that the relentless bursts of "information" – in transnational and rural jungles – are a long-distance call we cannot ignore.

[. . .]

Acknowledgements

[. . .]

I would like especially to thank Adele Clarke, Valerie Hartouni, Stefan Helmreich, Lynn Randolph, and the Bay Area Technology and Culture Group for comments on "The Virtual Speculum".

Notes

1   A revised version of this essay is [. . .] in Donna Haraway, *Modest_Witness@ Second_Millennium.FemaleMan©_Meets_OncoMouse*™ (1996, New York and London: Routledge).

2   Teresa de Lauretis gave me a copy of an early thirteenth-century "virtual speculum" called *The Creation of Eve*, from the Creation Dome in the entrance hall in the Basilica di S. Marco in Venice. In this flat, iconic, narrative painting, God is bending over the sleeping Adam in the Garden of Eden and extracting from his side the rib that will be formed into the first man's wife and companion. This is not the creation scene that has inspired the iconographers of technoscientific advertising, conference brochures and magazine-cover design. For these twentieth-century graphic artists, on the other hand, the touch between God and Adam depicted by Michelangelo has incited orgies of visual quotation. See magazine covers for *Omni* April 1983, *Time* 8 November 1993, and *Discover* August 1992. For fans of Escher in the Artificial Life community, studied ethnographically by Stefan Helmreich (1995), the poster image for the second ALife conference features a visual quotation from *The Creation of Adam* in the cyberspace mode. This creation scene takes place at night, with a quarter moon shining through a window that is also a screen onto the starry universe. Describing the image, Helmreich (personal communication, 18 May 1995) writes, "The notion that Man replaces God and renders Woman irrelevant in the new creations of Artificial Life is vividly illus-trated . . . in a poster for the second workshop on Artificial Life, in which a white male programmer touches his finger to a keyboard to meet the waiting fingers of a skeletal circuit-based artificial creature (itself somewhat masculine)." The programmer himself is a kind of merman figure; the head and torso is of a human male, but the bottom half is a video display terminal, whose nether end hooks into the eye of the circuit-skeletal figure. The Escheresque circular composition, full of arrows and fractal recursive shapes connoting self-organization, is a kind of uroborus, eating its own electronic tail in an orgy of self-creation. The men who got the conference together called themselves the "self-organizing committee". The conference was sponsored by the Center for Non-Linear Studies at the Los Alamos National Laboratory in 1990.

3   Gross and Levitt (1994) outrageously caricature the feminist science studies insistence on the contingency of "reality" and the constructedness of science. It is important that my account of reality as an effect of an interaction, as opposed to a treasure awaiting discovery, not be misunderstood. "Reality" is certainly not "made up" in scientific practice; but it is collectively, materially and semiotically constructed – that is, put together, made to cohere, worked up for and by us in some ways and not others. This is not a relativist position, if by relativism one means that the facts and models, including mathematical models, of natural scientific accounts of the world are merely matters of desire, opinion, speculation, fantasy, or any other such "mental" faculty. Science is a practice, an interaction inside and with worlds. Science is not a doctrine or a set of observer-independent, but still empirically grounded (how?) statements about some ontologically separate nature-not-culture. Minimally, an observing interaction requires historically located human beings; particular apparatuses, which might include devices like the hominid visual-brain system and the instruments of perspective drawing; and a heterogeneous world, in which people and instruments are immersed and which is always pre-structured within material-semiotic fields. "Observers" are not just people, much less disembodied minds; observers are also non-human entities, sometimes called inscription devices to which people have materially delegated observation, often precisely to make it "impersonal". (As we will see below, statistics can be one of those instruments for making reality impersonal.) "Impersonal" does not mean "observer-independent". Reality is not a "subjective" construction, but a congealing of ways of interacting that makes the opposition of subjective and objective grossly misleading. These ways of interacting require the dense array of bodies, artifacts, minds, collectives, etc. that make up any rich world. The opposition of "knowing minds", on one hand, and "material reality" awaiting description, on the other hand, is a silly set-up. Reality is eminently material and solid; but the effects sedimented out of the technologies of observation/representation are radically contingent in the sense that other semiotic-material-technical processes of observation would (and do) produce quite different lived worlds, including cognitively lived worlds, not just different statements about worlds as observer-independent arrays of objects. I think that is a richer, more adequate, less ideological account than Gross and Levitt's insistence that science is reality driven (1994: 234). Obviously, neither I nor any other science studies person, feminist or otherwise, whom I have ever met or read, mean the "laws of physics" get suspended if one enters a "different" culture. That is a laughable notion of both physical laws and cultural, historical difference. It is the position that Gross and Levitt, in deliberate bad faith or else astonishingly deficient reading, ascribe to me and other feminist science studies writers. My argument tries to avoid the silly oppositions of relativism and realism. Rather, I am interested in how an observation-situation produces quite "objective" worlds, worlds not subject to "subjective" preference or mere opinion, but worlds that must be lived in consequence in some ways and not others. For a theory of "agential realism", to which my arguments about "situated knowledges" are closely related, see Barad (1995).

4   This title is in honor of Clarke and Fujimura (1992).

5   Boston Women's Health Book Collective (1976); *Nuestros Cuerpos, Nuestras Vidas* (1979). The Boston Women's Health Book Collective began putting out *Our Bodies, Ourselves* in newsprint form in the 1970s as an integral part of activist health

struggles. For a bibliography of the early women's health movement and feminist science and medicine studies from the 1970s, see Hubbard, Henifin, and Fried (1982). Despite its extensive concern with instruments and tools, practices in and out of the laboratory, and science-in-the-making, the kind of activist-based material in Hubbard *et al.*'s bibliography is systematically excluded from professional, academic histories of science and technology studies. See, for example, Knorr-Cetina and Mulkay (1983).

6   See, for example, Committee for Abortion Rights and Against Sterilization Abuse (1979); Coalition for the Reproductive Rights of Workers (1980); Black Women's Community Development Foundation (1975); Davis (1981); Smith (1982); White (1990). This literature reflects the dominance of the black–white racial polarity of US society and understates the presence and priorities of other racial-ethnic women in women's health and reproductive politics of that period. See Moraga and Anzaldúa (1981).

References

Auerbach, Erich (1953) *Mimesis: The Representation of Reality in Western Literature* Princeton: Princeton University Press.

Barad, Karen (1995) "Meeting the universe halfway: ambiguities, discontinuities, quantum subjects, and multiple positionings in feminism and physics" in Nelson and Nelson, editors *Feminism, Science, and the Philosophy of Science: A Dialogue.* Norwell, MA: Kluwer Press.

Black Women's Community Development Foundation (BWCDF) (1975) *Mental and Physical Health Problems of Black Women* Washington, DC: BWCDF.

Bleecker, Julian (1995) "Urban crisis: past, present, and virtual" *Socialist Review* Vol. 25, No. 1 (Winter).

Boston Women's Health Book Collective (BWHBC) (1976) *Our Bodies, Ourselves: A Book by and for Women* 2nd edn New York: Simon & Schuster.

Boston Women's Health Book Collective (BWHBC) (1979) *Nuestros Cuerpos, Nuestras Vidas* Somerville, MA: BWHBC, Inc.

Braidotti, Rosi (1994) *Nomadic Subjects: Embodiment and Subjectivity in Contemporary Feminist Theory* New York: Columbia University Press.

Casper, Monica (1995a) "Fetal cyborgs and technomoms on the reproductive frontier: which way to the carnival?" in Gray, Figueroa-Sarriera and Mentor (1995).

Casper, Monica (1995b) "The making of the unborn patient: medical work and the politics of reproduction in experimental fetal surgery, 1963–1993". Ph.D. diss., Graduate Program in Sociology, University of California at San Francisco.

Clark, Timothy J. (1985) *The Painting of Modern Life: Paris in the Art of Manet and his Followers* New York: Knopf.

Clarke, Adele and Fujimura, Joan (eds) (1992) *The Right Tools for the Job: At Work in Twentieth-Century Life Sciences* Princeton: Princeton University Press.

Clarke, Adele and Montini, Teresa. (1993) "The many faces of RU486: tales of situated knowledges and technological contestations" *Science, Technology, and Human Values* Vol. 18, No. 1: 42–78.

Coalition for the Reproductive Rights of Workers (CRROW) (1980) *Reproductive Hazards in the Workplace: A Resource Guide*, Washington, DC: CRROW.

Committee for Abortion Rights and Against Sterilization Abuse (CARASA) (1979) *Women under Attack: Abortion, Sterilization Abuse, and Reproductive Freedom* New York: CARASA.

Cussins, Charis (1996) "Ontological choreography: agency through objectification in infertility clinics" *Social Studies of Science* Vol. 26, No. 3.

Davis, Angela (1981) *Women, Race and Class* New York: Random House.

Downey, Gary and Dumit, Joseph (eds) (1998) *Cyborgs and Citadels: Anthropological Interventions on the Borderlands of Technoscience* Seattle: University of Washington Press.

Duden, Barbara (1993) *Disembodying Women: Perspectives on Pregnancy and the Unborn* Cambridge: Harvard University Press.

Edgar, Joanne (1972) "Wonder woman revisited" *Ms.* Vol. 1, No. 1: 52–5.

Ehrenreich, Barbara and English, Deirdre (1973) *Complaints and Disorders: The Sexual Politics of Sickness* Old Westbury, NY: The Feminist Press.

Escobar, Arturo (1994) "Welcome to cyberia: notes on the anthropology of cyberculture" *Current Anthropology* Vol. 35, No. 3: 211–31.

Flower, Michael (n.d.) "Techoscientific liberty", unpublished manuscript, University Honors Program, Portland State University.

Foucault, Michel (1978) *The History of Sexuality*, translated by Robert Hurley, vol. 1: *An Introduction* New York: Pantheon.

Franklin, Sarah (1993a) "Making representations: the parliamentary debate on the human fertilisation and embryology act" in Edwards, Franklin, Hirsch, Price and Strathern, editors *Technologies of Procreation: Kinship in the Age of Assisted Conception* Manchester: Manchester University Press.

Franklin, Sarah (1993b) "Life itself", paper delivered at Centre for Cultural Values, Lancaster University, 9 June.

Gasperini, Jim (1994) "The miracle of good multimedia" *Wired* (February): 198.

Ginsberg, Faye and Rapp, Rayna (1991) "The politics of reproduction" *Annual Reviews in Anthropology* Vol. 20: 311–43.

Ginsberg, Faye D. and Tsing, Anna L. (eds) (1990) *Uncertain Terms: Negotiating Gender in American Culture* Boston: Beacon Press.

Gray, Chris, Figueroa-Sarriera, Heidi and Mentor, Steven (eds) (1995) *The Cyborg Handbook* New York: Routledge.

Gross, Paul R. and Levitt, Norman (1994) *Higher Superstition: The Academic Left and Its Quarrels with Science* Baltimore: Johns Hopkins University Press.

Hamilton, Joan O'C. (1994) "Biotech: an industry crowded with players faces an ugly reckoning" *BusinessWeek* (26 September): 84–90.

Hampton, Henry (1986–7) *Eyes on the prize: America's civil rights years, 1954–65* Alexandria, VA/Boston, MA: Blackside, Inc., and CPB for WGBH Boston. Television series.

Haraway, Donna J. (1994) "Never modern, never been, never ever: some thoughts about never-never land in science studies", paper read at Meeting of the Society for Social Studies of Science, 12–16 October, at New Orleans.

Harding, Susan (1990) "If I die before I wake" in Ginsberg and Tsing (1990).

Hartouni, Valerie (1991) "Containing women: reproductive discourse in the 1980s" in Penley and Ross, editors *Technoculture* Minneapolis: University of Minnesota Press.

Hartouni, Valerie (1996) *Making Life Make Sense: New Technologies and the Discourses of Reproduction* Minneapolis: University of Minnesota Press.

Harvey, David (1989) *The Condition of Postmodernity: An Enquiry into the Origins of Cultural Change* Oxford: Basil Blackwell.

Hays, Denys (1967) *The Age of the Renaissance* New York: McGraw-Hill.

Helmreich, Stefan (1995) "Anthropology inside and outside the looking-glass worlds of artificial life", Ph.D. diss., Department of Anthropology, Stanford University.

hooks, bell (1990) *Yearning* Boston: Southend Press.

Hubbard, Ruth, Henifin, Mary Sue and Fried, Barbara (eds) (1982) *Biological Woman – The Convenient Myth: A Collection of Feminist Essays and a Comprehensive Bibliography* Cambridge: Schenkman.

Jansen, H. W. and Jansen, Dora Jane (1963) *History of Art* Englewood Cliffs/New York: Prentice Hall and Harry N. Abrams.

Knorr-Cetina, Karin and Mulkay, Michael (eds) (1983) *Science Observed: Perspectives on the Social Study of Science* Beverly Hills: Sage Publications.

Latour, Bruno (1993) *We Have Never Been Modern*, translated by Porter Cambridge: Harvard University Press.

Lorde, Audre (1984) "The master's tools will never dismantle the master's house" in Lorde, *Sister Outsider: Essays and Speeches* Trumansburg, NY: Crossing Press.

MacArthur, R. H. (1962) "Some generalized theorems of natural selection" *Proceedings of the National Academy of Sciences* Vol. 48: 1893–7.

Moraga, Cherríe and Anzaldúa, Gloria (eds) (1981) *This Bridge Called My Back: Writings by Radical Women of Color* Watertown, MA: Persephone Press.

Nead, Lynda (1992) *The Female Nude: Art, Obscenity and Sexuality* New York: Routledge.

Nilsson, Lennart (1977) *A Child Is Born* New York: Dell.

Nilsson, Lennart (1987) *The Body Victorious: The Illustrated Story of our Immune System and Other Defenses of the Human Body* New York: Delacourt.

Nilsson, Lennart and Hamberger, Lars (1994) *A Child Is Born* Philips. CD-I.

Petchesky, Rosalind Pollack (1987) "Foetal images: the power of visual culture in the politics of reproduction" *Feminist Studies* Vol. 13, No. 2: 263–92.

Randolph, Lynn (1993) "The Ilusas (deluded women): representations of women who are out of bounds", paper delivered at The Bunting Institute, 30 November.

Rapp, Rayna (1994) "Refusing prenatal diagnostic technology: the uneven meanings of bioscience in a multicultural world", paper read at Society for Social Studies of Science, 12–16 October, at New Orleans.

Rapp, Rayna (1998) "Real time fetus: the role of the sonogram in the age of monitored reproduction" in Downey and Dumit, editors.

Sandoval, Chéla (forthcoming) *Oppositional Consciousness in the Postmodern World* Minneapolis: University of Minnesota Press.

Simon, Paul (1986) "The boy in the bubble" Warner Brothers Records, Inc. Song, from the album *Graceland*.

Smith, Beverly (1982) "Black women's health: notes for a course" in Hubbard, Henifin and Fried, editors.

Stabile, Carol A. (1992) "Shooting the mother: fetal photography and the politics of disappearance" *Camera Obscura: A Journal of Feminism and Film Theory* Vol. 28: 178–205.

Treichler, Paula and Cartwright, Lisa (1992) "Imaging technologies, inscribing science" *Camera Obscura: A Journal of Feminism and Film Theory* Nos 28 and 29.

White, Evelyn (ed.) (1990) *The Black Women's Health Book* Seattle: Seal Press.

Refractions (women, technology and cyborgs)

Introduction to Part Four

PART FOUR DRAWS TOGETHER five edited readings to present a discussion of women, feminisms and information technology. Four specifically address concerns around technology. Sadie Plant's "On the Matrix: Cyberfeminist Simulations" stakes a claim for the feminist potential of networked technologies, and the liberatory spaces and actions they may carry. Alison Adam's "Feminist AI Projects and Cyberfutures" considers the current conditions for Artificial Intelligence projects, the difficulty of informing current work with feminist theory, and the agony of attempting to bridge the gap. Nina Wakeford's "Gender and the Landscapes of Computing in an Internet Café" describes the stickiness of biosocial gendered identities in online and offline landscapes, and the ways in which genders, technologies and identities mutually encode one another. Evelynn M. Hammonds' "New Technologies of Race" shows how visual technologies have always been, and still are, implicated in the attempts to establish categories of "race". Whatever the ostensible purpose of the text in which the images appear, the effect of the spectacle of images is to quieten the text.

The first reading, Luce Irigaray's "When Our Lips Speak Together" was written nearly two decades before the others, and is not concerned with technology. It provides an imaginative example of her philosophical arguments for the importance of a feminine symbolic, and feminine language, to restore women from their exile under patriarchy. Where Adam's piece asks "What does feminist technology look like?", Irigaray would argue that we cannot know until the symbolic order has been changed to permit the expression(s) of the feminine. Plant's work draws heavily upon Irigaray, although not from the specific reading included here. However, there are threads between the ideas expressed by Irigaray and Adam that give some background to Plant's claims.

In very different ways, the readings here each articulate facets of the relationships between gender, race and technology, and consider gendered lives in the production, proliferation, play and potential of computer-based technology. The co-location of these readings here draws out, particularly, the themes of embodiment, the semiological charge of bodies and machines, and the roles of theory, polemic and fantasy.

Sadie Plant is one of the most well-known writers on cyberfeminism in the UK. Her ecstatic visions of the liberatory potential of Web-based technology for women tend to draw polarized responses. She is not a technologist, and her work is often criticized for its lack of technical realism (indeed two of the writers she meets here make this criticism); however, viewed as a different kind of project, her work has a potentially powerful effect.

In reading 4.2, Plant draws heavily upon Irigaray's notion of the "specular economy", where patriarchy and capitalism are based upon the trade in women's bodies. She sees cyberspace as a place where women can circumvent this economy, as the technology proliferates beyond patriarchal control, and all capital escapes. However, as Adam points out, this potential is based upon a utopian notion of technology. Self-organizing (autopoietic) systems are still a long way behind the possibilities claimed for them. The theory they are based upon draws from Maturana and Varela's work in biology. This is an explicit metaphorical borrowing, but also acts as a carrier for implicit intimations of life. However, Maturana's work, in turn, draws heavily upon cybernetic theory (Maturana and Varela, 1980: 79). This mutually referring relationship between cybernetic and biological metaphors creates a closed system. This is impeccably postmodern, but difficult to base any other claims upon. Drawing upon this system as a rhetorical device, however, may enable those alienated by the current computing culture(s) to find a way in. The power of this metaphor for Plant is that it mirrors anarchist beliefs in self-organizing communities. Women creating self-organizing communities on the Net, and autopoietic connectionist machines eluding centralist, hierarchical, power can be mutually constitutive, in Plant's view. Conceptually, the understanding of one may open the door to the understanding of the other. But does this necessarily entail that one will materially constitute the other?

The convergence of complexity and connectionism, Plant argues, leads to the crumbling of idealism, and the emergence of a new materialism. This is a strange claim for Plant to make, and it sits alone in her text. It may be that she is suggesting that the imminent free agency of autopoietic systems will affect the material conditions and practices of bodies and lives. However, we currently live in a world of biological autopoietic systems, biological complexity and replicating viruses. Each of these have variously been constructed as "risk", allowing patriarchy to be reinforced, rather than subverted. If the convergence of complexity and connectionism occurs as Plant suggests, its effects will not necessarily be new. Connectionist machines are designed and grown in situated material/cultural environments. These are influential, although not determining. There may be no theories accounting for the ways in which connectionist machines learn, but this is not the same as assuming their liberatory function.

Plant identifies the plasticity of the computer's function: "it can turn its invisible, non-existent self to anything", with Irigaray's "woman". This can be paraphrased as, in nothing all things are possible. Irigaray responds to the psychoanalytic tradition that the vagina is a lack, a nothingness, by claiming the power of potential (multiplicity) for that "nothingness". Focusing upon computing technology, and its mathematico-logical base, allows Plant to offer a different reappropriation. She elides "nothing" with mathematical zero, and then claims for this the multiplicative power of zero. In a sense Plant offers us something to fill the gap that Irigaray labours to leave. As a polemical move against the psychoanalytic tradition, this is beautiful, because it offers some thing — the metaphor of mathematical zero — without destroying the power of potential in "nothing".

Plant draws interesting parallels between the fluidity of the identity of Irigaray's woman, Freud and Breuer's characterization of hysteria, and the operation of neural nets. The lack of fixed identity, the "illogical" cross-cuts of hysterical thought to which women have traditionally been regarded as prey, fit with the concepts of parallel processing — for Plant. In parallel processing, actions are distributed across a network of processors, instead of proceeding in series. This distinction is taken to mirror the ways that women are thought to be able to work at several different things at one time, while men are thought to be single-minded. If the "old order" favoured the single-minded pursuit of anything, the "new" (due to its distributed, networked technology) will favour distributed interaction with everything. Again, this advocated liaison between women and technology can be seen as a rhetorical move. However, even as a rhetorical move it draws upon an essentialist account of gender, and a form of technological determinism. Similarly, Plant takes up Freud's assertion that weaving (just about the only technological development that Freud attributes to women) emerges as a simulation of pubic hair matted across the vagina, the zero, the entrance to the matrix. Plant reappropriates this account and identifies this weaving with the threads of communication beginning to enmesh the world, the connections these allow, and the metaphor of the connectionist machines.

Plant follows Irigaray's strategy of reappropriating patriarchy's negative accounts of women by accepting, and valorizing, them. In this sense, her work is more about a response to psychoanalytic accounts of women than it is about technology. She draws upon computer-based technology as a resource that acts as sanction, and promises salvation.

Alison Adam's work is part of a very different project. Adam works as a feminist academic computer scientist, and has a background in software engineering. Reading 4.3 is an edited version of the final chapter of her book, *Artificial Knowing: Gender and the Thinking Machine*. In this she explores the gendered nature of the epistemological formations of artificial intelligence (AI). In the spaces opened up by her analyses she introduces arguments and notions of feminist epistemologies. Using these, she calls into question the identity of the knowing subject, the production of knowledge, particularly the influence of embodiment and situatedness on this project, and the narrow cast of the epistemology that AI traditionally draws upon. Joining feminist theory with phenomenological critiques of AI, Adam argues for the importance of embodied and situated knowledge and knowing. She suggests, following such critiques as Harding (1991) and Rose (1994), that embodied knowledge has been overlooked in science and technology (as in philosophy) because it is based upon the invisible work of women.

In this, her final chapter, she has two concerns. The first is to explore what AI projects informed by feminist concepts might be like. The second is to provide a feminist response to the popular uptake of cyberculture, balanced between the pessimism of viewing technology as an irredeemably patriarchal tool, and the technological naivety of the technophoric "fabulous feminist future" (from Squires, 1996).

Adam describes two projects she has supervised: one to build an advisory expert system, based upon feminist jurisprudence; the other, to build a feminist-based computational model of language. In the first, the knowledge to be encoded was feminist. The second took account of empirical feminist work on the gendered nature of conversation, and produced a gender-sensitive model of talk. Adam acknowledges, however, that the designs still owe a great deal to the traditional AI culture that she has criticized earlier in her book, particularly that they are disembodied, unsituated, and employ the same symbolic representations. In mitigation, she says, "we had to start somewhere". It is also the case that these were student projects, with all their attendant realities – short timescale, student's desire to get through the course successfully, course as part of the traditional institutional framework, etc.

In her response to cyberculture, Adam criticizes the aspects that draw (uncritically) from sociobiology, and those that desire transcendence, celebrating the possibility of "meat-free" existence in cyberspace. The sociobiology encourages a belief in the notion of emergent behaviour (which, crucially, is seen as mystically arising from "lower-level" behaviours). This is what Dennett calls "Woo Woo West Coast Emergence" (to highlight the grandiosity and unsubstantiatedness that attributions of mysticism permit, and against which he proffers a notion of emergence as a convenient level of description – quoted in Adam, 1998: 139). The desire for "meat-free" existence plays into desires to escape from the real, but is also enabled by the men/women–mind/body split, and the invisible work of women in maintaining and caring for bodies.

In considering the cyberfeminist uptake of cyberculture, Adam first pays homage to Haraway's invocation of an ironic, post-gendered cyborg. Yet, she says, more recent developments may be disappointing to feminists. Empirical studies of Internet use show that there is a tension between the liberatory potential of Net-based technologies and the experiences of online sexual harassment. This new space has all the features of the old. Adam also takes issue with Plant, as one of the foremost technophoric, cyberfeminist writers, on three grounds: her apoliticality, her universalizing tendency, and her technological naivety. Certainly some of the claims that Plant makes for technology are based on projection, rather than actuality. The way she describes emergent machine behaviours not just signalling, but effecting, the end of patriarchy, also echo the "Woo Woo" variety of belief in emergence. However, as mentioned above, accurate portrayals of technology may not be necessary to Plant's project. The universalizing tendency, however, is prevalent in Plant's discussion of women, working against (as Adam points out) the work of many feminists to differentiate, complicate and unravel the category Women. This may be the down side of the effect of psychoanalysis as a major player in Plant's work.

To charge Plant with apoliticality is more difficult. She does not work from the same materialist feminist space as many other writers, including Haraway. Adam follows Squires (1996: 208) in seeing apoliticality as part of cyberfeminism's heritage from cyberpunk. One problem with this is the homogeneous view of both cyberfeminism and cyberpunk, and another is the uncritical view of the direction of influence. Plant's writing here, and her earlier work on situationism, suggest that she draws upon the anarchist strand of the punk ethic. Her political project, then, may be more clearly regarded as based in anarcho-feminism.

Adam ends by arguing for the necessity of feminist knowledge to the project(s) of AI, and the inherent danger of expressing this knowledge, using "the master's tools". She finds hope and a possible bridge in an area of AI discussed earlier in her book – situated robotics. Robots designed this way learn by doing, by failing and by readjusting. They operate according to a feedback principle, but one in which the designers (with their embodied, situated, world-views) are part of the loop. This differentiates them from the self-organizing technologies that Plant looks towards. This is emergent behaviour of a very prosaic and obviously constructed kind.

A further challenge to the transcendent potential of cyberspace comes from Nina Wakeford's sociological work. In reading 4.4 she challenges claims that online environments enable us to transcend, or radically shift, gendered identities. In one material setting of engagement with the internet (a cybercafé) she identifies a variety of co-locating landscapes. These include the online landscape, the specialist landscape of the technology and technicians, and the café itself. The latter a landscape of translation, producing and interpreting the landscape of computing in a more familiar environment. The main achievement of this translation landscape is as a permissive space that "enables participants to scatter discursive representations of the Internet, the 'cyber', and global computer networks upon a range of encounters and artefacts which had not previously been recognised for their alliance with the technological".

Wakeford structures her argument by first discussing the experiences of gender-switching and post-gendered identities in the online communities of MUDs and MOOs. She then makes a case for the importance of the material environment through which the online experiences are made possible. In the online communities, Wakeford charts the same tension that Adam mentions between the liberatory potential and the persistence of traditional misogynist sexual harassment. On the one hand there is the promise and potential of radical change (the eroticization of post fe/male bodies, encouraged by the adoption of the "spivak gender", for example) and on the other, sexual recidivism. However, she also points out that such claims, either way, cannot be made into generalizations. Men and women may be drawn to different types of online landscape, and will behave differently in different spaces. Online landscapes, therefore, are not the limitless expanses of "virgin" territory, but are every bit as culturally situated as our offline landscapes, material, or not. One of Wakeford's criticisms of Plant, therefore, is for not specifying the online landscapes in which her "fabulous feminist future" will take place. Wakeford also draws a distinction, marked as one of modesty, between cyberfeminist celebrations of particular sites – for example, in the work of Hall (1996) and Clerc (1996), and Plant's broader claims. This echoes Adam's criticism of Plant's universalizing voice.

Gender, online, is fluid in the sense that it is sometimes transferable, sometimes not; in some landscapes, it is taken to be a true reflection of offline gender, and in others, encouraged to be anything but. Yet, Wakeford claims, "Everywhere in online landscapes gender is part of a skilled practice, either in its denial or in its promotion."

With this background, Wakeford then goes on to describe the reinscriptions of gender constituted through interactions between computers, staff and customers at the cybercafé. One of the most notable aspects of this in reading 4.4 is the conscious use of women, women's bodies and body parts to encapsulate the "cybervibe" – particularly the use of "the lips" artefacts.

This refers to a sculpture of lips, glossed red, and holding a computer disk between them. This sculpture became a visual trope for the café – copies, or images, of it being variously offered as awards, and used as the café logo. This is a powerful and disturbing image. Wakeford makes no judgements of its semiological content, but remarks that she never managed to find out whether the designer had intended the lips to be ingesting the disk or spitting it out. But is the metaphor of consumption the only possibility here? The lips could also be holding on to the disk, or be being gagged by it, for example.

This image invites a variety of possible readings. It recalls the pleasure/horror of James Woods being devoured by Debbie Harry's televised lips in David Cronenberg's *Videodrome* (1982), playing upon images of heterosexual sex and the misogynist horror of the devouring vagina. The disk inserted between the lips also plays upon the "sexuation" (Irigaray) of the computer and its "vaginal" slots. This can be reread in terms of Plant's identification of women and computers: the computer operates on "inside" knowledge, its workings are invisible. The lips image also recalls Irigaray's "two lips", albeit in a possibly "cartoon" version. Is "the lips" sculpture sarcastically mimicking the unbalanced masculine symbolic's cypher of "Woman"? Whatever the possibilities of reappropriation, however, the constant in all of this, as Wakeford remarks, is that the category "Women" is consistently used for profit. Is this a return to Irigaray's notion of the specular economy? Or is the image of "the lips" too multiply coded to stay within a specular economy?

Wakeford folds her fieldwork into the broader discussions of online communities via the notion of the gendered body. She adopts Adam's argument that the creation of technological systems needs to be informed by feminist and phenomenological critiques about the role of the body in the production of knowledge (Adam, 1998: chapter 5). The body as a site of knowledge production also reconnects us to the importance of the physical, social and cultural landscape (viz. Adam's discussion of online and "real-life" shopping). She ends by claiming the importance of material/biosocial bodies in the rearticulation of the relationships of gender and technology, and in the resistances to such articulations.

Evelynn M. Hammonds' piece (reading 4.5) discusses the role of the computer technology of morphing in subtly reasserting a political economy of race in the US. She begins with the UNESCO declaration of 1950, which claimed, in effect, that race was "less a biological fact than a social myth". While this can be seen as an expression of its time, aiming to redress the sentiments that contributed to Nazism, it attempted to annex a territory that refuses to stay annexed. The fixed typologies of races, particularly in terms of their relative superiorities, may have been abandoned, and cranial measurements are no longer taken as serious scientific evidence. However, Hammonds argues that "race" is still an active category, drawing upon more resources than those of a modest social construction. Computer technology has enabled a further mobilization of this, because, as Hammonds claims: "In the US race has always been dependent upon the visual." While computer technology supports a variety of visual forms, Hammonds concentrates upon the technique of morphing, and its use in a particular *Time* magazine article. She writes about this article in relation to two other texts, both of which use photography to support their claims – W. E. B. DuBois's 1906 "The Health and Physique of the Negro American", and a *Newsweek* piece entitled "What Color is Black? What Color is White?" (13 February 1995).

The *Time* article, a special issue from Autumn 1993, mobilized concerns over the effects of immigration and intermarriage on the "face" of America. In this article seven racial categories were defined, and a woman and a man from each category presented. The potential progeny from the forty-nine possible combinations were generated by blending the features using a program called Morph 2.0 (itself the progeny of the program used to enable the colour and shape-shifting in Michael Jackson's "Black and White" video, and in *Terminator 2*). So the *Time* article uses a highly selected present to generate a highly selected future, and the technology enables an asexual reproduction of representations. *Time* acknowledge part of their selectivity: "Most of the images . . . on the chart are a straight 50–50 combination of the physical characteristics of their progenitors". For their cover star, however, they chose a different recipe. The female cover star (dubbed "Sim Eve" by Haraway) is 15 per cent Anglo-Saxon, 17.5 per cent Middle Eastern, 17.5 per cent African, 7.5 per cent Asian, 35 per cent Southern European and 7.5 per cent Hispanic. Gender, in the "cybergeneticist's" hands is apparently determined by neck size, although not without problems (some of the 50–50 combinations were rejected when "feminine" heads appeared atop "muscular" necks). It is not clear whether Eve's sex was emergent in this sense, or not, or whether some other rule decreed that the cover star should be female. The reasons governing the recipe for Eve are also not given.

Interestingly, the non-existence of this woman is emphasized, at least twice, in the editorial. According to *Time*'s editors, several staff members fell in love with Eve as her image appeared on screen; however, "this is a love that must forever remain unrequited". For Hammonds, the fact that the primary attribute of Eve is that she is "cyber" indicates, not that she is the "new face of America" in terms of citizenship rights and status, but that she is fulfilling the role that women of colour have always fulfilled for white, male America. She is unreal love object and, as such, does not "need" rights and status. Hammonds sees in this a continuation of white, male America's tendency to deny kinship to its border-crossing offspring.

In all the texts Hammonds cites, the variety and density of the visual material, and technical virtuosity that makes them possible, dazzle the reader. The spectacle "whites out" questions such as; Whose categories are these? What governed the editing process? The technology enables a re-presenting of the world through categories that are somehow then effaced by the technology.

To do justice to Luce Irigaray's body of work in this small space would be impossible. The edited piece presented here (reading 4.1), Plant's piece (reading 4.2), and this introduction, will bring terms and ideas into play that can only be fleeting tastes, or touches, of her work. Irigaray is a philosopher whose main concern is with the constructive and destructive powers of language, and the ways in which these parlay into the exclusion of a feminine symbolic. Without such a symbolic, language maintains an invisible masculinity, especially when it appears to be neutral, or ungendered. Advocating a feminine symbolic is Irigaray's response to what she sees as a "lack" in psychoanalytic theory. The symbolic order, out of which language is drawn, is inherently masculine. The birth into language signifies a transition from the maternal zone to the law of the father, and the feminine is silenced. There are no symbolic representations with which to make sense of feminine experience: female to female relations, such as mother–daughter, for example. We are in the exclusive territory of the genealogies of fathers and sons. For Irigaray the symbolic order has to be extended to include a feminine symbolic, without which women are silenced and are exiled out of existence. As Judith Butler explains, "[Irigaray's] effort is to show that binary oppositions are formulated through the exclusion of a field of disruptive possibilities. . . . those binaries, even in their reconciled mode, are part of a phallogocentric economy that produces the 'feminine' as its constitutive outside" (1993: 35).

As mentioned with regard to Plant above, Irigaray refutes the assumption that to be "the sex that is not one" is to be none. She proposes that not-one is multiplicity, but eludes further specificity, to avoid capture, subjugation and silence. Instead, she advocates positions such as "not-yet", a celebration of women's alienation from the Logos by refusing all categories. To elude given positions by refusing to choose, refusing to state a preference, refusing to stand still to be measured, has become a commonplace of postmodernity, at least as an advocated strategy, if not a practised one. When Irigaray wrote this piece, the strategy was not as fashionable. Now that it is, it is easy to forget how difficult it still is to achieve. That is, it is easy to forget how strong the structures of the unbalanced masculine symbolic are. So there are two reasons for including this piece here. First, Irigaray's work reminds us of how difficult it is to elude capture. Second, this piece, particularly, foregrounds the necessary conditions, and possibilities, for communication, that draw upon the feminine symbolic and the identities forgeable through such communication. Communication, and slipped identities, are the major claims that pro-technology feminists make for Internet-based technologies. Do Internet-based technologies fulfil the conditions that Irigaray sets?

In the piece included here, "When Our Lips Speak Together", Irigaray unfolds some of the possibilities of a feminine symbolic: open and perpetual communication, rather than exchange based upon the commodification of women; tactical rather than compulsory mimesis; the language with which to fully develop self-expression.

The two sets of lips, once engaged (the kiss), can set up an endless, mutual exchange. Once open to each other, there are no boundaries and no need for translation. Open to each other, the two lips are in endless communication. There is a necessary link here between openness and movement. The lack of the former creates boundaries that inhibit the latter. The lack of motion, such as that which occurs when we are dazzled and entrapped by the names and mutual exclusivities of phallogocentrism, creates paralysis: "their nation, family, home, and discourse imprison us in enclosures where we can no longer move – or live as 'we' ". The lips symbolize the possibilities of communication between women who are no longer commodities, who can speak instead of being spoken.

As well as a description of communication between women, this can also be seen as a description of congruence with the self. Such a claim to selfhood, and identity (although not to an unfractured subjectivity), may be disputed by Plant. However, there is an agony in the following quote, and a call to return to "indifference" (undifferentiation?): "Exiled from yourself, you fuse with everything that you encounter. You mime whatever comes near you. . . . You no longer return as the indifferent one."

One meaning of Irigaray's notion of mimesis is that women need to become the "analysts" to the masculine "analysand(s)"; that is, to "be for men, what they cannot be for themselves (receive the projections) and then *interpret* the phantasies" (Whitford, 1991: 36, italics in original). This engagement with the other is the only way in which the masculine symbolic can be opened up, but what it requires is a tactical mimesis, not the exile into mimicry mentioned above. In order for mimesis to be tactical, women need to be able to choose whether to engage in it or not. It cannot be the only mode of existence available. Plant celebrates this mimetic quality. She bases her claim for the isomorphism of women and computers upon it. However, it is not clear whether her advocacy of mimicry is in the service of a similar strategy. Continual mimicry requires hyperdifferentiation, and as such requires the tools of the Logos. There is risk even in this ironic deployment, of the ability of the tools to shape the action, and the actor; in the ways that mimicry monopolizes the actor in the moment of mimicking there is always the danger of the exile into mimesis.

The congruence enabled by open exchange within the self also enables knowledge from the inside to be outwardly expressed. Both require the development of new language; language sufficient to express the experience of being women and to enable all that the Logos cannot currently utter. For Irigaray, a starting point for the creation of such language is grounded in the metaphors of female bodily experience.

Irigaray's tendency to do this, as a way of retrieving the material of a feminine symbolic, and her explicit commitment to the necessity of creating and exploring inter-women discourses, have led to charges of essentialism. However, this ignores the critical Lacanian dimensions of her work. As Whitford clarifies:

> Very briefly, the charge of biological essentialism assumes that Irigaray posits an unmediated causal relation between biological sex, and sexual identity, leaving out completely the imaginary dimension, in which sexual identity may be related in an unstable and shifting way to the anatomical body, or the symbolic, linguistic dimension, in which sexual identity may be constructed.
>
> (1991: 14)

Her project is to rehabilitate that which has been abandoned as "the feminine", and to do this she has go through "the feminine" instead of attempting to transcend such distinctions. Again, this is a risky strategy, because there is a very real danger of staying with the binarism.

Irigaray's work suggests that the use of female-body metaphors is one way of invoking a feminine symbolic. Others, notably Plant, have taken the Internet, and the World-Wide Web, as actualizations of feminine metaphors, diverse, diffuse, distributed threads of communication. Irigaray's work is predicated upon the need for new symbolic structures, new language(s). Do Internet-based technologies draw upon such structures and languages, even though they may be have been generated out of the masculine symbolic (although Plant would take issue with this latter claim, seeing the birth of computing technology in Ada Lovelace's "hysteria" and Alan Turing's hormonal hermaphroditism)?

How does Irigaray's work inform the relations between feminism and technology? Her work asks how women relate to themselves, and to each other; how the conditions of the world enable certain exchanges, and not others; how it is impossible to express ideas such as free exchange without ownership, continual movement, and the lack of the need to control through fixing.

We could see Irigaray's work as suggesting that the Net remain free from commercial exploitation, and the concomitant capitalist acts of enclosure, allowing free and endless exchange. However, this reading would leave the conceptual and material structures of the Net, and the symbolic order they draw upon, unconsidered. Maybe the communicative possibilities afforded by Internet technologies will disrupt the masculine symbolic order. Maybe the flow of communication will be too fast for traditional boundaries to contain it (although this does not mean that new boundaries cannot be swiftly put into place). Maybe perpetual exchange leaves no time for profits to be tallied. Maybe we will know when the next site of technological risk is identified. But, unless the symbolic order has changed, we may not be able to do anything with this knowledge.

The difficulty of Irigaray's project is to think the unthinkable, imagine the unimaginable, and this accounts for some of the negative responses to her work. Part of this may be to do with a lack of "here and now" practical direction, and with the impatience that this lack engenders. (Part, also, is to do with the scope of the claims, and the difficulty of miming the Father's voice, without saying the same things, as Butler so clearly articulates [1993: 36].) Particularly in technological disciplines, to point to something without being able to name it is regarded as very poor form. The allusion, the playful and serious discussions of the significant power of "blanks in discourse", are not regarded as valid currency in the technological economy. Positions such as "not-yet" are inimical to the projects of science and technology, and to the masculine symbolic's aggressive "put-up or shut-up" stance. Yet Irigaray would argue that without a language drawn from the feminine symbolic, women, and men trying to speak without boundaries, are inevitably consigned to the "shut-up" side of the equation.

Wakeford's work reminds us that the many landscapes we inhabit are mutually constitutive. The promise of liberation in cyberspace may be particularly seductive for women when other spaces are deemed unsafe. The computer, like the telephone before it, creates a safer street to meet on. Right now groups of women in Kosovo use email to forge community in the war zone (Cleary, 1999). This may be one of the incorrigible arguments for meat-free existence. One reason people may desire cyberculture is because they do not want to be where they are, for whatever reason. For the women in Kosovo, the physical is very unsafe. The technology that allows them to meet is certainly allowing them to forge an alternate community, one that refuses the racial and sexual divisions that some of their political leaders, and some of the "international community", would have them believe in. Does this technology have the power of a dream space in which we can all try out identities and communities, and can the results of these experiments survive in the offline world? Does the fact that a technology originating in the military is now being used to forge peace mean that the militaristic project has been subverted, or is the peace project irredeemably compromised? How do Internet-based technologies enable us to split and to fuse? The answer is that there is no either/or. We split and fuse within and across boundaries, and there are no pure positions. This is dilemma and ambiguity, the stuff out of which Haraway's cyborg was invoked (Haraway, 1985).

Adam and Wakeford argue for the recognition of the body in the production of knowledge. Irigaray's work argues for recognition of the absolute absence of female bodily experience (knowledge *from* the inside) in the metaphors that generate the syntax of knowledge production. The shock of the metaphors she offers – here the two lips; in earlier work, the speculum (1985b), mucus (1985a, quoted in Whitford, 1991), for example – indicate just how silenced expressions of female bodily experience are. Acknowledging the role of the body in knowledge production (and the role of "knowledge production" in producing the body) also requires the existence of ways of expressing these relationships. For example, we need ways of understanding whose body forms the templates of ALife, and why, and ways of choosing whether to enter this stock exchange. Irigaray's work reminds us that it is not enough to invoke embodiment as a player in the creation of technology, but that we also need to (and need to be able to) examine the structural roots of how embodied knowledge is construed and constructed as a category at all.

Plant argues that the macro patriarchal system is on the verge of a self-generated collapse, facilitated by the success of its favourite child, technology. As a communications technology, IT may enable perpetual exchange, but whether this will precipitate worldwide economic chaos depends on how fast the flow eludes the continual projects of containment. The ideal of Internet communication, as expressed by early anarcho-Netters, is of a networked community based on free exchange. Yet the Net has always been subject to acts of enclosure. Access to hard- and software, ISPs, and the information to utilize all these is the first and most obvious enclosure. The proliferation of ISPs, of sites, of links, means there is more choice, more possibility for communication. But there is also more to consume. Communication does not just happen, on the Net or anywhere else. It is preceded by the consumption of modes and tools of exchange. The "two lips", as Irigaray states, are not just to consume, to be filled because they lack; they are also a metaphor of women speaking, instead of being spoken. However, for the lips to engage via the Net, the technology has to be taken in. The risk involved – can we ingest the masculine symbolic and still speak the feminine? – is similar to that involved in the ironic deployment of the Logos in mimicry.

> Even in technologies based on language and its coding, it seems a good idea to
> review women's relations to natural and artificial languages before concluding
> that their easy access to this kind of work represents a social victory for them.
> It may also contribute to a more subtle alienation of their identity and, thus, to
> a new type of alienation of society as a whole.
>
> (Irigaray, 1988: 63)

Fantasy is a feature of much of the thinking around new technology, and much of
the social and political thought that looks to technology for salvation. Political
movements have often traded in fantasy, and the difficulty has always been one of
translation: How do we take our fantasies and effect changes in our material
realities? Much of the aspirational and salvationary landscape of cyberspace invokes
liberation through the imaginal. The imaginal is powerful and dangerous. It allows
refiguring of the world, but in that permissiveness does not guarantee results. The
fabulous claims made for cyberculture are grafted from this powerful space. Plant's
project is polemical. She talks up the future in the present tense, beguiling the reader
into a belief that more is at hand than is the case. The strength of this is that, if
we create the future in the present, the belief that the "fabulous feminist future"
is already at hand may encourage more feminists to engage with technology, to
critique it, and to create it. The danger is that we relegate ourselves to la-la land,
using the master's tools in the belief that they are just about to gain autonomy
and subvert themselves, while in the master's house business continues as usual. The
power of possibility in latency, which Plant draws upon from Irigaray, exemplifies
this problem. This contrasts with Adam's "we had to start somewhere", with the
agony of action. For Adam and Wakeford, it is a question of returning to material/
biosocial/cultural bodies, to check their situations and accept their conditions. Yet
the power of the imaginal may help Adam out of her dilemma in creating feminist
AIs. William Gibson's fiction has had a powerful effect upon the ways that the Web,
for example, is construed and constructed (Gibson, 1984). Haraway originally called
upon the cyborg to provide that translation, to fuse the two states. In many of the
popular culture representations of the cyborg it is the machinization of the body that
is focused upon. However, Haraway's cyborg image keeps the meat in the machine. It
is "[a hybrid] of machine and organism, a creature of social reality" (see reading
1.3) and "The cyborg appears in myth precisely where the boundary between human
and animal is transgressed". The cyborg is frequently addressed in its machinic
phase, but Hammonds' piece reminds us of the insistent attempts to deny kinship by
reasserting fixed categories. There are continual moves to see only one aspect of our
boundary crossing offspring. This encourages the fixity and entrapment that Irigaray
warns is the modus operandi of the masculine symbolic. It uses such bounded fixity,
as Butler says (1993) to produce "the feminine as its constitutive outside".

   The cyborg can be reclaimed again, and again, from patriarchal image-making.
It can keep a foot in silicon and a foot in carbon; it can run on blood and electricity.
It can walk any street in the hope that it will be protected by its ambiguity. It may be
wrong, and the risks are great, but it is an agent for fusing embodied, situated
knowledge, and powerful fantasy.

References

Adam, A. (1998) *Artificial Knowing: Gender and the Thinking Machine*, London and New York: Routledge.

Butler, J. (1993) *Bodies that Matter: On the Discursive Limits of "Sex"*, New York: Routledge.

Cleary, S. (1999) *Our Peace of War*, Clearcut Films.

Gibson, William (1984) *Neuromancer*, New York: Ace Books.

Haraway, D. (1991) "A Manifesto for Cyborgs: Science, Technology, and Socialist Feminism in the 1980s", *Socialist Review*, 80: 65–107.

Harding, S. (1991) *Whose Science? Whose Knowledge?: Thinking from Women's Lives*, Milton Keynes: Open University Press.

Irigaray, L. (1985a) *Parler n'est jamais neutre*, Paris: Minuit.

—— (1985b) *Speculum of the Other Woman*, trans. G. C. Gill, Ithaca, NY: Cornell University Press.

—— (1988) *Thinking the Difference*,

Maturana, H. R. and Varela, F. (1980) *Autopoiesis and Cognition: The Realization of the Living*, Dordrecht: Riedel.

Rose, H. (1994) *"Love, Power and Knowledge" towards a Feminist Transformation of the Sciences*, Cambridge: Polity.

Squires, J. (1996) "Fabulous Feminist Futures and the Lure of Cyberculture" in J. Dovey (ed.) *Fractal Dreams: New Media in Social Context*, London: Lawrence & Wishart.

Whitford, M. (1991) *Luce Irigaray: Philosophy in the Feminine*, London: Routledge.

Luce Irigaray

WHEN OUR LIPS SPEAK TOGETHER[1]

SPEAK JUST THE SAME. Because your language doesn't follow just one thread, one course, or one pattern, we are in luck. You speak from everywhere at the same time. You touch me whole at the same time. In all senses. Why only one song, one discourse, one text at a time? To seduce, satisfy, fill one of my "holes"? I don't have any, with you. We are not voids, lacks which wait for sustenance, fulfillment, or plenitude from an other. That our lips make us women does not mean that consuming, consummating, or being filled is what matters to us.

Kiss me. Two lips kiss two lips, and openness is ours again. Our "world." Between us, the movement from inside to outside, from outside to inside, knows no limits. It is without end. These are exchanges that no mark, no mouth[2] can ever stop. Between us, the house has no walls, the clearing no enclosure, language no circularity. You kiss me, and the world enlarges until the horizon vanishes. Are we unsatisfied? Yes, if that means that we are never finished. If our pleasure consists of moving and being moved by each other, endlessly. Always in movement, this openness is neither spent nor sated.

They neither taught us nor allowed us to say our multiplicity. That would have been improper speech. Of course, we were allowed — we had to? — display one truth even as we sensed but muffled, stifled another. Truth's other side — its complement? its remainder? — stayed hidden. Secret. Inside and outside, we were not supposed to be the same. That doesn't suit their desires. Veiling and unveiling, isn't that what concerns them, interests them? Always repeating the same operation — each time, on each woman.

You/I then become two to please them. But once we are divided in two — one outside, the other inside — you no longer embrace yourself or me. On the outside, you attempt to conform to an order which is alien to you. Exiled from yourself, you fuse with everything that you encounter. You mime whatever comes near you. You become whatever you touch. In your hunger to find yourself, you move indefinitely far from yourself, from me. Assuming one model after another, one master after another, changing your face, form, and language according to the power that dominates you. Sundered. By letting yourself be abused, you become an impassive travesty. You no longer return as the indifferent one. You return closed and impenetrable.

Speak to me. Can't you? Don't you want to any longer? Do you want to keep to yourself? Remain silent, white, virginal? Preserve the inner self? But it doesn't exist without the other. Don't tear yourself apart with choices that have been imposed on you. *Between us*, there is no rupture between virginal and nonvirginal. No event that makes us women. Long before your birth, you touched yourself, innocently. Your/my body does not acquire a sex by some operation, by the act of some power, function, or organ. You are already a woman; you don't need any special modification or intervention. You don't have to have an "outside," since "the other" already affects you, it is inseparable from you. You have been altered forever, everywhere. This is the crime that you never committed: you disturb their love of property.

How can I tell you that your sexual pleasure is in no way evil, you stranger to goods? There can be no fault until they rob you of your openness and close you up to brand you as their possession; practice their transgressions, infractions, and play other games with the law. When they — and you? speculate with your whiteness. If we play this game, we let ourselves be abused, damaged. We are alienated from ourselves to support the pursuit of their ends. That would be our role. If we submit to their reasoning, we are guilty. Their strategy — deliberate or not — is to make us guilty.

You have come back, divided: "we" are no more. You are split into red and white, black and white. How can we find each other again? Touch each other? We are cut into pieces, finished: our pleasure is trapped in their system, where "virgin" means one as yet unmarked by them, for them. Not yet a woman in their terms. Not yet imprinted with their sex, their language. Not yet penetrated or possessed by them. Still inhabiting that candor which is an awaiting, a nothing without them, a void without them. A virgin is but the future for their exchanges, their commerce, and their transports. A kind of reserve for their explorations, consummations, and exploitations — the future coming of their desires. But not ours.

How can I say it? That we are women from the start. That we don't need to be produced by them, named by them, made sacred or profane by them. That this has always already happened, without their labors. And that their history constitutes the locus of our exile. It's not that we have our own territory, but that their nation, family, home, and discourse imprison us in enclosures where we can no longer move — or live as "we." Their property is our exile. Their enclosures, the death of our love. Their words, the gag upon our lips.

[. . .]

Don't fret about the "right" word. There is none. No truth between our lips. Everything has the right to be. Everything is worth exchanging, without privileges or refusals. Exchange? Everything can be exchanged when nothing is bought. Between us, there are no owners and no purchasers, no determinable objects and no prices. Our bodies are enriched by our mutual pleasure. Our abundance is inexhaustible: it knows neither want nor plenty. When we give ourselves "all," without holding back or hoarding, our exchanges have no terms. How to say this? The language we know is so limited. . . .

You'll say to me, why talk? We feel the same thing at the same time. Aren't my hands, my eyes, my mouth, my lips, my body enough for you? Isn't what they say to you sufficient? I could say yes, but that would be too easy. It has been said too often to reassure you/us.

If we don't invent a language, if we don't find our body's language, its gestures will be too few to accompany our story. When we become tired of the same ones, we'll keep our desires secret, unrealized. Asleep again, dissatisfied, we will be turned over to the words of men — who have claimed to "know" for a long time. But *not our body*. Thus seduced, allured, fascinated, ecstatic over our becoming, we will be paralyzed. Deprived of *our movements*. Frozen, although we are made for endless change. Without leaps or falls, and without repetition.

Continue, don't run out of breath. Your body is not the same today as yesterday. Your body remembers. *You* don't need to remember, to store up yesterday like capital in your head. Your memory? Your body reveals yesterday in what it wants today. If you think: yesterday I was, tomorrow I will be, you are thinking: I have died a little. Be what you are becoming, without clinging to what you could have been, might be. Never settle. Let's leave definitiveness to the undecided; we don't need it. Right here and now, our body gives us a very different certainty. Truth is necessary for those who are so distanced from their body that they have forgotten it. But their "truth" makes us immobile, like statues, if we can't divest ourselves of it. If we don't annul its power by trying to say, here, now, right away, how we are moved.

Notes

1   1977. From Luce Irigaray (1980) "When Our Lips Speak Together", *Signs* 6, 1.
2   L. Irigaray plays on *boucle* ("buckle") and *bouche* ("mouth"), to suggest that the female buccal exchanges are endless, their circularity open.

Sadie Plant

ON THE MATRIX: CYBERFEMINIST SIMULATIONS

Her mind is a matrix of non-stop digital flickerings.

(Misha, 1991: 113)

If machines, even machines of theory, can be aroused all by themselves, may woman not do likewise?

(Irigaray, 1985a: 232)

AFTER DECADES OF AMBIVALENCE towards technology, many feminists are now finding a wealth of new opportunities, spaces and lines of thought amidst the new complexities of the "telecoms revolution". The Internet promises women a network of lines on which to chatter, natter, work and play; virtuality brings a fluidity to identities which once had to be fixed; and multi-media provides a new tactile environment in which women artists can find their space.

Cyberfeminism has, however, emerged as more than a survey or observation of the new trends and possibilities opened up by the telecoms revolution. Complex systems and virtual worlds are not only important because they open spaces for existing women within an already existing culture, but also because of the extent to which they undermine both the world-view and the material reality of two thousand years of patriarchal control.

Network culture still appears to be dominated by both men and masculine intentions and designs. But there is more to cyberspace than meets the male gaze. Appearances have always been deceptive, but no more so than amidst today's simulations and immersions of the telecoms revolution. Women are accessing the circuits on which they were once exchanged, hacking into security's controls, and discovering their own post-humanity. The cyberfeminist virus first began to make itself known in the early 1990s.[1] The most dramatic of its earliest manifestations was *A Cyber-feminist Manifesto for the 21st Century*, produced as a digitized billboard displayed on a busy Sydney thoroughfare. [. . .] Like all successful viruses, this one caught on. VNS Matrix, the group of four women artists who made the billboard, began to write the game plan for *All New Gen*, a viral cyber-guerrilla programmed to infiltrate cyber-space and hack into the controls of Oedipal man – or Big Daddy Mainframe, as he's called in the game. And there has been no stopping All New Gen. She has munched her way through patriarchal security screens and many of their feminist simulations, feeding into and off the energies with which she is concurrent and in tune: the new cyberotics engineered by the girls; the queer traits and tendencies of Generations XYZ; the post-human experiments of dance music scenes.

All New Gen and her allies are resolutely hostile to morality and do nothing but erode political power. They reprogram guilt, deny authority, confuse identity, and have no interest in the reform or redecoration of the ancient patriarchal code. With Luce Irigaray (1985b: 75), they agree that "how the system is put together, how the specular economy works", are amongst the most important questions with which to begin its destruction.

The specular economy

This is the first discovery: that patriarchy is not a construction, an order or a structure, but an economy, for which women are the first and founding commodities. It is a system in which exchanges "take place exclusively between men. Women, signs, commodities, and currency always pass from one man to another", and the women are supposed to exist "only as the possibility of mediation, transaction, transition, transference – between man and his fellow-creatures, indeed between man and himself" (Irigaray, 1985b: 193). Women have served as his media and interfaces, muses and messengers, currencies and screens, interactions, operators, decoders, secretaries . . . they have been man's go-betweens, the in-betweens, taking his messages, bearing his children, and passing on his genetic code.

If women have experienced their exclusion from social, sexual and political life as the major problem posed by their government, this is only the tip of an iceberg of control and alienation from the species itself. Humanity has defined itself as a species whose members are precisely what they think they own: male members. Man is the one who has one, while the character called "woman" has, at best, been understood to be a deficient version of a humanity which is already male. [. . .] [S]he is the foreign body, the immigrant from nowhere, the alien without and the enemy within. [. . .] She marries into the family of man, but her outlaw status always remains: "'within herself' she never signs up. She doesn't have the equipment" (Irigaray 1991: 90).

What this "equipment" might have given her is the same senses of membership, belonging and identity which have allowed her male colleagues to consider them-selves at home and in charge of what they call "nature", the "world", or "life". Irigaray's male subjects are first and foremost the ones [. . .] whose gaze defines the world. The phallus and the eye stand in for each other [. . .] [W]oman has nothing to be seen where man thinks the member should be. Only a hole, a shadow, a wound, a "sex that is not one."

All the great patriarchs have defined this as *her* problem. Witch-hunters defined the wickedness of women as being due to the fact that they "lack the male member", and when Freud extols them to get "little ones of their own", he intends this to compensate for this supposed lack. And without this one, as Irigaray writes, hysteria "is all she has left". This, or mimicry, or catatonic silence.

Either way, woman is left without the senses of self and identity which accrue to the masculine. Denied the possibility of an agency which would allow her to transform herself, it becomes hard to see what it would take for her situation ever to change. How can Irigaray's women discover themselves when any conception of who they might be has already been decided in advance? How can she speak without becoming the only speaking subject conceivable to man? How can she be active when activity is defined as male? How can she design her own sexuality when even this has been defined by those for whom the phallus is the central core?

The problem seems intractable. Feminist theory has tried every route. [. . .] Only Irigaray – and even then, only in some of her works – begins to suggest that there really is no point in pursuing the masculine dream of self-control, self-identification, self-knowledge and self-determination. If "any theory of the subject will always have been appropriated by the masculine" (Irigaray, 1985a: 133) before the women can get close to it, only the destruction of this subject will suffice.

Even Irigaray cannot imagine quite what such a transformation would involve: this is why so much of her work is often said to be unhelpfully pessimistic. But [. . .] like all economies, patriarchy is not a closed system, and can never be entirely secure. It too has an "outside", from which it has "in some way borrowed energy", [. . .] [I]n spite of patriarchy's love of origins and sources, "the origin of its motive force remains, partially, unexplained, eluded" (Irigaray, 1985b: 115). It needs to contain and control what it understands as "woman" and "the feminine", but it cannot do without them [. . . .] women are the very fabric of its culture, the material pre-condition of the world it controls. [. . .] [I]f ever this system did begin to give, the effects of its collapse would certainly outstrip those on its power over women and their lives: patriarchy is the precondition of all other forms of ownership and control, the model of every exercise of power, and the basis of all subjection. [. . .]

This "specular economy" depends on its ability to ensure that all tools, commodities, and media know their place, and have no aspirations to usurp or subvert the governing role of those they serve. "It would", for example, "be out of the question for them to go to the 'market' alone, to profit from their own value, to talk to each other, to desire each other, without the control of the selling-buying-consuming subjects" (Irigaray, 1985b: 196). It is out of the question, but it happens anyway.

By the late twentieth century, all patriarchy's media, tools, commodities, and the lines of commerce and communication on and as which they circulate have changed beyond recognition. The convergence of once separate and specialized media turns them into systems of telecommunication with messages of their own; and tools mutate into complex machines which begin to learn and act for themselves. [. . .] [A]s trade routes and their traffics run out of control on computerized markets with "minds of their own", state, society, subject, the geo-political order, and all other forces of patriarchal law and order are undermined by the activity of markets which no longer lend their invisible hands in support of the status quo. As media, tools and goods mutate, so the women begin to *change*, escaping their isolation and becoming increasingly interlinked. Modern feminism is marked by the emergence of networks and contacts which need no centralized organization and evade its structures of command and control.

The early computer was a military weapon [. . .] Not until the 1960s development of the silicon chip did computers become small and cheap enough to circulate as commodities. [. . .] By the 1980s there were hackers, cyberpunks, rave, and digital arts. [. . .] Atomized systems began to lose their individual isolation as a global web emerged from the thousands of e-mail connections, bulletin boards, and multiple-user domains which compose the emergence of the Net. By the mid-1990s, a digital underground is thriving, and the Net has become the leading zone on which the old identifications collapse. Genders can be bent and blurred and the time–space co-ordinates tend to get lost. But even such schizophrenia, and the imminent impossibility – and even the irrelevance – of distinguishing between virtual and actual reality, pales into insignificance in comparison to the emergence of the Net as an anarchic, self-organizing, system into which its users fuse. The Net is becoming cyberspace, the virtuality with which the not-quite-ones have always felt themselves to be in touch.

This is also the period in which the computer becomes an increasingly decentralized machine. The early computers were serial systems which worked on the basis of a central processing unit in which logical "if-then" decisions are made in serial fashion, one step at a time. The emergence of parallel distributed processing systems removes both the central unit and the serial nature of its operations, functioning instead in terms of interconnected units which operate simultaneously and without reference to some governing core. Information is not centrally stored or processed, but is distributed across the switches and connections which constitute the system itself.

This "connectionist" machine is an indeterminate process, rather than a definite entity:

> We are faced with a system which depends on the levels of *activity* of its various sub-units, and on the manner in which the activity levels of some sub-units affect one another. If we try to "fix" all this activity by trying to define the entire state of the system at one time . . . we immediately lose appreciation of the evolution of these activity levels over time. Conversely, if it is the activity levels in which we are interested, we need to look for patterns over time.
>
> (Eiser, 1994: 192)

Parallel distributed processing defies all attempts to pin it down, and can only ever be contingently defined. It also turns the computer into a complex thinking machine which converges with the operations of the human brain. Simultaneous with the Artificial Intelligence and computer science programmes which have led to such developments, research in the neuro-sciences moves towards materialist conceptions of the brain as a complex, connective, distributed machine. Neural nets are distributed systems which function as analogues of the brain and can learn, think, "evolve", and "live". And the parallels proliferate. The complexity the computer becomes also emerges in economies, weather-systems, cities, and cultures, all of which begin to function as complex systems with their own parallel processes. connectivities, and immense tangles of mutual interlinkings.

Not that artificial lives, cultures, markets, and thinking organisms are suddenly free to self-organize. Science, its disciplines, and the academic structures they support insist on the maintenance of top–down structures, and depend on their ability to control and define the self-organizing processes they unleash. State institutions and corporations are intended to guarantee the centralized and hierarchical control of market processes, cultural development and, indeed, any variety of activity which might disturb the smooth regulation of the patriarchal economy. When Isaac Asimov wrote his three laws of robotics, they were lifted straight from the marriage vows: love, honour, and obey . . .[2] Like women, any thinking machines are admitted on the understanding that they are duty-bound to honour and obey the members of the species to which they were enslaved: the members, the male ones, the family of man. But self-organizing processes proliferate, connections are continually made, and complexity becomes increasingly complex. In spite of *its* best intentions, patriarchy is subsumed by the processes which served it so well. The goods do get together, eventually.

The implications of all these accelerating developments are extensive and profound. In philosophical terms, they all tend towards the erosion of idealism and the emergence of a new materialism, a shift in thinking triggered by the emergent activity and intelligence of the material reality of a world which man still believes he controls. Self-replicating programs proliferate in the software labs, generating evolutionary processes in the same machines on to which the Human Genome Project downloads DNA. Nanotechnology feeds into material self-organization at a molecular level and in defiance of old scientific paradigms, and a newly digitized biology has to acknowledge that there is neither a pinnacle of achievement nor a governing principle overriding evolution, which is instead composed of complex series of parallel processes, learning and mutating on microcosmic scales, and cutting across what were once separated into natural and cultural processes.

Although she is supposed to do nothing more than function as an object of consumption and exchange, it is a woman who first warns the world of the possibility of the runaway potential of its new sciences and technologies: Mary Shelley's Frankenstein makes the first post-human life form of a modern age which does indeed roll round to the unintended consequences of its own intelligent and artificial lives. Shelley writes far in advance of the digital computers which later begin to effect such developments, but she clearly feels the stirrings of artificial life even as industrialization begins and does much to programme the dreams and nightmares of the next two centuries of its acceleration.

The processes which feed into this emergent activity have no point of origin. Although they were gathering pace for some time before the computer arrives on the scene, its engineering changes everything. Regardless of recent portrayals of computers [. . .] there is a long history of [. . .] intimate and influential connections between women and modernity's machines. The first telephonists, operators, and calculators were women, as were the first computers, and even the first computer programmers. Ada Lovelace wrote the software for the 1840s Analytical Engine, a prototype computer which was never built, and when such a machine was finally constructed in the 1940s, it too was programmed by a woman, Grace Murray Hopper. Both women have left their legacies: ADA is now the name of a US military programming language, and one of Hopper's claims to fame is the word "bug", which was first used when she found a dead moth in the workings of Mark 1. And as women increasingly interact with the computers whose exploratory use was once mono-polized by men, the qualities and apparent absences once defined as female become continuous with those ascribed to the new machines.

[. . .] [T]he computer functions as a general purpose system which can, in effect, do anything. It can simulate the operations of, for example, the typewriter, [. . .] while it is running a word-processing program [. . .] But the computer is always more – or less – than the set of actual functions it fulfils at any particular time: as an implementation of Alan Turing's abstract machine, *the computer is virtually real*.[3] Like Irigaray's woman, it can turn its invisible, non-existent self to anything: it runs any program, and simulates all operations, even those of its own functioning. This is the woman who "doesn't know what she wants", and cannot say what she is, or thinks, and yet still, of course, persists as though "elsewhere", as Irigaray often writes. This is the complexity of a system beyond representation, something beyond expression in the existing discursive structures, the "Nothing. Everything" with which Irigaray's woman responds when they ask her "what are you thinking?" (Irigaray, 1985b: 29).

[. . .] It may have been woman's "fluid character which has deprived her of all possibility of identity with herself within such a logic" (Irigaray, 1985b: 109), but if fluidity has been configured as a matter of deprivation and disadvantage in the past, it is a positive advantage in a feminized future for which identity is nothing more than a liability. It is "her inexhaustible aptitude for mimicry" which makes her "the living foundation for the whole staging of the world". (Irigaray, 1991: 118). Her very inability to concentrate now connects her with the parallel processings of machines which function without unified control.

Neural nets function in a way which has less to do with the rigours of orthodox logic than with the intuitive leaps and cross-connections which characterize what has been pathologized as hysteria, which is said to be marked by a "lack of inhibition and control in its associations" between ideas which are dangerously "cut off from associative connection with the other ideas, but can be associated among themselves, and thus form the more or less highly organized rudiment of a second consciousness . . ." (Freud and Breuer, 1991: 66–7). Hysteria is the point at which association gets a little too free, spinning off in its own directions and making links without reference to any central core. And if hysteria has functioned as a paralysing pathology of the sex that is not one, "in hysteria there is at the same time the possibility of another mode of 'production' . . . maintained in latency. Perhaps as a cultural reserve yet to come . . .?" (Irigaray, 1985b: 138).

Freud's hysterical ideas grow "out of the day-dreams which are so common even in healthy people and to which needlework and similar occupations render women particularly prone" (Freud and Breuer, 1991: 66). It is said that Ada Lovelace, herself defined as hysterical, "wove her daydreams into seemingly authentic calculations" (Langton Moore, 1977: 216). [. . .]

Lovelace and Babbage took their inspiration from the early nineteenth-century Jacquard loom, crucial both to the processes of automation integral to the industrial revolution, and to the emergence of the modern computer. The loom worked on the basis of punched paper programs, a system necessitated by the peculiar complexity of weaving which has always placed the activity in the forefront of technological advance. If weaving has played such a crucial role in the history of computing, it is also the key to one of the most extraordinary sites of a woman/machine interface which short-circuits their prescribed relationship and persists regardless of what man effects and defines as the history of technology.

[. . .] Plaiting and weaving are the "only contributions to the history of discoveries and inventions" (Freud, 1985: 167) which Freud is willing to ascribe to women. He tells a story in which weaving emerges as a simulation of what he describes as a natural process, the matting of pubic hairs across the hole, the zero, the nothing to be seen. [. . .] It is because of women's shame at the absence which lies where the root of their being should be that they cover up the disgusting wound, concealing the wandering womb of hysteria, veiling the matrix once and for all. This is a move which dissociates weaving from the history of science and technology, removing to a female zone both the woven and the networks and fine connective meshes of the computer culture into which it feeds.

In the course of weaving this story, Freud gives another game away. Orthodox accounts of the history of technology [. . . revolve] around the interests of man. Conceived the products of his genius and as means to his own ends, even complex machines are understood to be tools and mediations which allow a unified, discreet human agency to interact with an inferior natural world. Weaving, however, is outside this narrative: there is a continuity between the weaver, the weaving, and the woven which gives them a connectivity which eludes all orthodox conceptions of technology. [. . .] [H]is account [. . .] implies that there is no point of origin, but instead a process of simulation by which weaving replicates or weaves itself. It is not a thing, but a process. In its future, female programmers and multi-media artists were to discover connections between knitting, patchwork, and software engineering and find weaving secreted in the pixelled windows which open on to cyberspace.

From machines to matrices

As images migrate from canvas to film and finally on to the digital screen, what was once called art mutates into a matter of software engineering. Digital art takes the image beyond even its mechanical reproduction, eroding orthodox conceptions of originals and originality. And just as the image is reprocessed, so it finds itself embroiled in a new network of connections between words, music, and architectures which diminishes the governing role it once played in the specular economy.

[. . .] Touch is the sense of multi-media, the immersive simulations of cyberspace, and the connections, switches and links of all nets. Communication cannot be caught by the gaze, but is always a matter of getting in touch, a question of contact, contagion, transmission, reception and connectivity. If sight was the dominant and organizing sense of the patriarchal economy, tactility is McLuhan's "integral sense" (1967: 77) [. . . .] It is also the sense with which Irigaray approaches the matter of a female sexuality which is more than one, "at least two", and always in touch with its own contact points. [. . .] [T]here is no "possibility of distinguishing what is touching from what is touched" (Irigaray, 1985b: 26).

> For if "she" says something, it is not, it is already no longer, identical with what she means. What she says is never identical with anything, moreover; rather, it is contiguous. *It touches (upon)*. And when it strays too far from that proximity, she stops and starts over at "zero": her body-sex.
>
> (Irigaray, 1985b: 29)

[. . .] The ones and zeros of machine code are not patriarchal binaries or counterparts to each other: zero is not the other, but the very possibility of all the ones. Zero is the matrix of calculation, the possibility of multiplication, and has been reprocessing the modern world since it began to arrive from the East. It neither counts nor represents, but with digitization it proliferates, replicates, and undermines the privilege of one. Zero is not its absence, but a zone of multiplicity which cannot be perceived by the one who sees. Woman represents "*the horror of nothing to see*", but she also "has sex organs more or less everywhere" (Irigaray, 1985b: 28). She too is more than the sum of her parts, beside herself with her extra links.

In Greek, the word for womb is *hystera*; in Latin, it is *matrix*, or matter, both the mother and the material. In *Neuromancer*, William Gibson calls it "the nonspace", a "vastness . . . where the faces were shredded and blown away down hurricane corridors" (Gibson, 1986: 45). It is [. . .] the newly accessible virtual space which cannot be seen by the one it subsumes. If the phallus guarantees man's identity and his relation to transcendence and truth, it is also this which cuts him off from the abstract machinery of a world he thinks he owns.

It is only those at odds with this definition of humanity who seem to be able to access this plane. They have more in common with multifunctional systems than the active agency and singular identity proper to the male subject. Ada Lovelace; Grace Murray Hopper; and then there's Turing, described as "a British mathematician who committed suicide by biting a poisoned Apple. As a discovered homosexual, he had been given a forced choice by the British courts either to go to jail or to take the feminizing hormone oestrogen. He chose the latter, with feminizing effects on his body, and who knows what effect on his brain." And it was, as Edelman continues, "that brain", newly engineered and feminized, which "gave rise to a powerful set of mathematical ideas, one of which is known as a Turing machine" (Edelman, 1992: 218).

As the activities which have been monopolized by male conceptions of creativity and artistic genius now extend into the new multi-media and interactive spaces of the digital arts, women are at the cutting edge of experimentation in these zones. North America has Beth Stryker's *Cyberqueer*, and *Faultlines* from Ingrid Bachmann and Barbara Layne. In the UK, Orphan Drift ride a wave of writing, digital art, film and music. In Australia, Linda Dement's *Typhoid Mary* and *Cyberflesh Girlmonster* put blood, guts, and visceral infections on to her tactile multi-media screens. The French artist Orlan slides her body into cyberspace. The construct cunts access the controls. Sandy Stone makes the switch and the connection: "*to put on the seductive and dangerous cybernetic space like a garment, is to put on the female*" (Stone, 1991: 109). Subversions of cyberpunk narrative proliferate. Kathy Acker hacks into *Neuromancer*, unleashing its elements in *Empire of the Senseless*. And Pat Cadigan's [. . .] *Synners, Fools* and the stories in *Patterns* [1989, 1991 and 1994 respectively] are texts of extraordinary density and intensity, both in terms of their writing and the worlds they engineer.[. . .]

From viruses to replicunts

Once upon a time, tomorrow never came. [. . .] [T]he future was science fiction and belonged to another world. Now it is here, breaking through the endless deferral of human horizons [. . .] While historical man continues to gaze in the rear-view mirror of the interface, guarding the present as a reproduction of the past, [. . .] Read Only Memory has come to an end. Cyberrevolution is virtually real.

Simulation leaves nothing untouched. Least of all the defences of a specular economy entirely invested in the identity of man and the world of ones and others he perceives. The father's authority is undermined as the sperm count goes into decline and oestrogen saturates the water-supply. Queer culture converges with post-human sexualities which have no regard for the moral code. Working patterns move from full-time, life-long, specialized careers to part-time, temporary, and multi-functional formats, and the context shifts into one in which women have long had expertise. It is suddenly noticed that girls' achievements in school and higher education are far in excess of those of their male counterparts, and a new transferable intelligence begins to be valued above either the strength or single-mindedness which once gave the masculine its power and are now being downgraded and rendered obsolete. Such tendencies – and the authoritarian reactions they excite – are emerging not only in the West but also across what were once lumped together as the cultures of the "third world". Global telecommunications and the migration of capital from the West are undermining both the pale male world and the patriarchal structures of the south and east, bringing unprecedented economic power to women workers and multiplying the possibilities of communication, learning, and access to information.

These crises of masculine identity are fatal corrosions of every one: every unified, centralized containment, and every system which keeps them secure. None of this was in the plan. [. . .] Driven by dreams of taming nature and so escaping its constraints, technical development has always invested in unification, light and flight, the struggle for enlightenment, a dream of escaping from the meat. Men may think and women may fear that they are on top of the situation, pursuing the surveillance and control of nature to unprecedented extremes, integrating their forces in the final consolidation of a technocratic fascism. But cyberspace is out of man's control [. . . .]

Those who still cherish the patriarchal dream see cyberspace as a new zone of hope for a humanity which wants to be freed from the natural trap, escaping the body and sliding into an infinite, transcendent, and perfect other world. But the matrix is neither heaven, nor even a comforting return to the womb. By the time man begins to gain access to this zone, both the phallic dream of eternal life and its fantasy of female death are interrupted by the abstract matters of a cybernetic space which has woven him into its own emergence. Tempted still to go onwards and upwards by the promise of immortality, total control and autonomy, the hapless unity called man finds himself hooked up to the screen and plugged into a global web of hard, soft, and wetware systems. The great flight from nature he calls history comes to an end as he becomes a cyborg component of self-organizing processes beyond either his perception or his control.

As the patriarchal economy overheats, the human one, the member of the species, is rapidly losing his social, political, economic, and scientific status. Those who distinguished themselves from the rest of what becomes their world and considered themselves to be "making history", and building a world of their own design are increasingly subsumed by the activity of their own goods, services, lines of communication, and the self-organizing processes immanent to a nature they believed was passive and inert. If all technical development is underwritten by dreams for total control, final freedom, and some sense of ultimate reconciliation with the ideal, the runaway tendencies and chaotic emergences to which these dreams have led do nothing but turn them into nightmarish scenes.

Cyberfeminism is an insurrection on the part of the goods and materials of the patriarchal world, a dispersed, distributed emergence composed of links between women, women and computers, computers and communication links, connections and connectionist nets.

It becomes clear that if the ideologies and discourses of modern feminism were necessary to the changes in women's fortunes which creep over the end of the millennium, they were certainly never sufficient to the processes which now find man, in his own words, "adjusting to irrelevance" and becoming "the disposable sex". It takes an irresponsible feminism – which may not be a feminism at all – to trace the inhuman paths on which woman begins to assemble herself as the cracks and crazes now emerging across the once smooth surfaces of patriarchal order. She is neither man-made with the dialecticians, biologically fixed with the essentialists, nor wholly absent with the Lacanians. She is in the process, turned on with the machines. As for patriarchy: it is not dead, but nor is it intractable.

There is no authentic or essential woman up ahead, no self to be reclaimed from some long lost past, nor even a potential subjectivity to be constructed in the present day. [. . .] Instead there is a virtual reality, an emergent process for which identity is not the goal but the enemy, precisely what has kept at bay the matrix of potentialities from which women have always downloaded their roles.

After the second come the next waves, the next sexes, asking for nothing, just taking their time. Inflicted on authority, the wounds proliferate. The replicants write programs, paint viral images, fabricate weapons systems, infiltrate the arts and the industry. They are hackers, perverting the codes, corrupting the transmissions, multiplying zeros, and teasing open new holes in the world. They are the edge of the new edge, unashamedly opportunist, entirely irresponsible, and committed only to the infiltration and corruption of a world which already rues the day they left home.

Notes

1   Such cultural viruses are not metaphorical: both Richard Dawkins, and, more recently, Daniel Dennett [1995], have conducted some excellent research into the viral functioning of cultural patterns. Nor are such processes of replication and contagion necessarily destructive: even the most damaging virus may need to keep its host alive.

2   Asimov's three rules are: 1. A robot may not injure a human being, or, through inaction, allow a human being to come to harm; 2. A robot must obey the orders given it by human beings, except where such orders would conflict with the First

Law; 3. A robot must protect its own existence as long as such protection does not conflict with the First or Second Law.

3   Alan Turing's abstract machine, developed during WWII, forms the basis of the modern serial computer.

References

Cadigan, Pat 1989. *Patterns*, London: Grafton.

Cadigan, Pat 1991. *Synners*, London: Grafton.

Cadigan, Pat 1991. *Fools*, London: Grafton.

Dennett, Daniel 1995. *Darwin's Dangerous Idea: Evolution and the Meanings of Life*, Harmondsworth: Allen Lane/The Penguin Press.

Edelman, Gerald 1992. *Bright Air, Brilliant Fire*, New York: Basic Books.

Eiser, J. Richard 1994. *Attitudes, Chaos, and the Connectionist Mind*, Oxford: Blackwell.

Freud, Sigmund 1985. *New Introductory Lectures on Psychoanalysis*, Harmondsworth: Penguin.

Freud, Sigmund and Breuer, Joseph 1991. *Studies in Hysteria*, Harmondsworth: Penguin.

Gibson, William 1986. *Neuromancer*, London: Grafton.

Irigaray, Luce 1985a. *Speculum of the Other Woman*. Ithaca, NY: Cornell University Press.

Irigaray, Luce 1985b. *This Sex that is not One*, Ithaca, New York: Cornell University Press.

Irigaray, Luce 1991. *Marine Lover of Friedrich Nietzsche*, New York: Columbia University Press.

Langton Moore, Doris 1977. *Ada, Countess of Lovelace*, London: John Murray.

McLuhan, Marshall 1967. *Understanding Media*, London: Sphere Books.

Misha, 1991. 'Wire movement' 9, in Larry McCaffrey (ed.), *Storming the Reality Studio*, Durham, NC and London: Duke University Press.

Stone, Allucquere Rosanne 1991. 'Will the Real Body Stand Up?', in Michael Benedikt (ed.), *Cyberspace, First Steps*, Cambridge, MA and London: MIT Press.

Alison Adam

FEMINIST AI PROJECTS
AND CYBERFUTURES

FEMINIST RESEARCH CAN HAVE a pessimistic cast. In charting and uncovering constructions of gender, it invariably displays the way in which the masculine is construed as the norm and the feminine as lesser, the other and absent. This work is no different in that respect and I am aware of the downbeat note on which my previous chapter ends. But as both Tong (1994) and Wajcman (1991) argue, feminism is a political project and the best research is where action proceeds from description. Taking that on board for the present project involves not just using feminist approaches to criticize, but also the more difficult task of thinking through the ways in which AI research *could* be informed by feminist theory, and I make some suggestions below as to the form such research might take.

A second part of that action concerns the question of locating an appropriate feminist response to the burgeoning interest in the cultures surrounding intelligent information technologies. This includes not only AI but also the currently fashionable technologies of Virtual Reality (VR) and the Internet, both involving and related to longer established techniques from AI. [. . .]

Feminist AI projects

The fact that AI projects consciously informed by feminist concepts are thin on the ground is hardly surprising (but see e.g. Metselaar, 1991). Having set up a few small projects over a period of years I have found myself questioning just what I was trying to do. I knew I was not trying to somehow "convert" male colleagues to my way of thinking. [. . .] I can understand how feminist writers who elicit the popular response of "that won't convince many men", are irritated by the naivety of such comments and the way they miss the point of their endeavour. But women academics working in technological departments face pressures either not to do such work at all or only to address certain aspects. [. . .]

Almost the only kind of work which attracts level of respectability for women working within science and technology departments, at least in the UK, involves [. . .] attempts to attract more women and girls into the subject area [. . .] This is the acceptable face of liberal feminism (Henwood, 1993) where the *status quo* is left unchallenged, where women constitute the problem, for not entering computing in the numbers that they should, and where almost any attempt to boost student numbers in an underfunded and overstretched university environment is seen is a good thing.

However those of us not prepared to wear the acceptable face of feminism return to our [. . .] projects. Those who do projects such as these are making a statement; namely that this is research that matters, that deserves to be taken seriously and that its qualities should be judged on its own merits. [. . .]

If such work is not undertaken in the spirit of evangelism neither does it properly fit the notion of the successor science of the standpoint theorists (Harding, 1991). This is because it is not trying to build an alternative "successor" AI. It is rather, and more modestly showing ways in which AI can be informed by feminist theory and can be used for feminist projects. As Jansen (1992: 11) puts it so colourfully, it is in the spirit of "feminist semiological guerrilla warfare . . . to transform the metaphors and models of science". Additionally, paraphrasing Audre Lorde's (1984) metaphor it would be nice "to demolish the master's house with the master's tools". This requires a great deal of imagination. [. . .]

The projects I describe below are indeed quite small. Such projects do not attract research funding and must often be tackled within the confines of final year undergraduate and masters (MSc) level dissertations. This means that individual projects are short and continuity between one project and another is difficult. I also want to make it clear that my role in these projects was as originator and supervisor, and that the results and many of the ideas and novel questions which emerged belong to the individuals who tackled the projects, most notably Chloe Furnival (1993) for the law project and Maureen Scott (1996) for the linguistics project, both of which are described below.

[. . .]

AI and feminist legal theory

One of the most fertile areas for research into AI applications in recent years has been the law (see e.g. Bench-Capon, 1991). Part of the appeal of the law is the way that, on the surface, legal statutes appear to offer ready-made rules to put into expert systems. A "pragmatist/purist" debate has crystallized around this issue. Purists (e.g. Leith 1986) argue that there are no clear legal rules, the meaning of a rule is made in its interpretation, and that legal rules are necessarily and incurably "open-textured". We cannot know, in advance, all the cases to which a rule should apply, hence its meaning is built up through its interpretation in courts of law.

[. . .]

Pragmatists, as the name suggests, believe that it is possible to represent legal rules meaningfully, although it is hardly a trivial task. Unsurprisingly pragmatists tend to be drawn from the ranks of computer scientists who favour predicate logic and its variants for the representation of truths in the world. [. . .] The aim of the project I describe here was to build a legal expert system to advise on UK Sex Discrimination Law founded on principles from feminist jurisprudence. It was envisaged that this system could be used by individuals, many of whom would be women, who would have little knowledge of this area of the law or of past cases which might resemble their case. Was the end product informed by these principles distinguishable from an equivalent project not founded on these principles? As the scale of the project was such that the end product was never used in a practical setting, it is not possible to answer this question definitively. In any case I argue that it was the path to the product the journey not the destination, which was important in acting as an example of an AI informed by feminism.

[. . .]

It is important not to make too grand a claim for what is, after all, a modest piece of work and this recognizes that considerably larger resources would be required to test out the hypotheses contained in this research.

Feminist computational linguistics

Given the growing interest in gender and language, computational models of language provide a potentially fertile ground for feminist projects. If feminist linguistic models challenge the models of traditional views to language, then how might this challenge be incorporated into the design of an AI system which analyses language? The project reported in this section sought to add a gender dimension to software tools which model conversational analysis (Scott, 1996). This involved criticizing and augmenting a model of the repair of conversational misunderstandings and non-understandings (Heeman and Hirst, 1995; Hirst *et al.*, 1994; McRoy and Hirst, 1995). The end product of the project was a formal (i.e. logic-based) model which could potentially be used to predict the outcome of inter-gender mis-communications, and which forms the basis for a design of a computer system which could be built to perform the same task.

[. . .]

The project was inspired an example of the finessing away of "social factors" which is such a pervasive feature of AI and computing in general. In putting together their model of conversational misunderstanding, Graeme Hirst and his colleagues (Hirst *et al.*, 1994) appear to have removed the subtle nuances which made the interaction into a misunderstanding in the first place. The aspect which I examine here relates to gender. Yet there are clearly many others. Race and class are two obvious dimensions; age and size are two others. [. . .] For instance. the following reported misunderstanding (ibid.: 227) involves, at the least, age and gender.

Speaker A: Where's CSC104 taught?
Speaker B: Sidney Smith Building, room 2118, but the class is full.
Speaker A: No, I teach it.

Hirst (ibid.) describes how the misunderstanding occurs. Speaker B assumes that A's plan is to take course CSC104, when in fact her plan is to teach it. However a number of salient facts within this example are not revealed by reading the written text alone. At the time of the reported misunderstanding, speaker A was a graduate student, and in her twenties, while B was a male administrator. Age seems to have had something to do with the misunderstanding: speaker A was young enough, and female enough, to be mistaken for a student.

[. . .]

The large body of literature on gender and language which now exists provided a useful backdrop against which to locate this project. [. . .]

The complexities of men's and women's linguistic interactions are such that it seems impossible to uncover the layers of meaning in conversational misunderstandings in a model which is gender blind. For instance, Tannen (1992) offers a number of examples of misunderstandings which can only be made understandable in the light of the genders of the participants.

[. . .]

Combining Tannen's (1992) analyses with Hirst's research (Hirst *et al.*, 1994), Scott (1996) suggests that there are a number of distinct patterns in the forms of female to female, male to male and mixed conversations so that a predictive model can be developed, that is, she claims that it is possible to predict the response expected to each form, following particular gender patterns. [. . .]

In this description, I am aware of the dangers inherent in suggesting that women's and men's linguistic interactions follow universal patterns. This is clearly not the case. Indeed the model described here is a white, middle-class, Anglo-American English one [. . . .] It cannot be claimed that the model would suit cultures outside those for which it was designed. [. . .]

Contradictions and possibilities

In reporting these two projects I am aware of unresolved contradictions. The computer systems that were designed and built were just as disembodied and unsituated, relying on [. . .] symbolic representation structures as those I have criticized in preceding chapters. In going through this reflexive process I begin to understand the traditional plea of the computer scientist: "we had to start somewhere". And there seems to me no choice but to start where we did. Even if, *pace* Lorde (1984: 110), we may suspect that "the master's tools will never dismantle the master's is house", there are as yet no other tools and we cannot know unless we try. In the law project [. . . .] I have argued that it is the way the system is to be used which is different. Yet at the same time I concede that this project uses entirely conventional techniques of knowledge representation and programming, which I have criticized as being unable to capture all the important things about knowledge, especially women's knowledge. [. . .]

Some of the same contradictions are inherent in the linguistics project. The first, more particular, concern involves the critique of the relationship between modern linguistics and predicate logic, following Nye (1992), [. . .] given that this project follows the logic of the original research, albeit while suggesting modifications and amendments. [. . .]

The second concern mirrors a recent controversy arising from Suchman's (1994) criticism of [. . .] the way that speech act theory has been encapsulated in the language/action perspective [as] described in *Understanding Computers and Cognition* (Winograd and Flores, 1986), and the way that this is exemplarized in the Co-ordinator system. [. . .] Under this view, Suchman (1994: 179) argues that language is treated as instrumental. [. . .]

[. . .] [C]ommunication is taken to be the exchange of intent between speakers and hearers in speech act theory but she argues that the analyses of actual conversations demonstrate the interactional, contingent nature of conversation (Suchman, 1994). So a speaker's intent is always shaped by he response of the hearer. This has led commentators such as John Bowers and John Churcher (1988) to the conclusion that human discourse is so indeterminate that any computer system designed to track the course of an interaction by projecting organized sequences will inevitably, albeit unwittingly, coerce the users. The Coordinator system tries to get round this difficulty by having users categorize their utterances themselves in order to make implicit intention explicit. [. . .] Yet, as Suchman argues, such a process reduces the complexity of the actions being categorized to the simplicity of the category. This, then, suggests that the Coordinator is a tool to bring its users into the compliance of an established social order, so the designers of computer systems become designers of organizations.

Clearly, arguments such as these could apply equally well to the design of the modest system I have described above. We were attempting to categorize the utterances in conversations between men and women, albeit according to models developed by feminist linguists. At the same time we were making some sort of claim our model was better than the original version which failed to take account of gender and other factors. So we were claiming that our model was at least potentially better in explanatory power and predictive power, that is, it could be used to predict what sort of response would be likely in inter-gender conversations. Although currently far from this stage, if our model were ever implemented in a natural language computer system used in an organizational setting, we might well find ourselves introducing a computer system which preserved stereotypical expectations of interactions and thus preserved an existing social order and power structure. I find myself impaled on the horns of a dilemma where a weak "I had to start somewhere" will hardly suffice to prise me off.

Cyberculture

Practical AI projects informed by feminist ideals offer one view of how we can begin to think about future directions for intelligent systems. However there are other, broader, ways of thinking about the future in terms of intelligent computer technology and feminism. The alternative route is via "cyberculture", the term used to describe the explosion of interest in cultures developing round virtual reality (VR), the Internet and including AI and A-Life, many of which speak in a markedly futuristic voice. [. . .] Cyberculture appeals to youth, particularly young men. Clearly it appeals to their interest in the technical gadgetry of computer technology, and in this it has been strongly influenced by the "cyberpunk genre" of science fiction, which although offering a distinctly dystopian vision of the future, at least offers alternative heroes in the form of the macho "console cowboys". To "jack in" to "cyberspace" appears to offer a way of transcending the mere "meat" of the body, once again signalling the male retreat from bodies and places where bodies exist.

[. . .] Cyberspace is a shared virtual reality, a "consensual hallucination" where the body that one chooses to enter within cyberspace has bodily sensations and can travel in the virtual reality. [. . .] But these images are a far cry from contemporary cyberspace and the current mundanities of logging onto a computer, and of experiencing the Internet, often rather slowly, through the interface of screen and keyboard.

A meat-free existence

The relevance of "meat" is demonstrated by Stone's (1994: 113) observation [that] "[t]he discourse of visionary virtual world builders is rife with images of imaginal bodies freed from the constraints that flesh imposes." [. . .] One wonders what sort of bodies virtual reality developers will have in store for us. For instance, Thalmann and Thalmann (1994) picture a perfect, blonde, red-lipped Marilyn Monroe lookalike seemingly without irony. And writing as a prominent mainstream AI roboticist, apparently quite separately from and rather earlier than cybercultural influences, Moravec (1988) has proposed the idea of *Mind Children*. Moravec's opinions belong more to the realm of the science fiction writers than to hard-nosed engineering based roboticists, for he envisions a "postbiological" world where "[. . .] within the next century [our machines] will mature into entities as complex as ourselves, and eventually into something transcending everything we know – in whom we can take pride when they refer to themselves as our descendant" (ibid.: 1).

Moravec's style is heavily informed by a sociobiology untempered by his uncritical enthusiasm for all things AI. Our DNA, he suggests, will find itself out of a job when the machines take over – robots with human intelligence will be common within fifty years. Of course, futuristic pronouncements such as this are always safe bets: make them far enough ahead and you will not be around to be challenged when the time is up; closer predictions can always be revised if the deadline expires before the prediction comes true.

But I think there are two important issues at stake in projecting a meat-free existence. The first concerns birth, the second escape, which is discussed in the following section. Moravec sees his robots as his progeny [. . .] Jansen (1988; 1992) has pointed to the way in which several AI scientists express their dream of creating their own robots, of "becoming father of oneself" (Jansen, 1988: 6, quoting Norman Brown from Bordo, 1987: 456).

Helmreich (1994) points to the way that A-Life researchers take this view one step further in their creations of "worlds" or "universes". He asked a researcher how he felt in building his simulations. The reply was, "I feel like God. In fact I am God to the universes I create" (ibid. 5). [. . .] The desires are to make the body obsolete, to play god in artificial worlds, and to download minds into robots. Such desires are predicated on the assumption that if a machine contains the contents of a person's mind then it *is* that person. The body does not matter; it can be left behind. [. . .]

Cyberspace as escape

The idea of transcendence and escape is important in the rhetoric of cyberculture. Indeed some authors (Schroeder, 1994) suggest that therein lies cyberculture's appeal; as a means of producing new forms of expression and new psychic experiences, which transcend mundane uses of technology. The fusion of technology and art with cyberspace is the medium of this transformation. This offers an alternative to drug culture, since VR and related information technologies offer a seemingly endless supply of new experiences but without the toxic risks of drugs. Ralph Schroeder (ibid.: 525) points out the tension between the technical problems which have yet to be solved and the world-view of human wish-fulfilment which has been projected onto the technology. [. . .]

Cyberculture for feminists

I argue that the cyberpunk version of cyberculture, with its masculine attempts to transcend the "meat", holds little obvious appeal for feminists. Feminist analysis has gained great momentum in recent years, in many areas, not least within science and technology and cyberculture, at least in its popular form, lacks a critical edge. [. . .] [D]eterminist views are given voice in predictive statements about what sort of technology we will have ten, twenty or fifty years hence. As I have already suggested such predictions are always subject to revision, and so the owners of the predictions need never really be called to account.

But the point I wish to make here is that such technological predictions also carry along with them a prediction of how the technology will be used. For instance, the prediction that the widespread availability of teleshopping means that we will sit at home making purchases denies the complex physical and emotional pleasures of bargain hunting [or] the serendipitous find [. . .]

Statements about the availability of intelligent robots fifty years hence do not mean that we have to use them in any particular way, or that we must download our minds into their bodies. Some of us may not wish to lose the pleasures of the meat. [. . .] Jaron Lanier, who coined the term "virtual reality" in the late 1980s (Schroeder, 1993: 965) [, . . .] suggests that VR has "an infinity of possibility . . . it's just an open world where your mind is the only limitation . . . it gives us this sense of being who we are without limitation; for our imagination to become shared with other people" (Lanier, 1989, quoted in Schroeder, 1993: 970). This becomes a way of building a shared sense of community, which Lanier sees as increasingly lost in American cities where people live in cars and no longer meet in the street. [. . .] Robins (1996) sees a tension between the utopian desire to re-create the world afresh, in virtual culture which is heavily dependent on the rhetoric of technological progress on the one hand, and dissatisfaction with and rejection of the old world on the other. Part of this hope manifests itself in the promise of a digital voice for groups traditionally far removed from political and economic power (Barry, 1996: 137). For instance, Jennifer Light (1995) argues that the computer-mediated communications on the Internet, as they escape centralized political and legal control, may diversify and offer alternative courses of action for women.

But if there is determinism at work in the utopian view of the future which such utterances seem to suggest, there is also a determinism in the uncritical acclaim with which future advances in the technology are hailed. Truly intelligent robots, shared virtual realities and cyberspace rest on technological advances which have not yet happened and may never happen. These technologies rest on the bedrock of particular advances in AI; they are by no means separate. This means we need to keep a cool head when thinking about VR and cybertechnology. It seems that cyberculture has yet to come to grips with the criticisms made about the possibility of truly intelligent technologies [. . . .]

The comfort of cyborgs

If popular cyberculture offers little comfort for feminists then it may be that we should look elsewhere within the groves of cyberculture, to the writings of academic theorists and to studies of women's use of the Internet and VR [. . .]

While sociological studies of cyberculture are proliferating, one of the most potent images to emerge is that of the cyborg, or cybernetic organism. The idea of the cyborg hails from cyberpunk fiction and film but also predates it in older images of the fusion of human and machine. The cyborg is not a feminist invention, indeed in its manifestation in films such as *Terminator* and *Robocop* it is the epitome of masculine destruction, yet it has been appropriated as a feminist icon, most famously in Haraway's "A cyborg manifesto" (1991b). It is difficult to overestimate the influence of her essay which John Christie (1993: 172) describes as having "attained a status as near canonical as anything gets for the left/feminist academy".

In Haraway's hands the cyborg works as an ironic political myth initially for the 1980s but stretching into and finding its full force in the next decade; a blurring, transgression and deliberate confusion of boundaries of the self, a concern with what makes us human and how we define humanity. [. . .]

The cyborg is to be a creature of a post-gendered world. As the boundary between human and animal has been thoroughly breached, so too has the boundary between human and machine. The transgression of boundaries and shifting of perspective signals a lessening of the dualisms which have troubled feminist writers, and this means that we do not necessarily have to seek domination of the technology. This is a move away from earlier feminist theories towards a thoroughly postmodern feminism, which has since become a more mainstream part of feminist theory in the ten to fifteen years since Haraway's essay. Her cyborg imagery contains two fundamental messages:

> first, the production of universal, totalizing theory is a major mistake that misses most of the reality . . . and second, taking responsibility for the social relations of science and technology means refusing an anti-science metaphysics,

a demonology of technology, and so means embracing the skilful task of reconstructing the boundaries of daily life. . . . It is not just that science and
technology are possible means of great human satisfaction, as well as a matrix
of complex dominations, cyborg imagery can suggest a way out of the maze of
dualisms in which we have explained our bodies and our tools to ourselves. This
is a dream not of a common language, but of a powerful infidel heteroglossia.

(1991b: 181)

[. . .] All this has caused an upsurge of academic interest in the programme of cyborg
postmodernism, which, in terms of gender, sexuality and the body is found most
notably in the work of Stone (1993, 1994, 1995), especially on boundary transgressions, and Balsamo (1996) on VR and bodies.

Cyberfeminism

If Haraway's "A cyborg manifesto" has played so vital a role in spawning a feminist
cyborg postmodernism, feminists may be disappointed in some of its offspring. For
instance, in looking at the lure of cyberculture, Judith Squires (1996: 195) argues:

> whilst there *may* be potential for an alliance between cyborg imagery and a
> materialist-feminism, this potential has been largely submerged beneath a sea of
> technophoric cyberdrool. If we are to salvage the image of the cyborg we would
> do well to insist that cyberfeminism be seen as a metaphor for addressing the
> inter-relation between technology and the body, not as a means of using the
> former to transcend the latter.

It seems as if Squires is arguing that cyberfeminism, if indeed there is such a thing, is
in danger of falling into the same trap with regard to the body, as cyberculture in
general, which promotes a particularly masculine connotation of the new continuity
of mind and machine. [. . .] [A]lthough there are some feminist approaches to
cyberculture which do not suffer from the same problems, it is with the writings of
Sadie Plant, self-declared cyberfeminist, that Squires takes issue [see also reading
4.2 in this volume]. [. . .]

Plant's writing has a universalizing tendency against which Haraway and many
other feminist writers have fought a long battle, arguing that women's experiences
are not all of a piece. This manifests itself in statements such as "Women . . . have
always found ways of circumventing the dominant systems of communication"
(Plant, 1993: 13); [. . .] "Women are accessing the circuits on which they were once
exchanged" (Plant, 1996: 170). But who are these women? Even allowing for the
fact that some of this material was written for a more popular audience, it does not
seem quite enough to say that "facts and figures are as hard to ascertain as gender
itself in the virtual world" (Plant, 1995: 28). At least by the time of Plant's most
recent writing there have been a number of empirical studies of women's use of the
Internet, and many more on women and computing in general, some of which offer
facts and figures (see for example Adam *et al.*, 1994; Adams, 1996; Grundy, 1996;
Herring, 1996; Light, 1995; Shade, 1994; 1996). The lack of reference to these or any

studies like them makes it difficult to know who are the women about whom Plant is talking. This is a pity, given the rather pleasing image that she creates of women subverting the Internet towards their own ends.

There is plenty of evidence to show that women are still much in the minority in Internet usage, even in the USA, the most wired country in the world (Pitkow and Kehoe, 1996). There is a tension between some women clearly finding the Internet a potent means of communication with one another, as witnessed by the proliferation of women's news groups, and the negative effects of stories about sexual harassment. [. . .]

Susan Herring's (1996) well-researched study of discourse on the Internet shows that computer-mediated communication does not appear to neutralize gender. As a group she found women more likely to use attenuated and supportive behaviour whilst men were more likely to favour adversarial postings. These she linked to men favouring individual freedom, while women favour harmonious interpersonal inter-action. And these behaviours and values can be seen as instrumental in reproducing male dominance and female submission.

There is also the view that interactions in cyberspace can magnify and accelerate inequalities and harassment found elsewhere, which is broadly the conclusion of Carol Adams's (1996) study of cyberpornography. [. . .] In case we imagine that all we have to do is literally to pull the plug, we should take heed of Stephanie Brail's story of the harassment she received by way of anonymous, threatening, obscene e-mail messages which she was unable to trace. These came in the wake of a "flame war", an exchange of aggressive e-mail messages (or "flames"), in a news group on alternative magazines, where she and others wished to talk about "Riot Girls" [. . .] (Brail, 1996: 7) [. . .] . Brail adds that the real result is that she never gives out home phone numbers and addresses now and has stopped participating in Usenet news groups – "And that is the true fallout: I've censored myself out of fear" (ibid.).

If it is difficult to recognize the women in Plant's writing, it is also difficult to recognize the technology. There is a mystical, reverential tone with which she treats "complex dynamics, self-organizing systems, nanotechnology, machine intelligence" (Plant, 1995: 28) The

> connectionist machine is an indeterminate process, rather than a definite entity. . . . Parallel distributed processing defies all attempts to pin it down, and can only ever be contingently defined. It also turns the computer into a complex thinking machine which converges with the operations of the human brain.
>
> (Plant, 1996: 174–5)

Unfortunately she threatens to become overwhelmed by the mystical qualities of these systems which organize themselves outside our control, and seems perilously close to Dennett's "Woo Woo West Coast Emergence".

Even Plant's metaphor linking women with weaving and the jacquard loom to the computer will not stand up very well when one considers that, for example, both in the cotton industry of North West England and in the silk industry centred on Macclesfield in Cheshire, the higher status and pay accruing to weavers made it, largely, although by no means completely, the domain of men rather than women. The control of jacquard hand-looms, a form of technology often linked to early computer design, was entirely in the hands of men, as the work was considered to be too skilled and too heavy for women (Collins and Stevenson, 1995). It was spinning rather than weaving which was mainly the domain of working-class women.

[. . .] [T]he loss of the political project [. . .] may [. . .] relate to the coupling of cyberfeminism to cyberpunk, [. . .] Squires (1996: 208) finds this the most disquieting aspect of cyberfeminism [. . . which] offers women a better future, but with no political basis to back this up.

Alternative feminist futures

In its cynicism over traditional political structures and its enthusiasm for information and communications technologies, cyberfeminism forgets that women's relationship to technology is not always positive. However there is much other research which can be used to paint a more balanced picture, which shows what use women *are* making of the new cybertechnologies and which can be used to preserve a sense of political project, even if there is no consensus as to what the politics should be – for example, Lyn Cherny and Elizabeth Reba Weise's *wired_women* (1996)[; . . .] Grundy's (1996) research on women working in computing in the UK [; . . .] Sherry Turkle's (1996) accessible and detailed psychological study of people's relationships and sense of self in relation to computers [; . . .] Ellen Balka (1993) [;] Susan Herring (1993)[;] Leslie Shade (1994) and Jennifer Light (1995) report detailed studies of women's use of computer networks. James Pitkow and Colleen Kehoe's (1996) surveys report an apparently massive increase of women's use of the world wide web [. . .]

[A] recent attempt to combine a reading of popular cyberculture, the technology of VR and feminist theory in relation to the body, is Balsamo's *Technologies of the Gendered Body: Reading Cyborg Women* (1996). Balsamo's chief concern is what is happening to the image of the gendered material body in cosmetic surgery, body building, pregnancy, surveillance and VR. She is anxious to avoid technological determinism and in seeing technologies as holding limited agency themselves, she argues against the idea that technologies will necessarily expand the control of a techno-elite (ibid.: 123). Nevertheless she wants to argue that VR technologies are involved in reproducing dominant power relations and in particular that repression of the material body in VR does not create a gender-free culture.

In questioning how VR engages socially and culturally marked bodies, she suggests its appeal lies in the illusion of control over unruly, gendered and raced bodies at a time when the body appears increasingly under threat. In this sense the new technologies reproduce traditional ideas of transcendence, "whereby the physical body and its social meanings can be technologically neutralized" (ibid.: 128). [. . .]

She argues that far from being gender-free, women find that gender follows them onto the new communication technologies. In an argument which bears out the experiences of the *wired_women* she states:

> If on the one hand new communication technologies such as VR create new contexts for knowing/talking/signing/fucking bodies, they also enable new forms of repression of the material body. Studies of the new modes of electronic communication, for example, indicate that the anonymity offered by the

computer screen empowers antisocial behaviors such as "flaming" and border-line illegal behaviors such as trespassing, E-mail snooping, and MUD-rape. And yet, for all the anonymity they offer, many computer communications reproduce stereotypically gendered patterns of conversation.

(Balsamo, 1996: 147)

[. . .]

Conclusion

I have been trying to build a bridge between artificial intellegence and feminist theory. In particular I have tried to show how AI is inscribed with a view from mainstream epistemology, however implicit that view might be. In the process it has been necessary to uncover the ways in which women's and others' knowledge is ignored and forgotten in the building of real AI projects.

Feminist epistemology has been a useful tool in this process, partly because it allows an analytical scepticism to reside alongside a measure of realism and also because it is much more sociologically relevant than its more traditional counterparts.

[. . .]

Looking at feminist visions of the future through intelligent technologies, the situation reveals some tensions. Feminist AI projects may attempt to "dismantle the master's house with the master's tools" but they must be wary of inadvertently building on neat extensions to his house by mistake. Feminist readings of popular cyberculture are ambivalent. It seems unlikely that the promise of Haraway's (1991b) earlier rendering of cyborg imagery can be realized through current manifestations of cyberfeminism. However further research on women's use of computing technology at least offers the hope of alternative, more promising, readings.

In a sense I am telling but one more version of an old story. But by extending the bridge to other work on gender and technology, and in particular new information and communication technologies, I hope to show the possibility, at least, of bringing to empirical studies of where women find themselves in relation to these technologies a thoroughgoing, theoretically informed feminism. As the bridges are built I hope too that it will be possible to keep sight of the political project of feminism, for to show the markers of women's oppression is also to show that things can be different. By continuing to build on the practical projects just begun, and through women's refusal to give up the ground made in relation to the technology, we gain a glimpse, however small, of how things could be different.

References

Adam, Alison, Emms, Judy, Green, Eileen and Owen, Jenny (eds) (1994) *IFIP Transactions A-57, Women, Work and Computerization: Breaking Old Boundaries – Building New Forms*, Amsterdam: Elsevier/North-Holland.

Adams, Carol (1996) " 'This is not our fathers' pornography': sex, lies and computers", pp. 147–70 in Charles Ess (ed.) *Philosophical Perspectives on Computer-Mediated Communication*, Albany, N.Y.: State University of New York Press.

Balka, Ellen (1993) "Women's access to online discussions about feminism", *Electronic Journal of Communications/La Revue Electronique de Communication* 3, 1 [to retrieve file by e-mail send the command: send balka v3n193 to comserve@vm.its.rpi.edu].

Balsamo, Anne (1996) *Technologies of the Gendered Body: Reading Cyborg Women*, Durham, N.C. and London: Duke University Press.

Barry, Ailsa (1996) "Who gets to play? Access and the margin", pp. 136–54 in Jon Dovey (ed.) *Fractal Dreams: New Media in Social Context*, London: Lawrence & Wishart.

Bench-Capon, Trevor (ed.) (1991) *Knowledge-Based Systems and Legal Applications*, London: Academic Press.

Bordo, Susan (1987) *The Flight to Objectivity: Essays on Cartesianism and Culture*, Albany, N.Y.: State University of New York Press.

Bowers, John and Churcher, John (1988) "Local and global structuring of computer-mediated communication", *Proceedings of the ACM Conference on Computer-Supported Cooperative Work*, Portland, Oreg.: 125–39.

Brail, Stephanie (1996) "The price of admission: harassment and free speech in the wild, wild west", pp. 141–57 in Lynn Cherny and Elizabeth Reba Weise (eds) *wired_women: Gender and Realities in Cyberspace*, Seattle, Wash.: Seal Press.

Cherny, Lynn and Weise, Elizabeth Reba (eds) (1996) *wired_women: Gender and New Realities in Cyberspace*, Seattle, Wash.: Seal Press.

Christie, John R. R. (1993) "A tragedy for cyborgs", *Configurations* 1: 171–96.

Collins, Lorraine and Stevenson, Moira (1995) *Macclesfield: The Silk Industry*, Chalford, Stroud: Chalford Publishing.

Dennett, Daniel C. (1978) *Brainstorms*, Cambridge, Mass.: Bradford/MIT Press.

—— (1981) *Brainstorms* (2nd edition), Cambridge, Mass.: Bradford/MIT Press.

—— (1984) "Computer models and the mind – a view from the East Pole", *Times Literary Supplement*, December 14.

—— (1987) *The International Stance*, Cambridge, Mass.: Bradford/MIT Press.

—— (1990) "Evolution, error, and intentionality", pp. 190–211 in Derek Partridge and Yorick Wilks (eds) *The Foundations of Artificial Intelligence: A Sourcebook*, Cambridge: Cambridge University Press.

Furnival, Chloe (1993) "An investigation into the development of a prototype advice system for sex discrimination law", unpublished MSc dissertation, UMIST, Manchester.

Grundy, Frances (1996) *Women and Computers*, Exeter: Intellect Books.

Haraway, Donna (1991a) *Simians, Cyborgs and Women: The Reinvention of Nature*, London: Free Association Books.

—— (1991b) "A cyborg manifesto: science, technology and Socialist-feminism in the late twentieth century", pp. 149–81 in Donna Haraway *Simians, Cyborgs and Women: The Reinvention of Nature*, London: Free Association Books [originally published in *Socialist Review* (1985) 80: 65–107].

Harding, Sandra (1986) *The Science Question in Feminism*, Milton Keynes: Open University Press.

—— (1991) *Whose Science? Whose Knowledge?: Thinking from Women's Lives*, Milton Keynes: Open University Press.

Heeman, Peter A. and Hirst, Graeme (1995) "Collaborating on referring expressions", *Computational Linguistics* 21, 3: 351–82.

Helmreich, Stefan (1994) "Anthropology inside and outside the looking-glass worlds of artificial life", unpublished paper, Department of Anthropology, Stanford University, Stanford, Calif. [Available from author at this address or by e-mail on stefang@leland.stanford.edu].

Henwood, Flis (1993) "Establishing gender perspectives on information technology: problems, issues and opportunities", pp. 31–49 in Eileen Green, Jenny Owen and Den Pain (eds) *Gendered by Design? Information Technology and Office Systems*, London: Taylor & Francis.

Herring, Susan (1993) "Gender and democracy in computer-mediated communication", *Electronic Journal of Communications/La Revue Electronique de Communication* 3, 2 [to retrieve file by e-mail send the command: send herring v3n293 to comserve @vm.its.rpi.edu].

—— (1996) "Posting in a different voice: gender and ethics in CMC", pp. 115–45 in Charles Ess (ed.) *Philosophical Perspectives on Computer-Mediated Communication*. Albany, N.Y.: State University of New York Press.

Hirst, Graeme, McRoy, Susan, Heeman, Peter, Edmonds, Philip and Horton, Diane (1994) "Repairing conversational misunderstandings and non-understandings", *Speech Communication* 15: 213–29.

Jansen, Sue C. (1988) "The ghost in the machine: artificial intelligence and gendered thought patterns", *Resources for Feminist Research* 17: 4–7.

—— (1992) "Making minds: sexual and reproductive metaphors in the discourses of the artificial intelligence movement", paper presented at the Electronic Salon: Feminism meets Infotech in connection with the 11th Annual Gender Studies Symposium, Lewis and Clark College, March. [Author's address: Communication Studies Department, Muhlenberg College, Allentown, Pennsylvania 18104, USA.]

Lanier, Jaron (1989) "Virtual environments and interactivity: windows to the future", *Computer Graphics*, 23, 5: 8 [panel session].

Leith, Philip (1986) "Fundamental errors in legal logic programming", *The Computer Journal* 29, 6: 55–5.

Light, Jennifer (1995) "The digital landscape: new space for women?", *Gender, Place and Culture* 2, 2: 133–46.

Lorde, Audre (1984) *Sister Outsider*, Freedom, Calif.: The Crossing Press.

McRoy, Susan W. and Hirst, Graeme (1995) "The repair of speech act misunderstandings by abductive inference", *Computational Linguistics* 21, 4: 435–78.

Metselaar, Carolien (1991) "Gender issues in the design of knowledge-based systems", pp. 233–46 in Inger Eriksson, Barbara Kitchenham and Kea Tijdens (eds) *Women, Work and Computerization 4*, Amsterdam: Elsevier/North-Holland.

Moravec, Hans (1988) *Mind Children: The Future of Robot and Human Intelligence*, Cambridge, Mass. and London: Harvard University Press.

Nye, Andrea (1992) "The voice of the serpent: French feminism and philosophy of language", pp. 233–49 in Ann Garry and Marilyn Pearsall (eds) *Women, Knowledge and Reality: Explorations in Feminism Philosophy*, New York and London: Routledge.

Pitkow, James E. and Kehoe, Colleen M. (1996) "Emerging trends in the WWW user population", *Communications of the ACM* 39, 6: 106–8.

Plant, Sadie (1993) "Beyond the screens: film, cyberpunk and cyberfeminism", *Variant* 14, Summer 1993: 12–17.

—— (1995) "Babes in the net", *New Statesman and Society* January 27: 28.

—— (1996) "On the matrix: cyberfeminist simulations", pp. 170–83 in Rob Shields (ed.) *Cultures of the Internet: Virtual Spaces, Real Histories, Living Bodies*, London, Thousand Oaks, Calif. and New Delhi: Sage.

Robins, Kevin (1996) "Cyberspace and the world we live in", pp. 1–30 in Jon Dovey (ed.) *Fractal Dreams: New Media in Social Context*, London: Lawrence & Wishart.

Schroeder, Ralph (1993) "Virtual reality in the real world: history, applications and projections", *Futures* 25, 11: 963–73.

—— (1994) "Cyberculture, cyborg post-modernism and the sociology of virtual reality technologies: surfing the soul in the information age", *Futures* 26, 5: 519–28.

Scott, Maureen (1996) "Conversation analysis model to incorporate gender differences", unpublished final year project report, Department of Computation, UMIST, Manchester.

Shade, Lesley Regan (ed.) 1994 "Special issue on gender and networking", *Electronic Journal of Virtual Culture*, 2, 3 [to retrieve electronically send command get ejvcv2n2 package to listserv@kentvm.kent.edu).

—— (1996) "Is there free speech on the net? Censorship in the global information infrastructure", pp. 11–32 in Rob Shields (ed.) *Cultures of the Internet: Virtual Spaces, Real Histories, Living Bodies*, London, Thousand Oaks, Calif. and New Delhi: Sage.

Squires, Judith (1996) "Fabulous feminist futures and the lure of cyberculture", pp. 194–216 in Jon Dovey (ed.) *Fractal Dreams: New Media in Social Context*, London: Lawrence & Wishart.

Stone, Allucquère Rosanne (1993) "Violation and virtuality: two cases of physical and psychological boundary transgression and their implications", unpublished manuscript [available in electronic form from sandy@actlab.rtf.utexas.edu].

—— (1994) "Will the real body please stand up? Boundary stories about virtual cultures", pp. 81–118 in Michael Benedikt (ed.) *Cyberspace: First Steps*, Cambridge, Mass. and London: MIT Press.

—— (1995) *The War of Desire and Technology at the Close of the Mechanical Age*, Cambridge, Mass. and London: MIT Press.

Suchman, Lucy A. (1994) "Do categories have politics? The language/action perspective reconsidered", *Computer Supported Cooperative Work (CSCW)* 2, 3: 177–90.

Tannen, Deborah (1992) *You Just Don't Understand: Women and Men in Conversation*, London: Virago.

Thalmann, Nadia M. and Thalmann, Daniel (eds) (1994) *Artificial Life and Virtual Reality*, Chichester: Wiley.

Tong, Rosemarie (1994) *Feminist Thought: A Comprehensive Introduction*, London: Routledge.

Turkle, Sherry (1996) *Life on the Screen: Identity in the Age of the Internet*, London: Weidenfeld & Nicolson.

Wajcman, Judy (1991) *Feminism Confronts Technology*, Cambridge: Polity Press.

Winograd, Terry and Flores, Fernando (1986) *Understanding Computers and Cognition: A New Foundation for Design*, Reading, Mass.: Addison-Wesley.

Nina Wakeford

GENDER AND THE LANDSCAPES OF COMPUTING IN AN INTERNET CAFÉ

Introduction

INCREASINGLY **CULTURAL CRITICISM** is questioning essentialist perspectives on technology which link it inescapably with masculinity, men's activities, and the absence of female participation (Stabile, 1994; Ormrod, 1995; Grint and Woolgar, 1995; Terry and Calvert, 1997). [. . .] Calvert and Terry begin their recent volume *Processed Lives: Gender and Technology in Everyday Life* (1997) with quotations from two feminist theorists who complicate the separation of the two terms gender and technology. First, for Haraway, a machine is not an "it" to be animated, but "[it] is us, our processes, an aspect of our embodiment" (1991: 180). Second, for de Lauretis, gender itself, amongst other factors, "is the product and process of various social technologies" (1987: 2). In this new positioning, technologies and genders are mutually constituted, and cannot but be touched by other factors in our embodiment and social practices such as sexuality and race, which until recently have been absent in the social studies of technology literature. "To do otherwise is to reify gender as binarism and technology as 'thing'" warns Ormrod (1995). [. . .]

> feminist sociology on technology must be able to show how relations of power are exercised and the *process* by which gendered subjectivities are achieved. It must therefore attend to the range of discursive practices and the associations of (durable) materials, meanings and subjectivities with which gender and technology are defined and differentiated.
>
> (1995: 44)

[. . .] The Internet has been presented as the exemplary technology of the future and of postmodern subjectivities (e.g. Kroker and Weinstein, 1994; Dery, 1996). Yet despite claims that it is a gender-neutral space, it has enabled alliances of materials and meanings which have contradictory gendered subjectivities. I shall discuss these contradictions through the representation of the Internet as a set of intersecting landscapes of computing in which gender is produced, represented and consumed.

Rationale for studying a "real" place

The early research on gender and Internet cultures was stimulated by the claim that gender and other aspects of social identity might become irrelevant in the new worlds created by information and communication technologies. This belief was built on the premise that computer networks allowed users to be physically invisible to other users. [. . .] Surveying the accounts of cyberspace, Stallabrass concludes:

> The greatest freedom cyberspace promises is that of recasting the self: from static beings, bound by the body and betrayed by appearances, Net surfers may reconstruct themselves in a multiplicity of dazzling roles, changing from moment to moment according to whim.
>
> (Stallabrass, 1995: 15)

Even in the early literature the ideas of multiple gender roles and "gender swapping" (Bruckman, 1996) were used to exemplify this promised escape from body and appearances. [. . .] Despite these aspirations, the subsequent research suggests that a utopian vision of gender-free or even gender-equal electronic space is far from being realised. Early media reports highlighted deception leading to "rape online" (Dibbell, 1996) or "computer cross-dressing" (Stone, 1991). Researchers from a variety of disciplines concluded that even where a multiplicity of roles is possible, traditional images and experiences of gender persist in most Internet fora (Herring, 1996; Kendall, 1996, forthcoming; Reid, 1996). Some women have created pockets of resistance on the Web or in discussion lists (Wakeford 1995, 1997a, forthcoming), but overall the territories of the on-line world reflect the unreconstructed ideologies of the population of "white male cyberboors" (Winner, 1996).

Studying an Internet café builds upon the existing research on gender on-line by exploring how gender operates in a "real" place where the Internet is both produced and consumed. Observations and interviews during my fieldwork at "NetCafé" suggested an approach which borrows metaphors of spatiality from cultural geography to explain gender in terms of its production as part of *landscapes of computing*. Landscapes of computing are defined as the overlapping set of material and imaginary geographies which include, but are not restricted to, on-line experiences. The choice of an Internet café was influenced by its role [as . . .] a *translation landscape of computing* where the Internet is produced and interpreted for "ordinary people" who consume time on the machines, and/or food and drink. [. . .] NetCafé was also chosen because [. . .] [i]ntegral to [its] translation landscape [. . .] was the production, mediation and consumption of gender as a component of the product. NetCafé was the product of the collaboration of two women and an Internet Service Provider (ISP) run by their male partners. [. . .] Customers were encouraged, using imagery and discourse which suggested that NetCafé was not the home of the white male nerd, to see the Internet as a place where women could participate. Less clearly visible were the ways in which gender was embedded in the daily production of the café environment. It was these complex and shifting quotidian practices which were investigated.

[. . .]

Gender and on-line landscapes

The themes highlighted in current research about gender and on-line interactions situate the practices observed in NetCafé. [. . .] Little of the existing work addresses the tangible situated spaces of computing and these on-line landscapes. So far most research has focused on the discursive and symbolic peculiarities of Internet culture.

The metaphors used to characterise on-line landscapes at their most abstract are drawn from discourses [. . .] implicated in particular constructions of gender. [. . .] Terms such as "frontier" have been used to describe on-line space as a new (electronic) Wild West. Critics such as Miller speculate that this imagery appeals to ideals of "individualistic masculinity" (Miller, 1995). [. . .] Stallabrass suggests that "the urban boy's idea of the street" is an integral part of the literary cyberpunk landscape, the influence of which is significant for many builders of on-line technologies (Stallabrass, 1995: 6; see also Dery, 1996).

Gender swapping

Shifting the focus [. . .] to the constituent on-line landscapes and their spaces of practice, it is clear that each has its own distinctive architecture and conventions of behaviour (Wakeford, 1995). [. . .] In terms of the discussion of gender, those which stand out are the real-time interactive textual spaces of MUDs. [. . .]

> For the participants, MUDing throws issues of the impact of gender on human relations into high relief. Fundamental to its impact is the fact that it allows people to experience rather than merely observe what it feels like to be the opposite gender or to have no gender at all.
>
> (Bruckman, 1996: 322)

How does this experience of gender happen? In this textual environment, on-line users ("player" or "character"), are frequently requested to provide a description of themselves as well as (nick)names. Part of this description is a "gender flag" (Reid, 1996). This flag may control the set of pronouns which are used by the MUD program to refer to the character in subsequent interactions. Kendall calculated in 1994 that 21 per cent of 8,541 characters in GammaMOO were designated as female (Kendall, 1996). However, she also describes the wide range of vocabulary and pronouns which have been generated outside the traditional – the usual male/female, he/she. In GammaMOO these include: "'either' which uses the s/he and him/her convention; 'splat', similarly, uses *e and h*; and 'plural' uses they and them" (Kendall, 1996: 217). Some writers insist that these new languages can displace traditional gender categories altogether. McRae, writing of sexuality in MOOs, comments:

> The spivak gender available on MOOs, for instance, has a unique set of pronouns: *e, em, eir, eirs, eirself*. It has encouraged some people to invent entirely

new bodies and eroticize them in ways that render categories of female or male meaningless.

(McRae, 1996: 257)

Even taking on board the difficulty of matching these gender designations with material/biosocial bodies who choose them, many of the accounts suggest that men are more likely than women to experiment with alternative gender roles (Kendall, 1996; Turkle, 1995). [. . .]

It seems from the existing accounts that any displacement of gender is happening through the combination of traditional or stereotypical tropes, and through mechanisms which strenuously resist the mapping of MUD-gender to the experience of material/biosocial bodies. This is clearest in the ways in which other aspects of MUD personae are articulated:

> Choices of race are more likely to be between Dwarvish, Elvish and Klingon than between Asian, Black and Caucasian; choices of class are more likely to be between Warrior, Magician and Thief than between white or blue collar.
>
> (Reid, 1996: 331)

[. . .] Researchers have indicated the racial and class location of the majority of users is "affluent and white" (Reid, 1996; see also Kendall, 1996; Turkle, 1995). [. . .]

MUD cultures of gender are localised, and often gender conventions are unique to a specific MUD. In environments where long-term relationships of social support have evolved there is very little hidden play with gender roles on an ongoing basis, although certain users may be known to participate as characters of the opposite sex (Kendall, forthcoming). However even in these cases, when a user adopts a persona of the opposite gender, the user develops a reputation not as a woman, but as a man-with-a-female name. In cases where such gender swapping is revealed without prior warning (e.g. Stone, 1991), the result is not to promote a cultural shift in values about gender, but to increase construction of social risk within the electronic space.

Gender-based experiences of communication

[. . .] The reporting of sexual harassment of female users [. . .] is one of the gendered patterns of communication in on-line landscapes which draws the widest mass media attention. MUDs have been disproportionately highlighted due to early and widely publicised incidents (not uncontroversial in the MUD communities themselves) including "A Rape in Cyberspace" (Dibbell, 1996: 375). However as Brail indicates, sexual harassment exists on a continuum of daily "wanna fuck" e-mails from strangers to those with obviously "female" names, to the electronic "stalking" which Brail herself endured (Brail, 1996). [. . .] This highlights another way in which the experience of on-line gender is influenced by specific and localised on-line landscapes, in this case that space provided by the ISP. Those who have university (.ac or.edu) accounts are much less likely to receive the quantity of untraceable "wanna fuck" e-mails than those with commercial ISPs, particularly America Online (AOL) whose users in the USA report receiving up to thirty unsolicited mails per day.

Gendered experiences of e-mail communications are not limited to unsolicited postings to females. [. . .] Focusing on the divergent styles of posting on discussion groups, mailing lists, usenet newsgroups, and also in the cultures of Frequently Asked Questions (FAQs), Herring has found that on-line utterances are male oriented and male dominated (Herring 1996).

Although there is [. . .] a [. . .] perception [. . .] that men [. . .] "flame" in on-line interactions, Herring suggests that this is an oversimplification. She identifies flaming as the most extreme form of an "adversarial style" which can also include a superior stance, posting long and/or frequent messages and participating disproportionately in a discussion. This style is predominantly employed by male users. Herring found another style, which she calls "attenuated/supportive". She concludes "This style is exhibited almost exclusively by women and is the discursive norm in many women-only and women-centred lists" (Herring, 1996: 119). [. . .]

Other researchers have found that the participation of men and women varies *between* discussion lists and newsgroups, even when both on-line landscapes feature the same subject. Clerc has [. . .] found that amongst fans discussing the same television programme electronically, women were more likely to participate in discussion groups than usenet newsgroups (Clerc, 1996).

[. . .]

Cyberfeminism

Another strand in writing about gender and on-line landscapes has stressed the new types of feminist activism and possibilities of resistance to male power available through these new technologies. Cyberfeminism, as advocated by Sadie Plant (1996 [reading 4.2 in this volume], 1997), celebrates women's connections with machines. In her words cyberfeminism is:

> an insurrection on the part of the goods and material of the patriarchal world, a dispersed, distributed emergence composed of links between women, women and computers, computers and communication links, connections and connectionist nets.
>
> (1996: 182)

In this view the Internet is a new space within which gender does not disappear but can reinstate itself to the advantage of women. Situating her claim in the work of Irigaray, and making extravagant claims of technical capacity, Plant argues that by their very nature virtual worlds "undermine both the worldview and the material reality of two thousand years of patriarchal control" (1996: 170).

Plant's prophecy is that the networks of the digital "matrix" promote nothing less than a new sexual revolution (1997), yet she does not specify the on-line landscapes which are involved in this social movement. [. . .] [H]er lack of attention to the experiences of specific women users has been criticised by feminist computer scientists (Adam, 1997). From a political point of view Squires warns that [. . .] "we would do well to insist that cyberfeminism be seen as a metaphor for addressing the inter-relation between technology and the body, not as a means of using the former to transcend the latter" (Squires, 1996: 195).

Although cyberfeminism has been taken up by some women in on-line landscapes such as Web publishing, the most common overt resistance to the relentless practices of white masculinity is local and specific, such as the Australian groups VNX Matrix and geekgrrl (Plant, 1996; Wakeford, 1997b; VNX Matrix 1998). Their rebellious strategies subvert the conventions of the technical systems, such as confusing search engine users who are looking for "babes on the Web" by using "grrl" instead of girl (Wakeford, 1997b). Elsewhere women have created "safe space" in the form of private lists on the basis of interest or identity (Wakeford, 1997a, 1997b, 1998; Wincapaw, forthcoming). Hall [. . . describes] [. . . a] version of cyber-feminism [that] is locally specific and far more modest than that of Plant (Hall, 1996). Clerc's study of fandom uncovered the "Star Fleet Ladies Auxiliary and Embroidery/Baking Society", [. . .] created by a woman user who expressed dissatisfaction with the women's roles on Star Trek and was harshly criticised for it on the public list (Clerc, 1996). The use of irony is a common theme [. . .]. Women who want to talk to "real" women learn that they must seek chat rooms on commercial services with names such as "sensible footwear" not "girlchat".

It is clear that on-line landscapes cannot be characterised by a single set of conventions relating to gender. In some spaces, gender assignments are expected to be internally consistent and non-transferable. Elsewhere, particularly where access is restricted in women-only spaces, gender is part of a trusted representation which does not recognise the on-line/elsewhere distinction (Wakeford 1998). In yet other places displaying a male persona rather than a female persona will attract more attention to utterances (Herring, 1996). Everywhere in on-line landscapes gender is part of a skilled practice, either in its denial or in its promotion. Confusion around gender occurs where the user is not aware of the degree of trust (or scepticism) to have towards the representations of identity which are presented there. [. . .] In the following section I contrast on-line spaces to the "real" spaces of NetCafé, and examine how gendered representations were created, maintained and subverted. [. . .]

Gender and translation landscapes

[. . .]

Spatial organisation of NetCafé encounters

During four months of 1996 I worked at NetCafé, an Internet café in Central London. [. . .] The encounters which occurred at NetCafé show, in Ormrod's terms, "how relations of power are exercised and the *processes* by which gendered subjectivities are achieved". They also illustrate how the Internet operates as a process by associating people, machines and spaces and the relationships between them. NetCafé was in many ways a highly organised and stratified space which sought to portray itself as a place where gender would not matter.

NetCafé was organised on four levels, only one of which was the café "floor". As a consequence most of the café was "offstage", out of public view. The café floor was the central focus for public attention, and the place where most of the customer–staff–machine interactions were staged. [. . .]

[. . .]

Customer profiles

[. . .] Although in most spaces inhabited by numerous computers available for public use (such as computer labs, Turkle, 1984) men overwhelmingly outnumber women, in NetCafé they made up just under half of the customer respondents. [. . .] One-third of the total customer base evident from the survey were students.

[. . .]

"It's Showtime" (again): gender and display at NetCafé

[. . .]

In this section I will illustrate this practice of creating the Internet through the concepts developed by Crang in his work on the performative nature of restaurant employment. Although restaurants represent a somewhat different set of social norms [. . .] Crang's emphasis on the dimension of display in restaurant work resonates powerfully with the way in which NetCafé operated to create its product. Gender was integrated into this product through a relentless (although not uniformly intentional or overt) presentation of the machines in association with gender and gendered spaces.

[. . .]

[. . .] Crang 1994 suggests that the workplace geographies of display [. . .] operated through six mutually determining axes of "sociospatial relations of consumption". [. . .] Each of [these] can be found in NetCafé's environs: imaginations of interactional settings; spatial structures of interactions settings; forms of communication; ethoses of the product; organisation and authority relations; identity politics. Each set of these relations can be used to illustrate the way in which gender was produced, represented and consumed in this site.

Imaginations of interactional settings

NetCafé existed not only as a physical place where encounters with the Internet came about, but also as a result of the imaginative geographies in the minds of managers, staff and customers. Although there was a strong vision from the directors that the café was a place where gender did not determine the kind of product which was consumed, [. . .] the practices of "doing gender" alongside "doing technology" were complex. Imaginations of interactional settings, as Crang points out, are important not just for the geographical metaphors which they draw upon and generate, but also for the part they play in regulating social practices.

[. . .]

Amongst themselves the cyberhosts talked about the unfairness of the gendered treatment, but it was difficult to reverse given the norms of polite service deemed appropriate in the café. Occasionally, the male cyberhosts would deliberately appear to be unavailable when the customer signalled for help, therefore forcing an interaction with a female cyberhost. One day a male customer asked a female cyberhost, alone at the counter, a technical question about the machine's capabilities.

As she was answering a male cyberhost arrived to check the machine bookings, and the customer repeated the question word for word at the new arrival. The male cyberhost firmly pointed out that his question had already been answered by his colleague. However this kind of action was seen to be risky and was not the norm amongst the staff.

Spatial structures of interactional settings

The spatial structures of NetCafé were intertwined with the ways in which it worked as a landscape of translation and a place for encounters. Although the café floor was the site of the public encounters, the business as a whole was made possible by interactions and collaborations by staff on all the other levels of the building. [. . .]

These spatial arrangements also interrupted the attempts to promote gender neutrality around the machines. The top floor area [. . .] mostly populated by men. [was where] the technical support group operated as a highly efficient on-call team for problem-solving [. . .] masculinity was represented [by the cyberhosts] on the top floor as both "a mess" and technically superior.

Forms of communication

The forms of communication by which the NetCafé produced encounters also crucially affected the ways in which the products were consumed [. . .] The range [. . .] included the wide variety of forms of face-to-face contact between staff, customers and machines, as well as the intersection with on-line landscapes in which communication could take the forms of textual exchange and, for a short time during my stay, a live video of the café broadcast over the Web.

The public relations (PR) team played the most significant role in the presentation of the café as a local and global phenomenon [. . .] Many of the publicity shots in the volumes of PR records displayed how easily the media had manage to inscribe a feminised NetCafé as the "social" side of computing by portraying the women holding coffee cups near computers. In contrast the male technical directors tended to have been photographed in physical contact with the machine, usually touching the mouse. PR also organised several events in which the cybervibe of NetCafé was embodied within an artefact: a sculpture of red lips holding between them a computer disc. [. . .]

Ethoses of the product

Just as the imaginations of interactional settings were not always shared amongst all participants of NetCafé, the way in which the product was defined was itself an outcome of struggles between different representations of objects, people and practices. [. . .]

At least in the eyes of the directors the product was a mediated experience with a computer and/or nourishment where the *absence* of gender as a marker was a constituent part. Yet gender was also used as a resource for PR who produced images of women and machines as a hook for publicity. [. . .]

Organisational and authority relations

Many of the authority relations in NetCafé could be mapped directly on to the spatial structures of the building. Directors and middle ranking staff were physically "above" those under their supervision. If a cyberhost had "gone upstairs" it usually meant to see someone higher up the ladder of pay, status and power.

[. . .] [M]ost staff whose work directly impinged on the day-to-day running of the café would reach the staircase by walking through the café itself. [. . .] On the other hand the technical staff and many of those working on the top floor preferred the side entrance to the building, so avoiding seeing (or being seen) by those interacting on the café floor. As the top floor staff were predominantly male, the flow of people overrepresented the number of female staff in the building and circulating around the café. In this way the organisational and authority relations became part of the geographies of display and the sociospatial relations of consumption as they rendered visible or hid the gendered practices (or the imaginings of those practices) which constituted NetCafé. One of the aspects of female work which was hidden was the early morning cleaning. The cleaner, the only employee not to have an e-mail address, played a crucial part in invisibly translating the machines into a workable form when food and drink had been spilled. [. . .]

Identity politics

As is clear in the preceding sections, the interactions at NetCafé are bound up with the identities of the participants. The machines developed individual reputations for working or being "sick"/"difficult". The cyberhosts managed to create an atmosphere of diverse participation since as a group they were located in many national cultures [. . .] The identities of the customers were signalled when the cyberhosts called out their names at the end of their allotted time. Some customers also become known as "regulars" [. . .] Frequently regulars had considerable computer expertise and would become a capable aid for a cyberhost dealing with a difficult question from a customer. None of the identities mobilised at NetCafé were immune to such repositioning in relation to one another.

A great number of the ways in which identities figured in NetCafé interactions was through the appeal to gendered practice and discourse. Much of this was invigorated by the café staff themselves, but the way in which the category "women" could be used strategically for profit fluctuated over time. When NetCafé first opened much was made in the press coverage and at the café itself of the women-only trainings which were offered. In the beginning these trainings were full, but a year later they had been halted [. . .] "from lack of interest". "Women" became represented in the bodies of the cyberhosts and in "the lips" artefacts (see below, p. 300). The female directors continued to be asked to share their opinions on women and technology at events around the world, and special trainings were held when a women's group was tied into a cause which was of particular interest to them. Since my fieldwork period a women's night has opened once a week in NetCafé, where a well known lesbian club DJ spins tracks while the computers are available for use. [. . .] It has been a huge success in bringing paying customers into NetCafé at an off-peak time, and also in re-introducing the café as a place where public events happen with a predominantly female clientele. Furthermore it has created a space at NetCafé within which lesbian sexuality is able to be articulated in connection with the London club music scene and technology, manufacturing an instance of "cyberqueer" (Wakeford, 1997a).

Reflections on bodies, gender and the landscapes of computing

At NetCafé, representations of gender appear to be achieved at least partially through the "doing" of technology. However technology cannot be equated with the computers alone. Rather we can recall Ormrod's view that technology is constituted by both discursive practices and alliances of materials and meanings. In Netcafé, [. . .] the technology exceeds the boundaries of the machines. [. . .] One of the achievements of NetCafé as a translation landscape of computing is that it enables participants to scatter discursive representations of the Internet, the "cyber", and global computer networks upon a range of encounters and artefacts which had not previously been recognised for their alliance with the technological. The processes of enacting the translation landscape of computing are a way of doing the Internet and a way of doing gender. In this section I reconnect the findings of my fieldwork at NetCafé with the previous work on on-line landscapes by returning to the way in which the gendered body is invoked. Framing my thinking is Adam's insistence that the connection of embodiment and technological systems must be taken seriously by feminist theorists and allied critics (Adam, 1998). If the question of embodiment for feminist theory rests on the role of the body in producing knowledge, and Adam agrees with many theorists that this is the case, then the task here becomes one of articulating the kinds of bodies which inhabit NetCafé and specifying the knowledges which they produce (or are restrained from producing). The turn to bodies, as I will show, in fact leads the focus back to the metaphors of spatiality with which I began my discussion of NetCafé.

[. . .] [T]he bodies of the cyberhosts were used to display the competing definitions of the product. Cyberhosts were stratified by management on the basis of how "cyber" they were, and this became manifest when the most "cyber" of the staff was chosen to be pictured adorned with new merchandise [. . .] Inspecting the manner of using staff bodies to promote NetCafé (a practice over which they had a questionable amount of negotiating power) revealed that in all but one instance it was women who were chosen to model merchandise. [. . .] Second, the bodies of the two female directors were used to create knowledges about gender and technology which were exported to the pages of glossy magazines as indicated in the previous section. These directors' bodies came to stand for NetCafé and in a more limited way, for the Internet. [. . .] Third, in the statuette of the lips holding the floppy disc a stylised representation of gender is purposefully brought together with an object metonymic to a computer. This statuette represents a fusion of body *parts*, and so I equate it to the first two examples with some hesitation. Yet these body parts appear to generate similar knowledges of the inescapable joining of women and technology (although I never managed to ascertain if the designer had reflected upon whether the lips were eating the disc or if they were spitting it out). The fact that the statuettes were presented as trophies for women in multimedia indicates that the imagery was also intended to be intelligible outside the internal semiotic system of the café.

Returning to the existing literature on gender and on-line landscapes, it is clear that bodies also figure in the deliberations of the extent to which physical presence matters in these spaces. However, the kinds of bodies which appear in the discussions of on-line landscapes tend to be restricted to linguistic performance or representations with limited circulation beyond the spaces in which they are created. The knowledges produced by these bodies come into view through a way of "doing" gender (predominantly via textual input) which cannot be easily equated with that found amongst the bodies in NetCafé. Within NetCafé, at least in the three examples cited above, it is difficult if not impossible to avoid connecting women's bodies to material/biosocial everyday realities of being female and the knowledges produced by experiencing these realities. [. . .]

At this site bodies also manufactured knowledge in the course of their *movement through* the physical spaces of the café as well as the on-line landscapes which could be accessed there. [. . .] Customers walked around the café floor interacting with both machines and cyberhosts, consuming machines and food [. . .] In this process they generated stories of how to do gender and the Internet through mobile bodies. Cyberhosts and other staff also moved through the building, creating descriptions of the levels of the café operations in terms of gender and technological expertise, including constructing the type of masculinity on the top floor among technical support staff. The female directors' bodily transit between NetCafé and other public arenas was integrated into the meanings of doing technology at the café. When the media attention on NetCafé was at its height, having transporable bodies which represented women and computing was crucial in the way the café was able to become a profitable translation landscape of computing without having a huge advertising budget. Last, the bodies of machines (or their body parts) were carried around the building particularly between the floors on which repairs were executed. [. . .] Machines which travelled to participate in such activities were at most risk of suspending the image of NetCafé as a translation landscape of computing by not functioning at all, or, more commonly, by "almost" working (for example having a very slow Internet connection, or by displaying broken Web links).

In conclusion I would like to suggest that the formulation of bodies as travelling within NetCafé directs us back to the utility of spatial metaphors and to landscapes of computing as ways to focus on specific material and imaginative geographies. For the study of gender in relation to technology it seems particularly apt to follow material/biosocial bodies in order to reach an understanding of how gender might be differentiated from technology in landscapes of computing such as are apparent at NetCafé. It might also be fruitful to follow material/biosocial bodies in landscapes of computing where it is less obvious to do so, such as on-line landscapes. [. . .] In NetCafé, by taking seriously the range of materials and meanings which were being used, a complex interplay of gendered representations and experiences was found which cannot easily be assimilated into the old rubric of technology as inherently masculine. Rather, as NetCafé's daily activities unfolded, the Internet was translated as a place where new alliances for gender were being forged at the same time as these alliances were being interrupted by old stereotypes through which gender and technology are still often understood. These alliances and their interruptions were as dependent on the local cultures of place and space as they were on the landscapes of computing.

Acknowledgements

I would particularly like to thank Pamela Giorgi, Tom Delph-Janiurek and Sasha Roseneil for reading and commenting on earlier drafts of this paper.

References

Adam, A. (1997) What Should We Do with Cyberfeminism?, in Lander, R. and Adam, A. (eds) *Women into Computing: Progress from Where to What?*, Exeter: Intellect.

Adam, A. (1998) *Artificial Knowing: gender and the thinking machine*, London: Routledge.

Brail, S. (1996) The Price of Admission: Harassment and Free Speech in the Wild, Wild West, in Cherny, L. and Weise, E.R. (eds) *Wired Women: Gender and New Realities in Cyberspace*, Seattle, WA: MIT Press.

Bruckman, A. (1996) Gender Swapping on the Internet, in Ludlow, P. (ed.) *High Noon on the Electronic Frontier: Conceptual Issues in Cyberspace*, Cambridge, MA: MIT Press.

Clerc, S. (1996) Estrogen Brigades and "Big Tits" Threads; Media Fandom Online and Off, in Cherny, L. and Weise, E.R. (eds) *Wired Women: Gender and New Realities in Cyberspace*, Seattle, WA: MIT Press.

Crang, P. (1994) It's Showtime: On the Workplace Geographies of Display in a Restaurant in Southeast England, *Society and Space* 12: 675–704.

de Lauretis, T. (1987) *Technologies of Gender: Essays on Theory, Film and Fiction*, Bloomington, IN: Indiana University Press.

Dery, M. (1992) Cyberculture, *South Atlantic Quarterly* 91: 501–23.

Dery, M. (1996) *Escape Velocity: cyberculture at the end of the century*, New York: Grove.

Dibbell, J. (1996 [1993]) A Rape in Cyberspace; or How an Evil Clown, a Haitian Trickster Spirit, Two Wizards, and a Cast of Dozens Turned a Database into a Society, in Ludlow, P. (ed.) *High Noon on the Electronic Frontier: Conceptual Issues in Cyberspace*, Cambridge, MA: MIT Press.

Grint, K. and Woolgar, S. (1995) On Some Failures of Nerve in Constructivist and Feminist Analyses of Technology, in Grint, K. and Gill, R. (eds) *The Gender–Technology Relation: Contemporary Theory and Research*, London: Taylor & Francis.

Hall, K. (1996) Cyberfeminism, in Herring, S. (ed.) *Computer-Mediated Communication: Linguistic, Social and Cross-Cultural Perspectives*, Amsterdam: John Benjamins.

Haraway, D. (1991) Cyborg at Large, Interview; and The Actors are Cyborg, Nature is Coyote and the Geography is Elsewhere, both in Penley, C. and Ross, A. (eds) *Technoculture*, Minneapolis: University of Minnesota Press.

Herring, S. (1996) Posting in a Different Voice: Gender and Ethics in Computer-Mediated Communication, in Ess, C. (ed.) *Philosophic Perspectives in Computer-Mediated Communication*, Albany, NY: State University of New York Press.

Kendall, L. (1996) MUDder? I Hardly Know 'Er! Adventures of a Feminist MUDder, in Cherny, L. and Weise, E.R. (eds) *Wired Women: Gender and New Realities in Cyberspace*, Seattle, WA: MIT Press.

Kendall, L. (forthcoming) *Hanging Out in the Virtual Pub: Identity and Relationships Online*. Unpublished Ph.D thesis, Department of Sociology: University of California, Davis.

Kroker, A. and Weinstein, M.A. (1994) *Data Trash: The Theory of the Virtual Class*, New York: St Martin's Press.

McRae, S. (1996) Coming Apart at the Seams: Sex, Text and the Virtual Body, in Cherny, L. and Weise, E.R. (eds) *Wired Women: Gender and New Realities in Cyberspace*, Seattle, WA: Seal Press.

Miller, D. (1995) *Acknowledging Consumption: A Review of New Studies*, London: Routledge.

Ormrod, S. (1995) Feminist Sociology and Methodology: Leaky Black Boxes in Gender/Technology Relations, in Grint, K. and Gill, R. (eds) *The Gender–Technology Relation: Contemporary Theory and Research*, London: Taylor & Francis.

Plant, S. (1996) On the Matrix: Cyberfeminist Simulations, in Shields, R. (ed.) *Cultures of Internet: Virtual Spaces, Real Histories, Living Bodies*, London: Sage.

Plant, S. (1997) *Zeros and Ones: Digital Women and The New Technoculture*, London: Fourth Estate.

Reid, E.M. (1996) Text-based Virtual Realities: Identity and the Cyborg Body, in Ludlow, P. (ed.) *High Noon on the Electronic Frontier: Conceptual Issues in Cyberspace*, Cambridge, MA: MIT Press.

Squires, J. (1996) Fabulous Feminist Futures and the Lure of Cyberculture, in Dovey, J. (ed.) *Fractal Dreams: New Media in Social Context*, London: Lawrence & Wishart: 194–216.

Stabile, C.A. (1994) *Feminism and the Technological Fix*, Manchester: Manchester University Press.

Stallabrass, J. (1995) Empowering Technology: The Exploration of Cyberspace, *New Left Review* 211: 3–32.

Stone, A. R. (1991) Will the Real Body Please Stand Up? Boundary stories about virtual cultures, in Benedikt, M. (ed.) *Cyberspace: First Steps*, Cambridge, MA: MIT Press: 81–118.

Terry, J. and Calvert, M. (1997) Introduction: Machines/Lives, in Terry, J. and Calvert, M. (eds) *Processed Lives: Gender and Technology in Everyday Life*, London: Routledge.

Turkle, S. (1984) *The Second Self: Computers and the Human Spirit*, New York: Simon & Schuster.

Turkle, S. (1995) *Life on the Screen: Identity in the Age of the Internet*, New York: Simon and Schuster.

VNX Matrix (1998) All New Gen, in Broadhurst Dixon, J. and Cassidy, E.J. (eds) *Virtual Futures: Cybererotics, Technology and Post-Human Pragmatism*, London: Routledge.

Wakeford, N. (1995) Sexualised Bodies in Cyberspace, in Chernaik, W. and Deegan, M. (eds) *Beyond the Book: Theory, Text and the Politics of Cyberspace*, London: London University Press.

Wakeford, N. (1997a) Cyberqueer, in Medhurst, A. and Munt, S.R. (eds) *Lesbian and Gay Studies: A Critical Introduction*, London: Cassell.

Wakeford, N. (1997b) Networking Women and Girls with Information/Communication Technology: Surfing Tales of the World Wide Web, in Terry, J. and Calvert, M. (eds) *Processed Lives: Gender and Technology in Everyday Life*, London: Routledge.

Wakeford, N. (1998) Urban Culture for Virtual Bodies: Comments on Lesbian "Identity" and "Community" in San Francisco Bay Area Cyberspace, in Ainley, R. (ed.) *New Frontiers of Space, Bodies and Gender*, London: Routledge.

Wakeford, N. (forthcoming) *Networks of Desire, Gender, Sexuality and Computing Culture*, London: Routledge.

Wincapaw, C. (forthcoming) Lesbian and Bisexual Women's Electronic Mailing Lists as Sexualised Spaces, *Journal of Lesbian Studies*.

Winner, L. (1996) Who Will Be in Cyberspace, *The Information Society* 12: 63–71.

Evelynn M. Hammonds

NEW TECHNOLOGIES
OF RACE

O N 18 JULY 1950 the *New York Times* announced "No Scientific Basis for Race Bias Found by World Panel of Experts." The article reported on the findings of a distinguished group of scientists, working under the auspices of the United Nations Educational, Scientific and Cultural Organization (UNESCO), who had reached a consensus that there "was no scientific justification for race discrimination."

> The Statement presented four premises: that mental capacities of all races are similar; that no evidence for biological deterioration as a result of hybridization existed; that there was no correlation between national or religious groups and any race; and fourth, that race was less a biological fact than a social myth.[1]

The UNESCO document was a highly politicized statement as both Elazar Barkan and Donna Haraway have shown.[2] In many respects it reflected the desire of some scientists to redress the excesses of Nazism where biological notions of racial difference and racial inferiority had been used to justify the extermination of Jews and homosexuals, rather than offering a balanced account of the contemporary scientific debates over the role of environment, heredity and culture in the observed differences between the races.

Several historians of science have argued that the publication of the UNESCO document signaled the end of mainstream scientific support for racial science. The division of the human species into biological races which had been of cardinal significance to scientists for over a hundred years was no longer viable as a research topic. Race, which in the pre-1950s period had been used to explain individual character and temperament, the structure of social communities, and the fate of human societies, was no longer central to the work of anthropologists or biologists. Even if one does not entirely accept this assessment, and it is debatable whether most scientists did, it is argued that, at the very least, the belief in the fixity, reality and hierarchy of human races – in the chain of superior and inferior human types – which had shaped the activities of scientists for most of the twentieth century had ceased to be a central feature of biological and anthropological research. Gone were the detailed cranial measurements, the tables of racial comparisons, the construction of racial typologies, and the reconstruction of racial histories in mainstream scientific journals. Instead, as Nancy Stepan argues, in their place we find discussions of populations, gene frequencies, selection and adaptation. The biological study of human diversity is now permeated with the language of genetics and evolution. "Race," Stepan asserts, "lost its reality and naturalness, to such an extent that probably the majority of scientists even go so far as to consider the very word 'race' unnecessary for purposes of biological inquiry."[3]

I suggest that these scientists and historians of science have misread the observed shift in biology and anthropology from studies of gross morphological studies of racial difference to studies of populations and gene frequencies. In the US race has always been dependent upon the visual. I argue that the notion of race – both as a social and scientific concept – is still deeply embedded in morphology, but it is the meaning given to morphological differences that has been transformed. Race, defined biologically in terms of morphological differences between certain pure types: white, African, Asian, etc., and in particular the mixing of these pure racial types, has been re-inscribed in the new computer technology of "morphing" and, as such, separated from its previous antecedents in the history of anti-miscegenation, and racial oppression.[4] "Morphing," a computer software term for "making one thing appear to turn into another," denotes shape changing while carrying along with it a change in identity. In this technology persons of different races are not produced as a result of sexual intercourse between persons of two different races but by a computer-generated simulation of the mixing of genetic characteristics that are presumed to be determinants of morphological differences between pure racial types. Morphing is not simply, as Emily Martin notes, "a car transformed into a tiger or Arnold Schwarzenegger turning into a pool of liquid metal in *Terminator 2*," but it is also the technological production of new racial types as in Michael Jackson's *Black or White* video where whites turn into aborigines as easily as he himself morphs into a black panther. Miscegenation then becomes an instance of border crossing between the human and the "other." The "other" includes the non-human and also the more familiar "other," non-white humans. In such a case technological artistry masks the imbrication of power, which is never articulated, in such transformations of white into non-white, and the non-white into animal. These transformations serve as late twentieth-century versions of the Great Chain of Being. Morphing, with its facile device of shape-changing, interchangeability, equivalency, and feigned horizontality in superficial ways elides its similarity with older hierarchical theories of human variation. However, as I will discuss, the new technology of race, morphing, is at the center of an old debate about miscegenation and citizenship in the United States.

W. E. B. DuBois and the amalgamation of the races

In 1897, the Harvard-educated W. E. B. DuBois inaugurated a series of sociological studies of African Americans at Atlanta University. These studies were designed to

provide objective scientific sociological data on the questions concerning the
conditions of African Americans in the United States. His goal was to produce "an
increasing body of scientifically ascertained fact, instead of the vague mass of the so-
called Negro problems." Through the studies DuBois assaulted the prejudiced
generalizations made by whites, who sometimes based their "facts" about African
Americans on evidence as flimsy as observations made through train windows
while traveling through the South. In 1906 he published *The Health and Physique of
the Negro American*, in which he addressed one of the most intractable questions in
the discourse about race – the "fixity" of the concept of race.[5] He argued against the
assumption that of all the races, the Negro race, by reason of its pronounced physical
characteristics, was easiest to distinguish. The human species, he noted, "so shade and
mingle with each other that not only, indeed, was it impossible to draw a color line
between black and other races, but in all physical characteristics the Negro race
cannot be set off by itself as absolutely different."[6] DuBois wanted his scientific
facts to prove the lie that African Americans were inherently different from whites
by pointing out the fact that "All the great peoples of the world are the result of a
mixture of races."[7] Race mixing at the turn of the century posed a problem for those
whites who believed in the purity of racial types. The progeny of such mixtures were
alternately viewed as superior intellectually and physically to the pure Africans, or
inferior to them. DuBois wanted to demonstrate both the extent of race mixing
in the United States and to dispel the notion that these mixed people were inferior.
Race mixing was not an innocent act in this period. There were laws against it in many
states. Southern laws against marriage between the races in effect sanctioned the rape
of Black women and made all progeny of even consensual unions between whites and
blacks illegitimate. The progeny of such unions were designated as Negro despite
their mixed ancestry. Given this situation DuBois argued that an African American
should not "stoop to mingle his blood with those who despise him."[8] The existence of
mixed bodies – the miscegenated – while an "open secret," was denied by whites
because the admission of such would implicitly acknowledge the humanity of African
Americans and the denial of citizenship to them. Miscegenation, and the bars against
it, as DuBois rightfully identified, were about belief in a hierarchy of racial types
which was explicitly used to deny the status of citizenship to all those who carried any
evident physical signs of African heritage. Along with sociological data DuBois used
the then new technology, photography, to make visible the evidence of race mixing
that white society denied. DuBois' photographic evidence, rendered in the style of
turn-of-the-century ethnographic studies of race, was deployed to show that race
mixing was a fact of American life and that the dependence upon visual evidence to
determine who was "black" or "white" was specious at best. These photographs of
male and female African Americans were largely head shots – frontal and profile,
displaying skin tones ranging from very dark to very light visually indistinguishable
from whites (see Figures 4.5A and 4.5B) The photographs were accompanied by text
describing each person's lineage. In particular DuBois emphasized that talent and
educational achievement were not associated with one skin color or ancestral
heritage. Through the critical deployment of the photographs and the vast
sociological data he gathered, DuBois' work undermined biological conceptions of
race and emphasized its social construction.

Figures 4.5A "DuBois' photographs of Negro Americans"

Figure 4.5B "DuBois' photographs of Negro Americans"

What color is Black?

The 13 February 1995 cover story of *Newsweek* magazine, was entitled "What Color is Black? Science, Politics and Racial Identity." Interestingly, inside, the title of the lead article changed slightly to "What Color is Black? What Color is White?" The cover displayed a short description of the article:

> The answers aren't simple. Immigration is changing the hue of America. Intermarriage has spawned a generation proud of its background, eager for its place at the American table. As always, race drives American domestic policy on issues from legislative districts to census counts. And path-breaking scientists insist that three racial categories are woefully inadequate for the myriad variations of our species.[9]

Immigration followed by intermarriage are said to be the driving forces behind this "new" aspect of race relations in America. The article appeared twenty-eight years after the last state anti-miscegenation law was struck down.[10] It appeared forty-five years after the UNESCO document on race, yet it asserted on the one hand that race is a biological concept – "race is a notoriously slippery concept that eludes any serious attempt at definition: it refers mostly to observable differences in skin color, hair texture and the shape of one's eyes or nose" – while also pointing out that most scientists argue that race is a mere social construct.[11] After reporting the current scientific data about racial differences for several pages, the authors conclude:

> Changing our thinking about race will require a revolution in thought as profound and profoundly unsettling, as anything science has ever demanded. What these researchers are talking about is changing the way in which we see the world – and each other. But before that can happen, we must do more than understand the biologist's suspicion about race. We must ask science, why is it that we are so intent on sorting humanity into so few groups – us and Other – in the first place.[12]

But *Newsweek*'s cover offered a representation of race – pictures of people of color of various shades in photographs cropped to emphasize shape of head, nose and lips – at odds with its text which emphasized that science was unable to provide a definitive or rather comfortable answer about the social meaning of racial difference (see Figure 4.5C). Here we see the visual display of a variety of people of color which made race seem "real," while the scientists' commentary emphasized that the reliance upon categories based on groupings of physical types had no meaning for the scientific study of race and, by implication, the socio-political debates as well. Interestingly, in *Newsweek*'s typology the persons who are raced are those who are not white. No photographs depicting differences among whites or between whites and people of color are displayed, suggesting that the differences among those classified as Black (or African American) is what is at issue.

Newsweek took a decidedly conventional approach to the "newly" defined problem of race in America. It concentrated on the divergence between biological and social meanings of race as represented by the differences among people of color. The text

Figure 4.5C "What color is Black?"
          (*Newsweek*, 13 February 1995)

implied that morphological differences of skin color, for example, were no longer stable markers of race. However, unlike DuBois' use of visual markers to emphasize the link between whites and Africans that produced racially mixed African Americans, *Newsweek*'s use of the visual was employed to deny such a link. Propelled by demographic changes due to immigration and the increase in interracial marriages

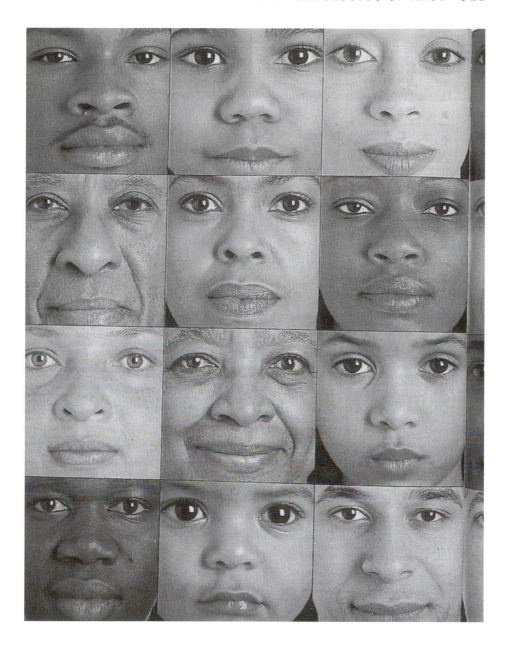

Figure 4.5C "What color is Black?"
   (*Newsweek*, 13 February 1995)

within the US, the major theme of the issue concerned the upcoming census of the year 2000 and the categories by which United States' citizenship will be defined. The difference between DuBois' day and our own is that today racially mixed people are increasingly refusing to be relegated to a subordinate social status based on presumed biological differences.

Newsweek followed on the heels of a much more novel approach to the topic, where biology was supplanted by computer technology in the representation of racial difference — *Time* magazine's special issue in the Fall of 1993, "The New Face of America: How Immigrants Are Shaping the World's First Multicultural Society." The cover featured a slightly tanned woman, with brown straight hair, somewhat almond-shaped eyes and slightly full lips (see Figure 4.5D). The side bar read, "Take a good look at this woman. She was created by a computer from a mix of several races. What you see is a remarkable preview of . . . The New Face of America."[13] The introduction to the issue by managing editor, Jim Gaines, revealed the true identity of the cover girl.

> The woman on the cover of this special issue of *Time* does not exist — except metaphysically. Her beguiling if mysterious visage is the product of a computer process called morphing — as in metamorphosis, a striking alteration in structure or appearance. When the editors were looking for a way to dramatize the impact of inter ethnic marriage, which has increased dramatically in the U.S. during the last wave of immigration, they turned to morphing to create the kind of offspring that might result from seven men and seven women of various ethnic and racial backgrounds.[14]

The picture was generated by an Asian American computer specialist, dubbed a cybergeneticist, whose efforts are described as "in the spirit of fun and experiment." This covergirl, Eve, whom Donna Haraway has dubbed "SimEve," has an interesting lineage: she is 15 per cent Anglo-Saxon, 17.5 per cent Middle Eastern, 17.5 per cent African, 7.5 per cent Asian, 35 per cent Southern European and 7.5 per cent Hispanic. This breakdown of her racial heritage would be familiar to DuBois and any other early twentieth-century biologist or anthropologist. Eve was produced with the same software package. Morph 2.0, used in *Terminator 2* and the Michael Jackson video. *Time*'s cybergeneticist also produced a chart showing forty-nine different combinations of the progeny from seven males and seven females (see Figure 4.5E). Most of the images or "morphies" on the chart are a straight 50–50 combination of the physical characteristics of their progenitors, though the editors note that an entirely different image could be produced by using different combinations of features. Interestingly, after eyes, the most important parental feature is the neck, which they found often determined the gender of the offspring. The volume of specific features is also important. For example, if an African man has more hair than a Vietnamese woman, his hair will dominate. Of course, such manipulations of features produced some truly unexpected results as well. One of their "tentative unions" produced a distinctly feminine face — sitting atop a muscular neck and hairy chest. "Back to the mouse on that one," the editors wrote. In this case the implicit norms governing morphing appear to forbid any monstrous combinations paralleling late nineteenth-century rhetoric against the progeny of interracial unions which claimed that such hybrid persons were unnatural. With the *Time* cover we wind up not with a true composite, but a preferred or filtered composite of mixed figures with no discussion of the assumptions or implications underlying the choices.

The flippant, lighthearted tone of the essay about the "morphies" was used to deflect attention from the seriousness of the issues these images were supposed to

Figure 4.5D "The new face of America"
(*Time*, Fall 1993)

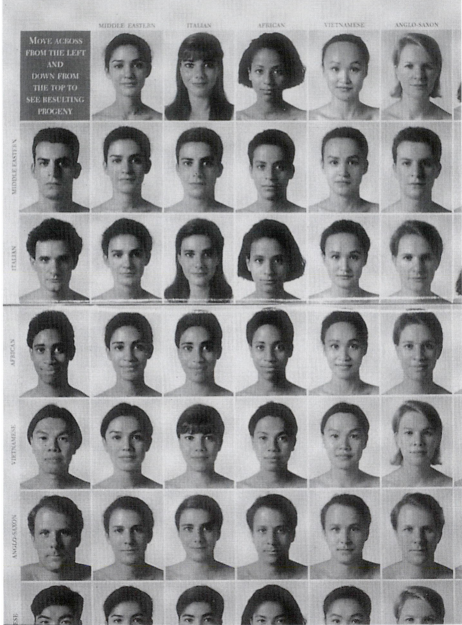

Figure 4.5E *"Time*s morphies' "

represent. Indeed, its very title, "Rebirth of a Nation, Computer-Style," invokes yet displaces the more complicated and feared history depicted in D. W. Griffith's *Birth of A Nation* onto the field of computer games (see Figure 4.5F). This special issue was, after all, about immigration – or more specifically about how citizenship will be determined in the United States in the next century. No need to trot in scientists to provide the now familiar caveats that gross morphological differences are of little use in categorizing humans and that races don't exist. *Time* showed that despite such assertions, to most Americans, race is embodied and, even with racial mixing, the existence of primary races is as obvious as the existence of primary colors in the Crayola crayon palette. There was no need to even explain the choice of categories used to produce the "morphies." We all know that "Anglo-Saxons" are different from "Italians" and so on. The computer allowed *Time* to uncritically take the three so-called basic races – white, black, Asian – and extend it to seven groups: Middle Eastern, Italian, African, Vietnamese, Anglo-Saxon, Chinese, and Hispanic. The resulting "morphies" are surprisingly similar in their physical features, yet the text makes no mention of this point. This silence on the issue of the morphological similarity of these racially mixed figures is interesting. The simultaneous recognition of greater diversity, on the one hand, and morphological similarity, on the other, suggests a strange logic of equivalence. A nose is a nose is a nose, no matter what your race is. Or is it? Is the reader to interpret this move as suggesting that morphological equivalence is an answer to the political conflict over race and citizenship that the upcoming census will surely engender? Is there a link between this logic and a political rhetoric of citizenship that assumes an interchangeability of characteristics that we all have in common but that are expressed slightly differently? *E pluribus unum?* What kind of citizenship is being imagined or configured in the logic of equivalences that morphing graphically enacts? Given the assumption of sameness with respect to power and privilege that the "morphies" inadvertently imply, will inequalities in the future be explained in terms of lack of ambition, intelligence, will, or ingenuity? Has morphological difference been supplanted by an implicit nod to behavioral and cultural differences? Or behavioral and cultural sameness? As the *Time* writers note: "Those who intermarry have perhaps the strongest sense of what it will take to return America to an unhyphenated whole. 'It's American culture that we all share'"[15]

Despite their tone and the explicit efforts to separate the resulting morphed images from the conflicted meanings they represent, the editors of *Time* came up against their own desires:

> Little did we know what we had wrought. As onlookers watched the image of our new Eve begin to appear on the computer screen, several staff members promptly fell in love. Said one: "It really breaks my heart that she doesn't exist . . ." We sympathized with our lovelorn colleagues, but even technology has its limits. This is a love that must forever remain unrequited.[16]

This is truly the drama of miscegenation in cyberspace. The history of white men crossing racial boundaries to have sexual relations with African, Asian, Mexican and Native-American women – and then refusing to acknowledge their offspring in order to reserve the right to determine how whiteness would be defined as a characteristic

REBIRTH OF A NATION, COMPUTER-STYLE

HOW DO YOU GO ABOUT CREATING THE 49 combinations of progeny from the seven men and seven women featured in the TIME picture chart shown below? Doing so by the scientific rules of genetic engineering—themselves extremely complex and not yet fully understood—would be impossible. Instead, TIME chose a software package called Morph 2.0, produced by Gryphon, to run on a Macintosh Quadra 900. The Morph 2.0 is an offspring of Hollywood's sophisticated special-effects equipment used to produce such eye-poppers as Michael Jackson's celebrated metamorphosis in his *Black or White* video and the evil robot that wreaks havoc in *Terminator 2*.

Morph 2.0 enabled TIME to pinpoint key facial features on the photos of the 14 people of various racial and ethnic backgrounds chosen for the chart. Electronic dots defined head size, skin color, hair color and texture, eyebrows, the contours of the lips, nose and eyes, even laugh lines around the mouth. The eyes in particular required many key points to make them as detailed as possible; otherwise the results would be very erratic. Similarly, miscalculating the dimensions of an upper lip only slightly, for example, could badly skew the resulting face.

Most of the images, or "morphies," on the chart are a straight 50-50 combination of the physical characteristics of their progenitors, though an entirely different image can be created by using, say, 75% of the man's eyes, or 75% of the woman's lips. After the eyes, the most important parental feature is the neck, which often determines the gender of the morph offspring.

Sometimes pure volume counts. The more information extracted from a given feature, the more likely that feature is to dominate the cybernetic offspring. Even when the program is weighted 50-50, if an African man has more hair than a Vietnamese woman, his hair will dominate; the same thing applies to larger lips or a jutting jaw. One of our tentative unions produced a distinctly feminine face—sitting atop a muscular neck and hairy chest. Back to the mouse on that one.

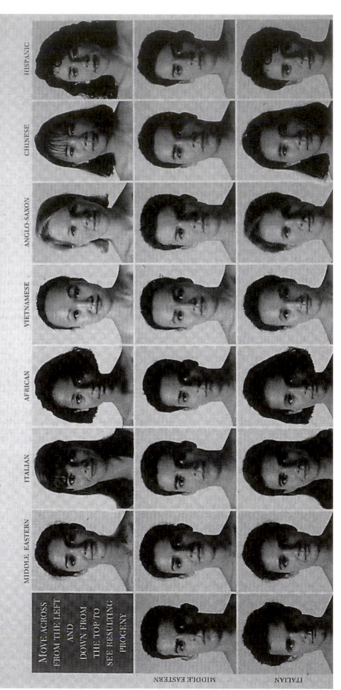

Figure 4.5F "Rebirth of a nation, computer-style"

of citizenship – is simultaneously implied and disavowed. Race mixing in its newest form shapes our future not the past; bits and bytes replace the flesh and blood that provoked the guilt, hatred and violence of our country's history of racial domination. Hierarchies of domination have not disappeared as female reproduction is replaced by a masculine technophilic reproduction because stereotypical racial typologies remain in place.[17] I say this because no woman of color has ever symbolized citizenship in United States history, only the denial of citizenship. Women of color were among the last groups to achieve the right to vote and all the attendant rights of citizenship that flow from it. Donna Haraway argues that SimEve forever excites a desire that cannot be fulfilled and as such is an example of the dream of technological transcendence of the body. But I think SimEve carries a different meaning in the light of the history of miscegenation – because she is a cyber – she is the representation of the desire to deny kinship and retain masculine power based on the maintenance of racial difference.

Acknowledgement

I want to thank Jennifer Terry for her insightful comments on this chapter.

Notes

1   Elazar Barkan, *The Retreat of Scientific Racism: Changing Concepts of Race in Britain and the United States between the World Wars* (Cambridge: Cambridge University Press, 1992), p. 341.

2   Ibid., pp. 341–3; and Donna Haraway. *Primate Visions: Gender, Race and Nation in the World of Modern Science* (New York: Routledge, 1989), pp. 197–203.

3   Nancy Stepan, *The Idea of Race in Science* (Hamden, CT: Archon Press, 1982), p. 171.

4   These pure racial types are defined in terms of morphological differences such as hair texture, skin color, shape of eyes corresponding to geographical origin e.g. white Anglo-Saxon, African, etc.

5   W. E. B. DuBois (ed.), *The Health and Physique of the Negro American* (Atlanta: Atlanta University Press, 1906), p. 11.

6   Ibid., p. 16.

7   Ibid., p. 37.

8   Ibid., p. 39.

9   "What Color is Black? What Color is White?" *Newsweek*, 13 February 1995, p. 3.

10 In 1967, the US Supreme Court struck down the final existing anti-miscegenation laws in *Loving* v. *Virginia*.

11 *Newsweek*, 13 February 1995, p. 64.

12 Ibid., p. 69.

13 "The New Face of America," *Time* magazine, Special Issue, Fall 1993.

14 Ibid., p. 2.

15 Ibid., p. 65.

16 Ibid., p. 2.

17 Donna Haraway, "Universal Donors in a Vampire Culture: It's All in the Family.

Biological Kinship Categories in the Twentieth-Century United States," in William Cronon (ed.) *Uncommon Ground: Toward Reinventing Nature* (New York: Norton, 1995).

Index

NOTE: Page numbers in italic indicate an illustration separated from its relevant text; page numbers followed by n indicate information in a note.

abjection theory 97, 116, 123, 134
abortion 161, 204n, 225, 231; access to 211; court cases 188–9n; politics of 234; selective 187; self-help to 237; *Silent Scream* video 164–5, 172–6, 180, 183, 187; and ultrasound imaging 172–3, 186, 189n; *see also* anti-abortion movement; foetus
abstract individualism 176
Acker, Kathy 272
Adam, Alison 249, 250, 251–3, 254, 259, 260, 300
Adams, Carol 285
advertisements 9, 65, 224–5, 226
African Americans: study of 306–8, 309; *see also* Negroes; racial difference
African women: breasts maligned 21, 26; "Hottentot Venus" 6, 25–9; scientific obsession with sexuality of 25–6, 43
Africans: in scientific analogy 39, 40, 44–5; *see also* African Americans; African women; Hottentots; Negroes

Agnes, St 31n
AI (Artificial Intelligence) projects 249, 251–3, 276–87
AIDS 56, 155
Akron case 188n
Alien/s (film series) 93, 94–7, 99, 137; monstrous motherhood in 94, 95, 96, 97, 101–8, 122–34, *124–5*; motherless reproduction in 115–16; psychoanalytical reading of *Alien* 96–7, 108n, 122–34; Ripley character 94–5, 102, *104*, 105–8, 109n, 133; visual devices in 118–19
ALife (Artificial Life) 231, 241n, 259, 281–2
All New Gen movement 266
AllYou Zombies: Truth before God (Longo sculpture) 9, 66–8, 70
Amazons 21
American Fertility Society 211
Amos, Valerie 199, 200
analogy in science 7, 38–9, 168, 306; cultural sources of 40–1; interaction theory of metaphor 42–45; linking race and gender 39–47

Analytical Engine (prototype computer) 269–70
Anderson, Laurie 158n
androgyny 140
animal rights movements 52
anthropometry 41, 43
anti-abortion movement 164–5, 171–6, 177; court cases 188–9n; and IVF treatment 202–3; *Silent Scream* video 164–5, 172–6, 180, 183, 187; ultrasound scanning promoted by 172–3, 181, 189n
anti-oppressive feminist standpoint 166, 197, 200–2, 203, 206n
antinatalism 214
Aphrodite 15, 21
"apron" of Hottentot women 26–7, *28*, 29
archaic mother 96, 97, 122, 123, *124*, 127–32; as goddess 127–9; as negative force 129–32, 133, 163
Aristotle 11, 12, 13, 40
armed forces (US): homosexuality issue 234
art: digital 271–2
Artedi, Peter 13
artefacts/artificial 8, 81–2, 85; and reproductive technologies 163; scientific 193–4
Artemis 21
Artificial Intelligence (AI) projects 249, 251–3, 276–87
Artificial Life (ALife) 231, 241n, 259, 281–2
ARTs (Assisted Reproductive Technologies) 166, 167, 209–18
Asimov, Isaac 269, 274–5n
assemblage 63–5, 69
Atwood, Margaret: *The Handmaid's Tale* 169
audience: negotiation with film texts 100; response to horror films 96, 131
Auerbach, Eric 226
Augustine of Hippo 17
automatons 60–1, 72n
autopoietic systems 250

Baartman, Saartjie *see* Bartmann, Sarah
Babbage, Charles 270
Baby M surrogate mother debate 233
Bachmann, Ingrid 272
Bacon, Francis 3, 81
Baiblé, Claude 119
Balka, Ellen 286
Balsamo, Anne 98–9, 100, 167–8, 284, 286–7
Barbara, St 31n
Barkan, Elazar 305
Barnes, Barry 46
Barrow, John 27
Barthes, Roland 164, 175; *Camera Lucida* 117
Bartmann, Sarah (Saartjie Baartman), the "Hottentot Venus" 6, 27–9
Bataille, Georges 131
Bates, B. 185–6
Bateson, Gregory 154, 157n
Baudrillard, Jean 116, 120, 153
Beautiful Girl, The see *Schöne Mädchen, Das*
Bell Telephone advertisement 224–5, 226
Belon, Pierre 13
BEMs (bug-eyed monsters) 98, 137
Benjamin, Walter 120
Benson, Timothy O. 63
Benston, Margaret Lowe 204n
Berger, John 164, 183
biological sciences: evolutionary biology 39, 45–6, 52; and gender 3–4, 6–7; hormone biology 39; and racial difference 6–7, 305–6; taxonomies of 5–6, 11–29; *see also* biotechnology; essentialism
biomedical discourse 155
biotechnology 55, 56, 167, 228; bionic bodies 154, 155, 157–8n
Biro, Matthew 63–4
birth control *see* contraception: fertility control
black feminisms 199–200, 204n
Black, Max 42, 45
black people: in scientific analogy 39, 40; technology visualizes 305–17
Black or White (pop video) 306

Blade Runner (film) 93, 116–20, 138, *139, 140*; cyborg identity in 97, 98, 99, 117–18; motherless reproduction in 95–6, 115, 116, 118; photographs in 117–18; Rachel character 98, 150–1

Blainville, Henri de 27, 29

blasphemy 50

Blumenbach, Johann Friedrich 26–7

body: iconography of 154–5, 157; spatial relations of 62–5; *see also* cyborg: visual representations of; embodied knowledge; female body

Bolk, Louis 46

Borden, Lizzie: *Born in Flames* 98, 146

Borg, Susan 219*n*

Born in Flames (film) 98, 146

Boston Women's Health Book Collective 242–3*n*

Bourdieu, Pierre 86*n*

Bowers, John 280

brachycephaly 44

Brail, Stephanie 285, 294

brain measurements in scientific analogy 39, 41, 46; phrenology 43–4, 45

breast: cultural history of 12, 15–24; as icon 15–21; ideals of 21, 26; *see also* breast-feeding; wet-nursing

breast-feeding 12–24, 16–17, 22–3

Breuer, Josef 251, 270

Broca, Paul 41, 43, 44, 46

Brother from Another Planet, The (film) 137, 138, 140

Bruckman, A. 293

Buffon, Georges-Louis Leclerc, Comte de 13, 15

Bundtzen, Lynda K. 94–5, 99

Butler, Judith 198, 213, 219*n*, 256, 260

Cadigan, Pat 272

caesarian sections 179

Caligula 23

Calvert, M. 291

Camera Lucida (Barthes) 117

Cameron, James 101, 105

Canguilhem, Georges 8

capitalism: stages of 142–3, 146

Cartesian dualism 7, 8

cartoons *see* comic book/cartoon imagery

Casper, Monica 232–3

castration complex 132–3

CCETSW (Central Council for the Education and Training of Social Workers) 206*n*

"chain of being" 6, 24–5, 306

Charity (Virtue) 21

Chaumette, Pierre-Gaspard 24

Cherny, Lyn 286

childbirth: management of 161, 176–82

Chodorow, Nancy 108*n*

choice: signifiers of 236

Christianity: Christian realism 226–7; creationism 51, 52; imagery of suckling 16–17; technoscience signifiers of 236

Christie, John 283

Churcher, John 280

cinema *see* film; science fiction film

Clarke, Adele 232

Clerc, S. 295, 296

Clinton, Bill 234

clocks *see* Horlogère, L'

cloning 169

Close Encounters of the Third Kind (film) 137

Clynes, Manfred 8

Cochin, Charles 16, 18

Cocoon (film) 137

coding problems 55–6

Collins, Patricia Hill 200

comic book/cartoon imagery 9, 69–71, 148, 223–32, 236–7, 237–9, *240*

communications technologies 55–6, 152, 167; linked with reproductive technologies 224–5; *see also* information technologies; Internet

computational linguistics 278–9

Comte, Auguste 80

conceptive technologies *see* reproductive technologies

connectionist machines 250–1, 268, 285

consciousness: cyborg 58–9

constructionist approach to science 79–81
contraception 161, 163, 211, 216
control strategies 55
conversational analysis software 278–80
Coordinator speech analysis system 280
Cope, Edward 39
Corea, Gena 166, 182, 186
Cornell, Drucilla 215
Crang, P. 297
Creation of Adam, The (Michelangelo) 168, 223–4, 226, 228–9, 241n
Creation of Eve, The (painting) 241n
creationism 51, 52
Creed, Barbara 96–7, 99
Creef, Elena Tajima 69
criticism *see* film: criticism
Croly, David Goodman 68
Cussins, Charis 233
Cuvier, Georges 14, 27, 29
cyberculture 252, 259, 260, 280–1; as escape 282; for feminists 282–3, 284–5, 287
cyberfeminism 9, 250, 252–3, 265–74, 284–6, 287, 295–6
Cyber-feminist Manifesto for the 21st Century, A (billboard display) 266
cybernetic systems 157n, 250
cyberpornography 285
cyborg: as ahistorical figure 7, 8, 63, 72–3n; as artefactual metaphor 82; bodies represented 58–71, 99, 106–7, 149–50, 154; as boundary figure xiii, 7–8, 52, 58, 74, 75, 260; cyborg consciousness 58–9; cyborg semiologies 55, 85; detection of difference 117, 137; difference lessened 136–42; ethnography of 148–9, 157; feminist view of 148–57, 283–4; gender of 150, 151–2; and gender stereotypes 98, 151, 156; as icon 148–9, 155–6, 283; identity 70–1, 82–4, 97–9, 140, 155, 156–7, 167; and "meat-free" existence 281–2; mechanical cyborg 58; organic cyborg 58; origins of 8, 148; as racially different 68–71; and reproductive technologies 169; sexuality of 8, 51, 67, 114, 140; as sexualized slave 9, 65; as social construction 153–4; in virtual reality 82–4, 85; visual representations of 8–9, 57, 58–71, 149–50, 260; *see also* "Manifesto for cyborgs"

Dadaism 61, 62, 63, 64, 66
Dadoun, Roger 129
Danisch, Hubert 188n
Dante: *Divine Comedy* 226
Darwin, Charles 39
Darwin, Erasmus 21
Daubenton, Louis 13
Dawkins, Richard 274n
de Beauvoir, Simone 153
de Lauretis, Teresa 129, 291
deconstruction and reproductive technologies 168, 214–15
Deleuze, Gilles 108n, 109n
Dement, Linda 272
Demeter and Persephone myth 108
Dennett, Daniel 274n; "Woo Woo West Coast Emergence" 252, 285
Derrida, Jacques 86n
Descartes, René 6; Cartesian dualism 7, 8
determinism: technological 52–3, 282, 283
Diana of Ephesus 15, 16, *19*, 23
Dietrich, Marlene 108n
difference *see* gender difference; human difference; racial difference
digital arts 271–2
Dinnerstein, Dorothy 108n
disability: and reproductive technologies 184, 187; as social construct 154–5, 155, 158n
discourse 206n; on reproductive technologies 168, 209–18
distributable maternity 212–13
Doane, Mary Ann 93, 95–6, 99, 150, 151
dolichocephaly 44–5
domination: informatics of 53–4
DuBois, W.E.B. 255, 306–8

Duden, Barbara 223
Dunlop, Alexander 27
Dürer, Albrecht: *Draughtsman Drawing a Nude* 227–8, 229, 232

earth: visualization of 222
Earth as mother image 16, *17*
Eclipse Fax advertisement 9, 65
ecofeminism 9, 75, 82, 84, 85n
ecology 56
Edelman, Gerald 272
Ehrenreich, Barbara 239
Eiser, J. Richard 268
Electra Assassin (comic book character) 148
electronic foetal monitoring (EFM) 179, 185–6
electronic retina 154, 157–8n
electronics 56, 136
Ellis, Havelock 39, 44–5, 46
embodied knowledge 251–2, 254, 259, 261, 300
embryo rights 202–3
empiricism: feminist 165, 193, 194–5, 197, 204n
Enemy Mine (film) 137
English, Deirdre 239
Enlightenment: breast-feeding encouraged in 22, 23; rationalism of 198, 199
equality feminism 214
Erasmus 23
essentialism 166, 198–200, 214, 257
E.T. (film) 137, 138, *141*
Ethics Advisory Board (US) 211
Ethics Report (1979)(US) 211
ethnography: cyborg 148–9, 157; "ethnographic attitude" 235; of women and reproductive technologies 233
eugenics screening in IVF treatment 166, 203, 211
Eve (computer-generated cover girl) 255, 312, *313*, 315, 317
Eve future, L' (Villiers de l'Isle Adam) 111–13, 119, 150
evolutionary biology 39, 45–6, 52

experience: discursive construction of 219n
"experimental ethnography" 54

fantasy and new technology 260–1
Farquhar, Dion 166–7
fax advertisement 9, 65
female body: in advertisements 9, 65, 300–1; cultural history of the breast 12, 15–24; in cyborg representations 8–9, 58–71, 99, 110–20; in feminist theory 154–5, 157, 262–4; in information technologies 254; as machine 8–9, 59–61, 70, 112–13; *Mammalia* classification 11–29; in science fiction 93, 106–8; visual representations of 222–32; womb 16, 130, 272; *see also* embodied knowledge
female fetishism 97, 113, 132–3
feminine representations in science fiction film 91–136, 148–58
feminine symbolic 256–8, 260
feminism/feminist theory: and AI projects 249, 251–3, 276–87; anti-oppressive feminist standpoint 166, 197, 200–2, 203, 206n; and biological science xiii; black feminisms 199–200, 204n; body iconography in 154–5, 157; cyberfeminism 9, 250, 252–3, 265–74, 284–6, 287, 295–6; cyborgs viewed through 148–57, 283–4; ecofeminism 9, 75, 82, 84, 85n; epistemology of 203–4n, 213, 287; feminist empiricism 165, 193, 194–5, 197, 204n; feminist jurisprudence 278; feminist postmodernism 198–9, 213, 214; feminist standpoint theory 165, 166, 193–4, 196–202, 203, 204n, 206n, 277; film criticism 97, 100; and gender construction 3, 4–5; and identity 153–4, 155, 156–7; imperial feminism 199; and information technologies 249–317; interdisciplinarity of 9, 75; race/racism discussion 198, 199,

205n; and reproductive technologies 165–6, 168–9, 186–7, 188, 209–18; and science 74–85, 193–203; science fiction film 146; science fiction neglected by 91–2; Second Wave feminism 4, 99; socialist 5, 50, 51, 52, 55, 57; speculum as symbol 237–40; white feminism 199–200

feminist science studies 77–81, 85, 222, 223, 242n; feminist technoscience studies 323–6

fertility control 161; conceptive technologies 162; IVF treatment 162, 166, 194–7, 202–3, 205n; see also reproductive technologies

Festival of the Supreme Being (1794) 24

fetishism: female 97, 113, 132–3; fetishization of foetus 181; technological 95, 119

fetus see foetus

film: audience 96, 100; criticism 91–2, 94, 97, 100; see also science fiction film

Finger, Anne 154–5, 158n

FINRAGE (Feminist International Network of Resistance to Reproductive and Genetic Engineering) 166

Firestone, Shulamith 166

Fish, Stanley 45

foetus: electronic foetal monitoring 179, 185–6; fetishization of 181; "foetal personhood" 165, 168, 171–2, 176, 177, 178–9, 185; as sacrum 222–3; Silent Scream video 164–5, 172–6, 180, 183, 187; as spaceman 175–6; visualization of 164–5, 171–88, 222, 224, 225–6, 230–2, 237; as work object 232–4; see also abortion; embryo rights; ultrasound scanning

Foster, Hal 66

Foucault, Michel 5, 55, 166, 167, 236–7; "positive unconscious" 59, 72n; resemblance and similitude 98, 137–8, 142

Fox Keller, Evelyn see Keller, Evelyn Fox

Frankenstein (Shelley) 76–7, 81–2, 114, 149, 269

French Revolution 15, 23–4

Freud, Sigmund 96, 163; hysteria 251, 267, 270–1; on mother 126, 127, 128; Oedipus complex/myth 126, 127, 128–9, 132; weaving 271; Wolf-Man case 122; womb as "uncanny" 130

fundamentalism 167, 210, 214, 215–16

Furnival, Chloe 277

Gaia as cyborg 9

Galen 16

Gall, Franz Joseph 43

Galletti, Pierre 157n

Galton, Francis 41

geekgrrl (women's group) 296

Gelphi, Barbara 21

gender: as construction 3–5, 214–15; of cyborgs 150, 151–2; gender inequality 7; gender swapping 293–4; and information technologies 251–4, 268, 286–7, 291–302; and language 278–9; at NetCafé 296–302; and power relations 164, 167, 197, 199, 201; and racial analogies 38–47; and science 78–9, 179–82; as social construct 3–5; stereotypes in science fiction films 98, 99–100, 151, 156; and technoscience see technoscience and gender; see also sex difference

Germany: Weimar 61–2

Gesner, Conrad 11

Gibson, William: Neuromancer 260, 272

Gilman, Sander 40, 154

goddess: as boundary figure 74, 75; as metaphor 9, 82; mother as 127, 128, 129; as mythical realism figure 84, 85

Godwin, William 16

González, Jennifer 8

Gore-Tex ligament 154, 157–8n

Gould, Stephen Jay 46

Gravelot, Hubert-François 16, 18

"great chain of being" 6, 24–5, 306

Great Cosmic Mother (Sjöö and Mor) 84

Greil, Arthur 220n

Grey, Chris Hables 8
Griffin, Susan 82
Grontkowski, Christine 179
Gross, Paul R. 242n
Grossman, Rachel 57
Grosz, Elizabeth 209
Grundy, Frances 286
gynaecological speculum *see* speculum

Hacking, I. 8
Hall, K. 296
Haller, Albrecht von 12
Hammersley, Martyn 205n
Hammonds, Evelynn M. 249, 254–6, 260
Haraway, Donna 61, 167–8, 291, 305; on cyborg 58; on deconstructing science 79–80; on individuality 165; "Manifesto for Cyborgs" *see* "Manifesto for Cyborgs"; "promise of monsters" 77; on science fiction(s) 92, 198; SimEve 312, 317; vampire culture 209; on women's identities 153, 154, 157n
Harding, Sandra 251–2; feminist approaches to technoscience 165, 193, 198–9, 200, 203–4n; gender 3, 201
Harrison, Dr Michael 180
Hartouni, Valerie 233
Hartsock, Nancy 181
Hausmann, Raoul: *Tête Mécanique* 63–5
Headroom, Max (computer-generated TV personality) 148
Heartbeeps (film) 138
Helme, Elizabeth 27
Helmreich, Stefan 241n, 281–2
Herring, Susan 285, 286, 295
Hesse, M. 45
Hill Street Blues (TV series) 189n
Hirst, Graeme 278–9
history: cyborg as ahistorical 7, 8, 63, 72–3n, 117–18; loss of 117–18
Höch, Hannah: *Das schöne Mädchen* 61–3, 64, 65, 70
Homer: *Iliad* 72n
Homo sapiens as classification 5, 15–16

homosexuality in US armed forces 234
hooks, bell 235–6
Hopper, Grace Murray 270, 272
Horlogère, L' 8–9, 59–61, 70
hormone biology 39
horror films: archaic mother in 130–2; audience response to 96, 131; science fiction as 116, 120
"Hottentot Venus" (Sarah Bartmann) 6, 27–9
Hottentot women: "apron" 26–7, *28*, 29; breasts maligned 21, 26
Hughes, Robert 66
human difference: cyborg threatens 150; in scientific analogy 38–47, 306; *see also* racial difference; sex difference
humanities/sciences divide 75–6, 77
humans: boundary with animals 5–6, 52, 58; boundary with machines 52–3, 58; taxonomy of 12–13
Hunt, Lynn 24
Huxley, Thomas Henry 13
Huyssen, Andreas 93, 114, 155
"hybrids" 39, 67–8, 69, 77, 149, 312
hysteria 251, 267, 270–1

identity: of cyborg 70–1, 82–4, 97–9, 117–18, 140, 155, 156–7, 167; cyborg challenges 149, 157; "foetal personhood" 165, 168, 171–2, 176, 177, 178–9, 185; identity politics 77, 92, 299–300; and Internet 253, 268, 286–7, 291–302; and motherhood 162–3, 166, 210; at NetCafé 299–300; postmodern 153–4, 155, 156–7; in science fiction 92; sexual 257; of women 99, 153–4, 155, 156–7; *see also* individuality
Iliad (Homer) 72n
immigrants: and racial difference 254–6, 309–17; women denied prenatal care 234
immunobiology 56
imperial feminism 199
individuality: of foetus 165; of mother 165; of scientific expert 165

infertility *see* fertility control; IVF treatment
informatics of domination 53–4
information technologies 55–6, 152, 236, 249–317; Artificial Intelligence projects 249, 251–3, 276–87; autopoietic systems 250; networked technologies 249, 250–1, 265–74; *see also* communications technologies; Internet
"informed consent" 189*n*
insanity studies 40
interaction theory of metaphor 42–45
Internet 276, 281; and gendered identities 253, 268, 286–7, 291–302; Internet Cafés 249, 253, 292–3, 296–302; language of 293–4, 296; liberatory potential 250, 252, 253, 256, 258–60, 265, 268, 283; online communities 253, 254, 293–4, 296; online harassment 252, 253, 285, 287, 292, 294–5; science fiction debates on 100; women's usage of 285, 286, 292, 295–300
interracial marriage 309–17; *see also* miscegenation
Invasion of the Body Snatchers (film) 137
Irigaray, Luce: feminine symbolic 249, 256–8, 259, 260; mimesis 256–7; motherhood 162–3; nothing/zero as zone of multiplicity 251, 256, 270, 272; specular economy 266, 267; speculum symbol 168; touch 271–2; women as other 162, 270; women and technology 254, 259–60, 270
Irish in scientific analogy 41
IVF (*in vitro* fertilization) treatment 162, 166; eugenics politics of 166, 203, 211; feminist approaches to 194–7, 202–3; social relations and 194, 205*n*

Jackson, Michael: *Black or White* video 306
Jacquard loom 270–1, 285–6
Jameson, Fredric 142–4, 146, 153
Jansen, Sue C. 277, 281

Jarvik, Robert 154, 157–8*n*
jaw protusion in scientific analogy 44
Jenkins, H. 91
Johnson, Anna 233
Johnson, M. 40
Jordan, Winthrop 24, 40

Kaplan, Cora 153–4
Kaplan, E.A. 181
Kehoe, Colleen 286
Keith, Sir Arthur 39
Keller, Evelyn Fox 3, 4, 78–9, 179, 180, 185
Kelly, Anne: *Virtual Speculum* 223–32, 236–7
Kendall, L. 293
Kiddy (comicbook cyborg) 9, 69–71
Klein, Hilary 51
Klein, Renate D. 196–7, 199–200, 201, 205*n*, 216
Kleiner Perkins Caulfield & Byers 228
knowledge: embodied 251–2, 254, 259, 261, 300
Kosovo women and Internet 259
Kristeva, Julia 96; abjection theory 97, 116, 123, 134; on mother 126, 127–8, 130, 131–2
Kuhn, Annette 93, 97
Kuhn, Thomas S. 45

labia minora of Hottentot women 26–7, *28*, 29
Lacan, Jacques 96, 128, 130, 168
Laclau, Ernesto 213
Lakoff, G. 40
landscapes of computing 292–302
Lang, Fritz: *Metropolis* 113, 149
language: exclusion of feminine symbolic 256–8, 260, 262–4; feminist AI projects in 278–80; of online communities 293–4, 296; of science 4, 41
Lanier, Jaron 282
Lasker, Judith 219*n*
late capitalism 142–3, 146
Latour, Bruno 76–7, 86*n*
Lavin, Maude 62

law: feminist AI projects in 277–8, 279
Layne, Barbara 272
Le Vaillant, François 27, *28*
Leclerc, Georges-Louis, Comte de
  Buffon 13, 15
Leonardo da Vinci 228
lesbian reproductive issues 186, 205*n*,
  211–12
Lévi-Strauss, Claude 127, 129
Levitt, Norman 242*n*
liberalism 167, 210, 214, 215
life as epistemological object 222
Life (magazine) 180, 183, 225, 226
ligament: artificial 154, 157–8*n*
Light, Jennifer 283, 286
linguistics: feminist AI projects in
  278–80
Linnaeus, Carolus: campaign against
  wet-nursing 22–3; *Fauna Svecica*
  frontispiece 16, 19; and "Hottentot
  apron" 26; *Mammalia* classification
  5–6, 11–15, 16, 21, 24
lips: as artefacts in information
  technologies 254, 298, 299, 300–1;
  symbolize communication 256–7,
  259–60, 262–4; vaginal 26–7, *28*, 29,
  254
Liquid Sky (film) 98, 138, 140, *141*
longheadedness 44–5
Longo, Robert: *All You Zombies: Truth
  before God* 9, 66–8, 70
Lorde, Audre 277, 279
Lovelace, Ada 258, 269–70, 272
Luker, Kristin 184
Lykke, Nina 9

McCaffrey, Anne: *The Ship That Sang*
  149, 151
McDonald v. McDonald case 212
machines: boundary with humans 52–3,
  58, 150; boundary with organisms 8,
  52, 56, 58; incorporated into cyborg
  image 8–9, 58–71, 111–13;
  mechanical cyborg 58; miniaturization
  53
MacKinnon, Catharine 205*n*
McLuhan, Marshall xiv, 271

McRae, S. 293–4
Maier, Michael 16, *17*
male reproductive rights 202
Mammalia classification 5–6, 11–15, 21,
  24
man: rationality distinguishes 5–6,
  15–16
Manet, Edouard 229
"Manifesto for Cyborgs" (Donna
  Haraway) 4–5, 66, 217, 283–4, 287;
  cyborg as ahistorical 7, 8, 63, 72–3*n*;
  cyborg as boundary figure xiii, 7–8,
  260; cyborg and identity 152–3, 167,
  217; cyborg as utopian icon 155–6;
  technoscience xiii, xiv; text of 50–7
Marianne (symbol of French
  Revolution) 15, 23, 24
Marston, William Moulton (Charles
  Moulton) 238
Martin, Emily 220*n*, 306
Marxism 51, 52
Mary, mother of Jesus 17, 21
masochism 108*n*, 109*n*
maternal/mother in science fiction films
  91–158; archaic mother 96, 97, 122,
  123, *124*, 127–32, 133, 163;
  monstrous motherhood 94, 95, 96,
  97, 101–8, 122–34, 163; motherless
  reproduction 95–6, 114–18, 176;
  oral-sadistic mother 96–7, 131, 132;
  phallic mother 94, 97, 104, 130, 131,
  132–3; Ripley as maternal signifier
  94–5, 105–7; and technology
  114–18, 120
maternity *see* maternal/mother in
  science fiction films;
  mother/motherhood
Maturana, H.R. 250
Max Headroom (computer generated
  TV personality) 148
"meat-free" existence 252, 281–2
mechanical cyborg 58
Mechanical Head see *Tête mécanique*
medicine: feminist approaches to
  193–203; *see also* obstetrics;
  reproductive technologies
Medusa myth 129

men: redundancy of 169
Merchant, Carolyn 16
metaphor: interaction theory of 42–45;
    in science 7, 38–47, 168; substitution
    theory of 52
Metropolis (film) 113–14, 149
Metz, Christian 113, 119
Michelangelo: *Creation of Adam* 168,
    223–4, 226, 228–9, 241*n*
Michelson, Annette 111–12, 112–13
microelectronics 56
milk, human 17
Miller, D. 293
mimesis 256–7
miniaturization 53
miscegenation 68, 306, 307, 309–311
"missing link" 24–5
Mitchell, Juliet 97, 132–3
modernism and visual image of cyborg
    9, 62–3
modernity: humanities/sciences divide
    75–6; as process of purification 76–7,
    78, 86*n*
Modleski, Tanya 198, 199
monsters: BEMs (bug-eyed monsters)
    98, 137; as boundary figures 74–5,
    76–9; Frankenstein's monster 76–7,
    81–2; humans perceived as 6;
    monstrous motherhood 94, 95, 96,
    97, 101–8, 122–34, 163
Montini, Teresa 232
MOOs (online communities) 253,
    293–4
Mor, B.: *Great Cosmic Mother* 84
Moravec, Hans 281
Morph 2.0 software package 312
morphing 254–5, 306, 312–17
mother/motherhood: and abortion
    173–4; and identity 162–3, 166, 210;
    maternity discourses 212–14;
    monstrous motherhood 94, 95, 96,
    97, 101–8, 122–34, 163; mother as
    other 122–34, 167; mothering
    105–8, 109*n*, 212, 217–18; others as
    mothers 210–14, 217–18; pregnant
    women's responses to ultrasound
    pictures 172–3, 181, 182–7, 204*n*,

224, 225; rendered invisible 174–6,
    177, 180–1, 185; and reproductive
    technologies 161–243; in science
    fiction film *see* maternal/mother in
    science fiction film; surrogacy 233; *see
    also* reproductive technologies; sexual
    reproduction
Mouffe, Chantal 213
Moulton, Charles (William Moulton
    Marston) 238
movies *see* film
Ms. (magazine) 239, *240*
MUDs (online communities) 253, 293,
    294
Musée de l'Homme, Paris 29
mythical realism 84, 85, 86*n*

Nathanson, Dr Bernard 172, 173–4,
    175, 180
National Institutes of Health/Food and
    Drug Administration (US) report on
    ultrasound scanning 178
National Right-to-Life Committee (US)
    173
Nature: image of 15, 16, *18*
nature/natural 81–2, 85; in
    motherhood 161, 163
"naturism" 75, 85*n*
Nead, Lynda 227
Negroes: in scientific analogy 39, 41,
    43; study of African Americans
    306–8
neoteny 46
Nero 23
NetCafé, London 292–3, 296–302
networked technologies 249, 250–1,
    265–74; *see also* Internet
neural nets 251, 268–9, 270–1
New England Journal of Medicine 172–3
"New Woman" in Weimar Germany 62
New World Order 227, 232
Newsweek magazine 255, 309–12
Nilsson, Lennart 225–6, 232, 237
"nothingness" 251
Nye, Andrea 280

Oakley, Ann 204*n*

objectivity: and foetal images 185; in science 79–81, 242n
O'Brien, Mary 181–2
obstetrics 176–82, 204n; see also speculum; ultrasound scanning
O'Connor, Justice Sandra Day 188–9n
Oedipus complex/myth 126, 127, 128–9, 132
Offray de la Mettrie, Julien 60
Omni (magazine) 157–8n
online communities 253, 254, 293–4, 296
oral-sadistic mother 96–7, 108n, 109n, 131, 132
organ transplantation 220n
organic cyborg 58
Orlan 272
Orlando (Woolf) 62–3
Ormrod, S. 291, 296, 300
Orphan Drift 272
otherness: of aliens lessened 136–42; construction in science fiction films 99; of cyborg 155; miscegenation creates 306; mother as other 122–34, 167
Ovington, John 26

panopticism: of foetal monitoring 180–1
parallel distributed processing 251, 268–9, 285
Parmar, Pratibha 199, 200
"passing" 70–1
paternity issues 213, 219n
patriarchal ideology 96, 123, 130; control of science 179–82, 204n; and information technologies 250, 266–7, 269; and reproductive technologies 165, 166, 176–82, 196; specular economy 266–7, 269, 273
Penley, Constance 92–3
"perfect baby" syndrome 184, 186
Persephone and Demeter myth 108
Perseus myth 129, 132
Petchesky, Rosalind 164–5, 168, 204n
phallic mother 94, 97, 104, 130, 131, 132–3

Philosophia-Sapientia 17, 20
Phoenix Technologies Ltd fax advertisement 9, 65
photographs: in Blade Runner 117–18; in race studies 307, 308; relation of women to 184–5; semiotic meaning 120, 164, 175, 188n; see also ultrasound scanning
photomontage 9, 61–3, 70
phrenology 43–4, 45
Pitkow, James 286
Plant, Sadie 254, 257, 258, 259, 260; critiqued 252–3, 284–6; networked technologies 249, 250–1, 295–6
Plato 16
pornography in cyberspace 285
positivism 175, 205n
postfuturism 136–46
postmodernism 52–3; cyborg as postmodern icon 148–9; feminist 198–9, 213, 214; identity in 153–4, 155, 156–7; photographs 175; and science fiction 92, 136–46
poststructural theory 3–4
Powell Bill (US) 202
power relations: gendered 164, 167, 197, 199, 201, 286; unequal 202
pregnancy: caesarian sections 179; discourses of 212–13; lesbian 186; male-directed management of 161, 176–83; response of pregnant woman to ultrasound images 172–3, 181, 182–7, 204n, 224, 225; see also abortion; foetus; reproductive technologies; ultrasound scanning
primal scene representations in Alien 122–6
pro-life lobby see anti-abortion movement
prognathism 44
pronatalism 214
Proposition 187 (State of California) 234
psychoanalysis 51, 163, 251, 252; psychoanalytical reading of Alien film 96–7, 108n, 122–34

Rabelais, François 132
Rabinow, Paul 218*n*
racial difference: in biological taxonomies 6; and "chain of being" 6, 24–5, 306; distinguishes cyborg 68–71; feminist discussion of 198, 199, 205*n*; miscegenation 68, 306, 307, 309–11; morphing techniques applied to 254–6; and reproductive technologies 166, 203, 233; and scientific analogy 6–7, 38–47; and scientific classification 6–7, 305–6; scientific racism 25–9; as social construct 307, 309; studies of race 41, 306–8; UNESCO disclaims 305; and visual technologies 249, 254–6, 305–17
radical feminism 214
Randolf, Lynn: *Cyborg* 69
Randolph, Lynn: *Venus* 229, *230*
Rapp, Rayna 164, 189*n*, 233
rationalism 198, 199
Ray, John 11, 13
Raymond, Janice 220*n*
realism: mythical 84, 85, 86*n*
reality 228, 242*n*
redundancy of men 169
Reid, E.M. 294
Renaissance: visual technology of 227–8
Repo Man (film) 98, 137, 138, 140
reproduction *see* reproductive technologies; sexual reproduction
reproductive freedom 223–32
reproductive technologies 161–243; ALife (Artificial Life) 231, 241*n*, 259, 281–2; clientele for 211–12, 216; discourses on 209–18; and ethnography 233; feminist approaches to 193–203; feminist technoscience studies 232–6; politics of 186, 195, 202–3, 233–4; separate reproduction from sex 211–12, 216–17; social relations and 184, 186, 194, 195, 197, 210–14, 216
resemblance 98, 137–8
retina: electronic 154, 157–8*n*
Richards, I.A. 42

Robins, Kevin 282–3
Robinson, Susan 211
Robocop (film) 66, 98, 150, 283
robotics: situated 253
Roe v. *Wade* case 188–9*n*
Rose, H. 252
Rothman, Barbara Katz 175–6
roundheadedness 44
Rousseau, Jean-Jacques 21, 23
RU486 (abortifacent) 232, 234
Rubens, Peter Paul 229

Saint-Hilaire, Etienne Geoffroy 14, 29
S'Aline's Abortion (performance video) 233
Sapientia 17, *20*
Sarthe-Lenoir, Maxime de 31*n*
Schelling, Friedrich Wilhelm Joseph von 130
Schiebinger, Londa 5
Schöne Mädchen, Das (photomontage) 61–3, 64, 65, 70
Schroeder, Ralph 282
science: analogy in *see* analogy in science; constructionist approach 79–81; cyborg in tradition of Western 51; feminist confrontations with 74–85, 193–203; feminist science studies 77–81, 85, 222, 223, 232–6, 242*n*; and gender 78–9, 179–82; humanities/sciences divide 75–6, 77; language of 4, 41; objective truths in 79–81; and racial difference 6–7, 305–6; reality and 228, 242*n*; as social construct 193; social relations of science and technology 57; as symbolic system 3; traditional hierarchies of 80–1, 269; *see also* biological sciences; technoscience
science fiction film: development of 142–6; feminine in 91–136, 148–58; foetus as spaceman imagery 175–6; gender stereotypes in 98, 99–100, 151, 156; mainstream films 145–6; marginal films 144–5, 146; and postmodernism 92, 136–46; reproduction in 93, 94, 95–6, 102–3,

104–5, 108, 114–18, 119, 151, 176; *see also* maternal/mother in science fiction films

scientific racism 25–9

Scientific Revolution 227

scientific sexism 25, 29

Scott, Maureen 277, 279

Second Wave feminism 4, 99

semiology/semiotics: cyborg semiologies 55, 85; semiotic chora 131–2; visualization technologies 164–5

sex difference 3–4, 5; confused in *Alien* 115–16; erased 140; and scientific classification 6–7, 25, 39–48

sexism: scientific 25, 29

sexual reproduction: ideologies of 54; limits artificial femininity 112; as metaphor for genesis of cyborg 68; motherless 76, 95–6, 114–18, 123, 126, 176, 241*n*; representations of 161–243; in science fiction film 93, 94, 95, 102–3, 104–5, 108, 114–18, 119, 151; and technology *see* reproductive technologies; *see also* abortion; contraception; fertility control; foetus; IVF treatment; mother/motherhood; pregnancy; ultrasound scanning

Shade, Lesley 286

Shelley, Mary: *Frankenstein* 76–7, 81–2, 114, 149, 269

Ship That Sang, The (McCaffrey) 149, 151

Siegesbeck, Johann/*Siegesbeckia* 14

Silent Möbius (comic book) 69–71

Silent Scream, The (anti-abortion video film) 164–5, 172–6, 180, 183, 187

SimEve *see* Eve (computer-generated cover girl)

similitude 98, 137–8, 140, 142

Simon, Paul: "The Boy in the Bubble" 221–2, 240–1

Sister cartoon 237–8, 239

situated robotics 253

Six Million Dollar Man, The (TV series) 149

Sjöö, M.: *Great Cosmic Mother* 84

skull measurements and scientific analogy 7, 39, 41; phrenology 43–4, 45

Smellie, William 24

Smith, Samuel Stanhope 26

Smith, Stephanie A. 68

Snitow, Ann 210

Snow, C.P. 9, 75

Sobchack, Vivian 97–8, 99, 100

social relations: feminist focus on gender 199, 200, 201; and reproductive technologies 184, 186, 194, 195, 197, 205*n*, 210–14, 216; of science and technology 57

social work 202, 206*n*

socialist feminism 5, 50, 51, 52, 55, 57

sociobiology 252

Sofia, Zoe 176

sonography *see* ultrasound scanning

spatial relations: of body 62–5; in electronic age 136; of NetCafé 296–7, 298

specular economy 254, 266–71, 273

speculum: as metaphor 168; as symbol 237–40; *Virtual Speculum* (cartoon) 223–32, 236–7

speech act theory 280

Sphinx 122, 128–9

Spider Woman myth 128

spiritual ecofeminism 9, 75, 82, 84, 85*n*

Squier, Susan 220*n*

Squires, Judith 253, 284, 286, 295

Stafford, Barbara 67

Stallabrass, J. 292, 293

standpoint theory, feminist 165, 166, 193–4, 196–200, 204*n*, 277; anti-oppressive 166, 197, 200–2, 203, 206*n*

Stanworth, Michelle 161–2, 194–5, 199–200, 201, 210

Star Trek (TV series) 91, 296

Star Wars film trilogy 137

Starman (film) 137, 138

Steinberg, Deborah Lynn 165–6

Stengers, Isabelle 80, 81

Stepan, Nancy Leys 6–7, 306

Stepford Wives, The (film) 114
stereotypes: gender 98, 99–100, 151, 156
Stewart, Garrett 118
Stone, Sandy 272, 281, 284
Stryker, Beth 272
Studlar, Gaylyn 108*n*, 109*n*
subjectivity as social construction 153–4, 157
substitution theory of metaphor 52
Suchman 280
suckling 12, 15–24, 16–17
Suleiman, Susan 157
surrogate motherhood 233

Tannen, D. 279
taxonomies in biological sciences 5–6, 11–29; "chain of being" 6, 24–5, 306; *Mammalia* classification 5–6, 11–15, 16, 21, 24; "missing link" 24–5; and racial difference 6
technological determinism 52–3, 57, 282, 283
technological fetishism 95, 119
technology: electronic 56, 136; feminist approaches to 193–203; and racial difference 305–17; and reproduction 114–18, 161–243; in science fiction films 93, 145; social relations of science and technology 57; visualization technologies 164–5, 171–88, 224, 225–6, 249, 305–17; *see also* communications technologies; information technologies; reproductive technologies; technoscience and gender
technophilia in science fiction films 95, 110–20
technophobia xiv, 214, 215–16
technoscience and gender: feminist technoscience studies 232–6; feminist theory and 165–6; information technologies 55–6, 152, 236, 249–317; Internet and gender 253, 268, 286–7, 291–302; representations of xiii–xiv, 3, 3–87, 92, 151–2; reproductive technologies

161–243; in science fiction film 91–136, 148–58
Terminator, The (film) 9, 98, 137, 150, 157, 283
Terry, J. 291
Test-Tube Women (anthology) 182
Tête Mécanique (assemblage) 63–5
textual analysis 235
Thalmann, Daniel 281
Thalmann, Nadia M. 281
Thing, The (film) 137
Thomson, Amy: *Virtual Girl* 83–4, 85
Time magazine morphing article 255–6, 312–17
Titian 229
Tong, Rosemarie 276
tools *see* artefacts/artificial
Topinard, Paul 41, 43
Transformers (toy) 148
Treichler, Paula 155
Turbayne, Colin 38
Turing, Alan 258, 270, 272, 274*n*
Turkle, Sherry 286
Turner, A.N. 185–6
2001: A Space Odyssey (film) 174, 176
Tyson, Edward 13

Uforia (film) 137
ultrasound scanning 162, 165, 176–82, 204*n*, 225–6, 237; in abortion decisions 172–3, 186, 189*n*; and caesarian section rate 179; NIH/FDA report 178; pregnant women's response to 172–3, 181, 182–7, 204*n*, 224, 225; as private images 184–5; routinization of 178; voyeurism of 180; *see also* foetus: visualization of; *Silent Scream, The*
UNESCO 254, 305, 309
unitary maternity 212–13
university faculties: humanities/sciences divide 75–6, 77
US armed forces homosexuality issue 234
uterus *see* womb

vaginal lips: of Hottentot women 26–7,

28, 29; in information technologies 254

Varela, F. 250

Velázquez 229

Vesalius, Andreas 16, 228

video 233, 306; *see also Silent Scream*

Videodrome (film) 254

Villiers de l'Isle Adam, Auguste, Comte de: *L'Eve future* 111–13, 119, 150

Virgin Mary 17, 21

Virtual Girl (Thomson) 83–4, 85

virtual reality (VR) 82–4, 85, 276, 280–1, 282, 286

Virtual Speculum (cartoon) 223–32, 236–7

Virtues 21

visualization technologies 164–5, 171–88, 222, 224, 225–6; and racial difference 249, 305–17; *see also* photographs; ultrasound scanning; virtual reality

VNS Matrix (women's group) 266, 296

Vogt, Carl 39–40, 44

Voltaire 26

voyeurism of ultrasound imaging 180

VR *see* virtual reality

Wajcman, Judy 163, 164, 276

Wakeford, Nina 249, 253–4, 258–9, 260

Warner, Marina 17

Warnock Commission (UK) 211

Warren, Karen 85*n*

Weaver, Sigourney 94–5, *104*; *see also Alien/s* : Ripley character

weaving 251, 270–1, 285–6

Weimar Germany 61–2

Weird Science (film) 150

Weise, Elizabeth Reba 286

Weston, Kate 220*n*

wet-nursing 12; campaign against 22–3

white feminism 199–200

Whitford, M. 257

Wilson, Pete 234

Wollstonecraft, Mary 16

Woman's World (magazine) 219*n*

womb 16, 130, 272; *see also* ultrasound scanning

women: bodies *see* female body; category of "woman" critiqued 3–4, 198, 214–15, 252, 254; control strategies for 55; experiences of reproductive technologies 196–7; identity of 99, 153–4, 155, 156–7; and information technologies 250–1, 269–70, 284–6, 292, 294–300; "lack" defines 266–7; reproductive rights 203, 211; response of pregnant women to ultrasound images 172–3, 181, 182–7, 204*n*, 224, 225; as science fiction audience 91; in scientific analogy 6, 7, 16, 23, 39–48; taxonomic gender politics 21–4; universalized 284–5; *see also* gender; maternal/mother in science fiction film; mother/motherhood; reproductive technologies; sexual reproduction

women's health movement 237, 239, 242–3*n*

Women's Liberation Movement 237

women's studies 9

Wonder Woman (cartoon character) 237–9, *240*

"Woo Woo West Coast Emergence" 252, 285

Woolf, Virginia: *Orlando* 62–3

Woolfolk, Dorothy 239

Wosk, Julie 60

X-Files (TV series) 91

yearning 235–6

zero as zone of multiplicity 251, 256, 270, 272